Between the Lines 11

Authors

Richard Davies

Glen Kirkland

Australia • Canada • Mexico • Singapore • Spain • United Kingdom • United States

Between the Lines 11

Director of Publishing:
David Steele

Publisher:
Carol Stokes

Program Manager:
Norma Kennedy

Project Manager:
Caron MacMenamin

Developmental Editor:
Susan McNish

Editorial Assistant:
Georgina Tresnak

Senior Managing Editor:
Nicola Balfour

Senior Production Editor:
Carol Martin

Production Manager:
Renate McCloy

Production Coordinator:
Julie Preston

Permissions and Photo Research:
Vicki Gould
Rebecca Hull

Interior Design:
Suzanne Peden

Cover Design:
Lori Klesmer

Composition Manager:
Marnie Benedict

Composition:
Erich Falkenberg

Printer:
Transcontinental Printing Inc.

Reviewers
The publishers gratefully acknowledge the contributions of the following educators:

Owen Davis, ON
Julianne Diubaldo, ON
Bernadette Homerski, ON
Wayne Hurley, NF
S. B. Kirby, NF
Gerard Lavelle, ON
Kristine van Leenen, AB
Colleen Lindsay, BC
Anne Manning, NF
Carol Mayne, AB
Glenda Weste, NF

COPYRIGHT © 2002 by Nelson Thomson Learning, a division of Thomson Canada Limited. Nelson Thomson Learning is a registered trademark used herein under licence.

Printed and bound in Canada
6 7 8   10 09 08

For more information contact Nelson Thomson Learning, 1120 Birchmount Road, Scarborough, Ontario, M1K 5G4. Or you can visit our Internet site at http://www.nelson.com

ISBN-13: 978-0-17-619705-6 (bound)
ISBN-10: 0-17-619705-2 (bound)

ISBN-13: 978-0-17-619704-9 (pbk.)
ISBN-10: 0-17-619704-4 (pbk.)

ALL RIGHTS RESERVED. No part of this work covered by the copyright herein may be reproduced, transcribed, or used in any form or by any means—graphic, electronic, or mechanical, including photocopying, recording, taping, Web distribution or information storage and retrieval systems—without the written permission of the publisher.

For permission to use material from this text or product, contact us by
Tel 1-800-730-2214
Fax 1-800-730-2215
www.thomsonrights.com

National Library of Canada Cataloguing in Publication Data

Davies, Richard
  Between the lines

(Nelson English)
For use in grade 11.
Includes index.
ISBN 0-17-619705-2 (bound)
ISBN 0-17-619704-4 (pbk.)

1. English language. I. Kirkland, Glen. II. Title. III. Series.

PE1112.D38 2001   428
C2001-930322-X

CONTENTS

Introduction vii

UNIT 1: CHARACTERS IN CONFLICT

Herman (The Haircut) *by Jim Unger* (cartoon). 2
Fear *by Anne Frank* (short story) 4
Bus Ride *by Ligaya Victorio Fruto* (short story) 7
One of These Days *by Gabriel García Márquez* (short story) 13
Nipikti the Old Man Carver *by Alootook Ipellie* (short story). 17
Relics *by Peter Cole* (poem) 21
denim blues *by Rita Wong* (poem). 24
The Man Who Finds That His Son Has Become a Thief
   by Raymond Souster (poem). 26
A Boy Grows Older *by Morley Callaghan* (short story) 28
Blood Knots *by Mallory Burton* (short story). 33
Wedge Island *by Lesley Choyce* (poem) 38
The Interlopers *by Saki (H.H. Munro)* (short story) 41
The Monsters Are Due on Maple Street *by Rod Serling* (teleplay) 47
Reflecting on the Unit. 60

UNIT 2: FAME AND GREATNESS

Outlasting the Fickleness of Fame *by Meg Murphy* (editorial) 62
Candle in the Wind *by Bernie Taupin* (lyrics) 66
The Cartoonist: Lynn Johnston *as told to Margo Roston* (profile) 68
Up Where She Belongs
   by Kathy Ullyott (with Buffy Sainte-Marie) (interview) 72
The TV Host: Oprah Winfrey *by Deborah Tannen* (profile) 76
The Moviemaker: Steven Spielberg *by Roger Ebert* (profile) 79
The Phenomenon: Pelé *by Henry Kissinger* (profile) 82
The Ordinary Superstar: Wayne Gretzky *by Ken Dryden* (profile). 86
Ex-Basketball Player *by John Updike* (poem) 91
Poems for Giovanni Caboto *by Filippo Salvatore* (poem) 93
The Nature of David Suzuki *by Jerry Buckley* (profile) 96
Rick Hansen: Still in Motion *by Cam Tait* (interview) 101
Mother Teresa: An Exemplary Life
   from The Edmonton Journal (editorial) 105
Reflecting on the Unit 108

iii

UNIT 3: CRIMES, CRIMINALS, AND JUSTICE

Let Me Tell You about the Crime I Committed
  by Sallie Tisdale (magazine article)... 110
It Was a Year Ago *by Grace Caguimbaga* (short short story) ... 114
Paid-up Member *by Will R. Bird* (short story) ... 116
D.B. Cooper *by Max Haines* (true crime story) ... 120
Flying off the Handle *by Christopher Elliott* (Web site news article) ... 124
Heat Lightning *by Robert F. Carroll* (play) ... 127
The Great Young Offenders Act Debate
  by Stephen R. Biss (Web site survey) ... 136
Debating the Death Penalty
  by David Matas and Andrew Allentuck (essays) ... 140
Herman (Good Behaviour) *by Jim Unger* (cartoon) ... 146
The Knife Sharpener *by Bonnie Burnard* (short story) ... 148
Thief *by Alice Major* (poem) ... 157
Citizen's Arrest *by Charles Willeford* (short story) ... 159
Reflecting on the Unit ... 166

UNIT 4: MEDIA/TECHNOLOGY INFLUENCES

Herman (TV) *by Jim Unger* (cartoon) ... 168
I would have e-mailed you *by GoTT* (birthday card) ... 170
clearNET (print ad) ... 172
Exercise Your Options *by Alen and Sandra Zukanovic* (print ad) ... 174
Nortel Networks (print ad) ... 176
Got Milk? (print ad) ... 179
Spilling Open *by Sabrina Ward Harrison* (photo essay) ... 182
October Sky *by Gary Johnson* (on-line movie review) ... 190
Web Safety: Information for Parents and Kids
  by the RCMP/GRC (Web page article) ... 194
News *by George Bowering* (poem) ... 197
Chatline lingo catching on
  by Michelle Macafee (newspaper article) ... 200
Ear *by Jane Yolen* (science-fiction story) ... 202
Reflecting on the Unit ... 210

UNIT 5: UNDERSTANDING AND ACCEPTANCE

Conceiving the Stranger *by Nigel Darbasie* (poem) ... 212
Don't Give Me Looks *by Maxine Tynes* (poem) ... 214
Filing a Complaint with the Canadian Human Rights Commission
  by the Canadian Human Rights Commission (instructions) ... 216
After the Wedding *by Marisa Anlin Alps* (poem) ... 220

Touch the Dragon *by Karen Connelly* (diary entry) 223
Grandma Weaver's Last Arrow *by Rosemary M. Huggins* (short story) . . 226
To Human Race *by Syeda Nuzhat Siddiqui* (poem) 229
Canada, My Canada *by Tomson Highway* (personal essay) 232
Arctic Plums *by Brian Fawcett* (memoir) 235
Jamie *by Elizabeth Brewster* (poem) 239
Paper Matches *by Paulette Jiles* (poem) 241
Doonesbury (Mother Goose) *by G.B. Trudeau* (cartoon) 243
Little Red Riding Hood *by James Finn Garner* (fairy tale spoof) 245
Reflecting on the Unit. 248

UNIT 6: RELATIONSHIPS

The Walk to Paradise Garden *by W. Eugene Smith* (photograph) 250
The Sea Shell *by Ed Kleiman* (short story) 252
One Woman's Story *by Michelle McColm* (essay) 256
Jamaican Dreams *by Cynthia Reyes* (memoir) 260
Thanks for being out there, brother *by Jennifer Champion* (letter) 267
First Kiss—First Lesson *by Jennifer Braunschweiger* (memoir) 271
First Date *by John McPherson* (cartoon) 276
Berrypicking *by Allison Mitcham* (poem) 278
Long Walk to Forever *by Kurt Vonnegut, Jr.* (short story) 281
"How do I love thee?" *by Elizabeth Barrett Browning* (poem) 289
Peanuts (How did I love thee?) *by Charles M. Schulz* (cartoon) 291
Fast Car *by Tracy Chapman* (lyrics) 293
Remember Africa? *by Jo Beth McDaniel* (narrative essay) 296
Reflecting on the Unit. 300

UNIT 7: YOUTH—THE AWAKENING YEARS

Designer Teens *by Ian Haysom* (newspaper article) 302
Cooks Brook *by Al Pittman* (poem) 307
Shamaya *by Susan Aglukark* (lyrics) 310
Powder *by Tobias Wolff* (short story) 312
In the Past *by Lesley-Anne Bourne* (poem) 317
What a Good Boy *by Steven Page* (lyrics) 319
For Better or For Worse ("Hi Mike") *by Lynn Johnston* (cartoon) 322
Teenage Wasteland *by Anne Tyler* (short story) 324
The Kids Who Make It in from the Cold
   by Bob Levin (magazine article) 334
"My Father Had Been Drinking"
   by William S. Pollack and Todd Shuster (monologue) 337
Write Me Sometime *by Taien Ng-Chan* (memoir) 340

The Slave Fort *by Ghassan Kanafani* (short story) 346
Celebration *by Al Pittman* (poem) 351
Reflecting on the Unit. 354

UNIT 8: OUT IN THE WORLD

Herman (The Job Interview) *by Jim Unger* (cartoon) 356
Preparing for an Interview
    by Grammy Asia Ltd. (self-help information) 358
Short-Order Cook *by Jim Daniels* (poem) 360
Ten Steps to Completing a Successful Application Form
    by Nancy Schaefer (instructions) 362
Preparing an Effective Résumé (instructions) 366
Writing for Business (letters, forms, memo) 368
Youth Employment Strategy
    by Youth Employment Canada (brochure) 378
Creating a Visual Package *by Marcelle Lapow Toor* (instructions) 380
"Hash for Cash" *by Gina Higgins* (poem) 385
How to Become a Millionaire *by Rod McQueen* (self-help article) 387
Are You a Risk-Taker?
    by M. Zuckerman and D.M. Kuhlman (questionnaire) 390
Speaking in Public (instructional essay) *by Lucy Valentino* 393
A is for Attitude! (feature articles) 397
Raiding the North *from What! A Magazine* (magazine article) 400
Reflecting on the Unit 406

Glossary 407
Acknowledgments 412

INTRODUCTION

To the Student—

Welcome to *Between the Lines 11*, an exciting new anthology for high-school students!

This book contains several popular themes, each having to do with relating and relationships. The selections themselves are mostly contemporary and Canadian, although many other cultures, countries, and time frames are represented.

We have included many famous and well-known writers such as Gabriel García Márquez, Roger Ebert, Max Haines, Jane Yolen, Tracy Chapman, and Kurt Vonnegut, Jr., as well as many popular or classic literary works, including "The Interlopers," "Paper Matches," "Teenage Wasteland," and "How do I love thee?".

As well, many of the people represented in this book will probably already be familiar to you: Anne Frank, Mother Teresa, Wayne Gretzky, Oprah Winfrey, Steven Spielberg, David Suzuki, and Marilyn Monroe.

You will notice, too, that there are also many different types of texts, including plays, cartoons, photographs, advertisements, lyrics, Web items, self-help instructions, humour pieces, interviews, and many selections tied in with media, technology, and the working world.

Before each of the eight units, there is a brief introduction to the theme along with several relevant quotations. With every selection, there are questions and activities to help you read between the lines, and for many selections, additional notes and author biographies are included.

At the back of the book, there is a useful glossary of terms to help you talk, write, and think about the book's selections.

We hope you enjoy *Between the Lines 11*. It is a book specially designed for you, your needs, and your interests.

> Wishing you a good year in English,
> Richard Davies
> Glen Kirkland

UNIT 1

"Without contraries is no progression."
–William Blake

"We have met the enemy and he is us."
–Walt Kelly

"Character cannot be developed in ease and quiet. Only through experiences of trial and suffering can the soul be strengthened, vision cleared, ambition impaired, and success achieved."
–Helen Keller

Characters in Conflict

As poet William Blake's quotation above suggests, there can be no progress or growth without conflict. *Pogo* cartoonist Walt Kelly's famous words remind us that, in times of conflict, we can often be our own worst enemy. Finally, Helen Keller points out that it is conflict that ultimately develops our character.

The first unit of this book examines literary characters in conflict with others and themselves. Conflict is defined as a struggle between opposing forces. When a character is in conflict, there are three possible outcomes: defeat, success, or a lack of resolution of the conflict.

As you read this unit, think about the following:

1) Who or what is in conflict?
2) What has caused the conflict (what are the problems or obstacles)?
3) What is revealed about the characters as they respond to the conflict?
4) What is the outcome of the conflict—is it resolved? Why or why not?

Before you read, cover the words below the illustration, and write your own caption.

As you read, note how the illustration and caption work together. Notice the body language and facial expressions, wording and punctuation.

Herman

Cartoon by Jim Unger

"There's just no pleasing you, is there? All week you've been telling me to get a haircut."

You take it from here ...

Responding

1. **Compare Captions**   In groups of two or three, read and compare the captions you wrote for this illustration. Discuss how they are alike or different.

2. **Speak the Part**   Imagine what the boy's attitude and tone of voice might be. Then read the caption aloud to a partner as you think the boy would have said it.

3. **Describe the Characters**   Make a two-column chart to list words describing each of the characters in the cartoon. Include what you guess about them (their relationship, attitudes) and words that give a physical description of the characters.

Man	Boy
tall	short
sitting	

4. **Make a List**   How does the style of the cartoon add to the humour? Working with a partner, list the details that make the cartoon funny and realistic.

Extending

5. **Write Dialogue**   Work with a partner to write what the man might have said just before and after the boy's answer. You could also write a longer conversation between the two. Then read the dialogue aloud for the class as you think the characters would have spoken it.

6. **Draw a Cartoon**   Draw your own cartoon showing two characters in a similar type of conflict. Add a humorous caption.

Before you read, discuss in class the experience of fear. When have you felt it? What caused it? How did the experience affect you?

As you read, make a short list of events that happen to the main character.

Fear

All I felt and knew was that I had to run.

Short Story by Anne Frank

Notes

Anne Frank wrote the most famous diary in world literature while she and her family were in hiding from the Nazis in Amsterdam. Her ambition was to become an author. The family was discovered just before the war ended, and Anne died at the Bergen-Belsen concentration camp at the age of 16.

It was a terrible time through which I was living. The war raged about us, and nobody knew whether or not he would be alive the next hour. My parents, brothers, sisters, and I made our home in the city, but we expected that we either would be evacuated or have to escape in some other way. By day the sound of cannon and rifle shots was almost continuous, and the nights were mysteriously filled with sparks and sudden explosions that seemed to come from some unknown depth.

I cannot describe it; I don't remember that tumult quite clearly, but I do know that all day long I was in the grip of fear. My parents tried everything to calm me, but it didn't help. I felt nothing, nothing but fear; I could neither eat nor sleep—fear clawed at my mind and body and shook me. That lasted for about a week, then came an evening and a night which I recall as though it had been yesterday.

At half past eight, when the shooting had somewhat died down, I lay in a sort of half doze on a sofa. Suddenly all of us were startled by two violent explosions. As though stuck with knives, we all jumped up and ran into the hall. Even Mother, usually so calm, looked pale. The explosions repeated themselves at pretty regular intervals. Then: a tremendous crash, the noise of much breaking glass, and an ear-splitting chorus of yelling and screaming. I put on what heavy clothes I could find in a hurry, threw some things into a rucksack, and ran. I ran as fast as I could, ran on and on to get away from the fiercely burning mass about me. Everywhere shouting people darted to and fro; the street was alight with a fearsome red glow.

I didn't think of my parents or of my brothers and sisters. I had thoughts only for myself and knew that I must rush, rush, rush! I didn't feel any fatigue; my fear was too strong. I didn't know that I had lost my rucksack. All I felt and knew was that I had to run.

I couldn't possibly say how long I ran on with the image of the burning houses, the desperate people and their distorted faces before me. Then I sensed that it had got more quiet. I looked around and, as if waking up from a nightmare, I saw that there was nothing or no one behind me. No fire, no bombs, no people. I looked a little more closely and found that I stood in a meadow. Above me the stars glistened and the moon shone; it was brilliant weather, crisp but not cold.

I didn't hear a sound. Exhausted, I sat down on the grass, then spread the blanket I had been carrying on my arm, and stretched out on it.

I looked up into the sky and realized that I was no longer afraid; on the contrary, I felt very peaceful inside. The funny thing was that I didn't think of my family, nor yearn for them; I yearned only for rest, and it wasn't long before I fell asleep there in the grass, under the sky.

When I woke up, the sun was just rising. I immediately knew where I was; in the daylight I recognized the houses at the outskirts of our city. I rubbed my eyes and had a good look around. There was no one to be seen; the dandelions and the clover-leaves in the grass were my only company. Lying back on the blanket for a while, I mused about what to do next. But my thoughts wandered off from the subject and returned to the wonderful feeling of the night before, when I sat in the grass and was no longer afraid.

Later I found my parents, and together we moved to another town. Now that the war is over, I know why my fear disappeared under the wide, wide heavens. When I was alone with nature, I realized—realized without actually knowing it—that fear is a sickness for which there is only one remedy. Anyone who is as afraid as I was then should look at nature and see that God is much closer than most people think.

Since that time I have never been afraid again, no matter how many bombs fell near me.

You take it from here ...

Responding

1. **Review the Plot**   With a partner, review what happened to the main character in the story. Start with the list you created while you were reading, and be sure to fill in any events or episodes you missed.

> **SELF ASSESSMENT**
> - What did you learn from making your list of events and sharing it with a partner?
> - Did the process help you read and understand the selection? How?

2. **Focus on Conflict**   In chart form, list the conflicts in the story. Identify what caused them and if and how they are resolved.

Conflict	Cause	Resolution

3. **Describe Mood**   In a group, answer and discuss the following questions: How did you feel about the narrator's situation as you finished the story? Choose and describe two details that made you feel this way. How do you think your feelings compare with those of the narrator?

Extending

4. **Write an Alternative Ending**   In the role of the narrator, write an alternative ending to this short story. Consider how the narrator would have reacted if she had not found her parents, or the difficulties she might have faced while rebuilding her life in a new town. You may want to take another look at "Fear" before you begin writing.

5. **Research the Author**   Find out more about Anne Frank, her life, and her writing. Choose a form of presentation (an oral or written report, a display, or a collage) and summarize your findings. Include a list of books, videos, or Web sites that you would recommend to others.

Before you read, discuss with a partner what it is like to ride on a crowded public bus. How do people usually behave?

As you read, ask yourself questions about the main character. What is she like? How can you tell?

Bus Ride

"Somebody," she gasped faintly, "somebody help."

Short Story by Ligaya Victorio Fruto

Notes

Ligaya Victorio Fruto was born in Rizal Province in the Philippines. This story is from a collection titled *Yesterday and Other Stories* (1969).

Lyda is pronounced "Lie-duh." The story is set in Manila, a city in the Philippines, during the Second World War.

Lyda watched the blue shining nose of the bus in fascination. Then she poked a finger at the pert tip of her own pretty nose. It isn't powdered, she thought stupidly. Noses shouldn't be shiny. Never allow your nose to get shiny, said a beauty article, if you intend to hold your man. My nose is seldom shiny, she thought in self-pity, and yet here I am losing my man. Hope that girl in his car will sport a shiny nose some time today.

Lyda stamped one foot impatiently. I am beginning to dodder, she thought in a sort of dull rage. Here I am thinking foolish thoughts while a female pirate steals my man away. But perhaps she is just a cousin, or a hitherto undiscovered sister-in-law. Even an aunt. She certainly looked old enough to be his mother.

She saw the bus toot smaller buses out of the way and slide to a stop. She looked at the quivering nose and dusty side. Then quickly, almost without thought, she moved close to the bus, her mind made up. I'll take it, she thought with subdued savagery. I won't wait for his car to pick me up. I'll take this bus and rush home and have a really good mad fit. Let him look for me till the balls of his eyes pop out. I won't give him the satisfaction of lying to me. Not just yet.

She waited with impatience while several passengers fought to get into the bus. Cattle, she thought with disdain. Creatures of instinct. They won't even file in order. How much time they would save if they spent a little more thought on boarding buses.

Once in the bus, she held herself apart from the perspiring crowd. She stood in a small pool of daintiness which the slightly awed passengers conceded her. She looked aloofly toward a desirable seat by a window, and as though her glance had pulled him up, the blue-shirted man with a bundle who occupied it rose and gave it to her. She moved slowly toward the seat and murmured her thanks. She glanced once at the hard

seat in doubt, then stepped by the trouser leg withdrawn to let her pass and sank upon the cool wood. Once settled in her seat, she looked out of the window, dismissing the bus crowd.

The city is different, she decided, from a bus seat. Somehow it looks dirtier, more crowded, more impossible to live in. Through a car window, one could regard it with impersonal disdain; one could hold oneself apart from it, secure from its smells and its sounds and its dirty humanity. She was beginning to regret having boarded the bus. Quite an experience, but she could have done without it.

A car—gleaming, magnificent—flowed by, and she turned her face sharply away from the street. There he was, alone this time, an anxious look framed by the windshield. He would never think of glancing up at the bus window, but she kept her face averted just the same. The hurt she had suffered moments before intensified in a fresh pain. You have done it. You have done it to me. How many more times will you do it before—and after—we get married? She recalled the pleasure on his face as he drove beside the laughing girl. The ghost of a girl's gay laughter was like a clean thrust of sound in the bus's stifling air. She would not stand for it, neither now nor later. And she sat rigidly upon her seat, dumb and proud with pain, doubt like an imp gnawing at her breast. And oddly mixed with her exquisite torture was a streak of annoyance because life could go on about her—active, noisy life borne upon bus wheels.

Behind her someone coughed. She sat straight up with disgust. What right had a man with a cough like that to ride in a public conveyance? The cough was repeated, more rackingly this time, and Lyda's irritation expressed itself in a glance of censure flung over her shoulder. He was sick, and not even her glance could summon enough blood to his face to proclaim his embarrassment.

"This cough is so bothersome," he was impelled to explain to the man who sat beside him. "The office doctor says ..." Here an interrupting cough. "But I cannot rest now. Wife's having a baby this month."

Lyda was shocked speechless. The things people said in buses. There should be a law.

"Same thing happened to a cousin of mine," another voice took up the subject in heavy sympathy. "My cousin took sick when his seventh child was about to be born. Poor fellow. He died two days before the birth of the child."

"Life is so difficult," the first voice sighed, and there was silence for a while.

Other voices, other sounds drifted to Lyda on the heels of his sigh. It was as though the cough had banished a spell which centred her senses solely on herself. She found her consciousness intruded upon with unwelcome frequency. Across the aisle, a group of labourers discussed the war. Their ignorance was like a needle pricking their earnestness, destroying for Lyda the balloons of thought which they flew with such assurance. Lyda was bored. What did she care about war? Her only resentment was that now her veil must come from New York instead of direct from Paris, as had been originally planned.

Two seats ahead of her, a man was talking to another about unions. What unions, she wondered in irritation. Weddings?

"I told you long ago that you were crazy not to join the union." The voice was raised to defeat the heavy purrings of the motor. "The union is the worker's friend, and a friend in need indeed. In companies like ours," the voice was raised further to drown out the tentative response from another, "the union was your life-saver. You need not worry about another job if you had joined when I told you. Let's take your case now. You were kicked out. There would have been investigations ..."

"There was no good reason." The other voice was sullen. "The cousin of the foreman had gotten married and needed my job."

"That's what I mean ..."

Lyda played deaf with an effort. I won't listen to soap-box orators, she thought firmly. I won't. Why don't people leave their miseries at home? Tie them to a post like dogs. Feed them, fondle them once they are home. Why carry them about in places where they will merely annoy people who have troubles enough of their own?

And at that thought a fresh flood of self-pity swept over her. She had not known real misery until she had glimpsed that laughing face and heard that airy sound as his car swept by. Perhaps they had driven out to the hills where he and she had gone so often. They had loved the clean fingers of wind which parted their hair as they drove past green slopes and quiet, blossom-bordered lanes. They had known what it was to laugh in the glare of the sun. And those pools of shade by the roadside where they had paused for lovely moments of talk and silence. The snowy tops of flowering weeds that they had passed again and again. Perhaps he had shown *her* those.

Pain sharpened within her and she stirred in her seat. A suffocating smell of gasoline mingled with the human odours which circulated within the hot interior of the bus. Lyda moved closer to the window and exposed her face further to the dust-laden breeze that brushed her cheeks. She looked at the houses which they now passed, filled with wonder that people could live in them. She glimpsed mats and blankets which obviously served as walls, and shuddered at the black dirt which for so many houses was a littered floor. Across the front of one rusty tin

hut, faded strips of bunting still clung, a hangover from a forgotten fiesta, like confetti on the face of dilapidation.

The bus gave a sudden jolt, and Lyda heard someone's head bump loudly against the sloping ceiling of the rear end. There was a child's sharp, short scream, and an equally sharp feminine voice which shushed this scream to a whimper. The man who had coughed behind Lyda rose from his seat and proffered his better place to the woman and her child. The woman looked at his pallid face uncertainly, then with a murmur of gratitude transferred herself and her child to the proffered seat.

Lyda looked up the thin length of the man who had offered the seat. He had refused the back seat and stood up to reach for the low beam of the bus ceiling. Lyda thought she saw his slight frame quiver as he sought to steady himself, then he swayed gently to the rhythm of the motor. Oh, well, she dismissed him scornfully, if he must be gallant ....

There was a sudden lurch, and Lyda grasped the wood bars of the window to keep from sliding off her seat. She directed an angry glance toward the driver. The fellow had no sense. Why, oh why did she take the bus? What spirit of folly had prompted her to take the bus when she could have ridden in comfort and safety in a taxi? The long ride home was a monotony of discomfort, thanks to her crazy impulsiveness. She looked about her, thoroughly irritated, and somehow the queer sick look of the man who swayed close to her heightened this irritation. Served him right, she thought unfeelingly, as she took in the intent unseeing look upon the almost bloodless face of the man. What on earth could have made him take this evil bus? She hoped savagely that he would not choose this moment to cough. That would be just a little too much.

She looked out of the window once more, noting without pleasure the crowded look of the road. Soon they would be on the provincial road, and there would be less noise and dust. She was a fool not to have waited for his car. She could have hailed him as he passed. By this time she would have been safely home and in the bath, while he smoked cigarette after cigarette on the porch and wondered about her icy remoteness. What could she gain with such tomfoolery as this bus ride? Funny into what discomfort love for a man could goad a woman. She imagined punishments for him while she was punishing herself.

She saw a small bus struggling through a tight space between their bus and a large truck, watching its imprudence without taking in its significance. Then she felt, rather than heard, the sharp grinding of brakes, and a man's weight flung sharply against her. Weak hands strove vainly to cling to something that would hold him away from the dirty floor of the bus. She moved closer to the corner of her seat, her face pale with nausea and horror, as she gingerly tried to lift the thin body off her knees.

"Somebody," she gasped faintly, "somebody, help."

The world was all movement and sound. There were the loud angry words of the driver, the squeals of the women, the indignant voices of the men who had rushed down to examine the trouble. She did not notice when the quarrelling voices lost their edge and softened to shocked pity. She was too stupidly intent on setting her frock to rights and freeing her frame of disgusted shivers. She looked about, pale and helpless, but even the women were not looking at her. They were too intent on a long burden that lately had sprawled against her knee.

There were sounds—too many sounds that made no sense to her. This would happen, this would happen to her. So many other women in the bus and this would happen to her. She felt the last vestiges of her control going. She thought of him and of the girl and of the love like a wounded bird within her. She thought of her beautiful home and her cool garden several minutes away from here.

And then she saw her shoes. With a mounting horror she stared at her once immaculate shoes, only just now beginning to feel the sticky warmth which streaked clear across her feet. She thought, I'm going to be sick. I mustn't be. Not here. I can't bear it here. But the muscles of her eyes refused to move, and she could not turn her gaze away from those horribly smeared shoes. She felt a fine dam loosening within her and the tears long pent were running down her cheeks. There is no one, she sobbed bitterly, no one at all, more miserable than I.

Bus Ride   11

You take it from here ...

Responding

> **TIPS**
> - A character sketch
>   - is usually about a paragraph long
>   - starts with a one-sentence overview of the character
> - Each adjective you use should be supported with an example from the story.

1. **Make a List**   What feelings does the main character experience during her bus journey? List her feelings in the order they arise.

2. **Write a Character Sketch**   Analyze the personality of the main character, and write a character sketch using adjectives (words that describe, such as "nervous," "reflective") and examples from the story.

3. **Consider Setting**   This story is set in Manila in the early 1940s during the Second World War. In a class discussion, consider how the historical context affects the story. How would the story be different if it were set in a different place and time—for example, in a Canadian city today? How might it be the same?

4. **Discuss a Sub-Conflict**   With a partner, discuss what has happened in the relationship between Lyda and her boyfriend. Describe the thoughts she has about him while she is on the bus.

Extending

5. **Compose a Letter**   When she finally arrives home, Lyda decides to write a letter to her boyfriend. Imagine and write that letter.

6. **Rethink the Story**   With another student, discuss what Lyda might have done differently to give herself a better day. Together, using either a serious or comic approach, compose a list of 10 ways to improve or avoid a bad day. Share your list with another pair of students.

7. **Give a Personal Response**   Does Lyda deserve the reader's sympathy? Write a paragraph explaining your opinion, and support it with your reasons.

> **SELF ASSESSMENT**
> - As you studied the story, did your view of Lyda change?
> - Did reading this story help you learn something about how you judge others? Comment.
> - How might you use this knowledge in your future dealings with others?

Before you read, discuss as a class what a power struggle is and what impact it has on the control of a situation.

As you read, decide which character is in control of the situation in the story.

One of These Days

"He says if you don't take out his tooth, he'll shoot you."

Short Story by Gabriel García Márquez

Notes

Gabriel García Márquez was born in 1928 in Aracataca, Colombia. He is considered one of the greatest authors of the twentieth century and was awarded the Nobel Prize in Literature in 1982.

Monday dawned warm and rainless. Aurelio Escovar, a dentist without a degree, and a very early riser, opened his office at six. He took some false teeth, still mounted in their plaster mould, out of the glass case and put on the table a fistful of instruments which he arranged in size order, as if they were on display. He wore a collarless striped shirt, closed at the neck with a golden stud, and pants held up by suspenders. He was erect and skinny, with a look that rarely corresponded to the situation, the way deaf people have of looking.

When he had things arranged on the table, he pulled the drill toward the dental chair and sat down to polish the false teeth. He seemed not to be thinking about what he was doing, but worked steadily, pumping the drill with his feet, even when he didn't need it.

After eight he stopped for a while to look at the sky through the window, and he saw two pensive buzzards who were drying themselves in the sun on the ridgepole of the house next door. He went on working

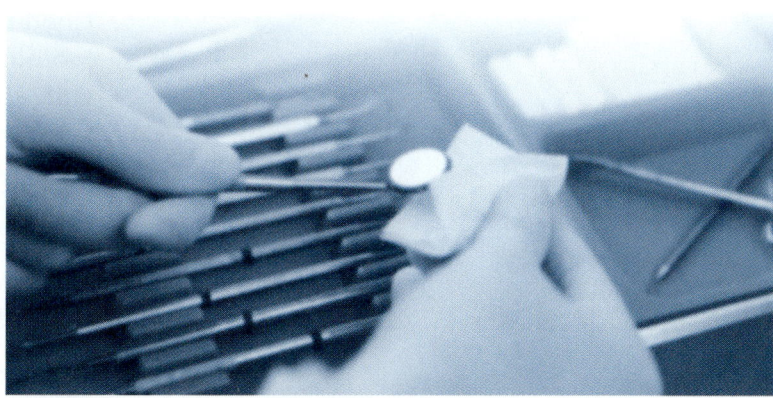

with the idea that before lunch it would rain again. The shrill voice of his eleven-year-old son interrupted his concentration.

"Papá."

"What?"

"The Mayor wants to know if you'll pull his tooth."

"Tell him I'm not here."

He was polishing a gold tooth. He held it at arm's length and examined it with his eyes half closed. His son shouted again from the little waiting room.

"He says you are, too, because he can hear you."

The dentist kept examining the tooth. Only when he had put it on the table with the finished work did he say:

"So much the better."

He operated the drill again. He took several pieces of a bridge out of a cardboard box where he kept the things he still had to do and began to polish the gold.

"Papá."

"What?"

He still hadn't changed his expression.

"He says if you don't take out his tooth, he'll shoot you."

Without hurrying, with an extremely tranquil movement, he stopped pedalling the drill, pushed it away from the chair, and pulled the lower drawer of the table all the way out. There was a revolver. "OK," he said. "Tell him to come and shoot me."

He rolled the chair over opposite the door, his hand resting on the edge of the drawer. The Mayor appeared at the door. He had shaved the left side of his face, but the other side, swollen and in pain, had a five-day-old beard. The dentist saw many nights of desperation in his dull eyes. He closed the drawer with his fingertips and said softly:

"Sit down."

"Good morning," said the Mayor.

"Morning," said the dentist.

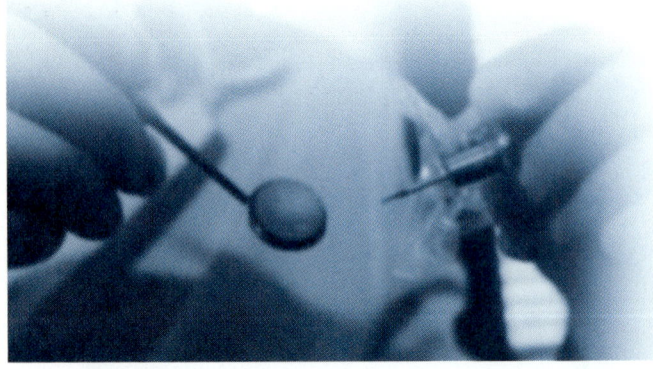

While the instruments were boiling, the Mayor leaned his skull on the headrest of the chair and felt better. His breath was icy. It was a poor office: an old wooden chair, the pedal drill, a glass case with ceramic bottles. Opposite the chair was a window with a shoulder-high cloth curtain. When he felt the dentist approach, the Mayor braced his heels and opened his mouth.

Aurelio Escovar turned his head toward the light. After inspecting the infected tooth, he closed the Mayor's jaw with a cautious pressure of his fingers.

"It has to be without anesthesia," he said.

"Why?"

"Because you have an abscess."

The Mayor looked him in the eye. "All right," he said, and tried to smile. The dentist did not return the smile. He brought the basin of sterilized instruments to the worktable and took them out of the water with a pair of cold tweezers, still without hurrying. Then he pushed the spittoon with the tip of his shoe, and went to wash his hands in the washbasin. He did all this without looking at the Mayor. But the Mayor didn't take his eyes off him.

It was a lower wisdom tooth. The dentist spread his feet and grasped the tooth with the hot forceps. The Mayor seized the arms of the chair, braced his feet with all his strength, and felt an icy void in his kidneys, but didn't make a sound. The dentist moved only his wrist. Without rancour, rather with a bitter tenderness, he said:

"Now you'll pay for our twenty dead men."

The Mayor felt the crunch of bones in his jaw, and his eyes filled with tears. But he didn't breathe until he felt the tooth come out. Then he saw it through his tears. It seemed so foreign to his pain that he failed to understand his torture of the five previous nights.

Bent over the spittoon, sweating, panting, he unbuttoned his tunic and reached for the handkerchief in his pants pocket. The dentist gave him a clean cloth.

"Dry your tears," he said.

The Mayor did. He was trembling. While the dentist washed his hands, he saw the crumbling ceiling and a dusty spider web with spider's eggs and dead insects. The dentist returned, drying his hands. "Go to bed," he said, "and gargle with salt water." The Mayor stood up, said good-bye with a casual military salute, and walked toward the door, stretching his legs, without buttoning up his tunic.

"Send the bill," he said.

"To you or the town?"

The Mayor didn't look at him. He closed the door and said through the screen:

"It's the same damn thing."

You take it from here ...

Responding

1. **Discuss in a Group**   In small groups, discuss the following questions: Why did the dentist refuse to help the mayor at first? Did the dentist have any choice about treating the mayor? What reason did he give for not using anesthesia? Do you think he was telling the truth? Explain.

2. **Analyze Dialogue**   Write a paragraph explaining the significance of each of these sentences:

    "Now you'll pay for our twenty dead men."
    "Dry your tears."
    "It's the same damn thing."

3. **Interpret the Title**   In your notebook or journal, write down what you think the title means. How is the title suitable? What else might the story have been titled?

Extending

4. **Role-Play a Scene**   With a partner, improvise a conversation between the mayor and the dentist in which the dentist refuses to pull the mayor's tooth.

5. **Compose a Monologue**   Write a short monologue the dentist might deliver to his son about the importance of doing the right thing—even if it isn't our first choice.

> **TIPS**
> - After finding each quotation, identify the speaker.
> - Think about the meaning and purpose of each quotation.
> - Consider whether the quotation could be ironic (whether it could have more than one meaning).

Before you read, discuss as a class what you know about Inuit carvings. What do they tell about the Inuit traditions and way of life?

As you read, notice how the main character responds to the obstacles he encounters during his errand.

Nipikti the Old Man Carver

"I should be able to sell the good carving for $150 easily," he said.

Short Story by Alootook Ipellie

Notes

Alootook Ipellie is a well-known Inuit artist and writer, and a contributor to *Nunavut* and *Nunatsiaq News*. His book *Arctic Dreams and Nightmares* was published in 1993.

There was a time when Inuit artists carved small sculptures for themselves. Some were made as toys for their children. Some were made in order to celebrate the people's deep belief in a world in which everything, even a stone, was inhabited by a soul and a personality. Nowadays, their spiritual art has also become a craft, a means of staying alive as they sell their stone carvings at the local co-operative, for strangers in the big cities to buy. How does an old Inuit, long past his hunting days, deal with having to sell his art in an increasingly Westernized world?

Nipikti was now an old man and took three times as long as any young Inuk to get from one point to another. Almost every week, he would get up from his small carving studio at home and start walking out to the Co-op where he sold at least a half a dozen carvings he had finished during the week. He hung the bag of carvings over his shoulder and started out the door, his walking stick leading the way for him.

"This is the day I will get the upper hand of the deal with the Co-op manager. I have no doubt that he will fall in love with the carving I finished today," he said as he closed the door behind himself.

On the way to the Co-op, Nipikti would stop several times to rest his tired old legs by sitting on the same rocks he had sat on for the last twenty years or so.

"Ahhh! Hi, Ojagajaak, it feels good to rest on you," he would say to the first rock, as if the rock was an old friend of his. "These legs of mine are a little weaker than last week, so I will have to sit on you for an extra five minutes if you do not mind."

There he sat to rest on Ojagajaak and looked across the land where he had lived as a young man. That is the place where he had hunted the good animals of the land. That is where he had taken care of his wife and family when they were growing up. "Those were good times of the past," he thought, "times when carvings like these were toys and tokens to us Inuit."

He got up slowly and continued on to the Co-op where he would get the money to support his family. The Co-op was still quite far away.

"If I had my way, I would prefer to carve the stones and ivory to make toys for my children, and hunt the animals like I used to. I wasn't such a bad hunter in those days," Nipikti said to himself.

"I never thought I would be living off the very carvings I used to make only to keep my children happy."

Nipikti finally came to the rock where he sat to rest the second time along the way to the Co-op and said, "How are you today, Ojagakaluk? I have come again to rest on you. I am an old man now, you know."

He sat on Ojagakaluk and took enough rest there to make it to the next rock. "I shall see you again on my way back. Just make sure the bulldozer doesn't push you under before then," Nipikti shouted back to the second rock as he slowly started walking on.

When he came to the third rock, he sat down and said, "You know, Ojagakutaaq, you are probably the most comfortable rock I have ever sat on in my life. I must say I will certainly miss you the day they remove you from this spot to make way for the new road. You have been a good rock to me and I must thank you in case they start building the road while I am at the Co-op."

He then got up to walk the last leg of the trip to the local Co-op and said to himself that it was time to think about how much he would persuade the Co-op manager to pay him for his carvings. Especially for the good one he finished earlier that day.

"I should be able to sell the good carving for $150 easily," he said. "I'm sure there isn't any other carving this week that was done any better than this one."

When he got to the Co-op, Nipikti took the six carvings out of the bag and laid them on the desk for the manager to look at.

The manager picked up the carvings one by one and looked them over carefully. When he came to the carving Nipikti had done that day, he immediately offered Nipikti $120 for it.

Nipikti stood leaning on his walking stick and counted on $150 as planned. Nipikti knew by experience that the carving was worth that much or even more. "$150," he said.

The manager looked up at Nipikti's face, then picked up the carving in question and mused over the fine detail of the work Nipikti had done. "Okay," he finally said, "I'll give you $130 for it."

Nipikti looked at the manager's face and thought about the last offer for $130. "If you think you are going to play games with me, you might as well be prepared to do it for the rest of the day. I am not going to play that long," he said in Inuktitut.

The manager clearly understood that Nipikti was not about to change his original asking price of $150. He knew that the price was right for the carving. But he decided to try once more to buy the carving for less than that. "140," he said.

Nipikti just stood there and cleared his throat, then said for the last time, "150." And with that, he tapped the top of the desk with his right hand. It was a sign that he meant business.

At that moment, the manager decided to give up trying to persuade the old carver to say yes to what he wanted and agreed to pay the $150 he was asking for.

Nipikti had won the battle this time around. He took the money for the carvings he'd brought in and went out the door to begin his journey back home with his walking stick in hand and money in his pocket to support the family for the next few weeks. He looked across the land and saw that the three rocks where he sat to rest each week were still there. No one had started to build the road yet. And he just smiled and said to himself that it was good.

"I had better make sure that they do not bulldoze my rocks away. The way I see it, I am sure to win my case over that too," he said for the last time, and he slowly moved on toward home where he would start the next carving.

Nipikti the old man carver lives on.

You take it from here ...

Responding

1. **Respond Personally**   In your notebook, write a sentence identifying what Nipikti wanted to achieve when he reached the Co-op. Did he succeed? Now write a paragraph telling about a time when you, like Nipikti, decided what you wanted and you persisted until you attained it.

> **SELF ASSESSMENT**
> - How was your experience the same as Nipikti's?
> - What did you learn from Nipikti's story about what it takes to achieve a goal?

2. **Chart Character Traits**   What does Nipikti think about each time he sits down on one of the familiar rocks? What do we learn about him as a character? Record your responses in a chart.

Rock	Nipikti thinks about ...	What it shows about Nipikti's character
1. Ojagajaak		
2. Ojagakaluk		
3. Ojagakutaaq		

Extending

3. **Write a Dialogue**   Imagine the conversation that might occur as Nipikti takes his next collection of carvings to the Co-op. Write it in the form of a scene in a play.

4. **Conduct an Interview**   With a partner, assume the roles of an interviewer and of an Inuit artist. Together, prepare questions and responses on what problems rapid social and technological changes in the North cause the independent Inuit artist. Write your work in script form, or present your interview to the class.

5. **Create a Fairy Tale**   Tell about an Inuit carving that comes to life for a child. You could write and illustrate a story, or create a cartoon, storyboard, or puppet show. Keep in mind that fairy tales are fantastic, imagined stories made up for young children and usually end with a moral or lesson.

> **TIPS**
> - For each speech, put the character's name on the left, followed by a colon. Put any stage directions or actions in parentheses. For example:
>
>   Nipikti: I want to sell these.
>   (Nipikti places the carvings onto the counter.)
>   Co-op manager: I'll give you $130.
> - You don't need to use quotation marks in this format.

Before you read, look up the word "relic" in a dictionary.

As you read, notice how the definition of "relic" applies to the subject of the poem. Also note whether the word is used in a positive or a negative way.

Notes

Peter Cole is of Celtic/West Coast Salish heritage. He says, "I write because it helps to centre me, to put ideas, feelings, and relationships into perspective." He enjoys the ambiguous, playful nature of language and poetry.

Relics

Poem by Peter Cole

I look at your beautiful war canoe, Grandfather
I feel the lines of its hull with my fingertips
stroke its ribs
inhale the length and depth and volume
of its smooth belly
sweet smell of cedar smudge

with sadness, Grandfather
I see your beautiful war canoe
hanging there on the wall
suspended from the ceiling
by wires spotlighted highlighted
caught in the glare like a spectacle
trapped in time and space
imported time white space

I look in awe, Grandfather, at this tree
you have transformed transfigured
from art of nature to art of mind formation
body formulation
I see the beauty that you carved
with your own hands the grace
that you drew from the spirit
of the living wood
carved from a single straight cedar
sixty feet long your canoe
a thousand years old

I watched you with your axes
and your knives and your chisels
I remember the arc of your hammer
the sound of your mallet

Grandfather, tell me
will your craft feel again the surge
and the roar of waves
the touch of sunlight the breath of sea wind
the scent of the rising mist
or will it rot within the spaces
and the time of these halls these walls
swept up each night
a sliver a speck a strand a mote
of bark of cambium of heartwood
will it decompose
with these other staged relics
with this annotated collection
of west-coast Indian artifacts?
memorabilia from ages times spaces
past memory

grandfather sun grandmother moon
mother earth father sky
powers and spirits and beings of the four directions
brothers and sisters of the wind and water
all my relations
I call on you ask that you give this canoe life again
pray that you grant wings to its spirit
let it fly through the canyons of hell's gate
through the rage and the clamour
let it crash onto the rocks
in the land of its birth
don't let it die here
in this climate-controlled mausoleum
this gallery of respectful silence
don't bury it like this crucified displayed
where everyone can watch it rot
for two dollars and fifty cents
half-price on thursdays

give me an axe and I will end its misery
and my own.

You take it from here ...

Responding

1. **Brainstorm Questions**   In your response journal or notebook, write down any questions you have about the poem. Share your questions in a small group, and work together to answer as many as you can.

2. **Write a Description**   Using details from the poem, describe the canoe. How was it made? What is special and magnificent about it? Your description could take the form of an illustration with an accompanying paragraph and/or a description of the details.

3. **Interpret the Meaning**   With a partner, discuss what feeling the poem expresses at the end. What do you think the poet means by the last two lines?

4. **Discuss with the Class**   Have a class discussion on the following questions: Why did the poet write this poem? How can you tell? Do you think it fulfills his purpose? Why?

Extending

5. **Do Internet Research**   Using a search engine on the Internet, type in the words "First Nations" or "Aboriginal peoples." Compile a list of three interesting Web pages or Web sites that give information on the topic. Report to the class on one of the Web resources you found and summarize what new information you learned about Native people.

6. **Create a Poem or Lyrics**   Write a poem or lyrics from the grandfather's point of view as he paddles his canoe.

> **Self Assessment**
> - How did you decide which style you would use to create your lyrics or poem?
> - Is it easier to write rhyming or non-rhyming poetry? Why?
> - What did you find interesting about this creative writing activity? Explain.

> **Tips**
> - You might find it helpful to write a song or poem in four-line stanzas with an end-rhyme scheme of A-B-C-B or A-B-A-B.
> - If you prefer, you can write free verse (non-rhyming poetry that has no regular or predictable structure or stanzas). "Relics" is an example of free verse.

Before you read, look at the title and brainstorm possible subjects of the poem.

As you read, write the numbers 1 to 6 for the six stanzas of the poem. Beside each, write a one- or two-word description of your reaction to each stanza.

Notes

Rita Wong grew up in Calgary and currently lives in Vancouver. She has taught English in China, Japan, and Canada. In 1997 she won the Asian Canadian Writers' Workshop Emerging Writers' award. Her first book of poetry, *Monkey Puzzle*, was published in 1998.

denim blues

Poem by Rita Wong

there are denim mountains in my closet:
well-worn cutoffs, raggedy jeans,
adolescent skin-tight pants, baggy prairie overalls,
years of tacky stampede outfits

nothing comes between me &
the labour of the garment workers
their fifty cents a day sweat
hugs me tight every morning

my auntie's fingers nimble
with the demands of piecework
how she churns dozens of jeans by dim lamplight
one more casualty for casual wear

cotton picked by hungry workers
beaten into fabric & submission in far-off factories
dissembled into department store offerings

black denim with amputated
fingers waving bloody threads from pockets
knotting in my chest as i look in the closet
find nothing to wear

nothing, that is, but
thin faded gauze ripping open,
spilling labour into consumer vision,
ragged with guilt, ignorance, fear
but still rippling, a necessary banner
in the wind for change

You take it from here ...

Responding

1. **Share Your Responses**   In small groups, discuss the purpose of each stanza and how each person responded. Then identify which two responses were the most interesting or insightful.

   > **GROUP ASSESSMENT**
   > - How did you reach a group decision? Was the process effective? Why?
   > - What did you learn about group decision-making?

2. **Read Between the Lines**   With a partner, discuss the following:
   a) What are the working conditions for the garment workers described?
   b) How old do you think the speaker is? On which lines do you base your opinion?
   c) Does the speaker identify with the workers? Explain.

3. **Analyze the Theme and Purpose**   In a paragraph, discuss the *pun* (a play on words where the words have more than one meaning) in the title. Then explain how that relates to the *theme* (main idea) of the poem. Conclude the paragraph with your thoughts about the poem's *purpose* (why the author wrote it). Hint: the last eight words may give you some ideas for answering the last question.

4. **Examine Style**   In a class discussion, comment on various effects in this poem:
   a) no periods
   b) no capital letters
   c) the last stanza being longer than the others
   d) the personification in stanza 2:
      "their fifty cents a day sweat
      hugs me tight every morning"
   How do these choices affect your reading of the poem?

Extending

5. **Create an Advertisement**   Assume that the garment workers are forming a union. Create a poster or an illustrated brochure inviting the workers to the meeting.

6. **Prepare an Oral Reading**   With a partner, rehearse a reading of the poem for the class.

> **TIPS**
> - Consider how you will divide up the poem.
> - You can use props or photographs or other images during your reading.
> - Taped background music can be very effective.
> - Practise your reading for a friend or family member and ask for constructive criticism.

> **Before you read,** use the title to imagine a picture of the poem's situation. In your notebook, write down the details you imagine.
>
> **As you read,** make a list of the changing feelings of the father.

Notes

Raymond Souster is a popular Toronto poet. His many books of poetry include *The Colour of the Times* (1964), which won the Governor General's Award. In his poetry, he likes to use natural speech rhythms rather than "poetic diction."

The Man Who Finds That His Son Has Become a Thief

Poem by Raymond Souster

Coming into the store at first angry
At the accusation, believing in
The word of his boy who has told him:
I didn't steal anything, honest.

Then becoming calmer, seeing that anger
Will not help in the business, listening painfully
As the other's evidence unfolds, so painfully slow.

Then seeing gradually that evidence
Almost as if tighten slowly around the neck
Of his son, at first vaguely circumstantial, then gathering damage,
Until there is present the unmistakable odour of guilt
Which seeps now into the mind and lays its poison.

Suddenly feeling sick and alone and afraid,
As if an unseen hand had slapped him in the face
For no reason whatsoever: wanting to get out
Into the street, the night, the darkness, anywhere to hide
The pain that must show in the face to these strangers, the fear.

It must be like this.
It could hardly be otherwise.

You take it from here ...

Responding

1. **Chart Changing Feelings**   With a partner, go over your prereading lists noting how the father's feelings change. For each feeling you noted, identify details in the poem that reveal those feelings. Chart your findings.

Father's feelings	Supporting details
angry (at the accusation)	
confident (in his son)	

2. **Focus on the Ending**   With the rest of the class, discuss the poem's last two lines. Has the author effectively recreated a parent's reaction to a teenager in trouble?

3. **Make a Prediction**   In a paragraph, state what the father is likely to do when he and his son arrive home. What do you think he *should* do? Why?

Extending

4. **Write a Letter**   As the son, write a letter of apology to the store manager. Suggest a way the incident can be resolved.

5. **Solve a Problem**   In a group of two or three, discuss the problem of shoplifting. Who does it hurt most: merchants? parents? the shoplifters themselves? consumers? society at large? How? Brainstorm a list of arguments against shoplifting, then select the top five to include on a poster or in a brochure aimed at shoplifting prevention.

> **Before you read,** have a class discussion about what it means to be "grown up." Is it a matter of age? attitude? something else?
>
> **As you read,** note how dialogue, actions, and details are used to show what each character is like.

A Boy Grows Older

"Speak to your father. It's his money."

Short Story by Morley Callaghan

Notes

Morley Callaghan (1903–1990) was a famous Toronto short-story writer and novelist. He began his writing career as a journalist in Montreal and Toronto. In 1951 he won the Governor General's Award for *The Loved and the Lost*.

In the bedroom Mrs. Sloane sat down and folded her hands tight in her lap and swallowed hard and said to her husband, "I've got something to tell you about Jim."

Holding the shoe he had just taken off in his hand, he said, "Were you talking to him today?"

"He's coming here for money. I've been giving a bit to him from time to time. I know I shouldn't, but he's got me completely distracted."

"He knows we've got no money to lend," he said, and as he got up and walked around excitedly with one shoe on, she knew he was thinking of their little bit of money disappearing day by day. "He knows we've only got our bit of a pension," he said. He had worked hard all his life and they had both denied themselves many little comforts and now she could see a look of terror coming into his eyes that she had seen for the first time the day he had to quit work and they had thought they would hardly be able to live. "Why, what'll happen to us?" he said, turning on her suddenly. "Where does he think we get it?"

She only sighed and shook her head, for she had been asking Jim that question for months, yet every time he got behind in his insurance collections he came around, scared, and got a little money from her.

"There's no use giving me a setting out," she said. "He'll never believe we won't give it to him till you tell him. If he understands we're through helping him maybe he'll get some sense."

As they sat there solemnly looking at each other and waiting for Jim, she had her old dressing gown wrapped around her and he was sitting on the bed with his white hair mussed from rubbing his hands through it. They took turns blurting things out, questions they never tried to answer, questions that worried them more and more and drew them

28   Characters in Conflict

closer together. When they heard Jim come in and call from the living room, she said, "Remember, I'm going to tell him I told you. I've done all I can. It's up to you now."

Jim was waiting for her, walking up and down with his hat on and his white scarf hanging out as if the wind had blown it free from his overcoat while he hurried along the street. He looked very unhappy but tried to smile at his mother. His face was so good-natured it was almost weak.

"What is it this time?" she asked.

"Oh," he said, sitting down and starting to rub his shoe on the carpet like an embarrassed small boy, "the same thing, I guess."

"More money again, you mean," she said.

"I guess that's it."

"In God's name, what for this time?"

"The same thing—I'm behind in my collections."

She had intended to shrug and say coolly, "Speak to your father," but instead she found herself walking up and down in front of him, wheeling on him and whispering savagely, "You'd take the last cent from us, and then what do you think is going to happen? Who are you going to run to then?" But he got up and took her arm and muttered, "I'll never ask you again—I promise—but I've got to have it. I'll give every cent back to you—I promise, I wouldn't ask you if there was a chance of getting it any place else." He felt sure of her. "I'll lose my job," he said.

"Maybe it would teach you to have some respect for yourself," she said, and then she added calmly, "I've told your father."

"You told him after all," he said, terribly hurt. "You promised not to."

"I'm through," she said.

He started to work himself up into a temper, which didn't fool her at all, because he always did it when he was trying to abuse her.

"You're mean," he said. "Plain mean." His words had no real anger and she smiled grimly. When he saw her smile he stopped and said helplessly, "Please, Mom, please—" But she said firmly, "Speak to your father. It's his money."

"Mom, just this once more," he pleaded, and when she saw how he dreaded facing his father, she was puzzled because he had never been afraid of him, they had never shouted at each other. "I've got to do it, I've got to do it," he kept saying to himself as he walked up and down, and then he turned to her, white-faced, and said, "Well, I've got to ask him, I can't help it," and he went into the bedroom with her following.

His father had gotten into bed and was reading, and he could just see the crown of his white head rising over the edge of the newspaper. When Jim went into the room, he stood over under the light on the wall. That was where he always stood when he was in trouble. Years ago when he

A Boy Grows Older 29

had been caught in a petty theft at school he had stood there; when he had started to work he used to come in late at night and stand under the light and tell them what had happened during the day, and it was where he had stood the night when he was eighteen and had told them he was going to get married. He was tilting back and forth on his heels, waiting for his father to look over at him, but when the paper wasn't lowered, he said at last in a mild, friendly tone, "Dad, could you loan me some money?"

His father put down his paper, folded it, shoved it under his arm and took off his glasses and said, "What do you do with your money, son?"

As his father stared at him steadily, a silly half-ashamed grin was on Jim's face. "I don't know, honestly I don't," he said shaking his head.

"Well, tell me what you think you do with it. You must remember something."

"Salesmen and collectors are all pretty much alike," Jim said. "They hang around together and it just slips through their fingers and then they're short at the end of the week."

"Then a man like you shouldn't have such a job."

"I guess you're right," Jim mumbled.

"Why don't you hunt for another job?"

"I will—I'll try hard," he said eagerly.

"How much do you need this time?"

"It's a lot, I've got to cover a whole week's collections," Jim said, his head down, his voice faint.

"All that?" his father said, and Mrs. Sloane knew by the way he swung his head toward her, startled, that he was thinking of the money he had saved for himself for his personal expenses such as tobacco, newspapers, a trip to the movies, and clothes for himself. As he swung the bedclothes off, his face was flushed a vivid red against his white hair and he kept on staring at Jim. Mrs. Sloane knew he had a bad temper and she grew afraid.

Jim, watching his father coming toward him in his bare feet, muttered hastily, "I guess you haven't got it. I guess I'll go."

"Wait, Jim," his father called anxiously, making it clear he was not going to challenge him at all. "I didn't say I didn't have it, did I?" He spoke as if Jim ought to understand they had always been close together. He was going over to his coat hanging on the closet door. When Mrs. Sloane saw how he fumbled in his pocket for his chequebook and how his hand trembled as he jerked his pen out of his vest pocket she knew he was scared of something. She thought he was scared of Jim: she resented it so much she turned to abuse Jim herself.

But she said nothing to Jim because she had never seen him look so hurt as he did standing there waiting and realizing that his father was scared. He was watching his father as if at last he understood everything his father felt, and he said in a whisper, "What are you scared of?"

"Nothing," his father said.

"What's the matter?"

"Maybe I was thinking it might be worse."

"What do you mean?"

"Supposing I didn't give it to you?" his father said, and while they kept looking at each other, Jim felt the fear in his father that came from knowing how weak he was, a fear that tomorrow or in a year something was apt to happen that would break him and jail him. He turned to his mother, begging her with his eyes to tell him what to do or say that would drive that scared look from his father's eyes. For the first time he seemed aware of their feeling for him. She nodded her head: she wanted to tell him she believed in him, but she was puzzled herself.

His father was writing the cheque on the top of the dresser. He wrote very carefully, and when he was finished he handed the cheque to Jim, saying, only, "Here you are, Son."

Looking at the cheque as if it were very hard for him to take it, Jim said in such a low voice she could hardly hear him, "I guess I've got to take it, but I'll pay you back. I wish you'd believe I'll pay you back. I don't want to take it if you won't believe it."

"All right, Son."

"Well, thanks, thanks," he said.

But at the door he stood for a while with his head down, waiting, as if he couldn't bear to leave them till he was sure they had some faith left in him. He was so grave it made him look years older.

When he had gone, his father waited a while for her to abuse him scornfully for not being firm with him, and then when she didn't speak, but stood there looking at the door, he got into bed and pulled the covers over him. After a few moments, she went over and got into bed too. But she couldn't lie down. She sat up stiffly, staring down at her husband's face. His head rolled away from her and his eyes were closed.

"I'm glad you gave it to him," she said.

He opened his eyes and said simply, "He's getting older. He was a little different. Didn't you notice it? It made me feel we hadn't been wrong helping him this far."

As she lay down beside him and reached to turn out the light, her hand trembled. She lay very still. Then she turned and put her arm around him, and they lay there together in the dark.

A Boy Grows Older 31

You take it from here ...

Responding

1. **Identify Conflicts**   Most conflicts are struggles within or between characters. In a small group, brainstorm and record three to five different conflicts in this story. Share and compare responses with another group.

2. **Explain Motivation**   Write a paragraph analyzing what caused the parents to give Jim a loan. What were their reasons? (Hint: focus on the last three paragraphs of the story.)

3. **Analyze Character**   In a class discussion, describe the characters of the mother and father. What are they like? Support your responses with examples from the story.

4. **Relate a Personal Experience**   Think about a time when you experienced or witnessed a "generation gap" conflict similar to the one in the story. Relate your experience to a partner and tell what you learned from it.

Extending

5. **Speculate on a Character's Thoughts**   Refer back to the story and speculate on how Jim felt after taking money from his parents. How do you think he felt about himself? about the position he had put his parents in? about his future? Record your deductions in point form and discuss them with the class.

6. **Role-Play a Scene**   With another student, improvise one of the following situations:
    a) a conversation between the mother and a family counsellor
    b) a conversation between one of the parents and Jim when he returns to request another loan

> **PEER ASSESSMENT**
> - View and then assess another pair's role-play scene. Did it tie into this story? Did the conversation make sense? Was it clear? Was the choice of detail interesting? How could the improvisation have been better?

> **Before you read,** look up the word "grief" in a dictionary. Do people grieve differently in response to a death? Discuss with another student.
>
> **As you read,** anticipate what the title may have to do with the plot.

Blood Knots

"Do you think it's strange, going fishing? At a time like this, I mean?"

Short Story by Mallory Burton

Notes

Mallory Burton lives in British Columbia. She is a teacher, linguist, and school administrator, and she has been a serious fly-fisher for more than 15 years. Her best-known book is *Reading the Water: Stories and Essays of Fly-fishing and Life* (with Holly Morris).

blood knot (also called a barrel knot): a uniform, difficult-to-tie fly-fishing knot

flies: natural or artificial flies used to catch fish

grommets: metal eyelets placed in a hole to protect a cable

leaders: short lengths of nylon, wire, etc. used to attach a lure or fly to a fishing line

rod: long lightweight pole used in fishing

I have neglected to tie the wading boots properly, to pull the braided laces tight against the metal grommets, to fasten them securely with a double knot. This is partly due to lack of effort and partly because the boots are much too big for me. They belong to my father. Belonged to my father. I suppose they are mine now. Neither my mother nor my sister fishes. I am the only one.

The boots are full of fine gravel, which chafes between my thick, outer wading socks and the lightweight fabric of these summer waders. I should get out of the river to empty the boots, but it doesn't seem worth the effort of battling the current all the way back to the bank.

A mosquito buzzes close to my temple. I can hear its thin whine over the rushing of the stream, see the dark fluttering blur out of the corner of my eye. The insect lands, and I feel its sting, such a tiny prick that I wonder why I have always made such a fuss about them, slapping at myself and smearing poisonous oil all over my face and limbs.

I slowly raise my hand to my temple and crush the mosquito. Not because I really want to, but because I feel I should. The same way that I felt I should wash my face and comb my hair and put on my clothes this morning, even though it seemed to make such little sense. It is unsettling, this doubting of routine, this absence of concern, this lack of energy. Perhaps I should not be here on the river at all.

"Go. Get out of the house for a while," my mother insisted. She extended her arms and flicked her hands at me as though I were a bothersome child. "There's really nothing you can do until this afternoon."

My father died two days ago. The funeral is today at four. Mother is handling it pretty well. My sister is distraught, sedated. I am still waiting for my own emotion to surface in what I anticipate will be a sense of

overwhelming loss. Every few hours, I test the depth of my grief, sounding its progress with tentative excursions into the past.

Earlier this morning, I sorted though my father's fly-fishing gear. I have gear of my own, of course, but it isn't something you think of packing when your father has died suddenly and you are trying to catch a plane at an impossible hour. I sorted his flies and mended his leaders. I removed the spool from his old Hardy reel to change it over from a right-handed to a left-handed retrieve. I had to unwind all the line in order to rewind it onto the spool in the opposite direction.

The gear was spread out all over the kitchen floor. A neighbour woman, who'd come by with a tray of baking for after the service, had to pick her way through the mess. Seeing the tangle of line on the floor, she offered to help. She held the line with a slight tension so that I could wind it more evenly onto the spool. She kept looking at the split-cane rod lying in sections near her feet. My father's name had been burned into the shaft in an old-fashioned, flowing script.

"This is beautiful old gear," she said. "Are you going fishing?"

"Yes."

"You're not," said my mother. She shut off the running water and turned, twisting her hands in her apron.

"You said get out of the house."

"I thought maybe a walk." She shrugged and left the room. I expected the neighbour woman to follow her; instead, she motioned me to continue my winding.

"Do you think it's strange, going fishing? At a time like this, I mean?"

The woman hesitated. Then she leaned forward and said, very quietly, "Sometimes it takes a while to catch up with you. When Alex passed away, I didn't even cry. A couple of weeks later I was coming through the door with my arms full of groceries, and the wind caught the door, slammed it shut behind me. I put down the groceries, opened the door and slammed it again. I must have slammed it twenty times."

I pictured the slight grey-haired woman slamming the door, understanding her satisfaction with the final, solid sound of it.

The hatch is beginning. At first there is just a handful of bugs coming off the water, teasing a few eager fish into splashy rises. The nearest fisherman is a hundred yards upstream, stationed in one spot, not casting. Presumably he is waiting for the better fish to show themselves. He looks alert, expectant as the swarm of swallows gathering overhead.

I know this river. The hatch will gradually accelerate over the next hour or so, until the smooth surface of the water is frothed and silver with feeding fish. Until the air is both noisy with lunging rises and soft with clouds of pale-winged mayflies.

The upstream fisherman has his rod in the air now, stripping line with his left hand while the length of his backcast grows. I have picked out my fish as well, a trout that shows the curved half-circle of his back with each leisurely rise. The fish is directly across from me.

I drop a delicate Pale Morning a few feet upstream, floating it dead-drift over his lie. I am in the right place, with just enough slack in my line to ensure a drag-free float, but my timing is off. The bugs are hatching in greater numbers now, and it is difficult to focus on the rhythm of my trout with fish rising sporadically on every side.

One larger fish, in particular, is coming up just a rod length away. His appearance is erratic, and his unexpected rises have twice startled me into lifting the tip of my rod, a reaction that makes the fly take a sudden skip over the water. Afraid that I will spook my fish, I decide to deliberately put down the erratic riser.

I face upstream, waiting for the fish to surface again, quickly stripping in my line until most of it lies in a tangle, bunched against my waist by the current. A cloud passes over the sun momentarily, and the water goes steel-grey. When the fish shows, I slap the line down hard on the water's surface just behind his head. The fish snaps up the natural that was his target, then lunges sideways, seizing my imitation and taking it down with him.

For a few seconds the leader disappears, its surface coils pulled straight down by the fish. Then, with a great sucking splash, the trout suddenly shoots through the air. He is coming fast, straight at me, eye level. His mouth is open, and I can see the fly lodged securely in his upper jaw. His gills are flared open. Looking into his mouth and out through his gills, I can see the trees on the far shore. The fish is wide-eyed, and I wonder if he has seen me. He drops just short of hitting my chest, clumsily on his side, throwing water in my face.

The fish changes direction, runs upstream. The current does not appear to be much of a deterrent. The pile of line at my waist diminishes rapidly, and somehow I have the sense to let it go, to keep my hand off the reel. The last of the slack disappears, and the line slaps tight against the rod, sending out a shower of tiny droplets. For an instant I feel the weight of the fish connecting at the other end of the line in one strong pull, and then he is gone.

Damn. Damn. I want that fish. I lift the rod tip, aching for the fish to be there. I will play the fish carefully and bring him gently to the net. I will hold him in the current, admire his colours until he is strong enough to swim away on his own; instead, the line comes back easily through the water.

The fish will jump again, trying to shake the fly that is still hooked in his jaw. I will see the gleam of silver as his twisting body catches the sunlight. I stand looking upstream, but he does not show.

It is difficult to retrieve the line. My hands are shaking, and I feel weak, disoriented. The current tugs at my legs with a new intensity, as if the river had suddenly risen six inches. In turning, I lose my footing. My feet slide over the smooth stones and gravel bottom of the river, carried by the current. It occurs to me that if I fall, I will not have the strength to regain a footing. I concentrate on remaining upright, leaning into the current, angling slowly across the river toward shallower water and the protection of a small island. Slowly I make my way to the water's edge and sit down heavily on the bank, where I lie back in the rushes, my feet trailing in the water.

My father's death was sudden, unexpected. The secretary found him face down on his desk when she went in with the morning mail. It is difficult to believe. He was the sort of man you'd expect to perish on the side of a mountain heading for the continental divide. Or on the bank of an icy river during the winter steelhead run.

The sun is warm on my face. A mayfly, a survivor, crawls up on the underside of a reed and hangs upside down on its tip, swaying. There is a cold spot on my right instep where the gravel in my father's boot has finally punctured a small hole. It is just as well. If I get off the river now, I will just have time to drive back and change for the funeral.

I sit up and quickly untie the boots, keeping one eye on the river. I dump the gravel, rinse the boots, and retie the laces with a secure double knot. I repair the leader, adding lengths of fresh tippet with a series of secure blood knots. I carefully attach a new fly. The hatch could go on for hours. There are still plenty of fish rising. I wonder if my mother and sister will understand.

You take it from here ...

Responding

1. **Discuss as a Class**   How has the narrator responded to the death of her father? Is she a cold person? Does she really miss him? Give details from the story to support your opinions.

2. **Analyze the Events**   In a small group, suggest answers for the following questions:
   a) Why has the narrator gone fishing?
   b) Why does the mother react as she does when she learns the narrator is going fishing?
   c) Why does the narrator get weak toward the end of the story?
   d) What do you think she will likely do after the story ends? Why do you think so?

3. **Examine the Title**   Write a paragraph telling how you think the title of this story relates to the plot and characters.

4. **Focus on Style**   In your notebook, quote three sentences you thought were especially effective. Using a chart, analyze what each sentence reveals or suggests about character or conflict.

Sentence	What it reveals or suggests

Extending

5. **Compose Journal Entries**   Taking the role of the narrator, write a journal entry for the evening of the story, revealing her thoughts and feelings after the funeral. Then write a second entry dated about a week later.

6. **Write a Personal Response**   Reflect on your discussion about how people grieve the loss of someone or something of importance to them. Consider how the narrator responded to the death of her father. What were her conflicts and how did she resolve them? Does the way she reacted make sense to you? Why or why not?

Before you read, recall a time when you walked by a lake, river, or the ocean. Think about the sights, smells, sounds, tastes, and feelings you experienced there.

As you read, create a mental picture of the scene drawn by the poem's words.

Notes

Lesley Choyce is an award-winning Nova Scotia author, publisher, teacher, TV host, musician, and all-season surfer. His books include *The Republic of Nothing*, which won the 1995 Dartmouth Book Award.

Wedge Island

Poem by Lesley Choyce

We walk the Wedge from inner tip,
a well-honed ridge of clay and rock
forgetting that it once was fat
and trussed a mighty headland
to the coast.
This acid sea again, at work,
in patient mutilation,
erasing, removing,
denying memory.

I remember a hike here once,
midstorm,
when seas rifled reports
and lemons bobbed around the foam,
a crate of yellow balls
loosed from some distant ship
for the waves to juggle
then toss toward shore.
I tasted one; it stung of sour
and salt and something else
not right for shores this far up north.

The gulls control this place
as the narrow splays out
into a broad green table top.
They gather by the hundreds
to eddy about—loud, threatening,
for we have arrived at their resting ground.
They shriek and dive
and carve long shadows with their wings
as they fence us in with their fury
and stage a frenzied ceiling
hung low beneath the clouds.

We meet one young, pedestrian gull,
then two,
both grey and downy
and confused by our shape.
Dead brothers and sisters appear,
caught in low alders,
picked clean by cruel relations
with careless hunger
and sharpened beaks.

You take it from here ...

Responding

1. **Record Initial Responses** In your notebook, record your answers to the following questions.
    a) What are the effects of the sea on Wedge Island? (stanza 1) How do these effects reflect conflict?
    b) Summarize the speaker's memory in stanza 2.
    c) Comment on the mood of stanza 3.
    d) What are the strongest words in stanza 4? How are they disturbing?

2. **Consider Structure** For each stanza in the poem, write a single sentence describing its main point or focus. Then write a two-sentence comment on how the poem is strategically organized to produce a strong reaction in the reader.

3. **Illustrate the Poem** Recall the mental picture you created on your first reading, and use it to help you illustrate the poem. You can draw your illustration or compile a collage of pictures or photos that effectively represent the poem.

> **TIPS**
> - Think in terms of images that capture the poem's moods.
> - Look at the scene as if viewing it with a camera. Is the scene viewed as a long shot or a close-up? Is it looking down to the beach, or up from it? What is in the foreground and background? Will you need human figures?

Extending

4. **Convey a Memory** Recall a place that affected you in a way similar to that described in the poem. Then write a paragraph or a 12-line (minimum) poem to describe the place you remember. Use forceful adjectives like those in the poem, and try to create a similar dramatic mood.

5. **Create a Display** With a partner, choose and photograph a selection of natural scenes in your area. Add descriptive paragraphs or poems for two of the pictures. Display your work in the classroom. If two groups photograph and caption the same scene(s), compare the artistic interpretation, both in terms of the image (layout, angles, lighting) and the description.

Before you read, look up the word "interloper" in a dictionary. On the basis of the meaning(s), predict what you think this story will be about.

As you read, notice how the interloper theme is woven into the story.

The Interlopers

doesn't belong

The two enemies stood glaring at one another for a long silent moment.

Short Story by Saki (H.H. Munro)

Notes

Saki (H.H. Munro) (1870–1916) was an English satirist, humorist, author, and journalist. He was best known for his short stories. He died in France during the First World War.

Fear—both authors were in setting

personal conflict

In a forest of mixed growth somewhere on the eastern spurs of the Carpathians, a man stood one winter night watching and listening, as though he waited for some beast of the woods to come within the range of his vision, and, later, of his rifle. But the game for whose presence he kept so keen an outlook was none that figured in the sportsman's calendar as lawful and proper for the chase; Ulrich von Gradwitz patrolled the dark forest in quest of a human enemy.

The forest lands of Gradwitz were of wide extent and well stocked with game; the narrow strip of precipitous woodland that lay on its outskirt was not remarkable for the game it harboured or the shooting it afforded, but it was the most jealously guarded of all its owner's territorial possessions. A famous lawsuit, in the days of his grandfather, had wrested it from the illegal possession of a neighbouring family of petty landowners; the dispossessed party had never acquiesced in the judgment of the Courts, and a long series of poaching affrays and similar scandals had embittered the relationships between the families for three generations. The neighbour feud had grown into a personal one since Ulrich had come to be head of his family; if there was a man in the world whom he detested and wished ill to it was Georg Znaeym, the inheritor of the quarrel and the tireless game-snatcher and raider of the disputed border-forest. The feud might, perhaps, have died down or been compromised if the personal ill will of the two men had not stood in the way. As boys they had thirsted for one another's blood, as men each prayed that misfortune might fall on the other. On this wind-scourged winter night Ulrich had banded together his foresters to watch the dark forest, not in quest of four-footed quarry, but to keep a lookout for the prowling thieves whom he suspected of being afoot from across the land

person named anne

boundary. The roebuck, which usually kept in the sheltered hollows during a storm-wind, were running like driven things tonight, and there was movement and unrest among the creatures that were wont to sleep through the dark hours. Assuredly there was a disturbing element in the forest, and Ulrich could guess the quarter from whence it came.

He strayed away by himself from the watchers whom he had placed in ambush on the crest of the hill, and wandered far down the steep slopes amid the wild tangle of undergrowth, peering through the tree-trunks and listening through the whistling and skirling of the wind and the restless beating of the branches for sight or sound of the marauders. If only on this wild night, in this dark, lone spot, he might come across Georg Znaeym, man to man, with none to witness—that was the wish that was uppermost in his thoughts. And as he stepped round the trunk of a huge beech he came face to face with the man he sought.

The two enemies stood glaring at one another for a long silent moment. Each had a rifle in his hand, each had hate in his heart and murder uppermost in his mind. The chance had come to give full play to the passions of a lifetime. But a man who has been brought up under the code of a restraining civilization cannot easily nerve himself to shoot down his neighbour in cold blood and without word spoken, except for an offence against his hearth and honour. And before the moment of hesitation had given way to action a deed of Nature's own violence overwhelmed them both. A fierce shriek of the storm had been answered by a splitting crash over their heads, and ere they could leap aside a mass of falling beech tree had thundered down on them. Ulrich von Gradwitz found himself stretched on the ground, one arm numb beneath him and the other held almost helplessly in a tight tangle of forked branches, while both legs were pinned beneath the fallen mass. His heavy shooting-boots had saved his feet from being crushed to pieces, but if his fractures were not as serious as they might have been, at least it was evident that he could not move from his present position till someone came to release him. The descending twigs had slashed the skin of his face, and he had to wink away some drops of blood from his eyelashes before he could take in a general view of the disaster. At his side, so near that under ordinary circumstances he could have touched him, lay Georg Znaeym, alive and struggling, but obviously as helplessly pinioned down as himself. All round them lay a thick-strewn wreckage of splintered branches and broken twigs.

Relief at being alive and exasperation at his captive plight brought a strange medley of pious thank-offerings and sharp curses to Ulrich's lips. Georg, who was nearly blinded with the blood which trickled across his eyes, stopped his struggling for a moment to listen, and then gave a short, snarling laugh.

"So you're not killed, as you ought to be, but you're caught, anyway," he cried; "caught fast. Ho, what a jest, Ulrich von Gradwitz snared in his stolen forest. There's a real justice for you!"

And he laughed again, mockingly and savagely.

"I'm caught in my own forest-land," retorted Ulrich. "When my men come to release us you will wish, perhaps, that you were in a better plight than caught poaching on a neighbour's land, shame on you."

Georg was silent for a moment; then he answered quietly:

"Are you sure that your men will find much to release? I have men, too, in the forest tonight, close behind me, and *they* will be here first and do the releasing. When they drag me out from under these damned branches it won't need much clumsiness on their part to roll this mass of trunk right over on top of you. Your men will find you dead under a fallen beech tree. For form's sake I shall send my condolences to your family."

"It is a useful hint," said Ulrich fiercely. "My men had orders to follow in ten minutes' time, seven of which must have gone by already, and when they get me out—I will remember the hint. Only as you will have met your death poaching on my lands, I don't think I can decently send any message of condolence to your family."

"Good," snarled Georg, "good. We fight this quarrel out to the death, you and I and our foresters, with no cursed interlopers to come between us. Death and damnation to you, Ulrich von Gradwitz."

"The same to you, Georg Znaeym, forest-thief, game-snatcher."

Both men spoke with the bitterness of possible defeat before them, for each knew that it might be long before his men would seek him out or find him; it was a bare matter of chance which party would arrive first on the scene.

Both had now given up the useless struggle to free themselves from the mass of wood that held them down. Ulrich limited his endeavours to an effort to bring his one partially free arm near enough to his outer coat-pocket to draw out his wine-flask. Even when he had accomplished that operation it was long before he could manage the unscrewing of the stopper or get any of the liquid down his throat. But what a Heaven-sent draught it seemed! It was an open winter, and little snow had fallen as yet, hence the captives suffered less from the cold than might have been the case at that season of the year; nevertheless, the wine was warming and reviving to the wounded man, and he looked across with something like a throb of pity to where his enemy lay, just keeping the groans of pain and weariness from crossing his lips.

"Could you reach this flask if I threw it over to you?" asked Ulrich suddenly; "there is good wine in it, and one may as well be as comfortable as one can. Let us drink, even if tonight one of us dies."

"No, I can scarcely see anything; there is so much blood caked round my eyes," said Georg, "and in any case I don't drink wine with an enemy."

Ulrich was silent for a few minutes, and lay listening to the weary screeching of the wind. An idea was slowly forming and growing in his brain, an idea that gained strength every time he looked across at the man who was fighting so grimly against pain and exhaustion. In the pain and languor that Ulrich himself was feeling the old fierce hatred seemed to be dying down.

"Neighbour," he said presently, "do as you please if your men come first. It was a fair compact. But as for me, I've changed my mind. If my men are the first to come you shall be the first to be helped, as though you were my guest. We have quarrelled like devils all our lives over this stupid strip of forest, where the trees can't even stand upright in a breath of wind. Lying here tonight, thinking, I've come to think we've been rather fools; there are better things in life than getting the better of a boundary dispute. Neighbour, if you will help me to bury the old quarrel I—I will ask you to be my friend."

Georg Znaeym was silent for so long that Ulrich thought, perhaps, he had fainted with the pain of his injuries. Then he spoke slowly and in jerks.

"How the whole region would stare and gabble if we rode into the market-square together. No one living can remember seeing a Znaeym and a von Gradwitz talking to one another in friendship. And what peace there would be among these forester folk if we ended our feud tonight. And if we choose to make peace among our people there is none other to interfere, no interlopers from outside. You could come and keep the Sylvester night beneath my roof, and I would come and feast on some high day at your castle. I would never fire a shot on your land, save when you invited me as a guest; and you should come and shoot with me down in the marshes where the wildfowl are. In all the countryside there are none that could hinder if we willed to make peace. I never thought to have wanted to do other than hate you all my life, but I think I have changed my mind about things too, this last half-hour. And you offered me your wineflask. Ulrich von Gradwitz, I will be your friend."

For a space both men were silent, turning over in their minds the wonderful changes that this dramatic reconciliation would bring about. In the cold, gloomy forest, with the wind tearing in fitful gusts through the naked branches and whistling round the tree trunks, they lay and waited for the help that would now bring release and succour to both parties. And each prayed a private prayer that his men might be the first to arrive, so that he might be the first to show honourable attention to the enemy that had become a friend.

Presently, as the wind dropped for a moment, Ulrich broke the silence.

"Let's shout for help," he said; "in this lull our voices may carry a little way."

"They won't carry far through the trees and undergrowth," said Georg, "but we can try. Together, then."

The two raised their voices in a prolonged hunting call.

"Together again," said Ulrich a few minutes later, after listening in vain for an answering halloo.

"I heard something that time, I think," said Ulrich.

"I heard nothing but the pestilential wind," said Georg hoarsely.

There was silence again for some minutes, and then Ulrich gave a joyful cry.

"I can see figures coming through the wood. They are following in the way I came down the hillside."

Both men raised their voices in as loud a shout as they could muster.

"They hear us! They've stopped. Now they see us. They're running down the hill toward us," cried Ulrich.

"How many of them are there?" asked Georg.

"I can't see distinctly," said Ulrich; "nine or ten."

"Then they are yours," said Georg; "I had only seven out with me."

"They are making all the speed they can, brave lads," said Ulrich gladly.

"Are they your men?" asked Georg. "Are they your men?" he repeated impatiently as Ulrich did not answer.

"No," said Ulrich with a laugh, the idiotic chattering laugh of a man unstrung with hideous fear.

"Who are they?" asked Georg quickly, straining his eyes to see what the other would gladly not have seen.

"Wolves."

You take it from here ...

Responding

1. **Interpret the Title**   Discuss with the class the significance of the title. Who are the interlopers in the story? In what ways are they interlopers?

2. **Review Conflict**   Create a chart to describe the course of the conflict between the two characters. List the following headings across the top of a page, then fill in the information below each.

Causes of the feud	Events leading feuders to friendship	Outcome of the conflict

   When you have finished, compare notes with a partner and discuss the following question: What does the author seem to be saying about feuding?

3. **Compare Characters**   In a paragraph, explain how the men are basically similar people.

4. **Focus on Setting**   In a small group, discuss the following questions. Follow up by sharing your views in a class discussion.
   a) What is the setting? Where and when does the story take place?
   b) How does setting create mood for the reader?
   c) How does the setting affect the plot, conflict, and characters?

Extending

5. **Evaluate the Story**   Write a review in which you give your personal response to the story. For example, do you think this is a good, entertaining story? Is it relevant today? What can readers learn from it?

   > **SELF ASSESSMENT**
   > - How did you arrive at your opinions and conclusions about the story?
   > - Have you read stories or novels with similar conflicts?

6. **Increase Vocabulary**   Make a list of at least six words in the story that are unfamiliar to you. Look up their definitions in a dictionary. Then write an original sentence for at least six of the words.

Before you read, predict what you think this teleplay might be about. Compare responses with a partner.

As you read, keep track of who the monsters are. Note how this record compares with your original prediction.

The Monsters Are Due on Maple Street

"They looked just like humans."

Teleplay by Rod Serling

Notes

Rod Serling (1924–1975) was best known as the host of the popular TV series *The Twilight Zone*. The series, for which he wrote most of the scripts, ran from 1959–1964. He was fond of stories that had an ironic twist or surprise ending.

Characters

NARRATOR
FIGURE ONE
FIGURE TWO

Residents of Maple Street:

DON MARTIN
STEVE BRAND
MYRA BRAND, Steve's wife
PETE VAN HORN
CHARLIE
CHARLIE'S WIFE
TOMMY
SALLY, Tommy's mother
LES GOODMAN
ETHEL GOODMAN, Les's wife
MAN ONE
WOMAN ONE

ACT ONE

Scene 1

(FADE IN ON SHOT OF THE NIGHT SKY. *The various heavenly bodies stand out in sharp, sparkling relief. As the* CAMERA *begins a* SLOW PAN *across the Heavens, we hear the Narrator.*)

NARRATOR: (*off stage*) There is a fifth dimension beyond that which is known to man. It is a dimension as vast as space and as timeless as infinity. It is the middle ground between light and shadow—between science and superstition. And it lies between the pit of man's fears and the summit of his knowledge. This is the dimension of imagination. It is an area which we call the Twilight Zone.

Scene 2

(THE CAMERA BEGINS TO PAN DOWN until it passes the horizon and stops on a sign which reads "Maple Street." It is daytime. Then we see the street below. It is a quiet, tree-lined, small-town American street. The houses have front porches on which people sit and swing on gliders, talking across from house to house. Steve Brand is polishing his car, which is parked in front of his house. His neighbour, Don Martin, leans against the fender watching him. A Good Humor man riding a bicycle is just in the process of stopping to sell some ice cream to a couple of kids. Two women gossip on the front lawn. Another man is watering his lawn with a garden hose.

At this moment Tommy, one of the two boys buying ice cream from the vendor, looks up to listen to a tremendous screeching roar from overhead. A flash of light plays on the faces of both boys and then moves down the street and disappears.

Various people leave their porches or stop what they are doing to stare up at the sky.

Steve Brand, the man who has been polishing his car, stands there transfixed, staring upwards. He looks at Don Martin, his neighbour from across the street.)

STEVE: What was that? A meteor?

DON: That's what it looked like. I didn't hear any crash though, did you?

STEVE: Nope. I didn't hear anything except a roar.

MRS. BRAND: (*from her porch*) Steve? What was that?

STEVE: (*raising his voice and looking toward the porch*) Guess it was a meteor, honey. Came awful close, didn't it?

MRS. BRAND: Too close for my money. Much too close.

(THE CAMERA PANS ACROSS VARIOUS PORCHES to people who stand there watching and talking in low conversing tones.)

NARRATOR: Maple Street. Six-forty-four p.m. on a late September evening. (*a pause*) Maple Street in the last calm and reflective moment ... before the monsters came!

(THE CAMERA TAKES US ACROSS THE PORCHES AGAIN. A man is screwing a light bulb on a front porch. He gets down off his stool to flick the switch and finds that nothing happens.

Another man is working on an electric power mower. He plugs in the plug, flicks the switch of the mower off and on, but nothing happens.

Through a window we see a woman pushing her finger back and forth on the dial hook of a telephone. Her voice sounds far away.)

WOMAN ONE: Operator, operator, something's wrong on the phone, operator!

(*Mrs. Brand comes out on the porch and calls to Steve.*)

MRS. BRAND: (*calling*) Steve, the power's off. I had the soup on the stove and the stove just stopped working.

WOMAN ONE: Same thing over here. I can't get anybody on the phone either. The phone seems to be dead.

(*We look down again on the street. Small, mildly disturbed voices creep up from below.*)

VOICE ONE: Electricity's off.

VOICE TWO: Phone won't work.

VOICE THREE: Can't get a thing on the radio.

VOICE FOUR: My power mower won't move, won't work at all.

VOICE FIVE: Radio's gone dead!

(*Pete Van Horn, a tall, thin man, is seen standing in front of his house.*)

VAN HORN: I'll cut through the back yard ... see if the power's still on on Floral Street. I'll be right back!

(*He walks past the side of his house and disappears into the back yard.* THE CAMERA PANS DOWN SLOWLY *until we are looking at ten or eleven people standing around the street and overflowing to the curb and sidewalk. In the background is Steve Brand's car.*)

STEVE: Doesn't make sense. Why should the power go off all of a sudden *and* the phone line?

DON: Maybe some kind of an electrical storm or something.

CHARLIE: That don't seem likely. Sky's just as blue as anything. Not a cloud. No lightning. No thunder. No nothing. How could it be a storm?

WOMAN ONE: I can't get a thing on the radio. Not even the portable.

(*The people again murmur softly in wonderment.*)

CHARLIE: Well, why don't you go downtown and check with the police, though they'll probably think we're crazy or something. A little power failure and right away we get all flustered and everything—

STEVE: It isn't just the power failure, Charlie. If it was, we'd still be able to get a broadcast on the portable.

(*There is a murmur of reaction to this. Steve looks from face to face and then over to his car.*)

STEVE: I'll run downtown. We'll get this all straightened out.

(*He walks over to the car, gets in, and turns the key.*

Looking through the open car door, we see the crowd watching Steve from the other side. He starts the engine. It turns over sluggishly and then stops dead. He tries it again, and this time he can't get it to turn over. Then very slowly he turns the key back to "off" and gets out of the car.

The people stare at Steve. He stands for a moment by the car and then walks toward them.)

STEVE: I don't understand it. It was working fine before—

DON: Out of gas?

STEVE: (*shakes his head*) I just had it filled up.

WOMAN ONE: What's it mean?

CHARLIE: It's just as if ... as if everything had stopped. (*Then he turns toward Steve.*) We'd better *walk* downtown.

(*another murmur of assent to this*)

STEVE: The two of us can go, Charlie. (*He turns to look back at the car.*) It couldn't be the meteor. A meteor couldn't do *this*.

The Monsters Are Due on Maple Street

(*He and Charlie exchange a look. Then they start to walk away from the group.*

Tommy comes into view. He is a serious-faced young boy in spectacles. He stands halfway between the group and the two men who start to walk down the sidewalk.)

TOMMY: Mr. Brand ... you'd better not!

STEVE: Why not?

TOMMY: They don't want you to.

(*Steve and Charlie exchange a grin and Steve looks back toward the boy.*)

STEVE: *Who* doesn't want us to?

TOMMY: (*jerks his head in the general direction of the distant horizon*) Them!

STEVE: Them?

CHARLIE: Who are them?

TOMMY: (*intently*) Whoever was in that thing that came by overhead.

(*Steve knits his brows for a moment, cocking his head questioningly. His voice is intense.*)

STEVE: What?

TOMMY: Whoever was in that thing that came over. I don't think they want us to leave here.

(*Steve leaves Charlie, walks over to the boy, and puts his hand on the boy's shoulder. He forces his voice to remain gentle.*)

STEVE: What do you mean? What are you talking about?

TOMMY: They don't want us to leave. That's why they shut everything off.

STEVE: What makes you say that? What ever gave you *that* idea?

WOMAN ONE: (*from the crowd*) Now isn't that the craziest thing you ever heard?

TOMMY: (*persistent but a little frightened*) It's always that way, in every story I ever read about a ship landing from outer space.

WOMAN ONE: (*to the boy's mother, Sally, who stands on the fringe of the crowd*) From outer space yet! Sally, you better get that boy of yours up to bed. He's been reading too many comic books or seeing too many movies or something!

SALLY: Tommy, come over here and stop that kind of talk.

STEVE: Go ahead, Tommy. We'll be right back. And you'll see. That wasn't any ship or anything like it. That was just a ... a meteor or something. Likely as not—(*He turns to the group, now trying very hard to sound more optimistic than he feels.*) No doubt it did have something to do with all this power failure and the rest of it. Meteors can do some crazy things. Like sun spots.

DON: (*picking up the cue*) Sure. That's the kind of thing—like sun spots. They raise Cain with radio reception all over the world. And this thing being so close—why, there's no telling the sort of stuff it can do. (*He wets his lips, smiles nervously.*) Go ahead, Charlie. You and Steve go into town and see if that isn't what's causing it all.

(*Steve and Charlie walk away from the group down the sidewalk as the people watch silently.*

Tommy stares at them, biting his lips, and finally calls out again.)

TOMMY: Mr. Brand!

(The two men stop. Tommy takes a step toward them.)

TOMMY: Mr. Brand ... please don't leave here.

(Steve and Charlie stop once again and turn toward the boy. In the crowd there is a murmur of irritation and concern, as if the boy's words—even though they didn't make sense—were bringing up fears that shouldn't be brought up.

Tommy is partly frightened and partly defiant.)

TOMMY: You might not even be able to get to town. It was that way in the story. *Nobody* could leave. Nobody except—

STEVE: Except who?

TOMMY: Except the people they'd sent down ahead of them. They looked just like humans. And it wasn't until the ship landed that—*(The boy suddenly stops, conscious of the people staring at him and his mother and of the sudden hush of the crowd.)*

SALLY: *(in a whisper, sensing the antagonism of the crowd)* Tommy, please son ... honey, don't talk that way—

MAN ONE: That kid shouldn't talk that way ... and we shouldn't stand here listening to him. Why, this is the craziest thing I ever heard of. The kid tells us a comic book plot and here we stand listening—

(Steve walks toward the camera, and stops beside the boy.)

STEVE: Go ahead, Tommy. What kind of story was this? What about the people they sent out ahead?

TOMMY: That was the way they prepared things for the landing. They sent four people. A mother and a father and two kids who looked just like humans ... but they weren't.

(There is another silence as Steve looks toward the crowd and then toward Tommy. He wears a tight grin.)

STEVE: Well, I guess what we'd better do then is to run a check on the neighbourhood and see which ones of us are really human. *(There is laughter at this, but it's a laughter that comes from a desperate attempt to lighten the atmosphere. The people look at one another in the middle of their laughter.)*

CHARLIE: *(rubs his jaw nervously)* I wonder if Floral Street's got the same deal we got. *(He looks past the houses.)* Where is Pete Van Horn anyway? Didn't he get back yet? *(Suddenly there is the sound of a car's engine starting to turn over. We look across the street toward the driveway of Les Goodman's house. He is at the wheel trying to start the car.)*

SALLY: Can you get started, Les?

(Les Goodman gets out of the car, shaking his head.)

GOODMAN: No dice.

(He walks toward the group. He stops suddenly as, behind him, the car engine starts up all by itself. Goodman whirls around to stare at it.

The car idles roughly, smoke coming from the exhaust, the frame shaking gently.

The Monsters Are Due on Maple Street

Goodman's eyes go wide, and he runs over to his car.

The people stare at the car.)

MAN ONE: He got the car started somehow. He got *his* car started!

(*The people continue to stare, caught up by this revelation and wildly frightened.*)

WOMAN ONE: How come his car just up and started like that?

SALLY: All by itself. He wasn't anywheres near it. It started all by itself.

(*Don Martin approaches the group, stops a few feet away to look toward Goodman's car and then back toward the group.*)

DON: And he never did come out to look at that thing that flew overhead. He wasn't even interested. (*He turns to the group, his face taut and serious.*) Why? Why didn't he come out with the rest of us to look?

CHARLIE: He always was an oddball. Him and his whole family. Real oddball.

DON: What do you say we ask him?

(*The group start toward the house. In this brief fraction of a moment they take the first step toward a metamorphosis that changes people from a group into a mob. They begin to head purposefully across the street toward the house. Steve stands in front of them. For a moment their fear almost turns their walk into a wild stampede, but Steve's voice, loud, incisive, and commanding, makes them stop.*)

STEVE: Wait a minute ... *wait a minute!* Let's not be a mob!

(*The people stop, pause for a moment, and then much more quietly and slowly start to walk across the street. Goodman stands alone facing the people.*)

GOODMAN: I just don't understand it. I tried to start it and it wouldn't start. You saw me. All of you saw me.

(*And now, just as suddenly as the engine started, it stops, and there is a long silence that is gradually intruded upon by the frightened murmuring of the people.*)

GOODMAN: I don't understand. I swear ... I don't understand. What's happening?

DON: Maybe you better tell us. Nothing's working on this street. Nothing. No lights, no power, no radio. (*then meaningfully*) Nothing except one car—*yours!*

(*The people's murmuring becomes a loud chant filling the air with accusations and demands for action. Two of the men pass Don and head toward Goodman who backs away from them against his car. He is cornered.*)

GOODMAN: Wait a minute now. You keep your distance—all of you. So I've got a car that starts by itself—well, that's a freak thing—I admit it. But does that make me some kind of a criminal or something? I don't know why the car works—it just does!

(*This stops the crowd momentarily and Goodman, still backing away, goes toward his front porch. He goes up the steps and then stops, facing the mob.*)

GOODMAN: What's it all about, Steve?

STEVE: (*quietly*) We're all on a monster kick, Les. Seems that the general impression holds that maybe one family isn't what we think they are. Monsters from outer space or something. Different from us. Fifth columnists from the vast beyond. (*He chuckles.*) You know anybody that might fit that description around here on Maple Street?

GOODMAN: What is this, a gag? (*He looks around the group again.*) This a practical joke or something?

(*Suddenly the car engine starts all by itself, runs for a moment, and stops. One woman begins to cry. The eyes of the crowd are cold and accusing.*)

GOODMAN: Now that's supposed to incriminate me, huh? The car engine goes on and off and that really does it, doesn't it? (*He looks around the faces of the people.*) I just don't understand it ... any more than any of you do! (*He wets his lips, looking from face to face.*) Look, you all know me. We've lived here five years. Right in this house. We're no different from any of the rest of you! We're no different at all ... Really ... this whole thing is just ... just weird—

WOMAN ONE: Well, if that's the case, Les Goodman, explain why—(*She stops suddenly, clamping her mouth shut.*)

GOODMAN: (*softly*) Explain what?

STEVE: (*interjecting*) Look, let's forget this—

CHARLIE: (*overlapping him*) Go ahead, let her talk. What about it? Explain what?

WOMAN ONE: (*a little reluctantly*) Well ... sometimes I go to bed late at night. A couple of times ... a couple of times I'd come out here on the porch and I'd see Mr. Goodman here in the wee hours of the morning standing out in front of his house ... looking up at the sky. (*She looks around the circle of faces.*) That's right, looking up as the sky as if ... as if he were waiting for something. (*a pause*) As if he were looking for something.

(*There's a murmur of reaction from the crowd again as Goodman backs away.*)

GOODMAN: She's crazy. Look, I can explain that. Please ... I can really explain that ... she's making it up anyway. (*Then he shouts.*) I tell you she's making it up! (*He takes a step toward the crowd and they back away from him. He walks down the steps after them and they continue to back away. Suddenly he is left completely alone, and he looks like a man caught in the middle of a menacing circle as the scene* SLOWLY FADES TO BLACK.)

ACT TWO

Scene 1

(FADE IN ON MAPLE STREET AT NIGHT. *On the sidewalk, little knots of people stand around talking in low voices. At the end of each conversation they look toward Les Goodman's house. From the various houses we can see candlelight but no electricity. The quiet which blankets the whole area is disturbed only by the almost whispered voices of the people standing around. In one group Charlie stands staring across at Goodman's house. Two men stand across the street from it in almost sentry-like poses.*)

SALLY: (*in a small, hesitant voice*) It just doesn't seem right, though, keeping watch on them. Why ... he was right when he said he was one of our neighbours. Why, I've know Ethel Goodman ever since they moved in. We've been good friends—

CHARLIE: That don't prove a thing. Any guy who'd spend his time lookin' up at the sky early in the morning—well, there's something wrong with that kind of person. There's something that ain't legitimate. Maybe under normal circumstances we could let it go by, but these aren't normal circumstances. Why, look at this street! Nothin' but candles. Why, it's like goin' back into the dark ages or somethin'!

(*Steve walks down the steps of his porch, down the street to Les Goodman's house, and then stops at the foot of the steps. Goodman is standing there; Mrs. Goodman behind him is very frightened.*)

GOODMAN: Just stay right where you are, Steve. We don't want any trouble, but this time if anybody sets foot on my porch—that's what they're going to get—trouble!

STEVE: Look, Les—

GOODMAN: I've already explained to you people. I don't sleep very well at night sometimes. I get up and I take a walk and I look up at the sky. I look at the stars!

MRS. GOODMAN: That's exactly what he does. Why, this whole thing, it's … it's some kind of madness or something.

STEVE: (*nods grimly*) That's exactly what it is—some kind of madness.

CHARLIE'S VOICE: (*shrill, from across the street*) You best watch who you're seen with, Steve! Until we get this all straightened out, you ain't exactly above suspicion yourself.

STEVE: (*whirling around toward him*) Or you, Charlie. Or any of us, it seems. From age eight on up!

WOMAN ONE: What I'd like to know is—what are we gonna do? Just stand around here all night?

CHARLIE: There's nothin' else we *can* do! (*He turns back, looking toward Steve and Goodman again.*) One of 'em'll tip their hand. They *got* to.

STEVE: (*raising his voice*) There's something you can do, Charlie. You can go home and keep your mouth shut. You can quit strutting around like a self-appointed hanging judge and just climb into bed and forget it.

CHARLIE: You sound real anxious to have that happen, Steve. I think we better keep our eye on you, too!

DON: (*as if he were taking the bit in his teeth, takes a hesitant step to the front*) I think everything might as well come out now. (*He turns toward Steve.*) Your wife's done plenty of talking, Steve, about how *odd* you are!

CHARLIE: (*picking this up, his eyes widening*) Go ahead, tell us what she's said.

(*Steve walks toward them from across the street.*)

STEVE: Go ahead, what's my wife said? Let's get it *all* out. Let's pick out every idiosyncrasy of every single man, woman, and child on the street. And then we might as well set up some kind of kangaroo court. How about a firing squad at dawn, Charlie, so we can get rid of all the suspects? Narrow them down. Make it easier for you.

DON: There's no need gettin' so upset, Steve. It's just that … well … Myra's talked about how there's been plenty of nights you spent hours down in your basement workin' on some kind of radio or something. Well, none of us have ever *seen* that radio—

(*By this time Steve has reached the group. He stands there defiantly.*)

CHARLIE: Go ahead, Steve. What kind of "radio set" you workin' on? I never seen it. Neither has anyone else. Who you talk to on that radio set? And who talks to you?

STEVE: I'm surprised at you, Charlie. How come you're so dense all of a sudden? (*a pause*) Who do I talk to? I talk to monsters from outer space. I talk to three-headed green men who fly over here in what look like meteors.

(*Mrs. Brand steps down from the porch, bites her lip, calls out.*)

MRS. BRAND: Steve! Steve, please. (*Then looking around, frightened, she walks toward the group.*) It's just a ham radio set, that's all. I bought him a book on it myself. It's just a ham radio set. A lot of people have them. I can show it to you. It's right down in the basement.

STEVE: (*whirls around toward her*) Show them nothing! If they want to look inside our house—let them get a search warrant.

CHARLIE: Look, buddy, you can't afford to—

STEVE: (*interrupting him*) Charlie, don't start telling me who's dangerous and who isn't and who's safe and who's a menace. (*He turns to the group and shouts.*) And you're with him, too—all of you! You're standing here all set to crucify—all set to find a scapegoat—all desperate to point some kind of a finger at a neighbour! Well now, look, friends, the only thing that's gonna happen is that we'll eat each other up alive—

(*He stops abruptly as Charlie suddenly grabs his arm.*)

CHARLIE: (*in a hushed voice*) That's not the *only* thing that can happen to us.

(*Down the street, a figure has suddenly materialized in the gloom, and in the silence we hear the clickety-clack of slow, measured footsteps on concrete as the figure walks slowly toward them. One of the women lets out a stifled cry. Sally grabs her boy, as do a couple of other mothers.*)

TOMMY: (*shouting, frightened*) It's the monster! It's the monster!

(*Another woman lets out a wail and the people fall back in a group staring toward the darkness and the approaching figure.*

The people stand in the shadows watching. Don Martin joins them, carrying a shotgun. He holds it up.*)

DON: We may need this.

STEVE: A shotgun? (*He pulls it out of Don's hand.*) Good Lord—will anybody think a thought around here? Will you people wise up? What good would a shotgun do against—

(*The dark figure continues to walk toward them as the people stand there, fearful, mothers clutching children, men standing in front of their wives.*)

CHARLIE: (*pulling the gun from Steve's hands*) No more talk, Steve. You're going to talk us into a grave! You'd let whatever's out there walk right over us, wouldn't yuh? Well, some of us won't!

(*Charlie swings around, raises the gun, and suddenly pulls the trigger. The sound of the shot explodes in the stillness.*

The figure suddenly lets out a small cry, stumbles forward onto his knees, and then falls forward on his face. Don, Charlie, and Steve race forward to him. Steve is there first and turns the man over. The crowd gathers around them.)

STEVE: (*slowly looks up*) It's Pete Van Horn.

DON: (*in a hushed voice*) Pete Van Horn! He was just gonna go over to the next block to see if the power was on—

WOMAN ONE: You killed him, Charlie. You shot him dead!

CHARLIE: (*looks around at the circle of faces, his eyes frightened, his face contorted*) But ... but I didn't know who he was. I certainly didn't know who he was. He comes walkin' out of the darkness—how am I supposed to know who he was? (*He grabs Steve.*) Steve—you know why I shot! How was I supposed to know he wasn't a monster or something? (*He grabs Don.*) We're all scared of the same thing. I was just tryin' to ... tryin' to protect my home, that's all! Look, all of you,

The Monsters Are Due on Maple Street

that's all I was tryin' to do. (*He looks down wildly at the body.*) I didn't know it was somebody we knew! I didn't know—

(*There's a sudden hush and then an intake of breath in the group. Across the street all the lights go on in one of the houses.*)

WOMAN ONE: (*in a hushed voice*) Charlie ... Charlie ... the lights just went on in your house. Why did the lights just go on?

DON: What about it, Charlie? How come you're the only one with lights now?

GOODMAN: That's what I'd like to know. (*a pause as they all stare toward Charlie*)

GOODMAN: You were so quick to kill, Charlie, and you were so quick to tell us who we had to be careful of. Well, maybe you *had* to kill. Maybe Pete there was trying to tell us something. Maybe he'd found out something and came back to tell us who there was amongst us we should watch out for—

(*Charlie backs away from the group, his eyes wide with fright.*)

CHARLIE: No ... no ... it's nothing of the sort! I don't know why the lights are on. I swear I don't. Somebody's pulling a gag or something.

(*He bumps against Steve who grabs him and whirls him around.*)

STEVE: A gag? A gag? Charlie, there's a dead man on the sidewalk and you killed him! Does this thing look like a gag to you?

(*Charlie breaks away and screams as he runs toward his house.*)

CHARLIE: No! No! Please!

(*A man breaks away from the crowd to chase Charlie. As the man tackles him and lands on top of him, the other people start to run toward them. Charlie gets up, breaks away from the other man's grasp, lands a couple of desperate punches that push the man aside. Then he forces his way, fighting, through the crowd and jumps up on his front porch.*

Charlie is on his porch as a rock thrown from the group smashes a window beside him, the broken glass flying past him. A couple of pieces cut him. He stands there perspiring, rumpled, blood running down from a cut on the cheek. His wife breaks away from the group to throw herself into his arms. He buries his face against her. We can see the crowd converging on the porch.)

VOICE ONE: It must have been him.

VOICE TWO: He's the one.

VOICE THREE: We got to get Charlie.

(*Another rock lands on the porch. Charlie pushes his wife behind him, facing the group.*)

CHARLIE: Look, look I swear to you ... it isn't me ... but I do know who it is ... I swear to you. I do know who it is. I know who the monster is here. I know who it is that doesn't belong. I swear to you I know.

DON: (*pushing his way to the front of the crowd*) All right, Charlie, let's hear it! (*Charlie's eyes dart around wildly.*)

CHARLIE: It's ... it's ...

MAN TWO: (*screaming*) Go ahead, Charlie, tell us.

CHARLIE: It's ... it's the kid. It's Tommy. He's the one!

(*There's a gasp from the crowd as we see Sally holding the boy. Tommy at first doesn't understand and then, realizing the eyes are all on him, buries his face against his mother.*)

SALLY: (*backs away*) That's crazy! He's only a boy.

WOMAN ONE: But he knew! He was the only one who knew! He told us all about it. Well, how did he know? How *could* he have known?

(*Various people take this up and repeat the question.*)

VOICE ONE: How could he know?

VOICE TWO: Who told him?

VOICE THREE: Make the kid answer.

(*The crowd starts to converge around the mother who grabs Tommy and starts to run with him. The crowd starts to follow, at first walking fast, and then running after him.*

Suddenly Charlie's lights go off and the lights in other houses go on, then off.)

MAN ONE: (*shouting*) It isn't the kid ... it's Bob Weaver's house.

WOMAN ONE: It isn't Bob Weaver's house, it's Don Martin's place.

CHARLIE: I tell you it's the kid.

DON: It's Charlie. He's the one.

(*People shout, accuse, and scream as the lights go on and off. Then, slowly, in the middle of this nightmarish confusion of sight and sound the* CAMERA STARTS TO PULL AWAY *until once again we have reached the opening shot looking at the Maple Street sign from high above.*)

Scene 2

(THE CAMERA CONTINUES TO MOVE AWAY WHILE GRADUALLY BRINGING INTO FOCUS *a field. We see the metal*

side of a space craft which sits shrouded in darkness. An open door throws out a beam of light from the illuminated interior. Two figures appear, silhouetted against the bright lights. We get only a vague feeling of form.)

FIGURE ONE: Understand the procedure now? Just stop a few of their machines and radios and telephones and lawn mowers ... throw them into darkness for a few hours, and then just sit back and watch the pattern.

FIGURE TWO: And this pattern is always the same?

FIGURE ONE: With few variations. They pick the most dangerous enemy they can find ... and it's themselves. And all we need do is sit back ... and watch.

FIGURE TWO: Then I take it this place ... this Maple Street ... is not unique.

FIGURE ONE: (*shaking his head*) By no means. Their world is full of Maple Streets. And we'll go from one to the other and let them destroy themselves. One to the other ... one to the other ... one to the other—

Scene 3

(THE CAMERA PANS UP *for a shot of the starry sky, and over this we hear the Narrator's voice.*)

NARRATOR: The tools of conquest do not necessarily come with bombs and explosions and fall-out. There are weapons that are simply thoughts, attitudes, prejudices—to be found only in the minds of men. For the record, prejudices can kill and suspicion can destroy and a thoughtless, frightened search for a scapegoat has a fall-out all its own for the children ... and the children yet unborn. (*a pause*) And the pity of it is ... that these things cannot be confined to ... The Twilight Zone!

(FADE TO BLACK)

You take it from here ...

Responding

1. **Discuss a Key Phrase**   As a class, discuss what the "twilight zone" is. Reread the narrator's opening remarks and consider how they relate to what happens in the teleplay. Then take a look also at the narrator's closing comments. What do they add to your understanding of the term "twilight zone"?

2. **Review Plot Elements**   A typical story includes most of the following elements of plot:

   - a complication (an event that starts conflict)
   - rising action (section where tension rises)
   - crisis (moment when conflict comes to a head)
   - climax (major turning point in the story; the moment of greatest emotional intensity)
   - falling action (events after climax)
   - resolution (moment where conflict is explained or resolved)

   Working with a partner, design a chart, line diagram, or other visual form of presentation to show how the plot progresses in this story, identifying events that correspond with each element.

Plot element	Example from text
complication	
rising action	
crisis	

3. **Analyze Characters**   Skim the story, and note as many things as you can about the following Maple Street residents:

   - Steve Brand
   - Tommy
   - Don Martin
   - Les Goodman
   - Charlie

   Take notes as you read. Compare notes with a partner, and discuss these characters' similarities and differences.

4. **Interpret Content** Write a paragraph explaining who the real monsters are in the story, giving examples of "monstrous" behaviour from the selection. Conclude with a sentence that tells what you think this story reveals about human nature.

Extending

5. **Make a Front Page** Create the front page of a newspaper for the day the play takes place. Include headlines and three news stories about the invasion, with at least one report focusing on Maple Street. Be sure to keep in mind that this story takes place during the 1960s, while you consider content.

6. **Create Trading Cards** Make five to seven trading cards featuring characters from the story. On one side, include the character's name and picture (which you can draw or cut-and-paste). On the other side, include a key quotation from the text and a brief description of the character.

   Decide whether you want to be serious or humorous. Be creative—use the text as a basis for the character, and use your imagination to fill in the details.

TIPS

- Use names from the teleplay for the Maple Street story.
- Include either hand-drawn illustrations, clip-art software, or pictures from newspapers and magazines.
- Include a banner (name of the newspaper) and the date, as well as some other typical front-page features (e.g., a news digest, table of contents, weather forecast).

Reflecting on the Unit

Responding

1. **Investigate a Theme**   Several selections in this unit feature characters who are in isolation as they face their conflicts. Record in chart form how isolation affects three individuals selected from "Fear," "Bus Ride," "Nipikti the Old Man Carver," "Relics," "The Man Who Finds That His Son Has Become a Thief," "Blood Knots," or "Wedge Island." Compare two of the three characters' responses to their situations.

2. **Deliberate on Unit Characters**   Discuss the following with a partner:
   a) Which character was the most interesting? Why?
   b) Which character did you sympathize with the most? Explain.
   c) Which character, in your opinion, was the least admirable? Why?
   d) Name two *static characters* (who don't change or develop).
   e) Name two *dynamic characters* (who changed significantly).

Extending

3. **Role-Play Conflict Resolution**   Work with a partner to choose an example of conflict between two characters in this unit, or create your own scenario. Write dialogue that expresses and then resolves the conflict. Rehearse the dialogue and present it to the class. Ask for their comments about your scene.
   From this discussion, make a list or chart of general rules of conflict resolution that can be applied to real-life situations.

4. **Compose an Ad**   Write five classified ads for a newspaper using characters and situations from the unit. Examples: bus pass for sale by Lyda in "Bus Ride"; house for sale from "The Monsters Are Due on Maple Street." Choose two of your ads, and recreate them in a different format (for example, billboard, radio ad, TV commercial). Present them to the class, and explain if, how, and/or why you made changes and additions to content to accommodate an alternate media form.

> **SELF ASSESSMENT**
>
> Review what you have learned from this unit regarding
> - how a theme or idea can be developed
> - what causes most conflicts and how they might be resolved
> - how mood is created by writers
> - how to organize an answer to a question
> - how to respond personally to a selection
> - how to work with others to accomplish a common purpose

UNIT 2

"I awoke one morning and found myself famous."
—Lord Byron

"Fame is a fickle food Upon a shifting plate ..."
—Emily Dickinson

"Some are born great, some achieve greatness, and some have greatness thrust upon them."
—William Shakespeare

"In the future, everyone will be world-famous for 15 minutes."
—Andy Warhol

Clockwise from top left: Alanis Morissette, Adrienne Clarkson, Ovide Mercredi, Elvis Presley, Bill Gates, Terry Fox, Albert Einstein, Roberta Bondar, Michael J. Fox, Nelson Mandela

FAME AND GREATNESS

As Lord Byron discovered, fame can come suddenly and unexpectedly. Poet Emily Dickinson and pop artist Andy Warhol suggest that fame is at best brief and changing, but many seek it nonetheless.

Greatness, however, may be one's destiny, or it can come from honest effort and hard work, according to Shakespeare.

In this unit, you will explore these topics in depth. In the process, you'll encounter several impressive individuals to whom, because they excel at what they do, these words can be applied.

As you read this unit, think about the following:

1) What is the nature of fame? Does it last?
2) In what ways can fame be a burden? How do the lives of the famous and great differ from the lives of others?
3) What are the main avenues to fame?
4) What distinguishes "great" people from mere celebrities?

Before you read, make a list of five very famous people. Share your list with one or two other students.

As you read, write in your notebook reasons why the fame of Sonny Bono and Chris Farley has not lasted.

Outlasting the Fickleness of Fame
by Meg Murphy

EDITORIAL

Chicago Tribune

For some celebrities, even death—what should be the final curtain call—fails to dim the public's fascination with their images and what they represent.

The 1997 death of comedian Chris Farley and the death of Cher's sidekick-turned-congressman Sonny Bono a few weeks later have prompted tributes and tears, but popular culture experts doubt that they or any number of other celebrities have what it takes to reach idol status.

It's a select group of stars whose lustre remains strong even decades after their careers and lives have ended.

For example, despite continuing tabloid reports to the contrary, the king of rock 'n' roll still is dead. But that did not deter Elvis fans who, in 1997, marked his birthday with pilgrimages to Graceland.

Why is it that some celebrities, such as Elvis, James Dean, and Marilyn Monroe, draw sighs from the public long after their final breath?

There's no set formula to predict exactly which celebrities will achieve idol status, popular culture experts say, but some points toward or away from eternal remembrance have been noted.

For one thing, at 62, Bono was too old.

"Most of the icons that die and go on to have great followings die young," according to Irv Rein, a professor at Northwestern University and the author of *High Visibility*, which talks about how people are transformed into stars.

A colleague agreed. "We do tend to care more about youth, particularly youth tragically lost, than we do about wise old age," said Alison Scott, of Bowling Green State University.

> "Most of the icons that die and go on to have great followings die young."

The stars who never fade oftentimes are rebels, with causes or otherwise. They stand for something in the public's mind, Rein said.

"They usually represent something tumultuous. Presley symbolized rock 'n' roll," Rein said.

While Farley, at 33, undoubtedly died young, "he didn't change the way we lived," an important prerequisite for legend status, said Mark Roesler, head of CMG Worldwide, which represents celebrity clients living and dead.

Chris Farley, 1997

His client roster includes Marilyn Monroe, James Dean, Liberace, and the racehorse Secretariat. Although Bono did manage to reinvent himself from a second banana to a fledgling statesman, neither he nor Farley were viewed as voices for much of their particular generations.

A fickle public dictates who achieves lasting fame, as well as who becomes an also-ran. The criteria are not necessarily fair or evenly applied; if they were, we might have seen a similar amount of Elvis-like hoopla devoted to the 20th anniversaries of the passings of crooner Bing Crosby, rocket scientist Wernher von Braun, and author Anais Nin, who also all died in 1977.

The reactions to the deaths of Diana, Princess of Wales, and Mother Teresa in the same month in 1997 show how the public's fancy is not based solely on the number or weight of worthwhile endeavours. How many stayed up to watch the princess's funeral? How many rearranged their schedules to tune in to Mother Teresa's memorial?

Diana was perceived as having a strong connection to women leading more typical lives, Rein said.

She had mother-in-law problems like many married women; in her case, they were exacerbated by her break from royal tradition that had kept the personal lives of the ruler's offspring relatively private.

"All of her faults have disappeared into this flame of martyrdom. Some celebrities we celebrate because they are not real to us, they're a myth, or they're someone we identify with," said Scott, noting that Diana managed to represent both fairy-tale princess and struggling mother.

The public's habit of elevating celebrities, breathing or not, to a higher plane is hardly a recent development. Autograph albums predate the Civil War in the United States. And British popular history is replete with heroes: Lord Byron, for instance, enjoyed an enormous following in his heyday, Scott said.

"It was not simply because he was a fine poet, but because of his reputation as a romantic hero," Scott said. "The fact that he died young in the Greek revolution did not do that celebrity a darn bit of damage."

Diana, Princess of Wales, 1997

"Celebrity worship intensified with the advent of motion pictures early in the twentieth century when the Hollywood film people discovered stars could sell movies," Rein said.

With the loosening of the chokehold that movies had on the national psyche after the Second World War, the system spread to include sports heroes, who now are armed with publicists in addition to athletic talent.

Also joining the ranks of celebrities on a course for icon consideration are hotshots from such formerly glamourless fields as business and the law. Bill Gates, who has youth, a geeky charisma, and let's not forget money, seems very promising.

Successful people in such fields always have enjoyed stature, but not on a national scale. Now, a bit of self promotion is beginning to change that. It might not be the most respect-worthy developer or accountant whose name comes first to mind; it might be the person most adept at tooting his or her own horn.

"The rules about being well-known have changed. Modesty is no longer in; now being flamboyant and talking about your skills is accepted," said Rein, noting the increasing appearances of practitioners from a variety of fields on television programs: Johnny Cochran, Martha Stewart, Donald Trump.

This type of celebrity still does not have the otherworldly type of staying power that seems to be the domain of movie and music stars.

Guiding living celebrities such as Sophia Loren in a way that will make icons of them is not a whole lot different from going to bat for the families of icons dead but established, such as Babe Ruth, Roesler said.

Any proposal that would distort the image of the celeb will get a swift thumbs down, Roesler said. For example, Dean's family members rejected a James Dean rubber duck bath toy.

James Dean, 1955

Dean and another movie idol, Marilyn Monroe, are by far the most popular images requested, Roesler said. He estimated that the firm evaluates between 600 and 800 pitches for Monroe a year. Even idols' property itself has a market, a tradition that dates back to the collection of saints relics, said David Redden, executive vice president of Sotheby's auction house in New York.

"To hold something in your hand that was held by somebody who you have some extraordinary feeling about has enormous meaning," said Redden. As the Internet joins television in providing an instantaneous forum for people to become famous, Redden said he would not be surprised to see an increase in celebrity auctions, as more wannabes achieve their 15 minutes in the spotlight. Whether such instant idols will endure is anyone's guess, but the search for them remains eternal.

"People need to believe in other people," Redden said.

"It's a wonderful human trait that there are some people we view as heroes and heroines."

You take it from here ...

Responding

1. **Discuss in a Small Group**   With another student, review the article and find answers to the following questions:
   - Why are Sonny Bono and Chris Farley not as famous as James Dean, Elvis Presley, and Marilyn Monroe?
   - How are ordinary people transformed into stars?
   - In what sense is the public fickle about fame?
   - Why were Princess Diana and Lord Byron famous?
   - How did the system of celebrity worship change after the Second World War?

2. **List Media Strategies**   According to the article, the best-known people are not necessarily the top ones in their field—rather, the most famous is "the person most adept at tooting his or her own horn." In pairs, identify three ways an individual can use mass media to become famous.

3. **Consider Audience and Purpose**   As a class, discuss the purpose and intended audience of this article.

4. **Understand Organization**   This article is actually organized into sections. Scan the article and identify what each section is about. Compare notes with another student.

Extending

5. **Share an Anecdote**   Make up a story in which you meet a celebrity—being as imaginative and as detailed as you can. (If you have actually met a celebrity in the past, then use that story.) What was the celebrity like in person? Did she or he behave like an ordinary person? How did you act or react toward her or him? Were you nervous or excited? Explain your feelings. Share your anecdotes in small groups.

   > **PEER ASSESSMENT**
   >
   > When all of the anecdotes have been told, provide feedback to the group:
   > - What anecdotes were most convincing? Why?
   > - What anecdotes were most entertaining? Why?

6. **Write Diary Entries**   Choose one celebrity and write three diary entries in which he or she describes the challenges of being famous and how it affects his or her everyday life.

Before you read, share what you know about Marilyn Monroe in a class discussion.

As you read, think about the meaning of the lines "Your candle burned out long before/Your legend ever did."

Notes

Since the 1960s, **Bernie Taupin** has co-written many songs with **Elton John**, with John writing the music to Taupin's lyrics. Their hits include "Your Song," "Crocodile Rock," "Daniel," and "Philadelphia Freedom." They continue to work together.

Marilyn Monroe (1926–62), born Norma Jean Baker, was an American film star, talented comedienne, and "sex goddess," whose personal life was tragic. She was a victim of child abuse and was later exploited by Hollywood executives and even by politicians. Her best-known movies include *Gentlemen Prefer Blondes*, *The Seven-Year Itch*, *Bus Stop*, *Some Like It Hot*, and *The Misfits*.

Candle in the Wind

Lyrics by Bernie Taupin

Goodbye Norma Jean
Though I never knew you at all
You had the grace to hold yourself
While those around you crawled
They crawled out of the woodwork
And they whispered into your brain
They set you on the treadmill
And they made you change your name.

And it seems to me you lived your life
Like a candle in the wind
Never knowing who to cling to
When the rain set in
And I would have liked to have known you
But I was just a kid
Your candle burned out long before
Your legend ever did.

Loneliness was tough
The toughest role you ever played
Hollywood created a superstar
And the pain was the price you paid
Even when you died
The press still hounded you
All the papers had to say
Was that Marilyn was found in the nude.

Goodbye Norma Jean
Though I never knew you at all
You had the grace to hold yourself
While those around you crawled.

Goodbye Norma Jean
From the young man in the 22nd row
Who sees you as something more than sexual
More than just our Marilyn Monroe.

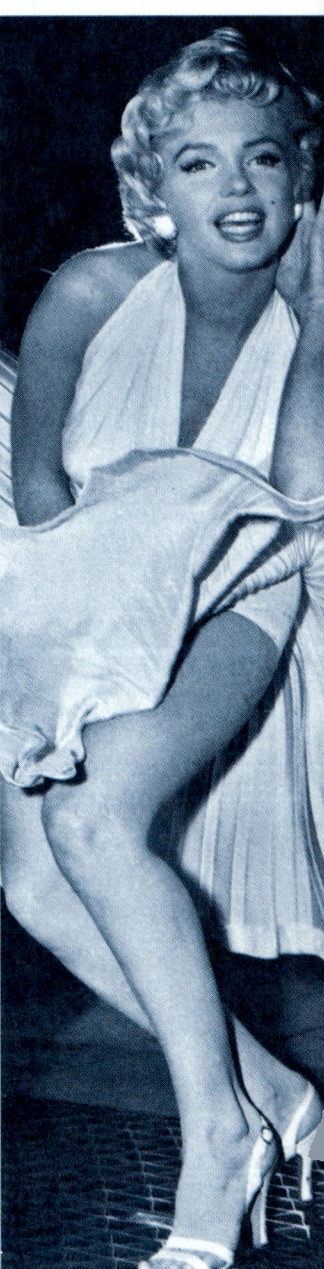

Marilyn Monroe in *The Seven-Year Itch*, 1954

You take it from here ...

Responding

1. **Discuss First Responses**   In a group, comment on how the lyrics make you feel. Do you think Monroe had a happy life? Did she have privacy? Do you feel sorry for her? Why or why not?

2. **Clarify Meanings**   With a partner, review the lyrics and arrive at an understanding of the following lines:
   - "Loneliness was tough/The toughest role you ever played."
   - "You had the grace to hold yourself/While those around you crawled."
   - "Your candle burned out long before/Your legend ever did."

3. **Develop an Idea**   Prepare a two-minute talk on one of the following themes dealt with by this song:
   - the high price of fame
   - the difference between public image and personal identity
   - why young people find celebrities of the past interesting
   - the difference between surface attractiveness and inner beauty

Extending

4. **Investigate Marketing**   Using the previous selection, "Outlasting the Fickleness of Fame," these lyrics, and other information, write a theory suggesting how Marilyn Monroe was marketed to the public. In what ways was she turned into a "commodity" for public consumption?

5. **Imagine a Different Outcome**   Imagine that Marilyn Monroe is still alive and is writing her memoirs, recalling the successes and struggles in her life and career so far. Choose an event—real or imagined—in her life, and write a passage presenting her reflections on that time. Share your account with the class.

6. **Conduct Research**   Select another movie idol from the past or present and find out some basic facts, such as
   - birth date and birthplace
   - significant people and events in his or her life—both before and after he or she became famous
   - career highlights
   - his or her most famous roles

   Present your findings in the form of your choice.

> **TIPS**
>
> Look for information and photos
> - in library books, magazines, and videos
> - on the Internet

> **Before you read,** brainstorm with a partner names of popular comic strips and discuss the features they exhibit that hook people into becoming faithful fans.
>
> **As you read,** write down words that describe Lynn Johnston's personality.

I always knew I'd make my living as an artist.

The Cartoonist: Lynn Johnston

AS TOLD TO MARGO ROSTON

PROFILE

It's amazing after 20 years (of creating *For Better or For Worse*), young people say to me, "I've been reading you since I was a little kid."

Art is something you do from the day you can pick up a pen. I think it's the same with dancers, musicians, and performers. When you're a little kid, people can see that you're sort of bent in that direction. (I grew up in North Vancouver) and my folks were wonderful and sent me to every art program that was available. I went to the Vancouver School of Art and took very serious courses—mostly life painting and life drawing, and that was wonderful because I love the body and I love the rhythm of it and just what you can say with the position of the body. That's about when the term "body language" first came out, which says it all because you can tell how someone is feeling and you can see if someone trusts you.

I love to draw, and it was my art teachers who would say "stop cartooning" and see what's there, look at the person. If it wasn't for that discipline I probably wouldn't be as artistic as I am in the work that I do.

A lot of people draw funny pictures. They don't look at a chair, they don't look at a car. If I want to draw a picture of a chainsaw, I've got to have a picture of a chainsaw there or else I'll go to the shed and find one. I like to be able to draw things the way they really are and I like to be able to write things the way they really are. Even if I fabricate a story, it's a story that could have happened to somebody, and invariably I'll get a letter from somebody who says "That happened to me this morning" or "That exact thing happened to my family."

I always knew I'd make my living as an artist somehow, but I didn't know how and I imagined I'd be a fine artist doing portraits or something—I have an aunt who is a quite well-known portrait painter in Vancouver—and yet I couldn't get away from the silliness. I was always being silly. If you were painting a moose on a landscape, I'd have him slipping on a rock. We had really serious anatomical drawing when I was in art school, and who was it who took the fruit display and packed the rib cage of the skeleton full of fruit with the banana in a strategic place? They always knew it was me. I was the one who glued wire wool under the statues' arms. I could never take anything seriously. (My teachers) had an affectionate hate. Even the employers who fired me missed me when I was gone.

I was working for an animation studio right out of art school and for the first time in my life I was with wacky people just like me. I just loved that environment. It was *Loony Tunes* and the people were just so much fun. I was apprenticing to be an animator and I was offered a job in Los Angeles, but I couldn't take it because I was married to a guy who wouldn't let me take it because he didn't get a job in L.A. It was when you followed your husband. I was just barely 20—drinking age, not thinking age.

That's my ex-husband, and I get a lot of material out of that. Every experience gives you material. He ran off with a voluptuous script assistant, but I never had a chance to thank her.

I was in Hamilton then and I got a job at McMaster University in the graphic art department of the medical school, and it was so wonderful because I love the body and the magic of what makes us work. When you go to an autopsy, you see that it's like taking the back off a television set and what have you got? All the wires and technical stuff, but what's the magic that turns it on? For five years I did such wonderful things and at the same time I was doing cartoons for the university—for dances and things for the children's ward and posters and cartoons for some of the lectures, and eventually I was doing nothing but cartoons.

One of the doctors there encouraged me, and I did some little books for him. The only reason I was offered the job (doing the strip) was because one of the publishers of the first books I did pitched it to Universal Press and said "If you don't syndicate her, I will."

I spend a lot of time on the phone and (have) a lot of e-mail and regular mail to answer. I work in clumps. Like, I'm writing a week of dailies on the road and, when I get home, I'll draw them and ink them. I'll write while I'm travelling. I write a little play. It's exactly like a script.

I try to do it in two-week lots. I'm going to be hiring someone to work on the weekly and Sunday comics. She's an inker and, I hate to

admit this, but I'm so busy. We're having a line of dolls and I travel a lot and we're going to be doing an animated series out of Ottawa very soon. We've just signed a contract. We'll be doing a series of 13 shows based on *For Better or For Worse*. I like to be involved in all elements of that—from the scriptwriting to the recording of all the voices.

I thought I'd be an animator, but I never thought anyone would animate my work and that's a marvellous compliment for what I've done. I could never ask for a greater honour than that.

My husband is a dentist, but his love is model trains and he's built a model railway you can ride on. It's about a quarter-mile of track around our property. He comes in looking like Hitler all the time because he's been breathing in the soot from the steam train. He makes many of the parts and refits the engines and puts the track down. He's a very patient person.

(My son) Aaron is a cameraman and our daughter (Katie) is at Western and she wants to be a dentist. I wanted another baby and couldn't have one so I made one up (April in *For Better or For Worse*). I think that's a good thing to do. I gained the weight, though.

In a way, my characters have their own lives. They say things you never thought they would say ... and sometimes the writing you do is like spirit writing. You'll often finish a project and it will take an entirely different course from the one you planned. That's the mystique of doing this work.

The characters are real personalities. The problem is that I have too many stories and not enough space to tell the stories, because each character has grown up past the nest of the family and they all have individual relationships with adult people and it's more complicated because I have to weave several stories together. People are forever writing saying they want to see more about Gordon and Lawrence.

Probably my favourite character in the strip is Michael. My son and I are very close. He and I are very similar people and we can have a two-hour conversation on the phone and my husband can't figure out why, but he can have a two-hour conversation with Katie because they are both academics.

Aaron and I talk more about how to survive, and he will be very open with me about his relationships with people, and I love to hear about that. That's helpful for the strip and I love that because someone who is 25 has a totally different perspective on things. Rod reads everything I do and he's perhaps my best editor, and he'll say "Oh, that's over the top" or "That's not funny," and I really respect that. Part of being a professional in any job is being willing to change something.

The strip goes to between 1700 and 2000 papers. It's being translated in about six different languages and appears in about eight to ten different countries.

I keep up with all the mail. I read every single letter that comes in and I write on the envelope what I want the answer to be and my assistant types it up on a nice piece of paper and I hand sign everything with a little drawing.

I get 40 a day. Very few are crabby, but the nastiest ones are about the proper use of English.

There are people who object to the controversial stuff. Some people still write and they tell me they don't like having a gay kid in the strip, but most of that has died down. With what you see on TV—all these things that have pushed every conceivable button; you can turn on daytime soap operas and see the most graphic stuff—there's still a real unwritten rule of decency in the comic strips. So when I did the story of Lawrence coming out, it was more a story of a kid desperately wanting to be understood. There was no graphic suggestive detail of any kind.

Comics go into so many different areas: into tiny little communities of maybe 3000 people where the editor knows everybody and if they printed something the people thought was outrageous and pornographic he wouldn't be able to get a doughnut at the corner store, right up to the *Chicago Tribune*, which was saying "Do more, we love to see you push the envelope." You have to gauge whether a story is worth telling. I had the dog (Farley) pass away because he was an old dog and Elly's mother passed away because my mother and dad both passed away and it was an experience I wanted to go through again and challenge myself—could I write this well?—so that it has enough happiness in it. Because there is tremendous humour in the passage of someone desperately ill. You have to get out of that blackness. It was a neat story and I was thrilled with the response.

I have a 10-year contract with United Media and I plan to see the 10 years as the busiest in my life. I'll be 61 when it ends. Then, pray God, I'm going to retire, and I'd like to not care about my body at that point. I want to go sit on a cruise ship and have that long table just slanted in my direction and four or five chefs with clean hands to just push the food (at me).

You take it from here ...

Responding

1. **Describe Character** Using the notes you made while reading, write a paragraph about Lynn Johnston, describing her personality, basic views, and values.

2. **Chart Information** Make a chart listing the members of Johnston's family. Beside each, write down information about them from the profile. Compare notes with a partner, then discuss your impressions: What is each person like? Do they seem like ordinary people? Do they seem like typical comic strip characters?

3. **Identify Influences** Scan the text and identify some key moments and turning points Johnston reveals about her past. Note as well which people influenced her. Make a timeline or another visual presentation highlighting how Johnston's career progressed, leading to her success as an important syndicated cartoonist.

Extending

4. **Examine Audience** Review some of Johnston's cartoons in the newspaper, in books, or on the Internet. Who would you say is the intended audience of her cartoons? How can you tell?

5. **Create a Cartoon** Using a single frame or a panel, draw an original cartoon about a situation involving your own family and friends. Make a week-long series of strips in which you develop your story more fully.

> **SELF ASSESSMENT**
> - Why did you choose the situation you did?
> - Does the cartoon give you a greater understanding of your family and friends and yourself?
> - In making your own cartoon, what did you learn about the conventions or techniques cartoonists use?

Before you read, as a class, identify three Native people who are celebrities.

As you read, summarize the highlights of Buffy Sainte-Marie's career.

"I was a terribly miserable teenager."

Up Where She Belongs

by Kathy Ullyott (with Buffy Sainte-Marie)

INTERVIEW

Notes

Martin Luther King, Jr.: a famous American peace and Black rights advocate

(Mohandas) Gandhi: famous East Indian leader and promoter of peace in his country

appropriation: taking over what does not belong to one; exploiting for one's personal advantage

co-opted: taken over; exploited

dreamcatcher: a Native artifact consisting of lacing, ring, beads, and feathers, intended to be hung by a sleeper's bedside in order to remove bad dreams (through the hole) and to catch good ones

Pocahontasize: A negative term used by some Natives to suggest the turning of Native peoples into Caucasian-like people. Specifically, it suggests the changing of Native beliefs, customs, and lifestyles into those more "acceptable" to non-Native people.

Fresh out of college, Buffy Sainte-Marie thought she'd move on, leaving the songs she'd written as a student behind. Instead, what started as a youthful pastime became a musical career that took her from the coffeehouses of Greenwich Village, where the young Bob Dylan was a fan, to a command performance for Her Majesty the Queen in the 1970s. She won an Oscar in 1982 for "Up Where We Belong," the theme song she wrote for An Officer and a Gentleman. *She was inducted into the Canadian Music Industry Hall of Fame at the 1995 Juno Awards. Her songs have been performed by hundreds of artists—including Elvis Presley, Barbra Streisand, Janis Joplin, and Indigo Girls. She's a Ph.D., a painter, a college lecturer, and a mom to her son, Cody. Those college songs—not to mention those protests—are still with her, and us, on her album* Up Where We Belong *(EMI).*

KU: What did you stand for in the '60s and '70s when you started singing, and what do you stand for now?

BSM: That was a very special time. Students ruled, coffee was the drug; conversation was the sport. And I really believed that if people understood the way it was for Native people, that they would change things, and to some extent they did. I tried to put a spotlight on what needed to be done on the reserves, because there wasn't anybody covering those bases then.

72   Fame and Greatness

KU: Has there been much change between then and now?

BSM: Oh, yes. In Canada, Native people ourselves have overcome amazing odds—to become teachers and lawyers and tribal leaders and telecommunicators and well-known artists, in spite of everything trying to Pocahontasize us.

KU: There's a trend now toward Native imagery in fashion and decor. Do you think that's a positive thing, or do you think that's an appropriation of Native culture?

BSM: For some people it's really meaningful, and for others it's just fashion. If you go out and buy a dreamcatcher from some hippie, believe me, it's not going to help Native people at all. But on the other hand, there are a lot of non-Indian people who take Native Studies in college. That's meaningful. Or get into a book like *Indian Givers* by Jack Weatherford—that's meaningful. Or who become nurses and work in Northern health care. That's meaningful. There are lots of meaningful things being done—but fashion, really, it's about as important as whether your cuffs are rolled up or rolled down.

KU: Has your generation accomplished what it set out to accomplish?

BSM: No. By 1968 I think it was all over. It was co-opted by the businessmen of our own generation who are now billionaires, with a "B." One of them called a friend of mine about two months ago and wanted to celebrate because he had just started working on his second billion—which used to be language that was reserved for countries. I think that's obscene. And if you wonder why some people don't have anything, it's because guys like that have it all. And that's what happened to the '60s. Somebody bought it. And shoved it up somebody else's nose.

Piapot Reserve, September 8, 1975

KU: Are you seeing anyone now?

BSM: Yes, I have a sweetheart. I'm not going to tell you his name. But he has two little kids. And he's been raising them by himself since his little boy was a year-and-a-half and his little girl was six months old—and boy, is he a good parent.

MW: Is [life after 50] what you had expected it to be?

BSM: No! It's a lot better! I'm real busy. And I have a track record. It's like if I look back on my life as a movie, it's a great movie. Sure, there are some real tragedies in there, but at least it's interesting. When I was 20, there wasn't that much to look back on, and who knew what was ahead? At this age, you know who your friends are. Now, I'm 20 years older than my boyfriend, so I figure he'll probably run off with a redhead in the next 10 minutes! But so far, so good.

Inducted Officer of the Order of Canada, 1998

KU: How would you like the first line of your obituary to read?

BSM: "She made it!" I'm very much looking forward to the next world. I don't care what anybody says—I hope folks have a party! I want one of those New Orleans funerals.

KU: Do you believe in heaven, then?

BSM: I don't think about heaven, I think of the next world. This world is like kindergarten. Every now and then you might be lucky enough to meet a first-grader, or a second-grader—who in my metaphor would be somebody like Gandhi or Martin Luther King, Jr. I feel as though we're a very young species, and the next world is a continuation of wherever it is that we leave off as individuals here.

KU: Is there any one event or moment in your life that you could point to and say, "That is where my life took the turn that brought me here"?

BSM: Yes. It's very personal; it's very private. I was a terribly miserable teenager; I wished that I could die. But I didn't have the courage to off myself. So I prayed. I just gave my life away. I said, "I don't know what I'm doing; just employ me." And that was it. Everything changed for me. I filled up with all kinds of energy; I became more positive. I came to grips with the fact that basically, we are alone and zipped into our own skins—and that that was wonderful and not a tragedy. So that's when things changed for me.

KU: If you could pass on one piece of advice to a woman turning 20, what would it be?

BSM: Don't be afraid to have a dream. Believe in yourself. Keep your nose to the joy trail. There are many, many people who want you to live their dream, but you're completely and totally unique and a blessing to the rest of us. And also: that the best thing in life is a good bath and a good night's sleep—it'll cure anything!

You take it from here …

Responding

1. **Analyze Content** As a class, discuss how the changing values of the 1960s affected the thinking and priorities of the young people of the time. Discuss Buffy Sainte-Marie's beginnings as a Native advocate during that period.

2. **Summarize Beliefs** Review the interview and list at least five basic beliefs and values expressed by Sainte-Marie. Share your list with a partner and discuss your own thoughts on each of the points you identified.

3. **Appreciate Humour** With a partner, find three examples of Sainte-Marie's sense of humour. Discuss the impression her humour makes on the reader: Does it make her seem more credible and realistic? Does it make you more or less likely to pay attention when she talks about serious issues?

Extending

4. **Research Music** With a partner, investigate Sainte-Marie's recording career, which spans four decades. Listen to several of her songs recorded over the years, and note the subjects they deal with. Choose one song to play to the class. Before you play it, present background information on the song, including a discussion of the song's subject and history (when it was recorded, and by whom) and why you chose it.

5. **Illustrate a Theme** Create a CD cover, poster, or other medium to illustrate one of the following ideas expressed by Buffy Sainte-Marie:

   - "Don't be afraid to have a dream."
   - "Believe in yourself."
   - "Keep your nose to the joy trail."

   Display your work on the classroom bulletin board.

6. **Investigate a Controversy** Using an Internet search engine and the search word "Pocahontas," find information about Native reactions to the popular 1995 movie. Write an editorial outlining the debate and giving your own response to it. Share your editorial with the class.

Before you read, write down a list of talk show personalities and hosts that, in your opinion, are entertaining to teenagers.

As you read, draft a timeline showing the main events in Oprah Winfrey's life.

Women, especially, listen to Winfrey, because they feel as if she's a friend.

The TV Host: Oprah Winfrey

by DEBORAH TANNEN

PROFILE

Notes

Deborah Tannen is a professor at Georgetown University and the author of *The Argument Culture*.

The Sudanese-born supermodel Alek Wek stands poised and insouciant as the talk show host, admiring her classic African features, cradles Wek's cheek and says, "What a difference it would have made to my childhood if I had seen someone who looks like you on television." The host is Oprah Winfrey, and she has been making that difference for millions of viewers, young and old, black and white, for nearly a dozen years.

Winfrey stands as a beacon, not only in the worlds of media and entertainment but also in the larger realm of public discourse. In her mid-40s, she has a personal fortune estimated at more than half a billion dollars. She owns her own production company, which creates feature films, prime-time TV specials, and home videos. An accomplished actress, she won an Academy Award nomination for her role in *The Color Purple*, and in 1998 starred in her own film production of Toni Morrison's *Beloved*.

But it is through her talk show that her influence has been greatest. When Winfrey talks, her viewers—an estimated 14 million daily in the U.S. and millions more in 132 other countries—listen. Any book she chooses for her on-air book club becomes an instant bestseller. When she established the "world's largest piggy bank," people all over the country contributed spare change to raise more than $1 million (matched by Oprah) to send disadvantaged kids to college. When she blurted that hearing about the threat of mad-cow disease "just stopped me cold from eating another burger!", the perceived threat to the beef industry was enough to trigger a multi-million-dollar lawsuit (which she won).

Born in 1954 to unmarried parents, Winfrey was raised by her grandmother on a farm with no indoor plumbing in Kosciusko, Mississippi. By age three she was reading the Bible and reciting in church. At six she moved to her mother's home in Milwaukee, Wisconsin; later, to her father's in Nashville, Tennessee. A lonely child, she found solace in books. When a seventh-grade teacher noticed the young girl reading during lunch, he got her a scholarship to a better school.

Winfrey's talent for public performance and spontaneity in answering questions helped her win beauty contests—and get her first taste of public attention.

Crowned Miss Fire Prevention in Nashville at 17, Winfrey visited a local radio station, where she was invited to read copy for a lark—and was hired to read news on the air. Two years later, while a sophomore at Tennessee State University, she was hired as Nashville's first female and first black TV-news anchor. After graduation, she took an anchor position in Baltimore, Maryland, but lacked the detachment to be a reporter. She cried when a story was sad, laughed when she misread a word. Instead, she was given an early-morning talk show. She had found her medium. In 1984 she moved on to be the host of *A.M. Chicago*, which became *The Oprah Winfrey Show*. It was syndicated in 1986—when Winfrey was 32—and soon overtook *Donahue* as the top-rated talk show in the U.S.

Women, especially, listen to Winfrey because they feel as if she's a friend. Although Phil Donahue pioneered the format she uses (mike-holding host moves among an audience whose members question guests), his show was mostly what I call "report-talk," which often typifies men's conversation. The overt focus is on information. Winfrey transformed the format into what I call "rapport-talk," the back-and-forth conversation that is the basis of female friendship, with its emphasis on self-revealing intimacies. She turned the focus from experts to ordinary people talking about personal issues. Girls' and women's friendships are often built on trading secrets. Winfrey's power is that she tells her own, divulging that she once ate a package of hotdog buns drenched in maple syrup, that she had smoked cocaine, even that she had been raped as a child. With Winfrey, the talk show became more immediate, more confessional, more personal. When a guest's story moves her, she cries and spreads her arms for a hug.

When my book *You Just Don't Understand: Women and Men in Conversation* was published, I was lucky enough to appear on both *Donahue* and *Oprah*—and to glimpse the difference between them. Winfrey related my book to her own life: she began by saying she had read the book and "saw myself over and over" in it. She then told one of my examples, adding, "I've done that a thousand times"—and illustrated it by describing herself and Stedman. (Like close friends, viewers know her "steady beau" by first name.)

Winfrey saw television's power to blend public and private; while it links strangers and conveys information over public airwaves, TV is most often viewed in the privacy of our homes. Like a family member, it sits down to meals with us and talks to us in the lonely afternoons. Grasping this paradox, Oprah exhorts viewers to improve their lives and the world. She makes people care because she cares. This is Winfrey's genius, and will be her legacy, as the changes she has wrought in the talk show continue to permeate our culture and shape our lives.

You take it from here ...

Responding

1. **Distinguish Terms**   In your notebook or journal, define "report-talk" and "rapport-talk." Compare notes with a partner, and then work together to decide which description best fits each talk show personality you listed before reading.

2. **Recognize Accomplishments**   In a small group, discuss the life and career of Oprah Winfrey. Consider the following questions: Why is she famous and successful? What are her greatest achievements? Does she have significant power and influence over her audience? Explain.

> **GROUP ASSESSMENT**
> - Did your group reach agreement on the answers?
> - Did your group respect the contributions of all members?

3. **Understand Media**   In a paragraph, explain Winfrey's views of television and talk shows. Do you agree with her views? Comment.

4. **Note Sentence Variety**   Find and quote, in your notebook, five sentences that use five different sentence structures.

> **SELF ASSESSMENT**
> - Which types of sentences are you already using?
> - What ideas do you get from the quoted sentences about how you can improve or vary your own sentence structure?

Extending

5. **Script an Interview**   Imagine and write the interview Winfrey might have had when she was hired as Nashville's first Black TV-news anchor.

6. **Identify Potential Topics for Further Research**   Think about and research topics suggested by this article, e.g., Oprah Winfrey, Winfrey's magazine, her book club, Deborah Tannen, other talk shows.

7. **Recommend a Book**   Write a letter to Oprah Winfrey telling her about a book you read that you would like to recommend to her book club. When you have finished, give your letter to another student for proofreading and feedback.

> **TIPS**
> - You should begin by telling her how much you enjoy her program.
> - In another paragraph, identify the book and tell a little about its plot and conflicts.
> - You could quote a passage from the book to create interest.
> - Conclude with reasons why you think she should recommend this book.

> **Before you read,** as a class, identify who Steven Spielberg and Roger Ebert are. What movies has Spielberg made? How is Ebert involved with movies?
>
> **As you read,** make a list of the Steven Spielberg movies you have seen.

"My dad took me out to see a meteor shower when I was a little kid."

The Moviemaker: Steven Spielberg
by Roger Ebert

PROFILE

Notes

Roger Ebert is an acclaimed movie critic of *The Chicago Sun-Times*.

Steven Spielberg

Dec. 18, 1946—born in Cincinnati, Ohio

1974—Directs first feature, *The Sugarland Express*

1976—directs suspense thriller *Jaws* at age 27

1982—directs *E.T. The Extra-Terrestrial*, a hugely popular science-fiction movie

1993—directs *Schindler's List*, what many critics consider to be his masterpiece, and *Jurassic Park*

1998—directs *Saving Private Ryan*, about the D-Day Invasion

Steven Spielberg's first films were made at a time when directors were the most important people in Hollywood and his more recent ones at a time when marketing controls the industry. That he has remained the most powerful filmmaker in the world during both periods says something for his talent and his flexibility. No one else has put together a more popular body of work, yet within the entertainer there is also an artist capable of *The Color Purple* and *Schindler's List*. When entertainer and artist came fully together, the result was *E.T. The Extra-Terrestrial*, a remarkable fusion of mass appeal and stylistic mastery.

Spielberg's most important contribution to modern movies is his insight that there was an enormous audience to be created if old-style B-movie stories were made with A-level craftsmanship and enhanced with the latest developments in special effects. Consider such titles as *Raiders of the Lost Ark* and the other Indiana Jones movies, *Close Encounters of the Third Kind*, *E.T.*, and *Jurassic Park*. Look also at the films he produced but didn't direct, like the *Back to the Future* series, *Gremlins*, *Who Framed Roger Rabbit*, and *Twister*. The story lines were the stuff of Saturday serials, but the filmmaking was cutting edge and delivered what films have always promised: they showed us something amazing that we hadn't seen before.

Directors talk about their master images, the images that occur in more than one film because they express something fundamental about the way the filmmakers see things. Spielberg once told me that his master image was the light flooding in through the doorway in *Close Encounters*, suggesting, simultaneously, a brightness and mystery outside. This strong backlighting turns up in many of his other films: the aliens walk out of light in *Close Encounters*, E.T.'s spaceship door is filled with light, and Indy Jones often uses strong beams from powerful flashlights.

In Spielberg, the light source conceals mystery, whereas for many other directors it is darkness that conceals mystery. The difference is that for Spielberg, mystery offers promise instead of threat. That orientation apparently developed when he was growing up in Phoenix, Arizona. One day we sat and talked about his childhood, and he told me of a formative experience.

"My dad took me out to see a meteor shower when I was a little kid," he said, "and it was scary for me because he woke me up in the middle of the night. My heart was beating; I didn't know what he wanted to do. He wouldn't tell me, and he put me in the car and we went off, and I saw all these people lying on blankets, looking up at the sky. And my dad spread out a blanket. We lay down and looked at the sky, and I saw for the first time all these meteors. What scared me was being awakened in the middle of the night and taken somewhere without being told where. But what didn't scare me, but was very soothing, was watching this cosmic meteor shower. And I think from that moment on, I never looked at the sky and thought it was a bad place."

E.T., The Extra Terrestrial

There are two important elements there: the sense of wonder and hope, and the identification with a child's point of view. Spielberg's best characters are like elaborations of the heroes from old *Boy's Life* serials, plucky kids who aren't afraid to get in over their head. Even Oskar Schindler has something of that in his makeup—the boy's delight in pulling off a daring scheme and getting away with it.

Spielberg heroes don't often find themselves in complex emotional entanglements (Celie in *The Color Purple* is an exception). One of his rare failures was *Always*, with its story of a ghost watching his girl fall in love with another man. The typical Spielberg hero is drawn to discovery, and the key shot in many of his films is the revelation of wonder he has discovered. Remember the spellbinding first glimpse of the living dinosaurs in *Jurassic Park*?

Spielberg's first important theatrical film was *The Sugarland Express*, made in 1974, a time when gifted auteurs like Scorsese, Altman, Coppola, De Palma, and Malick ruled Hollywood. Their god was Orson Welles, who made the masterpiece *Citizen Kane* entirely without studio interference, and they too wanted to make the Great American Movie. But a year later, with *Jaws*, Spielberg changed the course of modern Hollywood history. *Jaws* was a hit of vast proportions, inspiring executives to go for the home run instead of the base hit. And it came out in the summer, a season the major studios had generally ceded to cheaper exploitation films. Within a few years, the *Jaws* model would inspire an industry in which budgets ran wild because the rewards seemed limitless, in which summer action pictures dominated the industry, and in which the

Fame and Greatness

hottest young directors wanted to make the Great American Blockbuster.

Spielberg can't be blamed for that seismic shift in the industry. *Jaws* only happened to inaugurate it. If the shark had sunk for good (as it threatened to during the troubled filming), another picture would have ushered in the age of the movie bestsellers—maybe *Star Wars*, in 1977. And no one is more aware than Spielberg of his own weaknesses. When I asked him once to make the case against his films, he grinned and started the list: "They say, 'Oh, he cuts too fast; his edits are too quick; he uses wide-angle lenses; he doesn't photograph women very well; he's tricky; he likes to dig a hole in the ground and put the camera in the hole and shoot up at people; he's too gimmicky; he's more in love with the camera than he is with the story.'"

All true. But you could make a longer list of his strengths, including his direct line to our subconscious. Spielberg has always maintained obsessive quality control, and when his films work, they work on every level that a film can reach. I remember seeing *E.T.* at the Cannes Film Festival, where it played before the most sophisticated filmgoers in the world and reduced them to tears and cheers.

In the history of the last third of twentieth-century cinema, Spielberg is the most influential figure, for better and worse. In his lesser films he relied too much on shallow stories and special effects for their own sake. (Will anyone treasure *The Lost World: Jurassic Park* a century from now?) In his best films he tapped into dreams fashioned by our better natures.

You take it from here ...

Responding

1. **Respond Personally**   Focus on one Spielberg movie you have seen. Write a paragraph describing your reaction to it, noting its entertainment value, special effects, and your overall impression.

2. **Share Ideas**   In a class discussion, consider the following quotations about Spielberg and his work.
   - "[He makes movies] when marketing controls the industry"
   - "[M]ystery offers promise instead of threat"
   - "In his best films he tapped into dreams fashioned by our better natures."

Extending

3. **Write a Movie Review**   View one of Spielberg's movies and write a five-paragraph review of it. Present your review in class.

4. **Look Behind the Scenes**   In small groups, select a movie you have seen, and use library and Internet sources to research its production, including the role of the director. Then summarize the production process and present your findings to the class.

> **TIPS**
>
> Reviews typically
> - start with a short attention-grabbing paragraph
> - focus on a memorable moment or quotation from the film
> - summarize the plot and conflicts without giving away the ending
> - comment on casting and acting performances, editing, music, and special effects
> - conclude with the reviewer's overall impression and whether he or she recommends the film

Before you read, list up to 10 sports superstars. What do all these athletes have in common?

As you read, think about the game of soccer. Which countries have some of the best soccer teams in the world?

"This boy will be the greatest soccer player in the world."

The Phenomenon: Pelé

by HENRY KISSINGER

PROFILE

Notes

Henry Kissinger is a former U.S. Secretary of State. He brought World Cup soccer to the United States in 1994.

Pelé

Oct. 23, 1940—born in Tres Corações, in the Brazilian state of Minas Gerais

1956—begins pro career with Santos Football Club, nine championships between 1958 and 1969

1958—in his first World Cup appearance, leads Brazil to victory

1970—plays his final World Cup, a victory for Brazil

1974—signals retirement by picking up the ball 20 minutes into final game and kneeling in midfield

1975—in financial trouble, comes out of retirement to play for New York Cosmos

1977—retires from Cosmos

1994—long at odds with the world soccer authority, named Brazil's Minister of Sports

Heroes walk alone, but they become myths when they ennoble the lives and touch the hearts of all of us. For those who love soccer,

Edson Arantes do Nascimento, generally known as Pelé, is a hero.

Performance at a high level in any sport is to exceed the ordinary human scale. But Pelé's performance transcended that of the ordinary star by as much as the star exceeds ordinary performance. He scored an average of a goal in every international game he played—the equivalent of a baseball player's hitting a home run in every World Series game over 15 years. Between 1956 and 1974, Pelé scored a total of 1220 goals—not unlike hitting an average of 70 home runs every year for a decade and a half.

While he played, Brazil won the World Cup, staged quadrennially, three times in 12 years. He scored five goals in a game six times, four goals 30 times, and three goals 90 times. And he did

82   Fame and Greatness

so not aloofly or disdainfully—as do many modern stars—but with an infectious joy that caused even the teams over which he triumphed to share in his pleasure, for it is no disgrace to be defeated by a phenomenon defying emulation.

He was born across the mountains from the great coastal cities of Brazil, in the impoverished town of Tres Corações. Nicknamed Dico by his family, he was called Pelé by soccer friends, a word whose origins escape him. Dico shined shoes until he was discovered at the age of 11 by one of the country's premier players, Waldemar de Brito. Four years later, De Brito brought Pelé to São Paulo and declared to the disbelieving directors of the professional team in Santos, "This boy will be the greatest soccer player in the world." He was quickly legend. By the next season, he was the top scorer in his league. As the *Times* of London would later say, "How do you spell Pelé? G-O-D." He has been known to stop war: both sides in Nigeria's civil war called a 48-hour cease-fire in 1967 so Pelé could play an exhibition match in the capital of Lagos.

To understand Pelé's role in soccer, some discussion of the nature of the game is necessary. No team sport evokes the same sort of primal, universal passion as soccer. During the World Cup, the matches of the national football teams impose television schedules on the rhythm of life. Last year I attended a dinner for leading members of the British establishment and distinguished guests from all over the world at the staid Spencer House in London. The hosts had the bad luck to have chosen the night of the match between England and Argentina—always a blood feud, compounded on this occasion by the memory of the Falklands crisis. The impeccable audience (or at least enough of it to influence the hosts) insisted that television sets be set up at strategic locations, during both the reception and the dinner. The match went into overtime and

required a penalty shootout afterward, so the main speaker did not get to deliver his message until 11 p.m. And since England lost, the audience was not precisely in a mood for anything but mourning.

When France finally won the World Cup, Paris was paralyzed with joy for nearly 48 hours, Brazil by dejection for a similar period of time. I was in Brazil in 1962 when the national team won the World Cup in Chile. Everything stopped for two days while Rio celebrated a premature carnival.

There is no comparable phenomenon in the U.S. Our fans do not identify with their teams in such a way partly because American team sports are more cerebral and require a degree of skill that is beyond the reach of the layman. Baseball, for instance, requires a bundle of disparate skills: hitting a ball thrown at 90 miles per hour, catching a ball flying at the speed of a bullet, and throwing long distances with great accuracy. Football requires a different set of skills for each of its 11 positions. The U.S. spectator thus finds himself viewing two discrete events: what is actually taking place on the playing field and the translation of it into detailed and minute statistics. He wants his team to win, but he is also committed to the statistical triumph of the star he admires. The American sports hero is like Joe DiMaggio—a kind of Lone Ranger who walks in solitude beyond the reach of common experience, lifting us beyond ourselves.

Soccer is an altogether different sort of game. All 11 players must possess the same type of skills—especially in modern soccer, where the distinction between offensive and defensive players has dissolved. Being continuous, the game does not lend itself to being broken down into a series of component plays that, as in football or baseball, can be practised. Baseball and football thrill by the perfection of their repetitions, soccer by the improvisation of solutions to ever changing strategic necessities. Soccer requires little equipment, other than a pair of shoes. Everybody believes he can play soccer. And it can be played by any number of players as a pickup game. Thus soccer outside North America is truly a game for the masses, which can identify with its passions, its sudden triumphs, and its inevitable disillusionments. Baseball and football are an exaltation of the human experience; soccer is its incarnation.

Pelé is therefore a different phenomenon from the baseball or football star. Soccer stars are dependent on their teams even while transcending them. To achieve mythic status as a soccer player is especially difficult because the peak performance is generally quite short—only the fewest players perform at the top of their game for more than five years. Incredibly, Pelé performed at the highest level for 18 years, scoring 52 goals in 1973, his 17th year. Contemporary soccer superstars never reach even 50 goals a season. For Pelé, who had thrice scored more than 100 goals a year, it signalled retirement.

The mythic status of Pelé derives as well from the way he incarnated the character of

Brazil's national team. Its style affirms that virtue without joy is a contradiction in terms. Its players are the most acrobatic, if not always the most proficient. Brazilian teams play with a contagious exuberance. When those yellow shirts go on the attack—which is most of the time—and their fans cheer to the intoxicating beat of samba bands, soccer becomes a ritual of fluidity and grace. In Pelé's day, the Brazilians epitomized soccer as fantasy.

I saw Pelé at his peak only once, at the final of the World Cup in 1970. Brazil's opponent was Italy, which played its tough defence coupled with sudden thrusts to tie the game 1–1, demoralizing the Brazilians. Italy could very easily have massed its defence even more, until its frantic opponent began making the mistakes that would encompass its ruin. But, led by Pelé, Brazil paid no attention. Attacking as if the Italians were a practice team, the Brazilians ran them into the ground, 4–1.

I saw Pelé a few times afterward, when he was playing for the New York Cosmos. He was no longer as fast, but he was as exuberant as ever. By then, Pelé had become an institution. Most modern fans never saw him play, yet they somehow feel he is part of their lives. He made the transition from superstar to mythic figure.

You take it from here ...

Responding

1. **Define Words in Context**   Write what you think each of the underlined words means in the context of the sentence. Compare notes with a partner, then use a dictionary to confirm any definitions you're not sure about.

   - "But Pelé's performance transcended that of the ordinary star."
   - "... the World Cup, staged quadrennially ..."
   - "he did not [score] aloofly and disdainfully as do many modern stars."
   - "No team sport evokes the same sort of primal, universal passion as soccer."
   - "American team sports are more cerebral."
   - "Baseball and football are an exaltation of the human experience; soccer is its incarnation."

2. **Discuss the Title**   In a paragraph, explain how Pelé was a "phenomenon." Include your thoughts on why the author calls him a mythic figure. Discuss your ideas in a group of two or three.

3. **Pose Questions**   In your notebook, write down three questions you would have asked Pelé if you were a journalist. Then, for each, write what you think might have been his response.

4. **Make Comparisons**   With a partner, compare Pelé to other soccer stars and leading athletes in other sports. (Refer to the athletes you listed before reading.) Make a chart or use another format of your choice to show what qualities Pelé has in common with these other players.

Extending

5. **Research the Author**   Henry Kissinger, the author of this profile on Pelé, is also famous. Research to find out who he is and what he has done in the past that has made him famous. Decide why you think he was interested enough in Pelé to write this profile. Share your findings with the class in a media form of your choice (e.g., an oral report, an illustrated biography, a visual display, a timeline of his career, an essay).

6. **Profile an Athlete**   Choose an athlete or another individual whom you regard as a phenomenon—truly exceptional at what he or she does. Do some research on the person's life and career, and write a profile. Set it up as a magazine article, including illustrations and photographs where possible.

Before you read, discuss with a partner what it takes to become a superstar in sports today.

As you read, make a list of the points that contributed to Gretzky's success.

Even if Wayne Gretzky never lives in Canada again, deep in his bones he is Canadian.

The Ordinary Superstar: Wayne Gretzky

by KEN DRYDEN

PROFILE

Notes

Ken Dryden was a goalie for the Montreal Canadiens hockey team. He is currently president of the Toronto Maple Leafs.

Gretzky holds or shares 61 NHL records. The following are his career records.

—Goals: 894
—Assists: 1963
—Points: 2857
—Assists per game: 1.32
—Goals by a centre: 894
—Assists by a centre: 1963
—Points by a centre: 2857
—Overtime assists: 15
—Goals, including playoffs: 949
—Assists, including playoffs: 2023
—Points, including playoffs: 3239
—Hat tricks: 50
—40-goal seasons: 12
—50-goal seasons: 9
—60-goal seasons: 5
—Consecutive 40-goal seasons: 12
—Consecutive 60-goal seasons: 4
—100-point seasons: 15
—Consecutive 100-point seasons: 13

Ken Dryden

I never played against Wayne Gretzky. He came into the National Hockey League from the World Hockey Association with the Edmonton Oilers the October after I had played my last game in Montreal. I have met him and spoken with him a few times, but I know him mostly the way most of you know him—from the thousands of impressions I have gotten of him from TV and newspapers during these last two decades.

I don't know if he is the greatest player ever. He is certainly the best player of a time when hockey has been exposed to more people in more different places. He may also be hockey's most important player. He was, I think, the first Canadian forward to play a true team game. His predecessor superstars were always the focus of their team's strategy. The challenge was to get the puck to Howe or Richard or Hull or Mahovlich or Lafleur. Gretzky reversed that. He knew he wasn't big enough or strong enough, or even fast enough, to do what he wanted to do if others focused on him. Like a magician, he had to direct attention elsewhere, to his four teammates on the ice with him, to create the momentary distraction in order to move unnoticed into open ice where size and strength didn't matter. Then, he had to get the puck back, and accompanied by four players moving up the ice with him, and opponents backpedalling in sudden panic, to give it up again. Gretzky made his opponents stop five players, not one, and he made his teammates full partners to the game. He made them skate up to his level, pass and finish up to his level, or be embarrassed. He made them all be better players, not just statistically better players from riding his coattails. Bobby Orr had done the same a few years earlier, but as a defenceman, and while Orr's achievement may have been the more unexpected (imagine, a defenceman leading from behind), leading from in front is harder. Everything happens faster, there is less space and time to see the patterns and to make new ones, more reason to abandon the ideal and just do it yourself. The irony is that Gretzky, the greatest scorer of all time, by season with 92, and by career with 894, wasn't first of all a scorer. He was the artist who created the work of art and then left it to the artisan to finish it off.

His greatest contribution, however, may have come in other ways. This was never more apparent than in the days leading up to his retirement announcement. Happily for him, by the time the attention hit, he seemed genuinely

to have his mind made up. For in that kind of clamour, you cannot discover your own mind. He was emotional, and conflicted, as one would be, but he seemed relaxed, at peace, almost serene. As he had done so often on the ice, he had managed to put all his emotional/personal pieces together. Simply, he knew, it was time. "I'm done," he had said to his wife, Janet, the previous Sunday. So in the furor of his near week-long "death watch," he could just talk, openly, freely, with nothing to hide except his final words, which, everyone knew, would come soon enough. In Ottawa, after his last game in Canada, and the next day in New York at his final press conference, there was no rushing off, and no reporters in a race to beat their deadlines. Like after a season is over and the Cup is won, with all the pressure off and with experiences to share, everyone seemed content to just hang around and talk. And Gretzky listened, too. "Go ahead," he kept saying, encouraging the next questioner when it seemed to the media that they had already taken enough of his time. It's okay. He seemed utterly content with himself. But he always has, and maybe that's what is behind his biggest achievement. If you were to put Wayne Gretzky in a room of ordinary people, he would not appear ordinary—his clothes, his hair, how he speaks about himself, his bearing, and attitude—they would all set him apart. But if you were to put him in a room of superstars, he would stick out even more dramatically. There, he seems normal. Comfortably normal.

He is normal-sized. Every time he looks in the mirror, he knows he is not indestructible, and he has known that all his life. He also possesses a rare perspective on the game and his place in it that can only come from being a lifelong fan. He knows the names and records of all the great players. He has followed them, been inspired by their legends. Just watch him with Gordie Howe. Gretzky has caught up with and passed all of Howe's scoring records, and yet in his mind he knows he isn't Howe and he never will be. To his eight-year-old starry-eyed self, Howe was 10 feet tall, stronger than an ox, and able to skate and shoot faster than the wind. To the 20- or 38-year-old Gretzky, no matter what anyone else says, he can't match up. So Gordie Howe is the greatest of them all, and Wayne Gretzky is happily saddled with a humility he cannot deny. It is a humility that comes when one has a sense of history. Gretzky knows that time didn't begin and end with him. It comes from being a working-class kid for whom good things can never be assumed. He speaks about himself as if he is as mystified at the success he has had as everyone else.

The endless hours he spent as a young boy in his backyard rink have somehow more to do with his father, Walter, who built the rink and found time for him; the passion that kept him there he sees as a "gift" that came from somewhere else. He is not today's ubiquitous self-made man who worships his creator. Such self-image comes when one views one's immediate world as a burden and an obstacle to overcome. Gretzky doesn't see his world this way. He didn't grow up resenting the limits of small-town, working-class life, vowing to create a different future for himself. He likes what he is. He seems actually to like his father and mother, to like Brantford and Canada, and hockey. So when he went to L.A. and New York, he loved L.A. and New York the way any normal kid would, but without feeling the need to hate Brantford, without needing to give up Canada.

It is not supposed to be that way. We want each of us to carve out our own paths. To be responsible for our own destiny, to be beholden to no one. When most people go from the small time to the big time, they reject utterly their former existence. They make fun of the person they once were. Not Gretzky.

He is "the ordinary superstar." Former Heisman Trophy winner and Montreal Alouette football player Johnny Rodgers hung that same phrase on himself, but wanting to elevate himself, he put the emphasis on "superstar." With Gretzky, it is on "ordinary."

Wayne Gretzky did not go out at the top as a player. Michael Jordan did, so did Mario Lemieux and Jim Brown. No athlete who retires at age 38 can expect to. But the power and appeal of sport is far more than just in its wins and losses. Sport holds the attention of people with its compelling, unscripted, character-revealing dramas. I have at other times described hockey as Canada's national theatre. On its frozen stage, life lessons get played out, and millions watch and learn. And as in the theatre, what counts is not just what happens, but how it happens. Great athletes, though they may not know it, get paid not just for what they do, but for how they do it. For how he played on that stage, Gretzky, the superstar as person, clearly stepped down at the top of his game.

It is often said that Canadians love to lionize their stars and love even more to tear them down. There is some perverse sense of the democratic in Canadians that makes us chop off any head that rises above the others. I don't think so, or at least not any more so than Australians or Mexicans or Belgians or anyone else for whom centre stage lies in some other country. The standards of greatness in our world are established in New York or Paris or London or Hollywood. So people in smaller places wait for their stars to take to those stages, and then wait for the judgment of others. And to really make it, those home-grown stars often have to be so single-mindedly non-Canadian or a-Canadian that if they do succeed, we Canadians beat them up for not waving the flag when they get there.

To get to the top in hockey, you have to live a Canadian life, one of ice and snow, struggle and physical pain, even if you grow up in Kazakhstan or Sweden. And to stay at the top, you cannot stray very far from that life. Even if Wayne Gretzky never lives in Canada again, deep in his bones he is Canadian. With him, Canadians feel a bond. You could see it in the affection expressed toward him in those final days, and in the ease of conversation he had with the Canadian people. Canadians had watched him grow up. He is the first superstar to be recorded in the making.

We could see for ourselves the mythic normalcy of his childhood. His size, strength, and skating stride all could have been us. He had no advantages—family money, influential friends—that made his experience so different from our own as to set him apart. Even his hard work, his passion on the rink, looked to us like hard play, like the normal, natural passion we feel for this game.

He is the champion we all could have been. Hardworking, hard playing, skilled, knowing what he is and what he isn't, what he can and cannot do, respectful, and largely content, he is the face that Canadians would most like to present to the world.

You take it from here ...

Responding

1. **Recognize Accomplishments** According to the author, what were Gretzky's main accomplishments? What were the keys to his greatness in hockey? Discuss with others in a small group.

2. **Describe Character**   Write a half-page character sketch of Gretzky. Begin by brainstorming a list of words and phrases that describe his personal character, and use examples from the profile to support your points. Share your work with a partner.

3. **Examine Prejudice**   "It is often said that Canadians love to lionize their stars and love even more to tear them down." Discuss this statement in a small group—what does it mean? Come up with examples from your own observations of how Canadians have responded to Gretzky and other internationally famous Canadians. Do your observations support this claim? Comment.

> **GROUP ASSESSMENT**
> - Did the group respect individual members' contributions?
> - What was learned about the collaborative process?

Extending

4. **Research the Author**   Research the author of this profile, Ken Dryden. Who is he? What position did he play and for what team(s)? What did he do following his athletic career? What books has he written? Present your findings in a format of your choice, for example, a hockey card, a résumé, a biographical sketch, or a speech.

5. **Use Structure for New Text**   Using this profile as a model, research and write your own appreciation of another athlete or another great Canadian.

6. **Create a Children's Book**   Write and illustrate a children's book for the seven to nine age group about achieving a hockey-related dream. Be creative and entertaining. If possible, share a draft of your book with some children and invite their opinions. Consider their comments when you make your final copy.

> **SELF ASSESSMENT**
> - Was your book's language appropriate for the intended audience?
> - Using the children's comments, what did you do to make the book more interesting to them?

Before you read, discuss with another student how the lives of professional athletes change once they retire from competitive sports.

As you read, compare Flick's fame as an athlete with his current life at the garage.

Notes

John Updike is a famous American novelist and poet. His writing typically focuses on the lives of ordinary people.

Ex-Basketball Player

Poem by John Updike

Pearl Avenue runs past the high school lot,
Bends with the trolley tracks, and stops, cut off
Before it has a chance to go two blocks,
At Colonel McComsky Plaza, Berth's Garage
Is on the corner facing west, and there,
Most days, you'll find Flick Webb, who helps Berth out.

Flick stands tall among the idiot pumps—
Five on a side, the old bubble-head style,
Their rubber elbows hanging loose and low.
One's nostrils are two S's, and his eyes
An E and O. And one is squat, without
A head at all—more of a football type.

Once, Flick played for the high school team, the Wizards.
He was good: in fact, the best. In '46,
He bucketed three hundred ninety points,
A county record still. The ball loved Flick.
I saw him rack up thirty-eight or forty
In one home game. His hands were like wild birds.

He never learned a trade; he just sells gas,
Checks oil, and changes flats. Once in a while,
As a gag, he dribbles an inner tube,
But most of us remember anyway.
His hands are fine and nervous on the lug wrench.
It makes no difference to the lug wrench, though.

Off work, he hangs around Mae's Luncheonette.
Grease-grey and kind of coiled, he plays pinball,
Sips lemon cokes, and smokes those thin cigars;
Flick seldom speaks to Mae, just sits and nods
Beyond her face towards bright applauding tiers
Of Necco Wafers, Nibs, and Juju Beads.

You take it from here ...

Responding

1. **Analyze Character**   With another student, consider the following questions about Flick's career: Did he make the big leagues? Was he any good? How can you tell? Why is he working in a garage?

2. **Comment on Theme**   In your notebook, write down a *thematic statement* (the main idea reduced to one clear complete sentence) for this poem. Compare your statement with a partner's. If they are different, support your point of view.

3. **Examine Form**   Identify examples of the following poetic techniques:
   - personification (in stanza 2)
   - simile (in stanza 3)
   - metaphor (in stanza 5)

   For each example, describe how it is effective in revealing Flick's character and abilities. Compare your findings with those of another student.

Extending

4. **Make a Prediction**   Write another stanza describing Flick as he will be 10 years later. Try following the non-rhyming six-line stanza format that Updike uses.

5. **Role-Play an Interview**   With another student, role-play a situation in which the local newspaper is doing a series of nostalgia pieces entitled "Whatever Happened to ...?" Act out the meeting between a rookie reporter and Flick.

> **TIP**
> - A thematic statement should be put in general terms. For instance, you would likely use a general word like "athlete" rather than a specific name like "Flick."

Before you read, read the Notes. Discuss with the class: Who was Giovanni Caboto and what role did he play in Canada's history?

As you read, note the similarities and differences between the speaker's own experience and Caboto's.

Notes

Filippo Salvatore was born in Guglionesi, Italy, and immigrated to Canada in 1964. He teaches Italian literature at Concordia University in Montreal.

Giovanni Caboto, a.k.a. John Cabot, explored the coast of Labrador and Cape Breton in 1497. Like other explorers, he wanted to reach Asia by sailing west across the Atlantic Ocean. He had been sent by Henry V of England and claimed lands for that country. He died on a return voyage to England after his second trip to North America.

Eldorado: legendary city of wealth sought by early explorers

Maudit: accursed

Poems for Giovanni Caboto

Poem by Filippo Salvatore

I
Giovanni, I didn't need courage,
like you, I didn't set sail
toward the unknown on an unsafe boat,
I didn't have to fight the might
of the waves, I didn't suffer hunger,
I didn't look into death's eyes.

I travelled comfortably
with a DC 8 Alitalia plane,
flew over the perilous ocean,
closed my eyes,
dozed for a few hours and
arrived in the land of my dreams.

And to make me leave,
several bad crops, a sponsored
call, a visa sufficed.
It didn't take much to raise
my arms; despair let me surmount
my love for the native land
and my last indecisions.

Plenty of bread, and warm water too,
now I have, but the Eldorado
I was searching I didn't discover.
I discovered instead
scornful glances, a hostile
environment, an overwhelming
emptiness in my soul,
I discovered what it means
to be an emigrant.

And it didn't take much,
you know, it took so little!

II
Giovanni, they erected you a monument,
but they changed your name; here
they call you John. And you
look at them from your stony
pedestal with a hardly perceivable
grin on your bronze lips.

Where are you looking to?
Toward the new or the old world?
You don't answer me, of course,
you remain standing at Atwater and
keep on gazing afar.
How many Italians took the boat
with you? Today we are many, so many,
and most of us are young,
young and ambitious, like you,
young and forced to emigrate, like you,
to start a new life abroad, like you.

You were the first to plant
on the barren, wave-struck reef
the Lion of St. Mark beside the Royal Jack.
Today at the top of the skyscrapers
being built in this icy land
by so many of your fellow countrymen,
the tricolore flies
beside the maple leaf.
Listen: how many of them,
coming out of the Métro warmly
wrapped up speak about dollars
and houses to buy while they wait
for the 79 at the terminal
and rub their noses.
Only a few of them know you

as they see you impassable, with a shiny
ice-mantle on your shoulders,
heedless of the frenzied movement
and the blinding glimmers of this rush hour.

And I who had stopped at your feet
to talk to you, feel the top of my ears
getting frozen as an old drunkard
gives me a shake and mumbles
in his whisky-stinking mouth, maudit.

You take it from here ...

Responding

1. **Make a Comparison Chart** Use the notes you took while reading the poem to create a chart showing the similarities and differences between the speaker's experience and Caboto's. Compare notes with a partner's and discuss: How might their experiences compare to those of other newcomers to Canada?

2. **Discuss Bias** As a class, discuss the prejudices encountered by the speaker and Caboto. What is it that the transit passengers and the old drunkard do not understand and appreciate?

3. **Consider Purpose** Write a personal response commenting on what you think the author's purpose was in writing this poem. In your opinion, do most Canadians appreciate this country's history and its cultural diversity?

Extending

4. **Illustrate the Poem** Reread the poem and pay attention to the images that come to mind as you read. Create a drawing or a collage, or use another method to illustrate a moment or word images from this poem.

5. **Conduct Research** Find out more about Giovanni Caboto or another historical figure who was instrumental in the European settlement of Canada. Choose a form of presentation (for example, an illustrated news article, a speech, a song) and display or present your findings in class.

Before you read, as a class, discuss what you know about David Suzuki and *The Nature of Things*.

As you read, write down three things that you find interesting about David Suzuki's life and views.

"When I was a teenager, I wanted to have an eye operation, dye my hair, and change my name to Smith."

The Nature of David Suzuki

by Jerry Buckley

PROFILE

Notes

The Nature of Things TV series recently celebrated its 40th year on CBC. Topics range from the ethics of animal–human organ transplants to the greenhouse effect. David Suzuki is one of the most recognized scientists in North America.

The bad news rolls off David Suzuki's tongue all too easily these days. Whether he is addressing business executives at a tiny downtown Toronto club or preaching to an anti-nuclear rally from the pulpit of a neighbourhood church, Suzuki can't escape the grim statistics and dire predictions, evidence of what he considers man's mindless destruction of nature.

He talks of 3000 acres [1214 ha] of rain forests being destroyed every day and the possibility that the world's wilderness areas will all be gone in 30 years. He cries out against the dioxins leaking into the Great Lakes, and he echoes the prediction that in just three years, one species of plant and animal will be going extinct every hour. "There have been times," he admits, "when I've felt, 'okay, that's enough. I'm going to buy a piece of land in British Columbia and go off and just live there.' And I still may."

But Suzuki knows he can't do that, not now, perhaps never. "My anger is what sustains me," he says. "I'm too bloody mad."

Suzuki's anger, as anyone who knows him can attest, is genuine. Indeed, anger has been driving Suzuki for most of his years. A third-generation Japanese-Canadian, Suzuki spent three of his boyhood years, along with his sister, parents, and grandparents, in a detention camp in British Columbia during World War II. That bitter memory has dominated his life and it helps explain why today he is a world-renowned geneticist, science popularizer, television star, and environmentalist. "My father always told me

96   Fame and Greatness

that if I was going to compete with whites, I had to be ten times better," Suzuki says matter-of-factly. "He instilled in me a very powerful drive, that I had to achieve in order to be accepted."

In Canada, David Suzuki has achieved beyond even his most ambitious dreams. Everywhere from city playgrounds to prairie schoolhouses to Parliament Hill his name is now synonymous with science education and environmental activism. As host of *The Nature of Things with David Suzuki*, a Canadian Broadcasting Corporation series, Suzuki has helped to demystify science for millions of Canadians and millions more around the world. With an eight-part series called *A Planet for the Taking*, some years ago, he chronicled man's attempt to dominate nature—and brought the environmental problems of the world into stark view ... And he is passionate, driven, irreverent, brilliant, charismatic, and controversial, usually all in the same sentence.

"Nobody can touch him in this country, and around the world he is in the same class as Carl Sagan and Jacques Cousteau," says Stuart Smith, past chairman of the Science Council of Canada, once the national advisory agency on science and technology policy. Says Pamela Stokes, director of Environmental Studies at the University of Toronto, "He puts science over in a way that people can understand, and he does it without demeaning it or making it all Mickey Mouse. Fifteen or twenty years ago, the general public didn't know or care much about science. Suzuki has been a big part of changing that."

The Nature of Things ... attracts 1.3 million viewers each week, more than many of the drama shows carried by the CBC. The hour-long program is seen in the United States on PBS and in 80 other countries.

Nature covers a wide range of topics, from the dwindling population of cormorants in eastern Canada, to the fight between lumbermen and environmentalists over logging in the Queen Charlotte Islands in British Columbia, to the plight of the caribou in Labrador and northern Quebec, where 10 000 of the animals drowned some years ago. Whatever the topic, be it science, nature, or medicine (programs have covered AIDS and infant mortality in the Third World), the dominant theme is to question science and technology's impact on man and nature.

"We have become drunk with the power of our technology, and we have bought the illusion that we have control," Suzuki says. "It is estimated that there are 30 million species of plants and animals in the world, yet scientists have discovered only 1.7 million of them. How dare we think we can manage nature when almost 95 percent of it is a mystery?"

The crux of the problem, in Suzuki's view, is that the human species does not understand its position in nature. "Our whole definition of progress today is based on the notion that it is our role to dominate nature," he says. "If we come to understand weather, earthquakes, floods, and oceans, we call that progress. But of course that progress is a total illusion because what science and technology provide is a very crude, but very powerful, way of subduing nature in the short run. But you don't manage it or control it in the long run. We are only a part of the universe."

Some critics contend that the wizardlike Suzuki is overly pessimistic, a doomsday prophet who exaggerates problems. "I think he goes overboard sometimes," says Louis Simonovitch, head of the Research Institute at Toronto's Mount Sinai Hospital and an old friend of Suzuki. "All of us are against technology that goes too far, but I'm not sure David has come to grips with where you draw the line. He wants to cut off a technology

because it might be bad, but what about the good that it can do? It's fine to tell us that our values are screwed up and technology has gone wild. But we have to make choices."

The counter-argument is that someone has to sound the warnings. Because Suzuki feels so strongly about the problems afflicting the natural world, says Michael Perley, director of the Canadian Coalition on Acid Rain, "he would rather go out on a limb that's a little shaky than not go out on a limb at all."

Indeed, there is a kind of fire in Suzuki's eyes when he talks about nature. A listener senses that no matter how many times Suzuki says it, his intensity remains at the same fever pitch. For Suzuki, butterflies and bald eagles, caribou and black bears, salmon and starfish, and all creatures big and small are not simply words in a script, but each treasured parts of the universe.

And he still has the capacity to marvel at the natural world surrounding him. A few years ago, he was filming a show in the marshlands of Manitoba when, he recalls, he looked up to see dozens of flocks of geese moving south, making a wonderful noise as they went. "I knew that the marsh was part of the birds' migratory route, but I didn't know how beautiful the whole scene could be. I stood there looking at the sky and thought, 'My God, this is fantastic.' I was shivering with the thrill of it."

How this man came to be standing in a Manitoba marsh is best explained by looking back at his childhood.

"My father and Pearl Harbor."

That's Suzuki's answer when he is asked about the biggest influences in his life. "The most definitive event was Pearl Harbor," he says. "I was a Canadian, my parents were Canadian, but because of Pearl Harbor, Canada said we were the enemy." Unwelcome in British Columbia, where David had been born, the Suzukis moved east to Ontario.

But that didn't end the battle for young David. "I totally hated the Japanese people, but I couldn't avoid being one because the white society said, 'You're a Jap,'" he remembers. "So I grew up with a tremendous amount of self-hate. When I was a teenager, I wanted to have an eye operation, dye my hair, and change my name to Smith. I was terrified of whites, terrified of rejection. The only thing I could do well was school work."

Academics was David Suzuki's tool for coping with his troubled world. And his most important mentor was his father, Carr, a labourer on a fruit farm. "I loved school," David recalls. "The worst thing my father could ever do to me was to threaten to take me out of school and put me to work."

There was never much question about the young David's future profession. "Right from the beginning, it was nature," Suzuki remembers. "My father was an avid collector of plants of all kinds. He used to go up in the mountains and bring back plants for his garden. Plus no matter where we lived, he always had a pond with fish and water life. It was his love of nature that made me want to be a scientist."

The shy, angry young man became the president of his high school senior class and an accomplished public speaker.

Then in 1954, Suzuki won a scholarship to Amherst College in Massachusetts. "Amherst was the best thing that ever happened to me," Suzuki says. "It was the kind of educational experience that was simply not obtainable [then] in Canada. It opened all my horizons."

Entranced by genetics, Suzuki went to the University of Chicago for his doctorate and spent a year with the U.S. Atomic Energy Commission at Oak Ridge, Tennessee, before returning to Canada in 1962. As a professor of zoology at the University of British Columbia, he made his most significant scientific mark. Using the ordinary fruit fly, he demonstrated that in higher organisms, mutations exist in which genes can be controlled by simple factors like increases or decreases in temperature. Such mutations can be used to probe the mysteries of genetics, development, and behaviour.

But the more he learned as a scientist, Suzuki says, the more he realized he wanted to go beyond the lab and the classroom. "Scientists tend to be so focused on what they're doing, they're really not aware of the broader implications," he says. "I decided that it was not enough for scientists just to do good science, that you had to demystify your activity and warn the public of its implications."

Suzuki's media career began in earnest in 1969 when he hosted *Suzuki on Science*, a half-hour science-oriented talk show. Two years later, he was asked to become the host of a science program to complement the already existing *Nature of Things*. The program, *Science Magazine*, attracted a big audience, running for five years before the two shows merged to become *The Nature of Things with David Suzuki*.

Suzuki's television career has made him a star, but it has also humbled him. "My great conceit was that through the media, I was going to raise the public consciousness so they would take science more seriously and eventually vote for politicians who were more scientifically literate," Suzuki confesses. "But in terms of real political change and attitude toward science, there has been absolutely no effect. Our politicians are still every bit as ignorant about science as they were when I started."

One result is that Suzuki has in recent years shifted much of his emphasis to children. "Unfortunately, I don't believe adults are capable of changing very much," he says. "I've concluded that spending time hammering away at business people, for example, trying to get them to change, is far less productive than directing my energies at children who aren't already conditioned." Suzuki has written several books—including ones on plants, insects, the senses, the body, and weather—in a series aimed at giving children a hands-on look at science.

"The whole idea is to say to children that plants and insects are fascinating: they're not scary. They're important, and you can establish a relationship with them," Suzuki says. "The book on senses is to show them they are animals, too." Suzuki believes that when kids look at the world in this way, they will develop a different attitude toward nature. "I want children, when they see a chemical plant spewing junk into the air or water, to want to vomit. I want them to consider the water and the air and the soil their home," he says. "That may be airy-fairy, romantic talk, but I really believe the only way we're going to change the direction we're headed is to have that kind of spiritual connection with nature."

Suzuki is not one for grandiose statements, but he does admit to a certain sense of mission.

"Yes, I have a mission, which is to point out what is so obvious—that the planet is in deep trouble and it's in deep trouble for one reason—us. At the rate we're going, we're headed straight down the tubes."

What to do? Maybe do nothing, says Suzuki. "My own sense is that the only long-term solution is not to touch the environment. I don't think you can get a technological solution to a technological problem. It's an endless treadmill. Every technology has a cost. You have to have faith in the enormous resilience and flexibility of nature. And," he adds, "we have to put our hope in the children."

You take it from here ...

Responding

1. **Discuss in a Small Group**   With two or three other students, review your understanding of the article by addressing the following questions:

    - What aspects of human-caused destruction is Suzuki concerned about?
    - Why is he a successful TV and radio host and interviewer?
    - What is his fundamental view of human beings and their technology?
    - Why has Suzuki recently changed his target audience?
    - Based on his comments, do you consider him to be more of an optimist or a pessimist?

2. **Develop a Character Sketch**   Use the information in this profile to create a character sketch of David Suzuki.

3. **Discuss an Idea**   Write a paragraph expressing your views, supported with examples, on one of the following ideas presented by Suzuki. Then discuss your ideas with one or two other students.

    - "At the rate we're going, we're headed straight down the tubes."
    - "[T]he only way we're going to change the direction we're headed is to have [a] kind of spiritual connection with nature."
    - "We have to put our hope in the children."

Extending

4. **Write an Article**   Brainstorm with a partner a list of urgent environmental problems facing us today. Choose one of these and find out some more about it. Create an informative article or brochure describing the problem, its causes, and some solutions, based on your research. You could also include a "What you can do" section to show readers how they can personally contribute to the solution.

5. **Design a Poster**   Make a poster to raise awareness of the issue you researched in the previous activity.

> **TIP**
>
> First decide on
> - your intended audience
> - your message
> - your purpose, e.g.,
>   – to raise awareness
>   – to promote action

Before you read, gain an overview by scanning the heading, introduction, and photographs.

As you read, reflect on how Rick Hansen's work for people with disabilities has made him famous.

"People now know that individuals with disabilities are an important part of society."

Rick Hansen: Still in Motion

by Cam Tait

INTERVIEW

Rick Hansen wheeled into the Oakridge Shopping Centre in Vancouver to end his Man in Motion World Tour.

The West Coast sun shone brightly as Hansen, dressed in a blue spandex track suit, broke the yellow tape on stage in front of thousands of fans gathered at the centre.

The tour ended, but it was the start of a new chapter in Hansen's life. It meant adjusting to being Rick Hansen the man, the citizen, rather than Rick Hansen the athlete and hero.

Since his tour, Hansen has worked on various projects, including lobbying for wheelchair events to be included in the Olympic Games.

He lives in Vancouver with his wife, Amanda, and three daughters. Hansen was interviewed in Edmonton during his 1997 cross-Canada Tenth Anniversary Tour. He spoke about the tour and life afterward.

Q: How have attitudes changed toward people with disabilities since your tour?

"People now know that individuals with disabilities are an important part of society. As you see more people with disabilities in the community, you see that they are just people—they go to work, they socialize and they have friends and they're consumers.

"I'm not saying we're where we need to be. We have a long way to go. But we've made progress."

Q: Looking back, what would you have done differently with the tour?

"If I had been older and wiser I believe I could have levered up the level of change. I was a rookie—I was pretty naive with a lot of good intentions. I didn't know about the disability game, and I didn't know a lot about our community. I didn't know the political system, or how specific vehicles worked in social programming. I think now I'm a lot more mature in that area—I have some good scars now. And I've made mistakes. But in retrospect I think that the only thing I would have liked is to have had more sophistication. But perhaps it was the innocence of what we were doing that gave it some of its magic. I just know we gave it all we had and I can't ask any more than that."

Q: When the tour ended, was it hard to adjust to a normal life?

"What was really hard about it was trying to figure out who Rick Hansen was. The experience of the tour changed me, yet when I

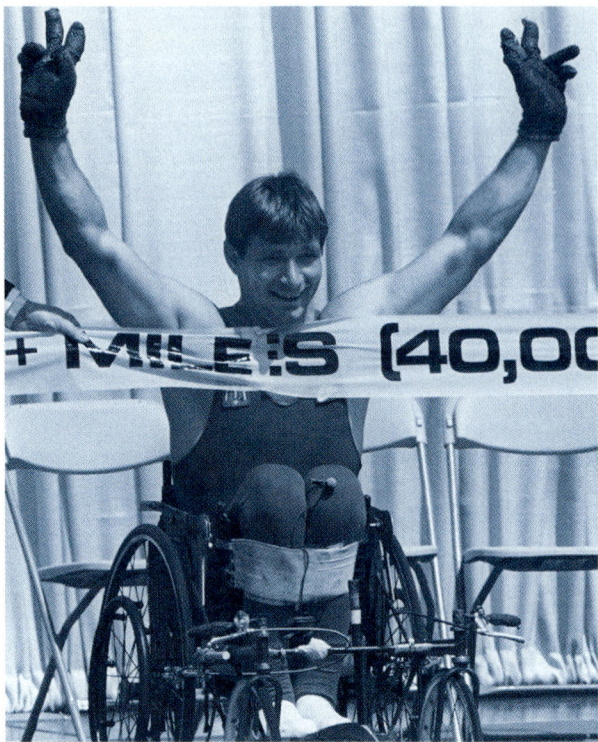

came back home, I still wanted to achieve the goals I had set two years earlier when I left on tour. One of the goals for me was to regain my world title as a wheelchair marathoner. During the first workout after the tour, I quit. You have no idea how frustrating that was to go from a guy who could wheel around the world with a vast amount of willpower to being a guy who couldn't even finish a workout. I realized then that my interests changed. I wanted to keep the issues of disability alive.

"When I broke the ribbon at the finish line, there was a welcome home sign and above that was a caption that said, 'The finish line is just the beginning.'

"I thought the guy who wrote that was nuts. I thought I was done. But in reality it was just the beginning. I was also getting married and I had to think about a career and all that. And as a by-product of what I did, I was becoming a celebrity. That was something new, but the way I handled that was getting on with my life and only going out in public when I was prepared to handle the responsibility. That was one of the things we wanted to achieve: to touch people and make them aware of disability."

Q: What are some issues facing people with disabilities today?

"I have to tell you one of the biggest things facing the disabled community today is unity. The community is fragmented. I think the future for us is greater cooperation and sophistication. There are 4.2 million people in Canada with a disability. In this election period I haven't heard any of the leaders speak on disability. How can they not deal with disability in their platforms or their strategy? The leaders obviously don't perceive 4.2 million people as a unified voting threat. If you look at the United States, the disabled community came together to form some alliances. Elections were being won and lost by the disabled vote. I think Canadians with disabilities and their families need to state their expectations. We don't have to apologize for being disabled, but to be on an equal playing field—without any special treatment—with the barriers removed.

"We also have to tackle the issues of education, training, and employment. Over 40 percent of Canadians with disabilities are not in the labour market. That's a huge number. It costs $13.2 billion a year alone in social assistance programs, not to mention other support programs. In this fiscal era, particularly here in Alberta, governments can no longer afford to confine people with disabilities. Take one example of a person with a disability going back into the labour market and making $35 000 a year. If they work for 30 years to age 65, benefits and social assistance and taxes generated by that individual amount to over $1 million in their lifetime. There are over 1.2 million Canadians with disabilities who are employable, but not working. If you multiply that by $1 million per person, the economics are staggering—not to mention they become consumers and have creativity for their own quality of life.

"I think we've got it all wrong. People with disabilities are not a burden to society—they're potential leaders."

Q: What are some of your current goals?

"I want to be a good father. Another goal is to take care of my health. After I was done with sport I gained 35 pounds. I was sick a lot—colds and that sort of thing. I realized I had lost one of my values in sport. And I want to give back to the community, because I have received so much."

Q: What is your favourite memory of Edmonton?

"I have a lot of them—before the tour, during the tour, and after the tour. I have great memories coming here, playing for the Vancouver Cable Cars wheelchair basketball team and beating the Alberta Northern Lights in the early '80's. Terry Fox, Peter Collistro, and Kevin Earl were some of the guys we played with and had some great rivalries. On the tour I have some great memories: the creation of the Rick Hansen Centre at the University, the legacy of the Premier's Council on the Status of People with Disabilities, created by Don Getty, speaking to schools, the event at West Edmonton Mall, the Oilers game with Score with Decore, going to the Aberhart Hospital. But the biggest one was the $2.6 million legacy fund for the Alberta Paraplegic Foundation."

Q: What makes you angry?

"Guys who try to keep me on schedule. (Laughs) I get cranky when I see injustices and when I see people exploiting others. It makes me mad to see the darker side of humanity. I try to focus on the positive side."

Q: You are a national hero. Does the pressure ever get to you?

"No. Because the only pressure you have is the pressure you put on yourself. There are always expectations from other people that I can't control. I never forget who I am and continue to follow my path. Some people might admire certain qualities I have. That's fine. I'm honoured. But if someone doesn't agree with what I'm doing, or if they're mad at me, that's their problem. I just have to be true to myself."

Rick Hansen: Still in Motion **103**

Q: You've often said one day you'll see a wheelchair in a museum. Do you still believe that?

"I do in two ways. I know through advancements and technology ... in the future people who are using wheelchairs are going to have some amazing ways to get around. In a more personal sense I think, one day, with research, the spinal cord will regenerate itself and people will be able to walk again.

"There's nothing we can't do if we set our minds to it."

You take it from here ...

Responding

1. **Comment on Tone**   As a class, discuss Rick Hansen's attitude toward his own disability, his past work, and the concerns of people with disabilities.

2. **Evaluate Heroism**   Write one or two sentences giving your own definition of a hero. Then write a paragraph evaluating Hansen's work and giving your opinion as to whether or not Hansen is a hero by your definition. Exchange views with a partner.

3. **Appreciate Organization**   Write down the interviewer's questions, paying attention to their order and sequence. What do you think was the best question and answer? Write two more questions the interviewer could have asked, and identify the point in the interview where they would fit best. Compare notes with another student.

Extending

4. **Write a Comparison**   Research the life and work of Terry Fox and his Marathon of Hope, and write a comparison essay showing the similarities and differences between the two men. Include any differences you find in their work and attitudes.

5. **Interview a Role Model**   Using a logical sequence of questions, in the manner of this article, interview someone in your school or community whom you admire and respect. Tape-record the interview and present a portion of it to the class.

> **TIPS**
> - Draw up a list of questions in advance.
> - Test your recorder and batteries before the interview.

Before you read, share what you know about Mother Teresa in a class discussion.

As you read, reflect on the statement "To call Mother Teresa a celebrity would only diminish her greatness."

To call Mother Teresa a celebrity would only diminish her greatness.

Mother Teresa: An Exemplary Life

EDITORIAL

Edmonton Journal

The world has lost one of the most outstanding and influential women of this century—a woman whose compassion, courage, and selflessness have been beyond measure.

Mother Teresa gave to our planet an example of the most noble aspects of humanity with her care of the poorest of the poor, the most desperate of the dying, the children that no one else wanted.

Her constant message to all was to love and care for one another—surely a much needed message in this fiercely competitive age.

That her death has been juxtaposed upon the funeral of Diana, Princess of Wales, adds an ironic context to the grief that much of the world already feels for the princess.

Yet this is not the senseless tragedy that took away a young life.

It is instead the ending of a long and productive life devoted to acts of mercy for those most in need.

Mother Teresa's passing will be mourned by millions of people moved by her exemplary acts of caring, helping, reaching out and touching those that no one else would touch.

The deeds of this frail, stooped follower of God had less of the glamour that surrounds other celebrities.

But to call Mother Teresa a celebrity would only diminish her greatness.

Certainly the founder of the Missionaries of Charity did not shun the glare of publicity, but she always used the media to bring the world's attention to the needs of the destitute and the sick and the abandoned.

How many times did people everywhere hear her words "Give until it hurts"?

There are so many examples of that compassion that they can't all be recounted here.

But a few notable examples should be contemplated by all of us as we consider Mother Teresa's astonishing accomplishments.

Against local opposition and a mob that threw stones at her, Mother Teresa established a home for the dying in Calcutta in 1962.

Although he promised to evict the nuns, the local chief of police was so moved by their care of these shunned people that he recruited other citizens to help the order.

It was to be the start of a growing movement aided by an increasing awareness of

the needs of the most underprivileged in that country.

Sister Teresa as she was then known—and largely unknown in the rest of the world—was asked sometimes how she would manage to raise money or food or clothing for all those in need.

"God will provide," she answered. God did provide and, through her, a miracle unfolded. More and more people donated to her homes and hospices.

Over the next 45 years, her founding hospice would receive 100 000 of India's unwanted dying and destitute people.

In 1953, Mother Teresa established an orphanage in Calcutta—its first occupant a premature baby wrapped in a newspaper found on a pile of garbage.

Although there were fears the three-pound baby would die, the woman in the white and blue habit saved the child.

In 1982, Mother Teresa persuaded battling Israelis and Palestinians in Beirut to stop shooting long enough to rescue 37 mentally disabled children from a hospital.

These were only some of the deeds of mercy that spawned a worldwide movement inspired by her dedication.

Today, the legacy she leaves is an order with 5000 nuns, 500 brothers, and four million lay workers in Japan, Europe, Australia, the United States, and Canada.

It is no wonder that she worked such a miracle.

We have only to consider the sentiments of love and humanity she expressed with such simple eloquence in each of her public appearances.

"I see God in every human being. When I wash the leper's wounds, I feel I am nursing the Lord himself.

"Is it not a beautiful experience?"

"The poor give us much more than we give them. They're such strong people, living day to day with no food ... We have so much to learn from them."

When she received the Nobel Peace Prize in 1979, Mother Teresa accepted it on behalf of those she cared for.

In her words:

"In the name of the hungry, the naked, the homeless; of the crippled, of the blind, of the lepers, of all those people who feel unwanted, unloved, uncared for throughout society, people that have become a burden to the society and are shunned by everyone."

These were words backed up by actions that have spurred millions to follow her example.

Residents of northern Alberta knew the power of her persuasion when she visited St. Paul in 1982, moving people to tears and awe. A branch of her mission was later established there following fund-raising efforts.

Looking back on that trip, even the most hardened of reporters spoke of witnessing the spell of wonder and love that she cast over those she moved among.

No doubt part of the intensity of the moment stemmed from the presence of a world-famous individual. But this was fame based on deeds beyond reproach.

Hers indeed was a life beyond reproach.

It is also one that will only grow in stature with passing time—as she moves into genuine realms of sainthood.

Catholics and people of other faiths have long considered her a candidate for that special category of holy person, one whose memory will live through the ages.

Whether Mother Teresa recognized what she had become is hard to discern, so humble was her own opinion of herself.

"God will find another person, more humble, more devoted, more obedient to Him, and society will go on," she said when announcing her intention to retire in 1989.

Now that she has left us, that just doesn't seem likely.

You take it from here ...

Responding

1. **Interpret a Statement**   Make a journal entry recording your thoughts on this statement: "To call Mother Teresa a celebrity would only diminish her greatness."

2. **Focus on a Trait**   Which do you think was Mother Teresa's strongest quality? Write down your opinion, supported with your reasons, and then share it with a partner.

3. **Analyze the Editorial**   Editorials typically present a point of view and a message for the reader. With a partner, review and discuss the text:
   a) What is the author's message? Is it effectively delivered?
   b) Is the message stated outright, or does the reader have to infer it ("read between the lines")?
   c) What is the *tone* of the editorial? (What is the writer's attitude toward Mother Teresa and her work?)

Extending

4. **Compose a Poem**   Write a free verse or rhyming poem as a tribute to Mother Teresa's achievements.

5. **Conduct and Present Research**   With a partner, research and then report to the class on one event in, or aspect of, Mother Teresa's life.

Reflecting on the Unit

Responding

1. **Define Fame and Greatness** Use a dictionary to define the words "fame" and "greatness." Then review the unit and list the people featured therein. Use a chart or diagram categorizing them as "great," "famous," or "great and famous." When you have finished, think about the process you used to decide whether someone was great, famous, or both. What features did you look at? Was it obvious in each case?

2. **Present Orally to the Class** Choose a real-life person who embodies the term "greatness" for you and give a presentation to the class about the person.

3. **Research Web Sites** Compile a list of Web sites pertaining to one of the people studied in this unit. Choose the site that you think others in the class would find most interesting, and share it with the class in an oral or written review. In your review, explain which of the site's features you liked best and why.

> **TIPS**
> - Tell how the person's past has influenced his or her career.
> - Summarize the highlights of the person's life.
> - What was the person's greatest achievement?
> - Define any unfamiliar terms and use appropriate visuals to create audience interest.

Extending

4. **Create a Game** With one or two other students, develop a plan for a board game called "Fame and Greatness." Decide what the object of the game will be, and then write out a description of the game and its rules—including rewards and penalties for players. Include a sketch of the game board and any playing pieces or cards that go with it.

5. **Read a Book** Go to your library and find a *biography* (book written about a famous person by someone else) or an *autobiography* (book written by the subject himself or herself). Prepare an oral review of the book to present to the class. The review should clearly emphasize the fame or greatness of your subject, and you should read aloud an important scene or section to create audience interest.

> **SELF ASSESSMENT**
> Review what you have learned from this unit regarding
> - what distinguishes greatness from celebrity
> - the relationship between fame and the mass media
> - the personal attributes of the great and famous
> - researching biographical information

UNIT 3

"Crime, like virtue, has its degrees."
–Jean Racine

"Society prepares the crime; the criminal commits it."
–Henry Buckle

"Let the punishment fit the crime."
–W.S. Gilbert

"Justice is mercy's highest self."
–Frances Hodgson Burnett

Crimes, Criminals, and Justice

French playwright Racine takes a relativistic view of crime, maintaining that some crimes are worse than others. British historian Buckle views crime as a result of both social conditioning and individual choice. As you study this unit, keep in mind the different motives behind what criminals do.

In his operetta *The Mikado*, lyricist W.S. Gilbert states that the punishment should fit the crime. What do you think? Compare this view with that of American author Frances Hodgson Burnett, who argues that it is mercy, not punishment, that is the basis for justice.

As you read through this unit, you will find that these and other perspectives will provide food for thought on the topic of crimes, criminals, and justice.

As you read this unit, think about the following:

1) What *is* a crime? How do you define "criminal"?
2) What are the consequences of crime? For whom?
3) Who decides what is just? On what basis?
4) Does everyone perceive crime and justice in the same way?

> **Before you read,** participate in a class discussion about any memorable actions from your past that you now wish you hadn't done.
>
> **As you read,** jot down in your notebook memories that this article brings to mind.

But the beast is always there.

Let Me Tell You about the Crime I Committed

by Sallie Tisdale

MAGAZINE ARTICLE

I haven't been arrested since I was caught skinny-dipping at the age of 15. Crime is something done by others—perhaps to me, but not by me. It's easy to presume the gulf that separates me from you, us from them, is wide and deep, but I know better.

I'm a criminal, and so are we all, and the difference between the crimes that send us to prison and the other kind is only one of degree. Like all criminals, I think we carry our crimes with us until we are done with them and they are done with us—until they are confessed and we are punished; and sometimes even after that.

When I teach writing to adults, I sometimes give them a phrase and start a clock, asking only that they keep writing until the clock stops, never taking the pen from the paper. I want them to stop editing in their heads, to put everything, anything down, and especially the unexpected, petty, surprising thoughts floating through their heads, which they never think to call writing. I like to use short, ambiguous words to get them started—words like "fired" or "dark"—and phrases with emotional gravity, like "doctor visit" or "lost object."

A few years ago, I happened upon a particularly useful phrase: "the crime I committed." I expected these beginning writers to take it literally. I was prepared for a series of anecdotes about teenage shoplifting and vandalism, perhaps a few confessions of drunk driving. My hope was to get the beginnings of storytelling and speaking from one's own experience.

I sure had that wrong.

It was a beginning of a different kind, the beginning of real writing—these raw, artless stories about the crimes that really mattered, the crimes they still carried hidden away, undeclared. One woman, crying, wrote about her failure to visit a dying friend. Another wrote about a cowardly escape from difficult circumstances. They wrote about yelling at their children. About broken promises. Faithlessness. Cruelty.

We're all bearers of a double standard, and not a simple one. This one has two sides to its doubleness: We forgive ourselves for acts we despise in others, despise ourselves for what we forgive in others, in a continual dance of separation. Hurting, we lash out; hurt by others, we retreat; and rarely do we just explain.

We visited my grandmother several times a year when I was a child. I committed one of my greatest crimes against her. I was about eight, and she'd been widowed only a short time. Nothing in her tidy house had changed—it was still a sunny, well-kept house with clearly delineated territories. She had a large yard, steadily tended, full of lush, continual growth of a fertile, warm valley. She had a number of prize plants; one of them, a split-leaf philodendron several feet tall and the deep green of jungle shadow, stood beside the back door.

I have no idea what angered me; I was simply angry, with the kind of anger that fills every space and controls every muscle, every word. The leash was off the beast, and I stood outside the back door of my grandmother's kitchen—my reserved and silent grandmother, her perfectly clean, white kitchen—and I tore her philodendron to shreds.

Not a second thought. No more thought than a pack of wolves spotting a weak caribou—ferocious, that anger. Cruel, ferocious, but carefully directed: I didn't tear up a neighbour's plant, after all, or pull up dandelions. Anger, and something weaker than me, something that couldn't fight back—something to kill—was all I needed. So I killed it—bit by bit, leaf by leaf, until there was nothing in the cool shadows of the brick patio but green confetti, me in the midst of it like a leprechaun after a night's debauch.

And then I realized what I'd done, and it wasn't killing a plant. My grandmother stood in the doorway, her face a stone mask. But behind her—my mother. That was the crime hidden inside the crime, that terrible act—exposing my mother to her mother like that, proving my mother inadequate, her child a terror. And her face—that was punishment.

A friend tells me one of his childish exploits—a chemistry-set experiment ending

with a big hole in the bathroom linoleum. He covered it with the clothes hamper and was on the phone, trying to arrange a repairman's visit, when his mother returned. But when I ask if this is his biggest crime, he says no. That was shooting a squirrel with a BB gun—wounding it and leaving it to die. He can outrun the sneaky attempt to cover up an accident, but he can't outrun the fact that he was a coward.

I think we all tend to presume that cowardice and destructive tantrums are childish things, something we outgrow, suppress, control. But the beast is always there. It isn't always angry, either; sometimes the beast is scared, sometimes the beast is sad, or just selfish, hungry for something it sees and wants. I've felt that leash slip many times as an adult, and I don't think I deserve much in the way of congratulations because I haven't done a lot of visible damage at those times. I've done lots of damage, wielded many weapons. We're like gardens, all flowers and weeds, not always sure which is which. Crimes of commission, mostly, and sometimes omission, crimes of intent, and lack of. Faithlessness, of so many kinds—petty dislikes and thoughts of disdain, dust motes of bad opinion and harsh judgment clouding the air. Little weeds, with long roots.

Little outlaw acts. An undercharged item at the grocery store. Too much change. A too-small tip. Misplaced blame. Exaggeration. They're all forms of stealing—robbing from others, taking what we want and have no title to, just because we want it. Intimate crimes, private ones: irritability, sarcasm, the short temper. Glib jokes at someone else's expense. Cheap shots. Abrupt ends to conversations, unanswered letters, unreturned calls, and wavering attention. The thank-you notes never sent, the presents never given.

The list is as long as our lives. What we so easily forget is how close to each other we are. The gap between an angry shout and a slap is very small. Weapons are always at hand, some deadlier than others. I keep reading the paper and listening to people talk about the criminals in the news, listening to the fear and anger and violent wishes for revenge. I try to remember that this fear, anger, this sense of powerlessness, these wishes are precisely the emotions that drive the acts we dread. Only humans can commit crimes against humanity, and no one is innocent of that.

You take it from here ...

Responding

1. **Write a Personal Response**   Write about a "crime" you have committed. How did you feel about it then? How do you feel about it now? Would you do anything differently if you had a second chance? Explain.

2. **Chart Ideas and Examples**   Working with a partner, review the article and identify some general ideas expressed by the author and specific examples she uses to illustrate each one. Copy the chart below and record your findings in it. (You should aim for at least three ideas and examples beyond the sample given.)

(General) idea	(Specific) example
the author is a "criminal"	She was once caught skinny-dipping

3. **Discuss as a Group**   This article contains many insightful views about crime. With two or three other students, talk about the ideas listed below. For each one, say whether you agree or disagree and give examples from your personal knowledge and experience or general observations. Then share your views with the class.

- Punishment for criminals is basically a form of revenge.
- We all steal at some level.
- We are all guilty of slights toward others.
- Small "crimes" have a significant impact on others, of which we are often unaware.
- People frequently do not know or understand their own destructive impulses.
- "We forgive ourselves for acts we despise in others."

> **GROUP ASSESSMENT**
> - How did your ideas compare to other groups' views?
> - Generally, were the views expressed by your group mostly conservative or mostly lenient?
> - Which group do you think expressed their viewpoints most convincingly?

Extending

4. **Write a Short Story**   Take the article's main theme—that ordinary people commit criminal acts—and write a story about a teenager who unintentionally commits a crime.

5. **Role-Play a Scene**   With one or two other students, draw on your own experience and observations to brainstorm a list of typical "crimes" people commit every day. Choose one or two of these to present in a role-play to the class.

> **TIPS**
> - Before you present your scene, explain the situation and identify the characters.
> - After the skit, explain the crime, why it's a crime, and how people are negatively affected. Then suggest a solution to the problem or issue.

Before you read, share in a class discussion your opinions about drinking and driving.

As you read, anticipate where the story is leading.

It Was a Year Ago

Short Short Story by Grace Caguimbaga

A slight breeze blew as Doug stood staring down at Joey.
   "Hello, Joey," said Doug.
   Silence surrounded the two of them.
   "Joey, I'm sorry. I didn't mean it. I didn't. And, Joey—Merry Christmas."
   Doug placed a rose on Joey's tombstone and walked away.
   "Can you ever forgive me," he asked, "for driving home drunk?"

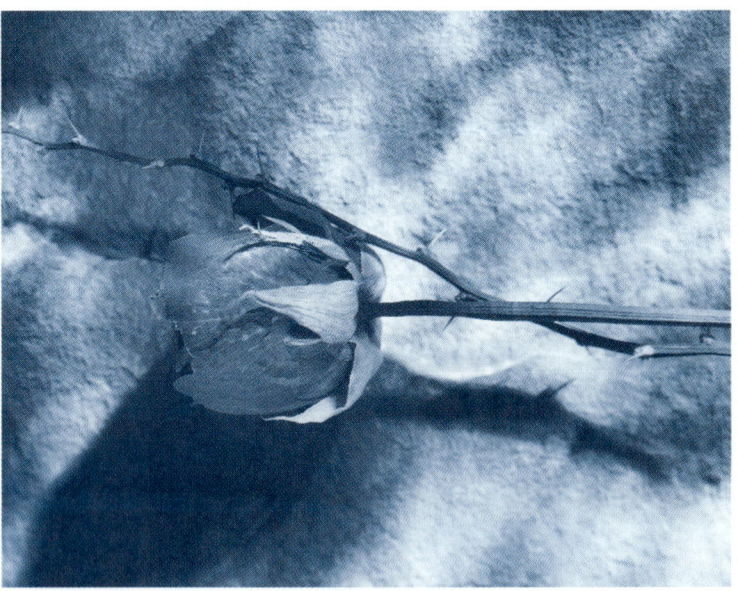

You take it from here ...

Responding

1. **Reviewing Structure**   For class discussion: At what point did you figure out what was going on in the story? Why would the reader be misled by the beginning of the story?

2. **Discuss Purpose**   With a partner, exchange thoughts about the author's reason for writing this short selection. Do you think the choice of the short short story genre was a good one?

3. **Create a "Prequel"**   Imagine the events that took place a year ago that led up to the scene in this story. Write about them in the form of a diary entry.

Extending

4. **Try the Form**   Using "It Was a Year Ago" as a model, write your own short short story with a surprise ending about another topic involving youth crime.

5. **Make a Public Service Announcement**   Drunk driving is a serious issue. Work with a partner to find out more about it and what is being done by various groups to prevent it. Create a public service announcement to promote the prevention of drunk driving (a full-page newspaper ad, or a radio or TV spot). Decide beforehand whether you want to target your message to a general audience or to young adults in particular. Present your PSA to the class.

6. **Do an Interview**   As a journalist or a talk show host, conduct an interview with Doug. Present it as a magazine article or role-play it as a live interview.

Before you read, discuss in a small group whether there is such a thing as the perfect crime.

As you read, see whether you can predict the ending before you get to it.

Paid-up Member

He flung the rifle in beside the dead man and shovelled hurriedly.

Short Story by Will R. Bird

Notes

William Richard Bird (1891–1984) was born in Nova Scotia. He fought in the First World War (in the 42nd Battalion, the Black Watch of Canada) and was awarded a military medal for bravery in the capture of Mons on the night of 10–11 November, 1918. He was a prolific editor and writer of fiction and nonfiction.

It was raining a little at noon, but Simon Lasher drove out to his corner lot with the disc harrow. He had seen Dickie go up the back road and he meant to intercept him as he returned; he had cleaned and oiled his old army rifle, and he meant to use it.

Simon gritted his teeth as he drove. Jim Dickie had asked for trouble. He had come into the settlement and bought the farm that Simon was on the point of buying. True, he and Hank Wheeler had disagreed on the price, but what right had an outsider to come in and pay more than the land was worth? Then, insult added to injury, Dickie had taken Simon's girl from him. It was carrying things too far.

Simon hurried his horses. He must get to the road corner a few minutes before Dickie came in sight. He held the rifle and a shovel between his knees, and he swung his whip sharply. Folks said Simon never drove without a whip, but how could one hurry horses without it? And where would he be if he had not hurried? In ten years he had paid for his farm, and now had his house in readiness for a bride.

At the corner of the field he stopped his horses. The ground dipped slightly, forming a small hollow, and he dug in the centre of it, scooping a short, shallow trench. He had not got it as deep as he wished when he saw his horses prick up their ears. Someone was coming. He dropped his shovel. Jim Dickie was plodding past, his head down to the fine rain. Simon sneered. No one but Dickie would go in a rain to Hank Wheeler's post office.

"He comes regular," Hank had reported. "He gets soldier magazines and Legion papers. He's a paid-up member if he does live out here."

"Paid-up member!" Simon had jeered. "What good's that to him? Will it help him farm?"

He pretended to be tinkering with the disc harrow. The rifle was on the ground behind the discs.

"Hi," he called. "Been for mail? Come over. I want to show you something."

Dickie turned, his pale face friendly. "Yes, I got something I been expecting, something special for returned men ..."

"Come and see where I've been diggin'," interrupted Simon.

He hated soldier stuff as he hated this man who had won Mary Hawkins from him, and the solemn way in which Dickie could recite "In Flanders Fields." Such rot!

Mary and he had quarrelled when he criticized the poem, and Mary had refused him her company. And now, a friend had told Simon in the morning, she and Dickie were to be married as soon as the school term ended. So Simon had cleaned his rifle.

Dickie carefully fished an envelope from his wet jacket as he came to where Simon had dug. "See what the Legion sent me," he said proudly, holding it out. "It's ..."

Crack! The sullen report of a rifle. Simon had looped the reins about his wrist before he fired, and for a moment he was busy jerking the horses to a standstill, then he swung them around to where the limp body was pitched, face down, half into the cavity. His aim had been true. A dreadful redness was welling from the collar of Dickie's shirt. "Blast you!" grated Simon. "You kin be a paid-up member of that hole till Kingdom Come."

The horses quieted and Simon caught up the shovel. He had heard the chug-chug of a wheezy motor in the distance. It was Hank Wheeler's car. A twist of his heel buried the envelope Dickie had dropped, a single push straightened the body in the trench. He flung the rifle in beside the dead man and shovelled hurriedly. When the old flivver came in sight, Simon was seated on his harrow and had just crossed the spaded earth. Twenty minutes later no one could have found the spot where he had dug.

At six o'clock Wheeler knocked at Simon's door. He was county sheriff as well as postmaster. "Did you see Jim Dickie this afternoon?" he asked bluntly.

"Yes, I did," said Simon. "He passed when I was harrowin'. Why?"

"He ain't been seen since," said Hank, as bluntly as before.

"That's strange." Simon simulated surprise. "Maybe he's at one of the neighbour's."

"I been all around," said Hank. "You don't know anything, eh?"

"Me? No, I don't," said Simon smoothly. "I'll send you word if I see him."

Three months had passed since Jim Dickie vanished. Simon went to his hoeing contentedly. Mary was recovering from the shock, had got her colour back. He would go and call on her in a few days.

Paid-up Member

He pulled weeds with a vim. Everything had gone better than he expected. There hadn't been much fuss over Dickie's disappearance, not as much as he had dreaded. And Dickie's Legion had been a joke. An official had come one day and talked with Hank, that was all that had been done. Paid-up member—pooh!

Hank had never seemed the same, but perhaps the sheriff's complete failure to find a clue to Dickie's murderer accounted for that. Simon had often looked at the corner lot, now a shimmering green, inches deep. Who would guess its secret? It was good ground and the grain was doing fine. In the fall he would scoop more earth in the hollow at the corner, fill it in.

When he reached the house at suppertime, Hank Wheeler and an officer from the city met him. Handcuffs were snapped on Simon's wrists before he could take in what had been said. Hank enlightened him.

"What—me—arrested for murderin' Dickie?" shouted Simon. "You're crazy. I don't know nothin' about him."

"No?" Hank's voice sent shivers up Simon's spine. "You'll have a hard time makin' the judge believe that. You harrowed that field the day Jim was killed—and it was your rifle we found beside him."

"You—you—found—" Simon's face whitened, became ghastly. He seemed to wilt.

"We did," said Hank grimly. "All I been doin' was watch that field of yours. I knowed they'd sprout if they was near the surface."

Simon licked his dry lips. "What—sprouted?" he whispered.

"Poppies," snapped Wheeler as they led Simon to his car. "Poor Jim got an envelope full of seed that day—a special good kind the Legion sent to paid-up members."

You take it from here ...

Responding

1. **Focus on Irony**   Working with a partner, review the surprise ending of the story. Explain how this ending contains *situational irony* (when events turn out differently from what is expected). Also discuss: How is the title ironic? How is the ending foreshadowed? Compare responses with another student pair.

2. **Explore Motivation**   In a paragraph, explain Simon's motivation for murdering Dickie. What was Simon's ultimate goal? In what ways was Dickie different from Simon? How did these differences contribute to the conflict?

3. **Follow up on an Allusion**   An *allusion* is a reference to someone or something famous from literature, history, or culture. Find and read the poem "In Flanders Fields" by John McCrae. List some aspects of the poem that you think Mary and Dickie probably liked about it. In two or three sentences, explain why you think Simon considered the poem "rot."

Extending

4. **Compose a News Story**   Write a news story about the discovery and solution of this crime as it might have been reported in the local newspaper.

5. **Develop a Film Script**   Assume you have been given a grant by CBC to make a film of this story. Write the opening scene of your script as you imagine it.

6. **Enter a Contest**   Find out about the annual student writing contest of the Royal Canadian Legion. Enter a poem, a prose work, or a visual in the competition.

> **TIP**
> - Remember to use the five Ws—*who*, *what*, *where*, *when*, and *why*—as well as *how* as you write the story.

Before you read, as a class, discuss the crime of hijacking. What is it and what are the usual motives for it? What are the punishments for it?

As you read, write down questions for a follow-up discussion about the story and fate of D.B. Cooper.

D.B. Cooper

"Do whatever he demands."

True Crime Story by Max Haines

Notes

Max Haines, known by some as the "Master of the Macabre" and "Mister Murder," introduced his popular "Crime Flashbacks" column in the *Toronto Sun* in 1971. He has researched thousands of crime cases and his books include *Murders: Strange but True* (1997) and *Celebrity Murders and Other Nefarious Deeds* (1996).

The 37 passengers responded to the announcement that Northwest Airlines Flight 305 was about to take off. Flying time for the 727 between Portland, Oregon, and Seattle, Washington, was 25 minutes. This flight would take much longer.

It was a trip none of the 37 passengers would ever forget. On that U.S. Thanksgiving evening of November 24, 1971, one of their number would become part of American folklore, as a cross between Robin Hood and Jesse James.

Dan Cooper unobtrusively strolled aboard the aircraft. Stewardesses Florence Shaffner and Tina Mucklow welcomed him aboard. D.B. Cooper, as he came to be known due to a reporting error, took a seat by himself at the rear of the aircraft.

Moments after takeoff, D.B. pressed the button requesting a stewardess's assistance. Miss Shaffner responded. Silently D.B. handed her a folded piece of paper. Miss Shaffner, an attractive brunette, had been approached in many different ways since becoming a stewardess. This was a novel move. She was later to tell authorities, "I thought he was trying to hustle me." Then she read the note.

In simple language it was a demand for 10 000 twenty dollar bills and two sport parachutes. Otherwise the plane, its passengers, and crew of six would be blown up. Miss Shaffner gulped as D.B. flipped open his suitcase and revealed two red cylinders attached to coils of wire. To this day no one knows if the contents of D.B.'s briefcase held a real bomb constructed of dynamite or merely highway flares. D.B. closed his briefcase and the contents were never seen by anyone again.

Miss Shaffner walked briskly to the cockpit and passed the note to Captain William Scott. He radioed Seattle for instructions. They, in turn,

120 Crimes, Criminals, and Justice

immediately contacted local police, the FBI, and Northwest Airlines president Don Nyrop. Instructions were not long in coming. Tersely they were told, "Do whatever he demands."

Scott informed his passengers that there would be a slight delay in landing due to minor mechanical difficulties. Meanwhile, officials on the ground were gathering up and photographing $200 000 in twenty dollar bills.

For three hours the 727 circled Seattle before beginning its descent. Once on the ground, the passengers were informed of the real cause of the delay. They breathed a collective sigh of relief when D.B. accepted a bag from a Federal Aviation Administration official. The laundry sack contained 21 pounds of twenty dollar bills. D.B. then inspected the two parachutes brought aboard as instructed. Satisfied, he dismissed all passengers and Miss Shaffner with a wave of his hand.

Flight 305 again took to the air. D.B. dictated notes to attendant Tina Mucklow, who passed them on to Captain Scott. Cooper instructed the pilot to head for Reno at an altitude below 10 000 feet, keeping flaps down and cruising at 200 miles per hour. After being assured that his wishes would be carried out to the last detail, D.B. escorted Tina Mucklow to the cockpit and gave firm orders that no one was to leave the cockpit area.

A few minutes later a red light flashed on Scott's control panel, indicating that the plane's rear boarding ramp had been unlatched. At 8:10 p.m. a second red light indicated that the ramp was fully extended. The aircraft was behaving somewhat erratically due to the extended ramp. Scott, at a loss for words, inquired over the P.A. system, "Anything we can do for you?" There was no reply.

It is believed that D.B. parachuted over a wilderness area north of Portland, which includes the tiny village of Ariel, Washington. A snowstorm was raging outside, while the temperature was 7 below zero. The crew of the 727 continued on to Reno, landing hours later without coming out of the cockpit.

Back in Seattle, passengers and stewardess Florence Shaffner were questioned extensively. They were able to provide surprisingly little in the way of helpful information regarding D.B.'s disappearance. Most had not really seen the skyjacker and had no reason to pay particular attention to him since they were not aware a skyjacking was taking place until they had landed. Miss Shaffner did her best. D.B. had been wearing a brown business suit and sunglasses. That was pretty well it. He wasn't noteworthy in any way. The 727 was searched for clues, but D.B. left nothing behind except unanswered questions.

Did he parachute out of the aircraft at 8:10 p.m. into a driving snowstorm, or did he parachute out later, extending the ramp as a subterfuge to throw police off his track? Did he survive? Above all, who in tarnation was D.B. Cooper?

For over eight years nothing was heard of D.B. Cooper. Many admired the idea of an individual planning and executing the daring skyjacking without hurting anyone. To police, he is the criminal responsible for hatching a diabolical plot which placed 42 lives in jeopardy.

Whatever your feelings, D.B. Cooper caught on. First came the t-shirts, then the movie, then the songs. You can even sip a D.B. Cooper cocktail in many western U.S. bars. No question about it, D.B. became an American folk hero.

On Feb. 12, 1980, the man without an identity again made his way into the headlines. Children on a family picnic about 32 kilometres outside of Portland found a bundle of decomposed twenty dollar bills. The FBI verified that the serial numbers of the bills, which totalled $6000, matched those of the bills handed over to D.B. eight long years before. They also verified that all the bills were from one bundle.

Did the recovered money provide any answers or did it lead to more unanswered questions? Was that rascal D.B. clever enough to toss away $6000 so that searchers would believe he died in the lonely woods upon landing, or did he really perish and was his body ravished by wild animals?

The mystery continues to intrigue Laurel and Dave Fisher, the owners of the Ariel Store and Tavern in Ariel, Washington. Each year, on the Saturday following the U.S. Thanksgiving, they celebrate D.B.'s dramatic jump on D.B. Cooper Day. Laurel tells me that there generally isn't that much excitement in Ariel, whose population is about 100, with another hundred or so "within shouting distance."

However, on D.B. Cooper Day all that changes. Over 450 patrons sign the guest book on the big day. Dave stocks up with 100 cases of beer and barrels of chili for the guests, some of whom come from as far away as England. You can purchase D.B. Cooper t-shirts and an engraved certificate attesting that you are a member of the D.B. Cooper fan club. The party starts at 10:00 in the morning and ends at 2:00 the next morning.

Did finding some of the ransom loot in 1980 put a damper on the fun in Ariel? "Not on your life," replies Laurel Fisher. "It added to the speculation. Among our customers it's about 50-50 whether old D.B. is dead or alive. We all hope he shows up for a bowl of chili and a beer on D.B. Cooper Day."

So does the FBI, Laurel, so does the FBI.

You take it from here ...

Responding

1. **Write a Personal Response**   In your notebook, jot down your first thoughts and feelings about D.B. Cooper's story. Then share your impressions with the rest of the class.

2. **Have a Panel Discussion**   With two or three other students, share the questions you wrote while reading and answer as many as you can. Include the following questions in your discussion: Who was D.B. Cooper? Did he commit a perfect crime? Do you think he escaped with the money?

3. **Express Your Views**   As a class, discuss what the terms "folk hero" and "social outlaw" mean. Was D.B. Cooper either of these? Why does Ariel, Washington, celebrate his crime?

4. **Comment on Style**   Consider the style of this story: it is a true story, but it is told in an entertaining way. In a paragraph, describe four or five things the author did to create interest in Cooper and his crime.

Extending

5. **Plan a Newscast**   As producer of an all-news TV station, plan the presentation of a 24-hour newswatch report for this story. Identify the types of information you will report, and make a list of the types of sources (people and graphics) you will need (e.g., maps, schematic diagrams, eyewitness reports, crime experts, aviation experts). Create an outline showing how the first hour of your program will look.

6. **Compose Lyrics**   You have been asked by the D.B. Cooper Day committee to write a theme song for this year's event. Try writing a rap, folk, country, or alternative version of the events of Cooper's story.

7. **Imagine a Sequel**   Continue the story, imagining that Cooper shows up for one of the annual D.B. Cooper Days in Ariel, Washington.

Before you read, brainstorm, in a small group, reasons why people lose their temper in traffic or on airplanes.

As you read, write down a definition of "air rage" or "sky rage" in your notebook.

"Once the rage starts, everything gets out of control."

Flying off the Handle
by Christopher Elliott

WEB SITE NEWS ARTICLE

It took two off-duty pilots, a military policeman, and a 5-foot-4, 98-pound flight attendant to subdue and hog-tie a menacing passenger on US Airways Flight 38.

The passenger had dropped acid and then tried to force his way into the cockpit to "bless the pilot." During the struggle, he tossed the flight attendant, Renee Sheffer, across three rows of seats into the overhead luggage compartment like a ragdoll. Now, less than a month before he goes to trial in a Baltimore federal court, most of Sheffer's physical wounds have healed, but not her psychological ones. She says she suffers post-traumatic stress syndrome and is on indefinite leave from work.

In the year since her violent encounter, she says, passengers have turned increasingly aggressive. Meanwhile, U.S. carriers seem oblivious. "I think it's going to take a plane crash before anyone does anything about this," she says.

BANNING HOTHEADS

Richard Branson shares her concerns. The Virgin Atlantic Airways chairman supports a plan to blacklist potentially deadly "air rage" passengers and ban them from flights worldwide. "It needs draconian measures like that to make people think twice before they behave in that manner on planes."

The German pilots' association recently suggested parcelling out nicotine gum to smokers who get cut off from their cigarettes. It also wants to limit the number of drinks served by flight attendants.

124   Crimes, Criminals, and Justice

And, although British Airways isn't marketing it as such, its recent move to redesign the fleet's economy class cabins at a cost of $251 million is sure to soothe some of the discontent over cramped conditions.

It's easy to see why the Europeans are troubled by air rage. A string of recent midair disruptions have tainted the skies over the continent.

On December 5, 1998, a Finnish passenger who assaulted several crew members on a Malev Hungarian airliner died after he was strapped to his seat and a doctor on board injected him with tranquilizers. An autopsy indicated he died from a mixture of the tranquilizer and another drug or alcohol.

In other recent incidents, flight attendant Fiona Weir was beaten over the head with a broken vodka bottle on a flight to Spain. British pop star Ian Brown was jailed for threatening to cut off a crew member's hand. Traveller Elisabeth Elliott (no relation to yours truly) reportedly bit and kicked a flight attendant and assaulted the co-pilot on a British Airways flight after being refused a drink. She went to jail for 15 months.

WHAT'S WITH THE YANKS?

American passengers are just as bad. But where's our sense of outrage? Where are our proposals to curtail this mile-high madness? There are none—at least on the order of the European ideas.

"It's a very serious situation," says Mary Kay Hanke, a spokeswoman for the Washington, DC based Association of Flight Attendants. "This problem continues to grow and escalate. The cases are more egregious. We have flight attendants who have required hospitalization, who can't return to work."

Hanke thinks there's a good reason for the lack of concrete proposals: no one really understands the cause of so-called cabin fever. Is

it the increasingly small seats? Something in the air? Too much alcohol? The endless delays?

"We need to do more research so that we can understand what's happening," she adds.

WARNING SIGNALS

A good start might be training flight attendants to recognize the telltale signs of in-flight rage, says Los Angeles psychologist William Glasser.

"Air-rage doesn't begin with rage—it starts with irritation," he says. "Flight attendants need to be as sensitive as they can to spotting problem passengers. Once the rage starts, everything gets out of control. You have to stop it before it becomes a problem."

Crew members should look for passengers who are trapped in a middle seat—Glasser says they're the most susceptible to losing their cool—or travellers who are cramped because the person in front of them leaned their seat back.

"One of these raging people could take a plane down," he warns.

What is it going to take for the U.S. airline industry to abandon its flawed "wait and see" approach? Do we really need to see a plane brought down over a populated area by an angry passenger as a wake-up call? Let's hope not.

You take it from here ...

Responding

1. **Discuss Organization**   With another student, go over the four sections of this article. Identify the subtopics in each section. Compare results with another pair of students.

   > **SELF ASSESSMENT**
   > - How did your analysis of the subtopics compare with that of the other student pair?
   > - What additional points did you pick up from sharing with the other students?
   > - How helpful did the other students find your points?

2. **Analyze Causes and Effects**   In a small group, review the examples of air rage mentioned in the article. Why do people become aggressive? What causes these incidents and what effects do the unlawful acts have on others?

3. **Expand Your Vocabulary**   Using a dictionary, write the definition for each of the following underlined words *in context* (to fit the meanings of the sentences in which they appear).

   - "… passengers have turned increasingly <u>aggressive</u>."
   - "It needs <u>draconian</u> measures … to make people think twice before they behave in that manner on planes."
   - "A string of recent midair disruptions have <u>tainted</u> the skies over the continent."
   - "This problem continues to grow and <u>escalate</u>. The cases are more <u>egregious</u>."
   - "… they're the most <u>susceptible</u> to losing their cool."

Extending

4. **Compose for Audience, Context, and Purpose**   Write the sort of letter an annoyed frequent flier might write an airline president. Suggest possible solutions to reduce the number of incidents of air rage.

5. **Design a Poster**   The federal government has decided to take action against air rage instigators. Create a poster to be displayed at an airline boarding gate to get potential troublemakers to think twice about "losing their cool."

Before you read, predict from the title what you think the play might be about.

As you read, refer to the scene description and envision the action.

Heat Lightning

"I couldn't see him very well—I was so frightened."

Play by Robert F. Carroll

Characters

GIRL: *About twenty-three years of age, blonde, small and delicate looking. She is dishevelled from the rain. Her hair hangs loosely about her head, almost all the wave gone. Her make-up is washed away. Almost constantly on the verge of hysteria. She has on what would seem to be a party dress, but now torn and dirty.*

FIRST MAN: *About thirty-five, tall, precise in his dress. He is wet from the storm, but tries to do what he can to alleviate this condition. He is nice-looking. Wears topcoat and soft felt hat, both of which are wet.*

SECOND MAN: *About thirty, not so tall as the first man and not so nice-looking. Determined in his manner. He wears a dark suit, the collar turned up. No hat. He is drenched.*

SCENE: *The drab interior of a bus station along a deserted highway somewhere in the midwest. There are two long benches stage right, back to back; one faces the audience and one faces the rear wall. A door up centre leads out onto the road. It has a single glass pane in the top, and the bottom is wooden. Two doors, up left and down left. Up left door reads "Men"; down left door reads "Women." The room is lighted by an overhanging light with a dull green shade. A large bus schedule is on the wall up right centre. A window is up right of centre and another at right.*

The sound of heavy rain can be heard outside. Lightning flashes outside followed by large bursts of thunder. With each flash of lightning the light in the room dims almost to the point of going out, but somehow feebly struggles back to its full strength.

When the curtain rises, the stage is bare. Then a man enters from the "Men's" room. He is a pleasant-looking man of about thirty-five. He takes off his hat and shakes the water from it; puts it on the bench downstage. He glances at the door up centre. Moves to it and peers out the glass; turns and moves to the schedule on the wall and reads it. He then moves downstage and sits on the bench facing the audience. He picks up a deserted newspaper that lies on the seat beside him. He glances back at the door, then turns his attention once more to the paper and begins going through it casually.

The door up centre suddenly bursts opens, and a girl of about twenty-three rushes into the room. She is sobbing and is out of breath. She throws her body against the door, slamming it. The man turns about quickly. She throws the bolt into place and turns slowly, seeing the man. The girl's clothes are wet and muddy. Her hair is dishevelled. She sobs and rushes to the man quickly.

GIRL: *(hysterically)* Thank God! You're here! Oh, thank God!

(She almost falls and the man catches her.)

MAN: My dear! What is it?

GIRL: Help me. Oh, please—please help me!

MAN: Good Heavens! You're in a terrible state. What has happened?

GIRL: Don't let him in. Please. He's after me. Please don't let him in.

MAN: Who? Who's after you?

GIRL: He'll be here any minute. Please—help me!

(The girl looks to the centre door. The lightning flashes and the light dims slowly. The girl looks at the light and begins sobbing again.)

MAN: Please, my dear, try to tell me what happened. You've locked the door. No one can come in. Now try to calm yourself.

(The light has recovered again.)

GIRL: You're waiting for the bus, aren't you? Oh, don't leave me! *(She rushes into his arms.)*

MAN: There, my dear! Of course I won't leave you!

GIRL: The bus. What time—Oh, tell me it will be here soon.

MAN: The last one's due any time now. The storm has probably slowed it down. Now, listen to me. I shall do whatever I can for you, but you must tell me what has happened.

GIRL: Yes—Yes—I must get hold of myself.

MAN: Here. Sit down. *(He brings her down to the bench facing the audience.)* There, now, that's better isn't it? Now—

GIRL: I was at a party. I—I could have stayed all night with a friend, but I thought I had enough gas to get home—

MAN: Where do you live?

GIRL: About eight miles from here.

MAN: I see.

GIRL: About a mile from here, I suppose—I don't really know—I ran out of gas—I took my flashlight and locked the car and started walking down the road. There are so few cars this time of the morning, but I thought—anyway—I knew I could get the bus when it came along and then—go back for the car later. *(She breaks off and glances at the door again. She shudders at her own thoughts.)*

MAN: Come on, now. You were doing fine.

GIRL: I must have walked—I don't know—just a little way, when I noticed a car pulled off into a lane. I saw the rear light burning. I wanted to call to them. I thought I'd just call out to them and ask if they could help me—if they might let me have some gas.

MAN: Did you?

GIRL: No—I—I didn't get the chance to. I walked near enough to the car to be heard if I called, but—before I could call out, I saw someone. The front door of the car was open and someone was standing by it. A man—he hadn't heard me—he was—he was pulling something out of the car. I couldn't tell what it was at first—and then the lightning—and I—I saw her hand fall to the running board—then—her head—her hair was light and long and it dragged in the mud.

MAN: This is dreadful!

(There is a flash of lightning and a crash of thunder.)

GIRL: He'll be here. He'll be here. I'm scared. Oh, God, I'm scared.

MAN: Did he see you?

GIRL: Maybe my flashlight—maybe I screamed—I don't know—I don't think I screamed. I was too frightened. He looked

up—I knew he saw me. I dropped the flashlight and started running. I could hear him behind me. I could hear the water splashing under his feet as he ran. I knew he was behind me—I was afraid I was going to faint. I ran crazylike all over the road—then I ran off the road and into the woods—I circled round and round hoping I'd lose him, but I kept hearing something behind me—I ran until I fell—I knew there was no use—I couldn't keep it up—but then I realized I must have lost him—because I didn't hear him anymore.

MAN: And you came straight here, then?

GIRL: Yes—Yes—Oh, he's still out there—somewhere. He'll be here. Oh, God! I know he will.

MAN: The bus will be here soon, and you'll be all right.

GIRL: Yes. Oh, God, please let it come quickly.

MAN: You'll have to get to the police immediately.

Heat Lightning

GIRL: No—I couldn't. I don't want to—I'm afraid.

MAN: But you must. It's your duty. This is a dreadful thing.

GIRL: I know, but—what could I tell them?

MAN: Tell them what you told me just now.

GIRL: That wouldn't be enough—they'd want me to describe him. Maybe identify him. I couldn't—I just couldn't.

MAN: Are you sure you couldn't think of something that might give them a lead. Anything?

GIRL: I don't even know what he looked like. I couldn't see him very well—I was so frightened.

MAN: Nevertheless, you've got to go to the police.

GIRL: I don't know—I—

MAN: They'll ask you a lot of questions, of course, but I'm sure you can answer most of them. After you tell them the story the way you told it to me, there'll be routine questions, but they'll be simple. They'll probably ask you something like—was he wearing a hat? How was he dressed?

GIRL: I don't even know that!

MAN: Or—was he tall? Was he short? How would you describe him generally?

GIRL: I don't know—I swear—I just don't know.

MAN: In the lightning—are you sure you didn't see his face at all?

GIRL: I don't remember. Maybe he was wearing a hat or something. I don't remember seeing his face.

MAN: But you saw a girl.

GIRL: No—I didn't.

MAN: But you said her hair was light—and you saw her hand.

GIRL: Yes, I did. In the lightning. I think—yes.

MAN: But you don't remember seeing him?

GIRL: No—I don't. *(She begins sobbing.)*

MAN: I'm sorry—I shouldn't be going on like this—you are much too upset to even think anymore about it. Don't worry about it anymore. Something will come to you later—that you've forgotten about right now. You'll see.

GIRL: Perhaps.

MAN: Your flashlight—for instance. You could identify that, couldn't you?

GIRL: Yes—but—

MAN: There, you see! Now—look—*(points to "Women's" room)* Go in there and dry your eyes and fix yourself up. You'll feel much better.

GIRL: You won't leave, will you?

MAN: Of course not, my dear. I'll be right here!

(She moves toward the door up left. There is a brilliant flash of lightning. The light begins to dim. The girl looks toward the centre door. There is a second flash of lightning illuminating the centre door. The girl screams. In the flash of lightning, a man's face can be seen pressed against the glass outside the door. The door rattles viciously. The light in the room has almost dimmed out.)

MAN: *(pushing her toward "Women's" room)* Get in there. Stay until I tell you to come out.

(The man pushes her into the room quickly.)

SECOND MAN: *(outside the door, rattles the door viciously once more)* Let me in. Open this door. Let me in!

MAN: What do you want?

SECOND MAN: *(outside)* I want to get out of this storm. What the hell do you think I want? What's the idea of locking this door? You think you own this place? *(The man goes to the door slowly and throws back the bolt, and the second man enters quickly. He is a nondescript sort of person; tall, nice-looking and about thirty years of age. He looks about the room as he enters.)* You've got no right to lock that door—keeping people outside in this kind of weather. *(The second man moves up to the schedule on the wall.)* Has there been a bus?

MAN: No—not yet.

SECOND MAN: Late, huh? Good.

MAN: Why?

SECOND MAN: Why? I'd have missed it if it were on time—wouldn't I?

MAN: Yes—of course—how stupid of me.

SECOND MAN: There's someone else here, isn't there?

MAN: What do you mean?

SECOND MAN: I saw somebody else when I looked in.

MAN: There—

SECOND MAN: A girl, wasn't it?

(The two men look at each other a moment; then the first man walks to the door where the girl has gone and knocks on it. The door opens slowly and the girl enters. When she sees the other man standing in the room, she starts to cry out, but the first man puts his finger to his lips conveying silence to her and then guides her downstage to the bench.)

SECOND MAN: I thought you said—

MAN: I didn't say anything.

SECOND MAN: You tried to tell me there was no one else here. I thought there was—

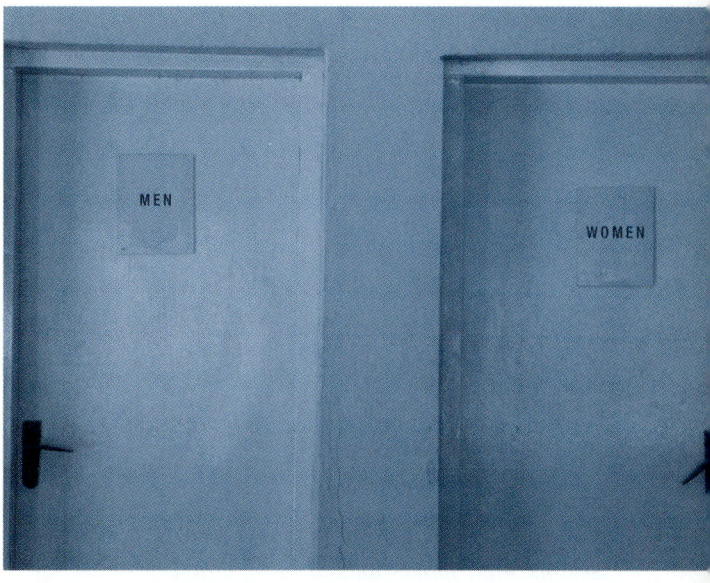

MAN: Did you?

SECOND MAN: Yeah, I was sure there was. What was the idea of lying?

MAN: I wasn't conscious of lying about anything.

SECOND MAN: Yeah? I guess I'm imaginin' things. Oh, well—forget it. How far you going?

MAN: Just into town.

SECOND MAN: How about you, Miss?

GIRL: Not far.

(The second man starts moving down toward the girl. She sees him coming, and moves over to the wall, appearing to read the schedule.)

SECOND MAN: It's pretty late, isn't it? I was in luck, don't you think? I told that to our friend here, but he didn't get it. *(to first man)* I'll bet she's smarter than you are.

MAN: Yes—I suppose she might—be.

SECOND MAN: *(noticing the girl's nervousness)* Say, you look pretty nervous about something.

Storm upset your plans? You can expect storms to slow up buses. If people were smart they wouldn't be out on a night like this. Just try to get somewhere when it storms—can't be done—especially if you're in a hurry.

GIRL: I'm—I'm in no particular hurry.

SECOND MAN: Well, I sure as hell am—but there's nothing I can do about it—I guess.

(There is another flash of lightning and the light dims very low again. The girl is pressed against the right window in fear. The light recovers.)

SECOND MAN: Say—you're really upset, aren't you? Has somebody been bothering you? *(The second man moves toward her again.)*

GIRL: It's—it's just the storm.

SECOND MAN: Afraid of storms?

GIRL: Yes—I—am.

(The girl seems as if she is about to faint. The first man pushes ahead of the second man and takes her by the arm and leads her down to the bench.)

MAN: She'll be all right. Why don't you leave her alone?

SECOND MAN: Yeah! Sure! *(He moves away, watching the girl.)*

(There is another brilliant flash of lightning and a crack of thunder. The light dims slowly and goes out. The girl lets out a muffled cry.)

MAN: Here! Have a cigarette, my dear.

(The man strikes a match, lights her cigarette and his. The second man pushes his head between them.)

SECOND MAN: Don't mind three on a match, do you?

MAN: No, of course not. *(Gives him a light.)*

(The light comes up slowly.)

SECOND MAN: Thanks. *(He strolls up toward the centre door.)* God! What a night! Always wonder what brings people out on nights like this. Wouldn't catch me out if it weren't pretty important. *(to man)* How about you?

MAN: I have early business in town.

SECOND MAN: *(to girl)* And you?

GIRL: I was visiting—with friends. I should have stayed the night.

SECOND MAN: Oh! You're not together, then?

MAN: Er—no—

SECOND MAN: I see. *(He moves down toward the girl.)* How far did you say you were going?

GIRL: Not far—about eight miles.

(The second man sits beside her, and she moves away suspiciously.)

SECOND MAN: I never saw anybody so afraid of a storm.

GIRL: It's the lightning—I—

SECOND MAN: Lightning. I used to be afraid of it, when I was a kid, but I got over it. All by myself too. *(He takes the girl's arm.)* Look! Come here. I'll show you. *(He leads her up to the window rear right.)* Watch the sky the next time there's a big flash. One of the really beautiful sights in this world if you look at it right—like a great big Fourth of July. *(There is now a brilliant flash of lightning.)* Look! See! What did I tell you? It's just like it were cutting the whole world in two. *(The girl breaks away and goes right.)* You wouldn't even watch it. You'll never get over being afraid of things if you won't face them.

GIRL: I can't.

(There is the hum of a motor in the distance. They all listen. The second man goes to the window.)

SECOND MAN: I guess that's it—Yep—Looks empty.

GIRL: Empty!

(There is a sound of brakes being applied. Each waits for the other to make the first move.)

SECOND MAN: Well—are we going?

MAN: No!

SECOND MAN: What?

MAN: I'm not going!

SECOND MAN: Why?

MAN: I don't see that I have to give you a reason for what I do.

SECOND MAN: No—I guess you don't at that— *(He looks at the girl, then moves to her, reaching for her arm.)* Well, in that case, I guess we'll just keep each other company, won't we?

(The girl is stunned. She looks to the first man, who stands behind the second man. The first man shakes his head "No." There is the sound of a horn outside.)

GIRL: *(backing away from the second man)* No—No—I don't think I'll go either. I'll wait—

SECOND MAN: I think you'd better come on. We'll have it all to ourselves.

GIRL: No—No—I won't. Leave me alone. I'm going to stay here—with him.

SECOND MAN: *(looks from one to the other)* I get it. Waiting for a bus! *(he laughs)* No wonder you had the door locked! *(The second man exits laughing.)*

(The girl rushes after him, slamming the door and throwing the bolt once more. She listens to the sound of the bus pulling away. Then she turns quickly to the man.)

GIRL: Thank God!

MAN: I tried to tell him you weren't here.

GIRL: But you let him in—In God's name—why?

MAN: He was making such a disturbance out there. Besides there was really no way to tell for certain that—

GIRL: No—He's gone—He's gone—I guess it wasn't—No—I somehow don't think it was—

MAN: You don't think it was he?

GIRL: No—I—don't—

MAN: You remember something, then?

GIRL: I seem—No—No—

MAN: Yes—You do! You know that wasn't the man. Why? That's a step to remembering.

GIRL: No—only that he—left. He left—

MAN: Yes, you do! I knew it would come back slowly—that you'd remember something.

GIRL: No!

MAN: First, you would say—That wasn't the man because I remember—and then later—That was the man because I remember. Yes. You would remember!

GIRL: No! *(There is another brilliant flash of lightning and the light begins to dim.)* Oh—no—the light—Dear God—No!

MAN: Don't worry, my dear. You'll have light.

(He has taken a flashlight from his coat pocket. The girl stares at it as the lightning flashes again and the already very dim light dies completely. The piercing light of the flashlight is the only light in the room. The girl runs up to the centre door and pulls at it; she doesn't have time to throw the bolt before the man is almost on her. The light plays crazily over her. She runs right and the light follows, jumping its crazy pattern about her. She runs downstage, but she can't escape it. She runs up left and is pressed into the corner facing the man as he approaches. She gropes wildly about the wall. The light dances about her face, blinding her, as he comes nearer and nearer. She shuts her eyes against its brightness. She screams terribly—as the curtain falls.)

Crimes, Criminals, and Justice

You take it from here …

Responding

1. **Analyze Suspense**   Reflect on your emotional reaction to the play and think about the moments at which the suspense was heightened. Review those moments in the play and compare the ways in which the suspense was created in each instance. Discuss your analyses in groups.

2. **Examine Atmosphere**   Scan the play and list the references to different forms of light. As a class, discuss how light and dark have been used to create the atmosphere of the play.

3. **Reveal Clues**   In a group, review the play and see if you can identify clues that, in retrospect, might have indicated how it would end. Compare your conclusions with those of another group.

> **TIP**
> Pay attention to
> - stage directions
> - character descriptions
> - character actions/reactions
> - dialogue

Extending

4. **Create a Newspaper Ad**   Make an ad to promote the play. Use a combination of text and visuals, making up such elements as the names of the actors, director, and producer; reviewers' endorsements; and the name of the theatre.

5. **Spoof the Play**   A *spoof* is a "take-off" or humorous version of something serious. In a group, perform the play as a comedy for either stage or radio. Record your performance on video- or audiotape and play it for the class.

> **TIPS**
> - Look in a newspaper entertainment section for examples.
> - Visuals can be from
>   – clip art
>   – magazines
>   – the Internet
>   or drawn by hand.

> **GROUP ASSESSMENT**
> - Did your group readily agree on roles and responsibilities?
> - Did you agree on how best to present the characters and situations in order to turn the play into a comedy?

6. **Write a Police Report**   Imagine that you are a police officer arriving at the bus station just after the crime occurred. Search for and record clues or evidence found at the scene and then write a police report speculating on what happened.

Before you read, as a class, discuss which youth crimes are serious enough to warrant a jail sentence or something harsher.

As you read, make a chart showing which points raised in the survey you agree and disagree with.

I think kids should go to jail if they kill someone.

The Great Young Offenders Act Debate

Compiled by Stephen R. Biss

WEB SITE SURVEY

Visitors to Stephen Biss's Web site were invited to e-mail their thoughts on the following questions:

- For what criminal offences should young persons receive sentences of jail (open or secure custody)?
- For what criminal offences should young persons receive non-custodial sentences?

✉ I think that it would be appropriate for anyone who breaks the law by killing or having possession of a gun to be charged as an adult. I believe this because this is a serious crime and should be treated seriously.

✉ You should start jailing young people when you see a pattern in their behaviour. If they have stolen something once, it could have been peer pressure from their friends. I am not saying that they shouldn't get in trouble for their crime, but they also shouldn't get jailed for it. If they continue stealing, then jailing them would be appropriate. If they kill someone, on the other hand, they should be locked up right away. If a child is 10 years old and he/she kills someone, he/she should not be able to get off as easily as the YOA lets them. I believe they knew what they

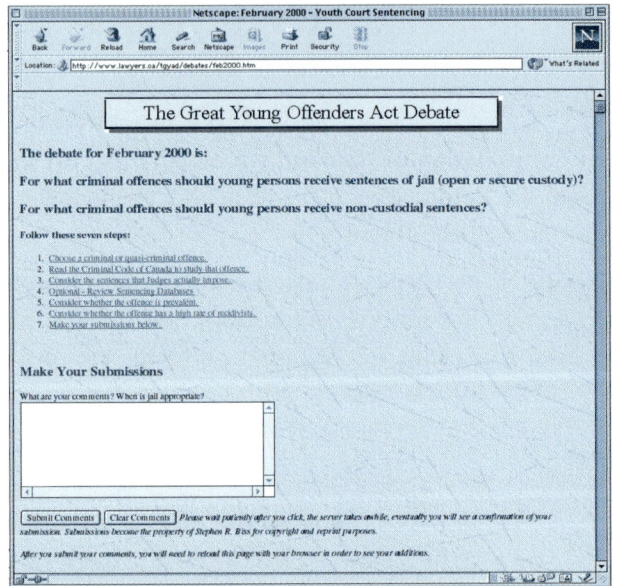

were doing and should be punished for their crime. If you just get the kids therapy, then they are going to think they can get off that easily the next time they go out and shoot someone.

✉ The root cause of 80 percent of cases starts with family problems such as divorce between parents, lack of attention, love, caring, etc. given to children by their parents. It is the parents' responsibility to teach their children good things.

136 Crimes, Criminals, and Justice

Therefore, if a child makes any trouble, I would say the parents deserve punishment too.

✉ Jail is appropriate for any age and gender.

✉ I think that this is a very tricky question to answer. The basis of our entire justice system is rehabilitation and *not* punishment. Many of the respondents have replied "whatever fits the crime," like rape and murder. But I believe every case is different, and every child has a different background to their cases. When a six-year-old shoots and kills another six-year-old, we have to realize that *they* might have no understanding of what they have done. To send them to jail is to dismiss society's problems without truly looking at the circumstances and consequences as such.

✉ Jail is appropriate when the person has done something to ruin someone's life completely. Suppose I kill someone—it would be only right to send me to jail or give me the death penalty.

✉ Jail is appropriate for all offences no matter how small.

✉ I think the Young Offenders Act is a great way to teach youths that there are other people around them and that they should care more for others. I think jail is appropriate for people 12 and over. If they are younger, then their parents should be charged for letting this situation grow over the years to get so bad.

✉ I think that we have to realize the consequences of putting young people in jail. By isolating them from society and placing them in a situation where they are surrounded

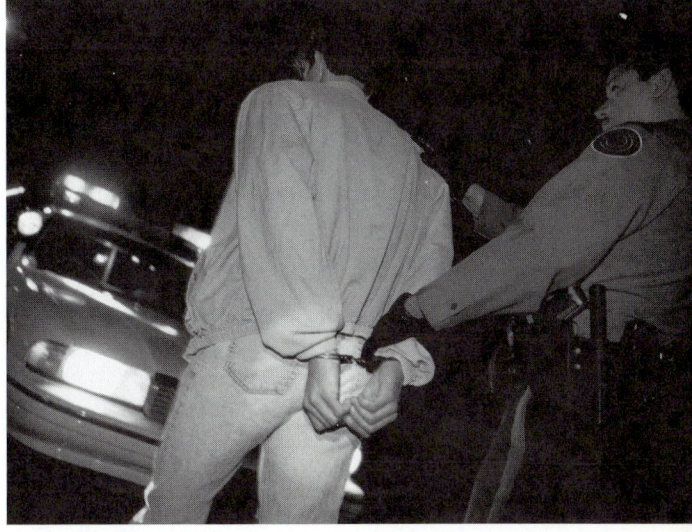

by hardened criminals, we are alienating these troubled youths from the society in which they must exist. Surely we as Canadians have decided that our justice system is based on rehabilitation (hence the absence of a death penalty), and we must promote the socialization of juveniles over the potentially dehumanizing experience of years in prison.

✉ Jail is appropriate whenever the person is old enough to understand what they are doing!

✉ Youths who commit crimes, regardless of what their crimes are, should be tried as adults. It doesn't make sense that a 17-year-old can commit the same crime as an 18-year-old, and the 17-year-old's maximum sentence is considerably shorter than the adult's. They both knew what they were doing, it's just that one was lucky enough to fall under the Young Offenders Act. If you do the crime you must be able to do the time, regardless of your age.

✉ Jail is appropriate when the crime is irreversible. If the offender can express remorse, undergo counselling or some form of rehabilitation, and make up for what they have done, then jail time is not necessary. Jail should only be enforced upon the people who continue to re-offend and show no desire to change, when the last resort is hard time. Although "hard time" is somewhat of a joke in Canada.

✉ I think kids should go to jail if they kill someone.

✉ I think that jail is never right for anyone under the age of 18.

✉ I am a student who is attending college and I know that the justice system is not tough enough on young offenders. My goal is to become a police officer, and I don't want to see so many young people throw everything away by committing petty crimes. I hope that our system can find a way to deal with people fairly. There are many people who are accused of crimes where they have never got into trouble with the law, and the courts have to see that something wrong may have happened and the person may have been innocent. I hope that things can change for the better for everyone in our society.

✉ I feel that as long as the person the crime was committed against was not seriously hurt, and the juvenile perpetrator can show evidence of positive supervision in the home and community, the child should be sentenced to house arrest. I think that throwing these kids into jail or juvenile detention is ensuring that these children return to society even more violent and angry. If we do not begin to show our children some compassion, we can be assured that eventually a more violent and savage society will be created in the near future.

✉ I have a 16-year-old stepbrother who is involved with the law. He has a lot of charges and now is being charged with breach of probation, fraud, and theft under [$5000]. When will the law finally realize that the sentencing they give has to be increased? The law is too light on young offenders, and I think that in order for them to learn, sentencing has to be high!

✉ I do not believe in jail cells for our young people. Each person should be judged individually. We have to address the reasons behind the crime. I know many misunderstood youths, and what they need is a clinic, some wins in life, some direction, and faith in themselves to clear the hurdles they encounter in the cruel world they live in. People have been too critical. It's so easy to judge others. Try walking [a mile in the shoes] of one of these kids and see how you cope.

✉ Juveniles must be made to serve long-term sentences for presumptive offences (murder, aggravated sexual assault, assaults involving serious violence and grave bodily harm), repeat violent offences, and crimes involving the use of weapons (knives, knuckledusters, spiked bats, machetes). If we are to be serious about curbing senseless and barbaric acts of violence, a step in the right direction would be to make these brave individuals serve their entire sentence in prison without parole, give them a mat to sleep on and a few changes of garb. Regardless of what anybody says about rehabilitation, when you're dealing with hardened anti-social behaviour, time is the best form of rehab. We must realize that no matter how hard we work on the preventive end of things, crimes of serious violence will continue to occur in Canada. We can do little to stop it. But we can do a lot to manage it, especially when it comes to preventing repeat offences. Minors who choose to perpetrate violence against other human beings must realize and be made to pay for their actions. Why as Canadians do we continue to clutter our natural instincts and simple logic by diving into the minds of sociopaths and trying to alter their thought patterns? I've never understood that. It's like trying to change the shape of the leaves on a tree. It just doesn't work. Let the sociopaths have life, but make sure it's different from the life that law-abiding and non-violent Canadians are entitled to. There's nothing wrong with living the rest of one's natural life in prison. There is everything wrong, however, with risking the lives of other potential innocent victims to appease the wishes of the sociopath to return to society. We take far too many risks with criminals in Canada.

You take it from here ...

Responding

1. **Explore Viewpoints**   In a small group, discuss the chart you made while you read. Find out what other students think, and try to reach a consensus on which crimes deserve jail sentences. Designate a note-taker to record the overall position of the group. Then present your group's views to the rest of the class.

2. **Develop an Argument**   Select the point of view expressed in the survey that most closely reflects your own opinion. Use it as a starting point to write your own personal response to the questions under debate.

Extending

3. **Suggest Solutions to a Problem**   Assume you are submitting an article to a magazine for teenage readers on the topic of rehabilitating young offenders. What solutions can you suggest for this social problem?

4. **Create a Web Page**   Plan and set up a Web page on another issue related to crime, punishment, and justice such as drunk driving, the death penalty, hate crimes, or road rage. Include background information on the issue as well as space for a discussion forum.

5. **Write a Letter**   Write a letter to the Minister of Justice suggesting how the problems of juvenile delinquency and juvenile crime could be addressed effectively.

> **TIPS**
> - Do some research on the topic before you draft your letter.
> - Exchange letters with another student for proofreading and feedback.

Before you read, as a class, discuss capital punishment as a method to discourage and prevent crime.

As you read, write down two or three questions to ask in a follow-up class discussion on capital punishment.

Even the most premeditated murderer never bargains on being caught.

Debating the Death Penalty
by David Matas and Andrew Allentuck

ESSAYS

I. THE DEATH PENALTY IS FUNDAMENTALLY UNJUST

Justice implies a concept of fairness, of equality, of proportion. However, the death penalty is unfair, unequal and disproportionate.

The notion that the death penalty is just stems from the belief that it is fair to do to a murderer what he has done to his victim. Yet that is a notion society applies to no other crime. The government does not steal from thieves, burn the houses of arsonists, or rape rapists.

Why does the government not, say, rape rapists? The reasons are many. It would be degrading to the penal authorities. It would appear to condone the crime by repeating it. It would be a wanton cruelty. All of these reasons apply to the death penalty. Justice requires punishment of the crime, not inflicting the crime on the perpetrator.

There are several other reasons besides why the death penalty is unjust. Executing an innocent person is unfair, and wherever there has been the death penalty, there has been an inevitable number of documented cases of the innocent executed. Of course, punishing any innocent person is unjust, no matter what the punishment. At least other punishments can be either reversed or compensated. The death penalty is irreversible and beyond compensation.

What is more, the death penalty actually leads either to the acquittal of the guilty or to the conviction of the innocent, both unjust results. The result in death penalty cases depends on whether there are death-qualified juries or not. A jury that is death qualified, i.e., the jurors all believe in the death penalty, is more likely to convict than a jury randomly chosen. The very process of death qualification has been found to predispose the jurors that survive that process to believe the defendant is guilty. Those who believe in the death penalty have been found more likely to believe that a defendant's failure to testify is indicative of his guilt, more hostile to the insanity defence, more mistrustful of defence lawyers, and less concerned about the danger of erroneous convictions.

A jury not death qualified, where some of the jurors oppose the death penalty, is more likely to acquit because of the death penalty than if there were no death penalty. A murderer who would be convicted if there were no death penalty is acquitted because there is a death penalty.

Same penalty

Justice requires that like cases be treated in like manner. If two people commit the same crime in the same circumstances and there is the death penalty, either both accused should be sentenced to death, or neither should be sentenced to death. Yet, wherever there is the death penalty, like cases are treated differently. In the United States, blacks who kill whites are more likely to be executed than others. In Canada, before the death penalty was abolished, native Indians, Ukrainians, and French Canadians were more likely to be executed than others.

There is, as well, the disproportion in cruelty. Killing a murderer is not doing exactly the same thing to the murderer as the murderer did to his victim. Both the murderer and his victim are killed. However, in addition, the murderer is detained for years in isolation and told he will die. The cruelty of the death watch is separate from the murder, above and beyond what murderers do to their victims.

There is the injustice to the family of the victim. Execution draws attention away from the victim and forces it on the executed prisoners. The feelings of rejection experienced by relatives of victims are increased.

There is a notion of a death bargain behind the argument of justice in the death penalty. The implied argument is that once there is a death penalty, a person knows he will be executed if he kills. It cannot be unfair to the murderer to execute him when he was told in advance that that would be the consequence of his actions.

The notice of a death bargain assumes a level of rationality to murder that does not exist. The people who impose the death penalty may think through this sort of bargain, but the people who kill do not. The people doing the killing and the people doing the thinking are two different sorts

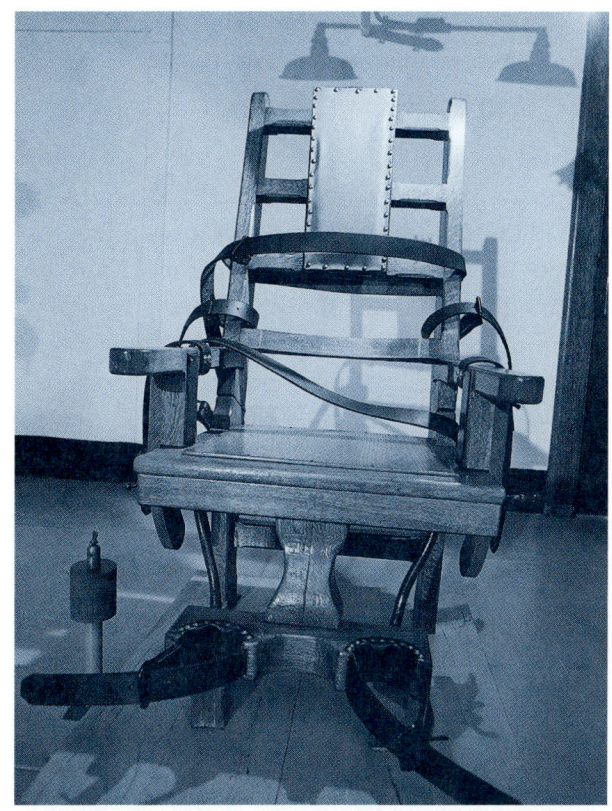

of people. Murder is fundamentally an irrational act, done most often emotionally, on the spur of the moment, in reaction to unexpected events. Even the most premeditated murderer never bargains on being caught. The belief that a murderer makes some sort of Faustian bargain of death for his crime is a sheer fiction.

The bargain of the death penalty is, in a sense, even more diabolic than the one Faust negotiated with the devil. Faust entered into his bargain willingly, in advance. Murderers do not agree to the death penalty. Once in place it is simply imposed on them. The logic that leads a person to say murderers, in all justice, must accept the death penalty because it is there when the crime was committed, is a logic that would justify the most horrible punishments, say drawing and quartering, or boiling in oil, for the most trivial offences. For any criminal can be taken to know the punishment in place when the crime was committed.

Ethnic origin

The death penalty is fundamentally arbitrary. If Canada were to have the penalty, only a few people would be executed. The choice of those executed would depend more on the ethnic origin of the criminal, the quality of the defence, the quality of the prosecution, and the ethnic origin of the victim, than it would on the nature of the crime. The execution would be a human sacrifice to the public anger over crime. Where is the justice in human sacrifice?

Statistics do not support the death penalty. Neither does justice. All that really does is raw emotion. Members of Parliament should base decisions on more than that.

—David Matas

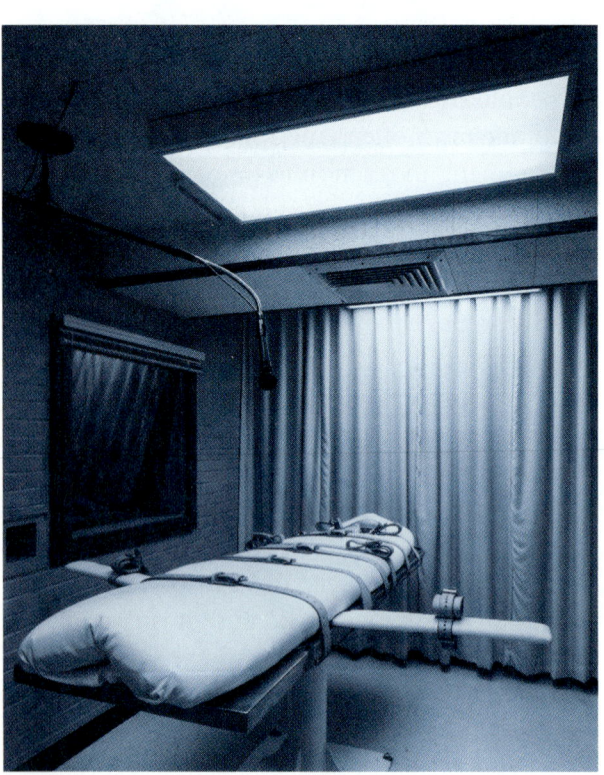

II. EXECUTION SHOULD BE USED AS AN OPTION

Pragmatic people today should be able to agree on some conditions for a return to capital punishment. It is all a matter of numbers. If a nation-wide poll were taken and respondents were asked to balance both rules of evidence and method of punishment, there should be a point at which the voters would find a consensus.

Few of the polled would choose rules of evidence so favourable to the prosecution and so damning to the accused that three innocent people would die for every genuine murderer convicted and executed. How about one guilty one for one innocent? One innocent for every 10 murderers? I think that even people reluctant to return to capital punishment would be willing to accept a ratio of one innocent person executed for 100 000 murderers condemned to death.

Kill again

That is less destructive to the innocent than the system we have now, for some innocent people do die when murderers go free and kill again. Clearly, the innocent–guilty kill ratio is merely the other side of the problem of murderers leaving custody and repeating their crimes. Had they been executed they obviously could not have had more victims.

A balance of rules of evidence and deterrent punishments becomes terribly difficult to determine when one puts theory aside and examines the practical world of criminological fact. Paradoxically, the existence of a death penalty may have the effect of putting more murderers on the street. Juries, aware that their decision may kill an accused, tend to acquit more often in cases where execution is possible than they do in which long imprisonment is the only penalty.

In Canada from 1956 to 1960, for example, 33 percent of all accused murderers were convicted, compared to 76 percent of all persons charged with manslaughter. In England, Australia, and New Zealand, the same disparity has been observed. Recently, a Canadian study by University of Toronto psychologist Jonathan Freedman has shown that as many as 30 percent of jurors in first-degree murder trials in which the accused was found guilty would have voted for acquittal if confronted with the knowledge that conviction would result in execution. So much for the idea of using capital punishment to keep murderers off the streets. It has the opposite effect in our system of law.

From the point of view of the criminal, the existence of capital punishment so decreases the likelihood of conviction that it actually makes a capital crime easier to get away with than a lesser offence. University of Victoria criminologist Ezzat A. Fattah compiled statistics on death sentences in Canada from 1881 to 1960. He found that even though capital punishment was mandatory upon conviction for murder, a person charged with murder had only one chance in three of being sentenced to death. Once sentenced to death, he had more than three chances out of four of escaping execution. In all, murderers had only an 8 percent chance of losing their lives.

As a result of the tortuous appeals process, found criminologist C.W. Topping in a famous 1952 article published while capital punishment was in its prime, "the net result of the administration of justice in Canada as it relates to capital offences is that murder has become the least risky of any or all the offences which a citizen might choose to commit."

Judicial error

Opponents of capital punishment stress the problem of judicial error. Judges and juries can convict the innocent, as we know from the case of Donald Marshall, jailed for more than a decade for a murder he did not commit. An unknown number of other convicts now in jail are in the same situation. One may reprieve and compensate those imprisoned. It cannot be done for those killed by court decision.

Among criminals, murderers are a good bet to go straight once they have been released into society. In Canada, data from the National Parole Board show that from 1920 to 1967, 119 capital offenders who had their death sentences commuted were granted parole. Only one of the 119 committed a second murder. Obviously, 118 did not repeat their crime, and the one repeat murderer was hanged for his second murder. Among the 119 parolees, 0.84 percent were likely to commit murder, 99.16 percent were likely never to kill again. Those seem good odds for society, yet compared to Canada's current murder rate of 2.19 per 100 000 inhabitants, it is 383 times greater. Should society kill the 119 to save one innocent victim's life, or let the 119 live and then lose an innocent life? That is the equation and the trade-off.

I believe that there is no practical argument for imposing capital punishment on the murder of one person by another. Yet where a person is a menace out of the equation's scale, where, for example, he commits mass murder, serial murder, murder for hire, terrorism, or arson resulting in many deaths, then capital punishment should be a sentencing option.

Judicial error and the much-used defence of insanity have to be weighed against the chance the convicted person could escape or, years later, be pardoned, and kill again. Capital punishment should in the final analysis be seen as a tool for protecting the living, not as a means of retribution, of infliction of biblical justice, as an instructive means of deterrence of others.

If a person has demonstrated to a court through proven multiple murders or paid murders that he is a menace out of the ordinary scale, then the balance of evidence and error, of predictive doubt and the future costs of yet uncommitted crimes suggests that society is well served by his execution. This special category of murder punishable by execution would then be reserved for and applied to Clifford Olson (who has not repented his acts), whoever bombed the Air India plane, and executioners for biker gangs and other criminal organizations. This is pragmatism, not idealism. There is, after all, no ideal to be preserved in the taking of life by the state.

—*Andrew Allentuck*

You take it from here ...

Responding

1. **Clarify Meaning**   As a class, share the questions you came up with while reading the essays. Paraphrase the main ideas expressed in the essays, and define any unfamiliar terms. Is there information you would add to the two sides that you think the authors missed? Which view most closely resembles your own? Explain.

2. **Make a Chart**   In a small group, go over the two articles. Make a chart showing the pros and cons (arguments for and against) about the death penalty. Decide which arguments you find most convincing, then share your views in a class discussion.

Arguments for	Arguments against
it is fair to do to a murderer what he has done to his victim	the government does not steal from thieves, burn arsonists' houses, or rape rapists— so why treat murderers differently?

3. **Identify Thesis Statements**   A *thesis statement* is the most important sentence of an essay and presents an overview of the main idea or argument. In your notebook, jot down the thesis statements for these two essays.

Extending

4. Conduct Library Research   Visit your school library and find out what information is available on the subject of capital punishment. Identify three available sources. Record all relevant information about the sources (author, publisher, date and city of publication) as well as similarities, differences, and any other interesting information you uncover. Share your research with the class.

5. Organize a Debate   Hold a debate on the following resolution: The death penalty should be reinstated in Canada.

6. Compose Diary Entries   Imagine what it would be like to be someone on "death row" awaiting response to a last-minute application for a pardon. Write two diary entries for such a prisoner.

Before you read, as a class, discuss the effectiveness of the justice system and sentencing today.

As you read, examine the details of the cartoon and, in your notebook, list at least three things that make it humorous.

Herman

Cartoon by Jim Unger

"A 300-year sentence is not so bad nowadays. With good behaviour you can be out by August."

You take it from here ...

Responding

1. **Explore Humour**   With a partner, discuss what is ironic about the caption. Look up the word *satire*. How is the cartoon satirical? Is there truth to what is said in it? Why do you suppose Jim Unger chose this topic?

2. **Comment on Style**   In a paragraph, address the following questions.

    a) Who are the two people in the cartoon? What is their relationship to each other?
    b) What are they feeling or thinking? How can you tell?
    c) What details of the drawing are specifically funny?

3. **Analyze Content**   As a class, discuss the issues this cartoon is dealing with, such as lenient sentencing of criminals and failure of courts to render true justice. Do you think these are serious problems? Do you think they're appropriately addressed in a cartoon? Why or why not? After the discussion, write a follow-up paragraph in your notebook summarizing the points made.

Extending

4. **Draw a Cartoon**   Imagine another ironic situation involving crime or justice. Create a single-frame cartoon about it in the same ironic style as Jim Unger uses. (Your caption will probably be as important as the picture itself.)

5. **Support Your Opinion with Facts**   Review the issues you discussed in Activity 3. Use these as the basis for an editorial criticizing or defending the justice system of Canada or your province. Illustrate your points with factual examples. You will need to do some research beforehand to make your arguments convincing.

Before you read, debate with others in a group whether it is always dangerous for children to talk to strangers.

As you read, pay attention to your emotional response, noting what parts of the story raise feelings of tension.

The Knife Sharpener

"Please don't call the police," he said.

Short Story by Bonnie Burnard

Notes

Bonnie Burnard is a Canadian author and creative writing teacher whose fiction has been gaining international attention in recent years. She won the Commonwealth Best First Book Award in 1989 for *Women of Influence* and in 1999 won the Giller Prize for her novel *A Good House*.

"Now tell me again," Janet said, wrapping the yellow scarf around her daughter's neck. Erin was dark, like her mother, with unruly curly hair framing an open face. She began her singsong.

"Don't dawdle, don't play with the dogs, don't talk to anyone I don't know. Go right to Kathleen's house." Kathleen was the twelve-year-old daughter of a friend and she had agreed to walk Erin to school the first year.

"Right." Janet opened the back door. "Off you go. See you at lunch."

Mitsy ran up with Daniel in tow.

"Kiss and hug," she demanded. "Kiss and hug for me."

Daniel threw himself into the huddle, his arms raised and eager. After a minute Janet broke them up. "Okay, okay, enough." She herded the little ones back into the den. "Play," she said.

Erin stood hanging on the doorknob, waiting for her mother's hug. She accepted it like a talisman, safer after. "Love you Mom. Bye." She hurried down the steps.

Janet closed the door. She walked back up through the kitchen, grabbed her cigarettes, and went to the living room window. From there she could watch Erin march down the driveway and across the street, making her way to the corner, where she turned out of sight. The neighbour, the older woman whose children were grown, sometimes watched Erin too. She'd told Janet that the child walked just like her mother. It was a kind of hurried saunter, a shuffle, anything but graceful. Janet lit her cigarette. Here and there, patches of the road had been worn by traffic to blue-black ice. The smaller kids on the street ran to those patches, sliding as fast and as far as they could, but always later in the morning, when the neighbourhood traffic had ceased and the street was quiet. For the past few years Janet and the other mothers had taken informal turns supervising the play and even when she was not on

148   Crimes, Criminals, and Justice

patrol, pacing and jumping in her parka and mukluks, she watched from the living room window. This year Erin would not be involved in the games. She was off, on her own.

Mitsy and Daniel stood with Janet now, their hands pressed against the cold window. Mitsy wrapped her arms around her mother's leg. "Time for toast," she said.

Daniel joined in, happy to hear a word he could echo. "Toast," he said. "Toast, toast, toast and jam."

"Okay." Janet took a hand in each of her own. "Let's do it."

The kids hauled themselves up to their places at the table while Janet dropped some bread into the toaster and eased the handle down to catch. She got the peanut butter and jam out and cleared Erin's cereal and juice away. The kids sat quietly, eyeing each other. Any minute some squabble would break out and then in another minute they would be best friends again. It would go on like that all day. She wondered when real long-lasting malice would begin. She'd seen hints of it in Erin, big hints.

The toast popped up.

"There it is," Daniel yelled.

She made herself a cup of coffee and sat down with them. Erin will be in school by now, she thought, will be taking off her coat and scarf and boots and sitting down at her desk, ready.

When the kids had finished eating, she took them to the TV in the den. They settled down in front of *Romper Room*, waiting for their instructions from the young woman who would lead them through their romps. Janet looked at the woman's perfect face. "You do a fine job," she said. "You're a good broad."

She spoke to the backs on the floor. "I'm going up to shower now. I'll leave the bathroom door open." They ignored her.

She hurried upstairs and made the beds. One of her husband's jackets hung on the bedroom door. That meant it needed a button; the button would be in the pocket. She stripped in the hall, tossing her nightie down the chute before going to the bathroom to turn on the water. Then back to the top of the stairs to listen for any noise other than the voice of Miss whatever-her-name-was on TV. Then into the shower. She sudsed her hair and groaned into the steamy water. Someday she would stand there for an hour, just stand, steaming, wasting water.

Afterwards, downstairs to check the kids and downstairs again to the wash in the basement. Left, right, white, coloured; left, right, white, coloured. She threw the white into the washer. Then upstairs to the bananas. They were past eating raw, ready to be made into muffins. She'd do this, check the mail, have another coffee. Then the kids. Hold them. Tell them there would be muffins.

She was mashing the bananas when the back doorbell rang. Oh go away, she thought, leave me be. But she went to the door and opened it. It was an old man.

"Yes?" she said.

"Morning." He tipped an imaginary hat to her. "I was wondering if you'd have any knives that could use sharpening?"

He was tall but his shoulders were stooped under the sloppy sleeves of a heavy grey curling sweater. It was not zippered and she could see suspenders. They held up dingy brown draped pants, the kind the young guys were wearing again now, but these were from some former life in the world of fashion. A satchel hung over his shoulder, bulky with something heavy. His face, fleshier than the rest of him, was a sickly, ashen colour. Her eyes finally settled on his. They were clear and alert, under bushy grey eyebrows. Well, he's not a drunk, she thought.

"Knives?" she asked.

"Maybe you've heard from your neighbours. I come round every March. Do mowers as well." He bundled his sweater around his chest, moving his weight from one foot to the other.

"Come in," Janet said. "You're cold." She closed the door behind him. "I guess I likely have some that aren't as sharp as they might be. How much do you charge?"

"That's up to you, Mrs.," he said.

Janet started toward the kitchen. "Come this way. I'll give you the knives. The mower's in the basement."

Mitsy and Daniel erupted from their play trance. "Hi," Mitsy said. "Who are you?"

Janet shooed them away from the knife sharpener. She led him to the kitchen drawer and handed him the knives, one after another. "These, I guess."

Downstairs in the basement, she pointed to her husband's workshop. "The mower's in there. I'll leave you to it."

She watched him look around. He dragged a lawn chair over to the workbench, opened his satchel and took out his whetstone.

Janet went to the washer, emptied the white load into the dryer, threw in the coloured and left him to go upstairs. The kids were busy with Lego. She finished the muffins.

Then Mitsy was at her knees.

"Hi, sweetheart," she said. "I'm coming to sit with you." She led her by the hand down into the den. They sat on the floor with Daniel and he pointed to the abstraction he'd built. "Tree," he said.

She played with them, letting them roll over and around her like bear cubs. Between squeals, she could hear from the basement the rhythmic scrape of steel against whetstone. She wondered if he could hear the squeals. The timer buzzed.

"Muffins!" she said.

The kids ran ahead of her, stopping just short of the stove. She pushed them back so she could open the oven door. "They have to cool a bit." She dumped the pans upside-down on the counter. Steam rushed up to her face and a sweet banana smell filled the kitchen. The kids danced around her. "In a minute," she said.

She put the kettle on for tea. He can likely smell the muffins, she thought. She reached for the cups and got the tray out from behind the spices. Two hands reached up over the counter and she put a steaming muffin in each. "Blow on them," she warned. "I'm going downstairs. You eat your muffins with Big Bird." They wandered off, watching their muffins as they carried them.

When the tea was ready, she arranged the pot and cups on the tray with a plate of muffins and carried it down to him. He was bent over his work, his knees braced under his thickly muscled arms. He didn't see her until she was right in front of him. He jumped a little.

"Thought you might like some tea and muffins." She put the tray on the workbench.

"Don't mind if I do," he said. He set the knife he was working on down beside him on the floor, the whetstone on his lap, "This is one fine old house," he said. "Tell by the shape of the basement." He waited for her to pour his tea.

"Yes," she said. "It's got some creaks and cracks but we like it." She leaned against the wall.

He took a muffin. "What line of work's your husband in?" he asked.

"He's an architect," she answered.

"That'd be interesting," he nodded.

"Are you retired from something?" Janet asked. "I'm guessing this is sort of a hobby?"

He leaned back to give her room as she poured his tea. "Retired from a lot of things," he chuckled. "Never been very lucky with a career." He took a sip of tea and added some milk. "Had jobs, though. Some good, some not so good."

Janet thought about her father. He'd been lucky; he'd made it. All the men in her life had made it, one way or another.

"I quit regular work when my wife died," he said. "She needed money more than I ever did."

"I'm sorry," Janet offered.

"Oh, that's all right," he said. "We didn't get along anyway. She spent most of her time hanging over a Bingo card, anxious for the big win. Did make a good pot of tea, though. Like you. I miss a woman pouring my tea."

"You have children?" Janet asked.

"Two," he said. "The young lady took off with the scum of the earth when she was sixteen and my boy's over in the North Sea, drilling for oil. He don't write much but I follow the papers to see what's going on over there. His mother used to worry over him but I don't. He's a hell of a swimmer. If the thing threatened to blow, he'd be the first one off, guaranteed." He broke a muffin open and wiped his mouth with the sleeve of his sweater.

Janet saw that the cuff was unravelling, eating away at itself. "That would be a good high-paying job for a young man," she said.

"He's not so young," he said. "He came home two years ago to bury his mother and he was thirty-five then."

Janet was sorry she'd poured a cup for herself and she finished it quickly.

He put his teacup on the tray. "Thanks a million," he said. He picked up his whetstone. "I better get to work here."

"And I better get back upstairs," Janet said. "My oldest will be home soon. I'll leave the muffins for you."

"How old's she?" the knife sharpener asked.

"Six," Janet answered.

"That's a nice age," he said.

She left him to finish, got the clothes out of the dryer and put the coloured load in. Upstairs, she dumped the clothes on the floor with the kids and began to fold. The back door flew open.

Erin ran across the rug and threw herself into the mess of clothes and arms on the floor. "I'm home," she said.

"Boots off," Janet said. "How was school this morning?"

Erin trudged back to the door, kicking off her boots. "We did art," she said. "Real art."

The kids looked at something behind Janet. It was the knife sharpener.

"Finished," he said.

"Oh, good." Janet got up from the floor. "I'll get my purse."

Erin came back into the room. "You're not the plumber," she said.

"No," he answered. "I just had tea with your mommy and sharpened some things for her."

Janet stood beside him, offering a ten dollar bill. "Is this all right?"

"That's good, Mrs. Thank you."

Erin had come to stand in front of her mother, wrapping Janet's arms around her chest.

"I was wondering if you'd like to stay and have lunch with us?" Janet asked. "Just soup."

"No," he said. "I'll be off, thank you." He walked over to the door, turning to wave at the kids as he let himself out.

They all admired Erin's school work, her bold triangles and shaky circles, then Janet went up to put the soup on to heat. She saw the knives on the counter. She was glad she'd had them sharpened. They were overdue. She gathered them up in a bunch and put them into an upper cupboard. They'd have to stay there for a while; the kids wouldn't know how sharp they were until one of them was cut and bleeding.

After lunch, Janet stood at the living room window again, watching Erin, admiring the way she swung her book bag. As the child crossed the street, she took a good run at a sheet of ice, skidding across it and tripping up onto the sidewalk. Erin, the name book said: a fair jewel set in a tranquil sea. Janet wondered if hard work and luck would bring her a good old age with her children. She wondered about the places downtown that offered some warmth, some company. Old hotels, there were six or seven of them, close to the Bay.

She saw him clearly, standing at the corner, his hand outstretched to Erin. Erin gave a little skip then took his hand; Janet had seen her take her grandfather's hand just that way. They walked together around the corner.

The Knife Sharpener

She ran back to Mitsy and Daniel in the den. They were watching *Mister Rogers*. "Don't move," she said. "I just have to go out for a minute."

She grabbed her coat from the closet and was out the door and halfway down the driveway before she had it on. She ran as hard as she could, down to the corner and around it. Nothing. They were gone. There were two lanes mid-way down the block, one going south, one north, back toward the house. Don't call her name, she told herself. Don't call her name. There are garages, empty yards, shrubs to hide in. She decided on the lane going south. That's where he'd take her. She ran across the street. Her slippers were slapping hard on the icy pavement, loud. She kicked them off and started down the lane in her stockinged feet. She looked in the yards on each side as she ran, looked in every filthy garage window, in every overgrown space between house and fence.

She saw Erin's scarf snagged around the stuccoed corner of a garage twenty yards ahead. She let loose, let everything she had go to her legs.

She found Erin tucked into an evergreen hedge. The knife sharpener was crouched down talking to her in a gentle old man's voice. Janet pulled her away from him, turning the small face into the front of her coat.

The knife sharpener stood up and started to back away from them. "I wouldn't have hurt her, Mrs."

"Just what the hell would you have done with her then? Just what the hell do you think ..." Janet heard the ugly edge to her voice and she knew she'd have to stop. Erin had taken her hand.

The knife sharpener was edging back, along the wall of the garage. "Please don't call the police," he said.

"What choice do I have?" Janet asked. She saw Erin watching, listening.

They turned their backs on him, walking down the lane and out into the street. She found her slippers there, overturned in the snow and she put them on. Erin hadn't said anything. Just keep quiet, Janet told herself, let her questions sort themselves out. She'll ask the right one. They were nearly at Kathleen's house.

"I shouldn't have gone with him, should I?" Erin looked down at her boots. "He was a stranger."

"No," Janet said. "You shouldn't have. You can know strangers a little bit, but they're still strangers."

Erin kicked at the snow. "I thought he was a friend of yours."

Kathleen ran noisily toward them. "Where've you been?" she asked. "My mom's been phoning. We're late. C'mon."

"Hi," Erin said calmly, as though nothing had happened to her. She took her friend's hand. "See you later, Mom."

"Wait, Kathleen." Janet put her hand on the girl's book bag. "You be sure you don't talk to anyone you don't know. All right?"

"I never do. What's wrong?" she asked.

"Just make sure, that's all. I'll talk to your mom this afternoon." Janet watched the two of them go off down the street. Erin was leaning, just slightly, into Kathleen's shoulder. She turned back toward the house and, remembering Mitsy and Daniel, began to run again.

They were fine. They had all the muffins, some half eaten, spread out around them on the floor. *Mister Rogers* was still on. Janet looked at the screen, at his kind face, at his kind cardigan sweater. She felt her feet stinging from the cold.

She went to the living room window with her cigarettes. The snow on the lawns was blue-white in the sun, and the black ice on the street had been covered with a light dusting of snow she hadn't seen fall.

She had choices. She could call her husband, who would likely call the police. She could describe the knife sharpener. She could make it so bad for him that he'd never show his face in their world again. Or she could say absolutely nothing, to anyone, ever.

She could take a calm liberal stance. She could get in the Toyota and find him, talk to him, listen to him. She could remind him of his own daughter, when she was small and trusting on his knee. Before she took off with the scum of the earth.

Or she could take the grey ceramic ashtray from the coffee table and hurl it across the room at the fireplace where it would shatter and come to rest in pieces among the ashes.

You take it from here ...

Responding

1. **Locate Suspense**   *Suspense* refers to feelings of uncertainty or nervousness that people have as they read a story. Note three moments, sentences, or bits of dialogue that increase the tension of this story. Compare notes with one or two other students.

2. **Comment on Theme**   With another student, discuss the main idea of the story. How does it relate to the following: trust, poor choices, safety, family, or crime? Write a sentence stating the theme of the story. Give two or three examples of events from the story to support your theme choice.

3. **Assess Atmosphere and Mood**   *Atmosphere* is the feeling presented in a story, whereas *mood* is the feeling created in the reader by the story's atmosphere. Working with a partner, develop a paragraph response in which you describe story details that create atmosphere and tell about what moods you felt at various times in the story.

Extending

4. **Role-Play a Scene** In pairs, write a dialogue that might have taken place between Janet and her daughter, her husband, the police, or the knife sharpener. Make sure that it focuses on the concerns and reactions of both parties. Role-play the scene for the class and ask for their critique of your presentation and interpretation.

> **PEER ASSESSMENT**
> - What were the strong points of the dialogue presented?
> - What could have been done to make the scenes even better?

5. **Organize Information** Assume Janet decides to take action to make her neighbourhood safer. With a partner, make the kind of flier she might have produced after her encounter with the knife sharpener. Before you begin, decide on the purpose of her flier (e.g., to warn people about the knife sharpener, to organize a meeting to establish a Neighbourhood Watch program, to remind people to streetproof their children).

Before you read, as a class, discuss what feelings a break-in would raise in the victims.

As you read, make notes about how this poem made you feel about the thief and break-ins in general.

Notes

Alice Major was born in Scotland and now resides in Edmonton. She is the author of several books of poetry, including *Time Travels Light* and *Tales for an Urban Sky*. She is a president of the League of Canadian Poets and a long-time member of Edmonton's Stroll of Poets.

Thief

Poem by Alice Major

You have made the others in this house
more careful. Locks drilled
      in doors. Boards nailed
to basement windows.
      The cats prick cautious ears
at the covert crumble of leaves
      in outer dark.

You pawed the intimate, clinging
confusion of drawers. Your breath
mingled with the potpourri that scents
my shelves. All the time, your face
in shadow. Your hands hasty, random,
stupid for what they take
      and what they leave behind.

But you will not make me take
precautions. I know your face too well.
You are the thief who, one day, will
      seize all
that I hold precious. You will come
again, lock-breaker, thug with thick fingers.
No care that I can take, no shutter
on my heart, can keep you out. I know
the scythe-curve of your shadow
      on the wall.

You take it from here ...

Responding

1. **Build on Notes** With one or two other students, review the notes that you made while reading and discuss the following questions, answering them in your notebook.

   - Who is "you"? How can you tell?
   - How does the speaker feel about the thief and the break-in?
   - Why will the speaker not take "precautions"?

2. **Find Images** *Images* are words that form vivid sense impressions for the reader. In a class discussion, offer examples of images in this poem. How are they effective?

3. **Focus on Poetic Techniques** One common effect used by poets is *alliteration* (the repetition of consonant sounds at the beginning of a sequence of words). Find one example in this poem.

   Another device used by poets and other writers for emphasis is called *parallel structure* (in which sentences start with or follow the same grammatical pattern; e.g., subject-verb, subject-verb). Find one example of parallel structure.

   Still another technique used in *free verse* (unrhymed poems) is purposeful line breaks to create effects in a first and following line. Identify an example of an interesting line break in this poem.

Extending

4. **Script Dialogue** Imagine that the thief has been caught and is at the police station. The speaker has asked police if she could talk to the thief for a few minutes. Write what she says to him.

5. **Do Internet Research** Using a search engine on the Internet, look up the search words "home invasion." Define the term and find some information about this crime. How is it similar to a break and entry? Report your findings to the class.

> **TIPS**
> - Dialogue is set up with the speaker's name on the left, followed by a colon. If this is done, no quotation marks are needed.
> - Stage directions appear in parentheses. Example:
>   VICTIM: (angrily) Why did you break into my house?

Before you read, define "shoplifting" and "citizen's arrest." Do you think citizen's arrests are common or recommended by police?

As you read, decide whether you would report a shoplifter if you saw one trying to steal something.

Citizen's Arrest

There had been no mistake. I had seen the man take the lighter.

Short Story by Charles Willeford

Notes

Charles Willeford (1919–1988) was a Miami author of many novels and short stories, including a series of crime novels about Miami. He also wrote nonfiction and poetry, and he reviewed mystery and suspense fiction for *The Miami Herald*. As a tank commander in the Second World War, he received the Silver Star, Bronze Star, and Purple Heart, among other awards.

attentively: paying attention in a concentrated way

effusive: gushingly, in a demonstrative way

gabardine: twill-woven cloth

indignantly: angrily

inventory: stock

It was fairly late in the afternoon when I stopped at Gwynn's Department Store on my way home to look at some new fishing tackle. Gwynn's is the best store in the entire city; there are three full floors of everything imaginable. So I always took my time shopping at Gwynn's; a man who's interested in the outdoors can spend several hours in there just looking around.

My back was to the man at the counter—the thief, I should say—because I was looking at the shotguns in the rack behind the locked glass doors. He must have seen me, of course, but he didn't know, I suppose, that I could see his reflection in the glass doors as he stood at the next counter. There was no clerk in the immediate vicinity; there were just the two of us in this part of the store on the ground floor. Casually, as I watched him in the polished glass, he snatched the heavy lighter off the counter and slipped it into the deep right-hand pocket of his green gabardine raincoat.

I was pretty well shocked by this action. As a kid, I had pilfered a few things from ten-cent stores—pencils and nickel key-rings, and once a twenty-five-cent "diamond" ring—but this was the first time in my life I had ever seen anybody deliberately *steal* something. And it was an expensive table lighter: $75 not counting tax. Only a minute or two before I had examined the lighter myself, thinking how masculine it would look on the desk in my office or on the coffee table in a bachelor's apartment. Of course, as a married man, I couldn't afford to pay that much money just for a cigarette lighter, but it was a beautiful piece of work, a "conversation piece," as they say in the magazine ads. It was a chromium-plated knight in armour about six inches tall. When you flipped up the visor on the helmet a butane flame flared inside the empty head, and there was your light. There had been a display of these lighters in shining armour on the gift counter, and now, as the big man sauntered toward the elevators, there was one less.

If I'd had time to think things over I am inclined to believe now that I would have ignored the theft. As I've always said, it was none of my business, and nobody wants to get involved in a situation that is bound to be unpleasant, but at that particular moment a young clerk appeared out of nowhere and asked me if I needed any help. I shook my head, and pointed my chin in the general direction of the elevators.

"Do you see that man over there in the green raincoat? I just saw him take one of those knight table lighters off the counter and put it into his pocket."

"Do you mean he stole it?" he asked, in a kind of stage whisper.

"No." I shook my head again. "I didn't say that. All I said was that he put the lighter into his pocket and then walked over to the elevators."

The big man entered the elevator, together with a teenaged boy who badly needed a haircut, and the operator clanged the door closed.

The clerk, who couldn't have been more than twenty-two or three, cleared his throat. "I'm afraid, sir, that this sort of thing is a little out of my province. Would you mind talking to our floor manager, Mr. Levine?"

I shrugged my reply, but there was a sinking sensation in my stomach all the same. By mentioning the theft, I had committed myself, and now I knew that I had to go through with it no matter how unpleasant it turned out to be.

The clerk soon returned with Mr. Levine, a squat bald man in his early forties. He wore a plastic name tag and a red carnation on the left lapel of his black silk suitcoat.

I briefly explained the theft to Mr. Levine. He pursed his lips, listened attentively, and then checked out my story by going over to the glass case of shotguns to prove to himself that the gift counter was reflected perfectly in the polished surface.

"Would you be willing, Mr. ...?"

"Goranovsky."

"Would you be willing, Mr. Goranovsky, to appear in court as a witness to this shoplifting? Providing, of course, that such is the case."

"What do you mean, if such is the case? I told you I saw him take it. All you have to do is search him, and if you find the lighter in his raincoat—in the right-hand pocket—the case is cut and dried."

"Not exactly, sir. It isn't quite that simple." He turned to the clerk, whose eyes were bright with excitement, and lowered his voice. "Call Mr. Sileo, and ask him to join us here."

The clerk left, and Mr. Levine steepled his fingers. "Mr. Sileo is our security officer," he explained. "I don't want you to think that we don't appreciate your reporting this matter, Mr. Goranovsky, because we do, but Gwynn's can't afford to make a false accusation. As you said, there was no clerk in the vicinity at the time, and it's quite possible that the gentleman might have gone off to search for one."

I snorted in disgust. "Sure, and if he can't find one on the second floor, maybe he'll find one on the third."

"It's possible," he said seriously, ignoring my tone of voice. "Legally, you see, no theft is involved unless he actually leaves the store without paying for the item. He can still pay for the lighter, or put it back on the counter before he leaves."

"Sure, I see. Why not forget the whole thing? I'm sorry I brought the matter up."

"No, please. I merely wanted to explain the technical points. We'll need your cooperation, and it's Mr. Gwynn's policy to prosecute shoplifters; but you can't make charges without an airtight case and a reliable witness. If we arrest him within the store, all the man has to say is that he was looking for a clerk, and there isn't anything we can do about it. He very well may be looking for a clerk. If such is the case, we could very easily lose the goodwill of a valuable customer."

"I understand; I'm a businessman myself. In fact, I hope I'm wrong. But if I'm not, you can count on me to appear in court, Mr. Levine. I've gone this far."

We were joined by Mr. Sileo. He was slight, dark, and businesslike. He looked more like a bank executive than a detective, and I had a hunch that he had an important job of some kind with Gwynn's, that he merely doubled as a security officer. In a businesslike manner, he quickly and quietly took charge of the situation.

I was directed to stand by the elevators and to point out the thief when he came down. Mr. Levine was stationed in the centre aisle, and Mr. Sileo took up his post by the Main Street entrance. If, by chance, the shoplifter turned right after leaving the elevator—toward the side exit to 37th Street—Mr. Levine could follow him out, and Mr. Sileo could dart out the main door and circle around the corner to meet the man outside on 37th Street. Mr. Sileo explained the plan so smoothly, I supposed it was some kind of standing procedure they had used effectively before. The eager young clerk, much to his disgust, was sent back to work by Mr. Levine, but he wasn't needed.

To my surprise, when I looked at my watch, only ten minutes had passed since I reported the theft. The next ten minutes were much longer as I waited by the elevators for the man in the green raincoat to reappear. He didn't look at me as he got off, and I pointed him out by holding my arm above my head, as Mr. Sileo had directed, and then trailed the man down the wide corridor at a safe distance. I wondered if he had a gun, and at this alarming thought I dropped back a little farther, letting Mr. Levine get well ahead of me. Mr. Sileo, who had picked up my signal, went out the front door as soon as it became apparent that the man was going to use the Main Street exit. I could see Mr. Sileo through the glass door as he stood on the front sidewalk; he was pretending to fumble a cigarette out of his pack. A moment later, just about the time I reluctantly reached the Main Street doorway myself, Mr. Levine and Mr. Sileo were escorting the big man back inside the store.

I couldn't understand the man's attitude; he was smiling. He had a huge nose, crisscrossed with prominent blood veins, and he had a large mouth, too, which probably looked bigger than it was because of several missing teeth.

The four of us moved silently down the right side aisle a short distance to avoid blocking the doorway. For a strained moment nobody said anything.

"I'm sorry, sir," Mr. Sileo said flatly, but pleasantly, "but this gentleman claims that you took a desk lighter off the counter and put it into your pocket without paying for it."

I resented the offhand way Mr. Sileo had shifted all of the responsibility onto me. The big man shrugged and, if anything, his genial smile widened, but his bluish white eyes weren't smiling as he looked at me. They were as cold and hard as glass marbles.

"Is that right?" He chuckled deep in his throat. "Is this the lighter you mean?" He took the chrome-plated knight out of his raincoat pocket.

"Yes," I said grimly, "that's the one."

He unbuttoned his raincoat and, after transferring the lighter to his left hand, dug into his pants pocket with his right.

"This," he said, handing a slip of paper to Mr. Sileo, "is my receipt for it."

Mr. Sileo examined the receipt and then passed it to Mr. Levine. The floor manager shot me a coldly furious look and returned the slip of paper to the man. The thief reached into his inside jacket pocket for his check book. "If you like," he said, "you can look at the cheque stub, as well."

Mr. Sileo shook his head, and held his hands back to avoid taking the chequebook. "No, sir, that's quite all right, sir," he said apologetically.

Mr. Levine made some effusive apologies for the store which I thought, under the circumstances, were uncalled for—but the big man cut him off in the middle of a long sentence.

"No harm done," he said good-naturedly, "none at all. In your place, I'd have checked, too. In all probability," he qualified his remark.

"It was my mistake," I said, finally. "I'm sorry you were inconvenienced." And then, when neither Mr. Levine nor Mr. Sileo said anything to me, and the big man just stood there—grinning—I turned on my heel and left the store, resolving, then and there, never to spend another dime in Gwynn's as long as I lived.

There had been no mistake. I had seen the man take the lighter, and there had been no clerks anywhere near us at the time. I stood beside my car at the curb, filled with frustration as I ran things all over again in my mind. A trick of some kind had been pulled on the three of us, but how the man had worked it was beyond my comprehension. I opened the door on the sidewalk side and slid across the seat. As I fastened my seat belt, a meaty hand opened the door and the big man in the green raincoat grinned in at me. He held out the shining knight for my inspection.

"Want to buy a nice table lighter, buddy?" he said, chuckling deep in his throat. "I can let you have it without any tax."

I swallowed twice before I replied. "I knew you stole the lighter, but how did you get the receipt?"

"Will you buy the lighter if I tell you?"

"No, damn you; I wouldn't give you ten cents for it!"

"Okay, Mr. Do-Gooder," he said cheerfully, "I'll tell you anyway. This morning there were several lighters on the counter, and I bought one of them at ten a.m. After stashing the first one in a safe place, I came back late this afternoon and got this one free. Unfortunately, you happened to see me pick it up. The receipt I got this morning, however, served me very well for the second. The store stays open until nine-thirty tonight, and I had planned to come back after dinner and get another one. So long as I took them one at a time, one receipt is as good as three, if you get my meaning. So the way I figure it, you ought to buy this one from me because I can't come back tonight for my third lighter. You cost me some money, fella."

"I've got a good mind to go back in and tell Mr. Sileo how you worked it."

"Really? Come on, then. I'll go in with you."

"Get the hell out of here!"

He chuckled, slammed the door, and walked away.

My fingers trembled as I lit a cigarette. There was no mistaking my reaction now—I was no longer frustrated, I was angry. If the man had been my size—or smaller—I would have chased after him and knocked out the remainder of his front teeth. I also considered, for a short moment, the idea of telling Mr. Levine how he had been cheated. All they had to do was to inventory their remaining lighters (there couldn't be too many of them in stock, an expensive item like that) and they would soon find out that they were one short. But after the cold way they had treated me, I didn't feel like telling them anything.

A policeman's head appeared at the car window. "Is this your car, sir?"

"Of course."

"Will you get out, please, and join me on the sidewalk?" He walked around the front of the car and I unfastened my seat belt and slid back across the seat; I was more than a little puzzled.

"Take a look," he said, pointing at the curb when I joined him on the sidewalk. "You're parked well into the red zone."

"That isn't true," I said indignantly. "Only the front bumper's in the zone; my wheels are well behind the red paint. There's supposed to be a little leeway, a limit of tolerance, and I'm not blocking the red zone in any way—"

"Don't argue with me, sir," he said wearily, taking a pad of tickets out of his hip pocket. "Ordinarily, I'd merely tell you to repark or move on, but this time I'm giving you a ticket. A good citizen in a green raincoat reported your violation to me at the corner just now, and he was a gentleman who had every right to be sore. He said he told you that you were parked in the red zone—just as a favour—and you told him to go to hell. Now, sir, what is your name?"

You take it from here ...

Responding

1. **Discuss Irony**   With a partner, answer the following questions.
   - As you read the story, what did you think the narrator was going to do at different times?
   - How did the thief get away with his crime? What was his trick?
   - What is ironic about the ending?
   - Why did the thief betray the narrator to a policeman?
   - In your opinion, is the story believable?

2. **Fill in a Chart**   Make a chart to show various characters' initial reactions to the theft. Suggest reasons for each.

Character	Reaction to theft	Reasons
Mr. Goranovsky		
clerk		
Mr. Levine		
Mr. Sileo		
thief		

3. **Write a Personal Response**   In a paragraph, indicate what you would have done in the narrator's place. Would you have turned the thief in initially? What would you have done when the store personnel didn't believe you or back you up? What would you have done when the thief confessed his method to you or offered you a deal on the stolen lighter? Exchange paragraphs with a partner and discuss your views.

4. **Focus on Theme**   One of the themes of this story is that the justice system is not always "just." Write a paragraph about this idea based on the events and outcome of this story.

5. **Argue a Related Issue**   In a small group, discuss the narrator's initial inclination to ignore the theft. In your opinion, should people get involved in reporting crimes that don't personally or immediately affect them? Is it better to be honest and speak the truth or to be silent and not tell? Share your group's opinions with the rest of the class.

Extending

6. **Rewrite an Ending**   Write a different ending for this story starting with the scene before the narrator got a ticket.

7. **Write a Complaint Letter**   In the role of the narrator, write a four-paragraph letter to the police protesting the ticket.

> **TIPS**
> - In paragraph 1, indicate what the ticket was for and that you are protesting it.
> - In the middle paragraphs, recreate the situation, explaining how and why you got the ticket and what was really going on. Tell why you are protesting.
> - In the final paragraph, say what you hope the police will do in the light of the facts.

Reflecting on the Unit

Responding

1. **Write about a Subtheme**   Pick one of the following subthemes as the basis for an essay:
   - ordinary people commit most crimes
   - people need to become more responsible for their actions
   - justice can be complicated by prejudice or discrimination
   - young people should be treated more like adults in matters of law and sentencing
   - punishment for crimes should generally be harsher

2. **Compare/Contrast Two Selections**   With a partner, find two thematically related selections and discuss how they are similar and different in their plots, themes, and views of crime. Share your findings with the rest of the class.

Extending

> **TIP**
> - You may want to include music and sound effects to create more interest and urgency.

3. **Create Radio Ads**   Your community is fighting back against crime. Write two one-minute spots on the idea that crime is everybody's business. Tape a reading of the spots and play them for the class.

4. **Have a Panel Discussion**   With three other students, talk about what can be done about crime in our society. Make notes, then summarize the group's position and present it to the class.

5. **Debate Wrongful Convictions/Insufficient Evidence**   In groups, study and debate the high profile cases of Canadians David Milgaard and Guy Paul Morin, as well as American Football Hall of Famer O.J. Simpson. Consider the charges laid against these men and debate the end results. Were the outcomes just? Consider lost years, reputations, impact on families, etc.

> **SELF ASSESSMENT**
>
> Review what you have learned from this unit regarding
> - using different forms of writing and genres
> - how to find information
> - how to select information for a purpose
> - stating a theme
> - developing an argument
> - working with others effectively

UNIT 4

"Any sufficiently advanced technology is indistinguishable from magic."
—Arthur C. Clarke

"Technology—the knack of so arranging the world that we don't have to experience it."
—Max Frisch

"All our advertising is propaganda, of course, but it has become so much a part of our life, is so pervasive, that we just don't know what it is propaganda *for*."
—Pauline Kael

Clockwise from top left: Shawn Fanning (Napster creator), Tom Jackson, Julia Roberts, Stephen King, Alexander Graham Bell, Jim Carrey, Mike Bullard, Jann Arden

Media/Technology Influences

Technology is something we are bombarded with each day—e-mail, the Internet, cell phones, DVDs, video games. These new technologies create excitement and have what science-fiction author Arthur C. Clarke describes as a kind of "magic" about them.

Swiss writer Max Frisch implies that one danger of technology is that it may become a substitute for real-life experience. Think about his words when you read Jane Yolen's story "Ear."

One ever-present feature of our technological society is advertising—a type of propaganda, according to film critic Pauline Kael, that attempts to shape our opinions and behaviour.

As you read and view this unit, think about the following:

1) What audiences are these ads aimed at?
2) What is actually being sold or promoted?
3) Why are these ads effective?

Before you read, assess your own reading and TV viewing habits. How many hours do you read and watch TV in a typical week? Share your answers with a partner.

As you read, think about the last sentence of the caption. Is it true?

Herman

Cartoon by Jim Unger

"I don't need to learn reading. It's all on TV."

You take it from here ...

Responding

1. **Compare Notes**   With another student, discuss the caption and compare your responses to the "As you read" question. Do you agree that TV makes reading unnecessary?

2. **Write a Reply**   Imagine and write the father's response to his son's comment. Write a short speech, one paragraph long, in which the father explains his point of view to his son.

3. **Comment on Humour**   Discuss as a class the roles of the following in creating humour:
   - choice of subject
   - contrasting characters and attitudes
   - facial features and body language
   - drawn lines (i.e., smooth, round, broken, missing)

4. **Respond to an Argument**   In a group, discuss whether reading is as popular and necessary as ever. What would be your comment on the recent popularity of mega-bookstores? What about the rise in the number of specialty magazines and the rapid expansion of information sites on the Internet? Do you think that all information is available on TV and videos?

Extending

5. **Design a Poster**   Create a poster aimed at young children to promote the benefits of reading. Consider how reading helps children use their imaginations, experience adventures, and learn about new and interesting people, places, and things.

6. **Debate an Issue**   As a class, debate one of the following propositions:
   - that print media should be eliminated to save the environment
   - that all reading in the future should be done on computers or e-books
   - that the number of hours that children watch TV and videos and play video games should be strictly limited
   - that students should be expected to read books in print form before seeing any related movie adaptations

Before you read, discuss with another student the impact that computers and e-mail are having on our society, relationships, and communications.

As you read, summarize the story told by the pictures in your own words.

I would have e-mailed you ...

Birthday Card by GoTT

but my computer crashed.

Happy Birthday

You take it from here ...

Responding

1. **Share Your Summary**   With another student, share what you wrote about the pictures. What does the punch line have to do with the pictures?

2. **Compile a Glossary of Computer Terms**   Working with a partner, use a dictionary and other information sources to define the following computer terms:

attachment	graphics	modem	toolbar
CD-ROM	hard drive	monitor	upgrade
crash	hardware	mouse	username
cyberspace	home page	netiquette	virus
desktop	icon	newsgroup	Web site
downloading	inbox	on-line	World Wide Web
DVD	Internet	scanner	(www)
e-mail	joystick	software	
FAQ	keyboard	spam	
font	Listserv	surfing	

Extending

3. **Compose a Greeting**   Brainstorm other computer-related *puns* (a type of play on words) to choose from to create another greeting card for a specific occasion—birthday, get well, promotion, friendship, etc.

4. **Design and E-mail a Card**   Using a computer graphics program, design a simple card for your greeting. E-mail your card to one of your classmates and request that he or she e-mail you back an assessment of your design focusing on the relationship between the graphics and the words.

> **TIP**
> - You might want to use the glossary of computer terms in Activity 2. What words could you make a word play on?

> **PEER ASSESSMENT**
> - Was the card a clear communication?
> - What was unique about its style?

5. **Write a Personal Response**   Compare and contrast e-mail to "snail mail" (regular hand-delivered posted mail) and telephone calls. Which would you rather receive and send? What advantages and disadvantages are there to each of the three modes of communication?

Before you read, as a class, discuss what you pay attention to when you look at an advertisement.

As you read, notice the order in which elements in the ad catch your eye.

clearNET

Print Ad

Now you can use your Clearnet phone to play games online. You can also use it to do your banking, go shopping, and get news. To see how simple it is to get on the wireless Web, visit www.myclearnet.com The future is friendly.

Unlimited wireless surfing starting at $10 a month

Play games online.

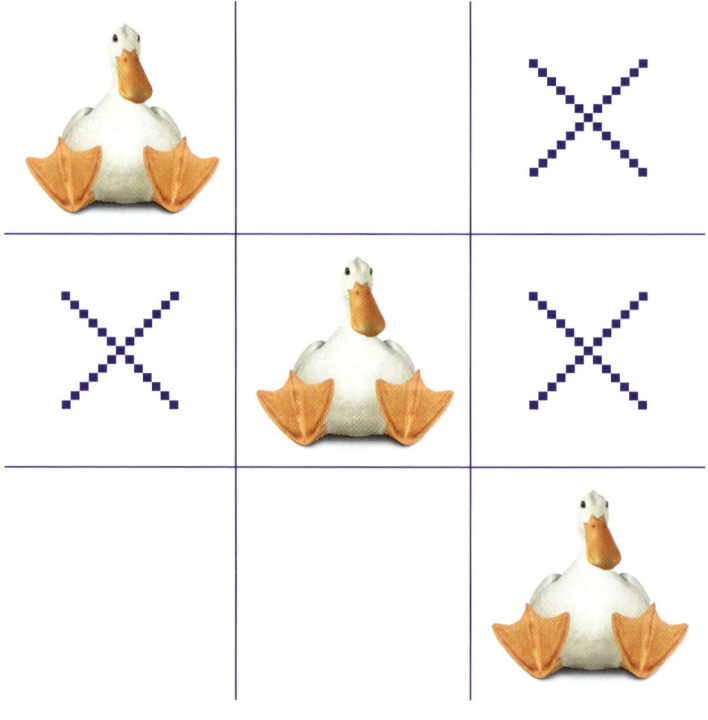

clearNET pcs

More content is being added all the time. To find out what's new, visit us at www.myclearnet.com

You take it from here ...

Responding

1. **Discuss First Impressions** Discuss with a partner what the ad is promoting and to what target audience(s). Compare your impressions with those of another student pair.

2. **Analyze Appeal** As a class, talk about why you think the advertiser would use the image of a duck to promote wireless services. Brainstorm a list of TV and print ads that use similar visual appeal.

3. **Consider Design** Write a paragraph commenting on the limited use of colour and the large amount of white space in this ad. Is it effective? Explain.

Extending

4. **Research Other Ads** Find three to five other magazine ads that you find exceptional. Compile a portfolio of these ads, and write a paragraph for each identifying what elements make them effective. Then share your portfolio in class.

5. **Create an Ad** Borrowing techniques used in this ad, create a new one to promote a fictional product, service, or cause. Design a logo and write the advertising copy. Present your ad to the class.

> **PEER ASSESSMENT**
> - Was the design of the ad well thought-out? Explain.
> - Were all the required elements in place?

Before you read, discuss with another student what the phrase "exercise your options" means.

As you read, discuss with the same partner how the above phrase means something different in this ad.

Exercise Your Options

Print Ad by Alen and Sandra Zukanovic

You take it from here ...

Responding

1. **Study the Visuals**   In your notebook, write down what is going on in each of the three squares occupied by human figures. What do they have in common? What first attracts your eyes to this ad? Share your impressions with another student.

2. **Relate the Parts**   In a paragraph, comment on
   a) what the purple square has to do with the other three squares
   b) the meaning of the ad's title

3. **Discuss Purpose and Related Issues**   In a group, discuss why the authors created this ad. Is it true that a "healthy mind lives in a healthy body"? What does the ad imply about technology and technology users? What larger social issues does it suggest?

Extending

4. **Respond Creatively**   Write two captions for each of the three illustrations. Share your work with a partner.

5. **Create a Collage**   Using the title "Exercise Your Options," make a collage using images and words from newspapers, magazines, the Internet, and other sources to create a different interpretation of the phrase.

6. **Design a Satirical Ad**   Using cut-out pictures or hand-drawn images, produce an ad that satirizes an existing commercial product or service. You can also make a social criticism in your ad. Present your work to the class.

Before you read, scan the ad and write down your first impressions.

As you read, jot down the claims made about the advantages of Wireless Internet.

Nortel Networks

Print Ad

Wireless Internet

Well, Danny, hop aboard. You've been cleared for takeoff. We're building the high-performance Internet. It's faster, more reliable and designed to a higher le quality. Allowing things once only dreamed of, to become possible. Like Wireless Inte anytime, anywhere, access via phone, laptop, PDA, you name it… without pluggi

Nortel Networks, the Nortel Networks logo, the Globemark and "How the world shares ideas." are trademarks of Nortel Networks. "What do you want the Internet to be?" is a service mark of Nortel Networks. ©1999 Nortel Networks. All rig

Media/Technology Influences

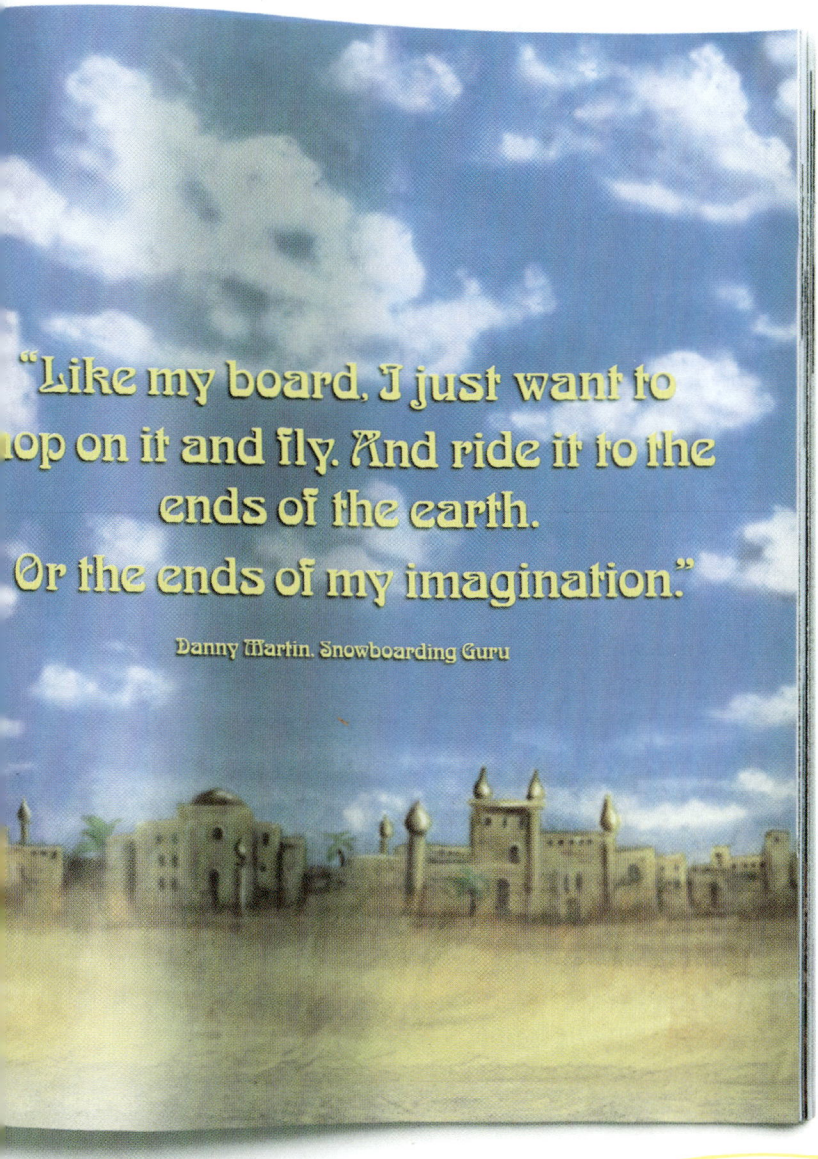

You take it from here ...

Responding

1. **Discuss First Impressions**   With a partner,
   a) discuss and compare your first impressions prior to reading.
   b) discuss who you think is the target audience for the ad. Support your opinion.

2. **Focus on Diction**   In print ads, the words are as important as the visuals. Review the text and notice how the information is presented. In a paragraph, describe how this approach affects the message.

3. **Discuss Imagery**   As a class, discuss how the image of "snowboarding guru" Danny Martin flying on a magic carpet is linked to the idea of "surfing the Net." Is the choice of image effective? Give reasons to support your opinion.

Extending

4. **Create an Ad**   With a partner, imagine a product targeted at a particular audience (e.g., teenagers, women, men, families). Design and create a promotional ad for the product using creative techniques similar to those used in the Nortel Networks ad (e.g., creative visual and text imagery, celebrity endorsement). Present your ad to the class, identifying the techniques you used.

   > **PEER ASSESSMENT**
   > - Was the ad effectively directed toward its target market? Explain.
   > - What suggestions could you offer to improve it?

5. **Perform a Skit**   With another student pair, create a TV-commercial version of one of your print ads. As a group, record what changes were required to adapt the ad from one format to another. Present your skit in class.

Before you read, with another student, brainstorm ads that use celebrities to endorse products.

As you read, write down two reasons why you think the Backstreet Boys agreed to do this ad.

Got Milk?

Print Ad

Notes

The Backstreet Boys is an American group who sing new jack ballads, hip-hop R & B, and dance-club pop. Their first album was released in 1995. Their hits include "Quit Playin' Games (with My Heart)," "As Long as You Love Me," "I Want It That Way," and "Shape of My Heart."

You take it from here ...

Responding

1. **Discuss Purpose and Audience**   As a class, discuss what the purpose of the ad is. Who is the company or organization behind the ad? What are they trying to sell? Based on the use of the Backstreet Boys in the ad, who would you say is the audience?

2. **Analyze Appeal**   Write a response explaining the appeal of this ad. Address the following ad features:

   - the caption "It takes more than a hit single to reach the top."
   - the way the group members are dressed
   - the sentence "15% of adult height is added during teen years."
   - the slogan "got milk?"

3. **Focus on Endorsement**   *Endorsement* is an ad technique in which a product is promoted by a celebrity. Why do you suppose the Backstreet Boys agreed to appear in this ad? In what way does the wording of the ad reflect their claim to fame and style? In what way do their poses reflect their reputation and projected public image? Why do you think the advertisers wanted the group to endorse their product?

4. **Comment on Ad Impact**   In your opinion, is this an effective ad? Is the message appealing? Do you think it might influence someone to drink more milk? Explain. Organize your answers into a written response.

Extending

5. **Check the Facts**   In small groups, do research on whether the ad's claims are true—that 15% of adult height is added during the teen years and that drinking milk can influence growth. Does your research show that milk is the best source of calcium, or are there others that are just as good or better? Share your group's findings with the rest of the class.

6. **Analyze a Technique**   Survey several magazines or TV commercials and make a list of at least five celebrities you see endorsing various products and services. Evaluate how your feelings about the product are influenced by the celebrity's endorsement of it—for example, would you be more likely to buy this particular brand as a result? Would you feel differently without the celebrity endorsement?

Celebrity	Product or service	Your response

7. **Create an Ad**   Design an ad featuring your favourite performer promoting a product—real or fictional—targeted to teens. You can choose to make a print, TV, radio, or Internet ad; your ad might be humorous or serious. Share your ad concepts with the class.

TIPS
- You might want to use a computer illustration program to
  - lay out your print ad or storyboard
  - download pictures of celebrities you are going to use
- You might consider using a video camera or tape recorder if you are creating a TV or radio ad.

Got Milk?   **181**

Before you read, write a personal response explaining what it's like to be a teenager today.

As you read, write down images and phrases from this photo essay that you particularly like or agree with.

Spilling Open

Photo Essay by Sabrina Ward Harrison

Notes

Sabrina Ward Harrison is a writer and artist. She wrote *Spilling Open: The Art of Becoming Yourself*, a personal journal combining text, photos, drawings, and collage, when she was between the ages of 18 and 21.

Tracy Chapman: popular Black American folksinger and songwriter

Walt Whitman: nineteenth-century American poet who prided himself on his independence, joy of living, and love of the United States

182   Media/Technology Influences

introduction

The great American poet Walt Whitman said that there is a time we must "wash the gum from our eyes and dress ourselves for the dazzle of the light."

He looked at men and women struggling with their lives and said,

"Long have you timidly waded holding a plank by the shore, now I will you to be a bold swimmer, to jump off into the midst of the sea, rise again, nod to me, shout! and laughingly dash with your hair."

today was just one of THOSE DAYS
I woke up wanting to go to Italy by car.
perhaps if I really drove fast enough I might
CATCH AIR to FLORENCE
instead of Typography class this morning
Sometimes I forget about the magic.
like the moon and red leaves and HOW
the apples grow AGAIN and AGAIN
Outside my windows.
Life HAS felt overwhelming lately
today in class I had to climb
under the desks during the critique
to get a grip of my "meish-ness" (thats what megan
to find myself again... I don't calls being all
think anyone noticed me DISAPPEAR. yourself)
I can feel so suffocated at school —
WATCHING + THINKING + WONDERING
HOW I fit-in the world...
it can look so easy. "JUST RELA

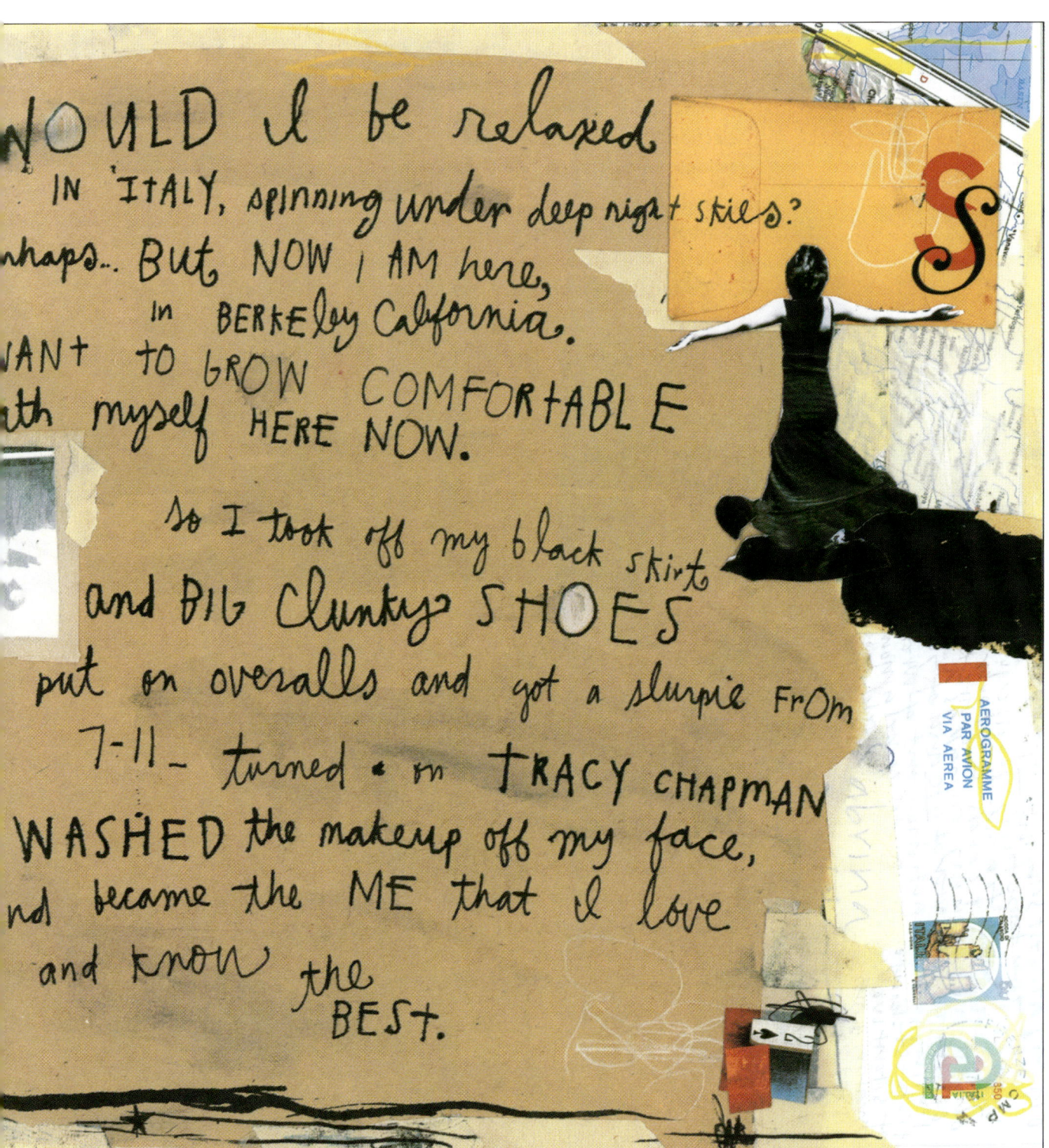

WOULD I be relaxed
IN ITALY, spinning under deep night skies?
perhaps... BUT NOW I AM here,
in BERKELEY California.
I WANT TO GROW COMFORTABLE
with myself HERE NOW.

So I took off my black skirt
and BIG clunky SHOES
put on overalls and got a slurpie From
7-11 — turned on TRACY CHAPMAN
WASHED the makeup off my face,
and became the ME that I love
and know the BEST.

You take it from here ...

Responding

1. **Consider Content and Relevance**   With a partner, discuss how this selection is relevant to you and other young people. Then write your response in a paragraph, including the following points:

    a) State in two or three sentences what this photo essay says about what it means to be a teenager today.

    b) In a single sentence, state the main idea of this photo essay.

    c) Indicate what words and images are used to develop this theme.

2. **Define a Form**   As a class, discuss the term *photo essay*. What is it? As you look again at "Spilling Open," describe the features and methods that are used in this photo essay.

3. **Analyze Visuals**   In a group, discuss your responses to the following images, and give reasons why you think they are included.

    a) girl with oranges

    b) person by the water

    c) child with the stroller

    d) drawing of the girl with her hand behind her back

    e) young woman with the scrapbook

    f) shot of woman's sandals

    g) airmail stamps

    h) blue map

4. **Explore Style**   *Style* is a word used to describe the unique manner in which something like this photo essay is done. Have a class discussion on the effects you liked best about the selection—and any you did not like—and respond to the following:

    a) mix of writing and print

    b) mix of lower- and upper-case letters

    c) display of words and images that caught your attention most of all

    d) collage effect of having words mixed with photos, clippings, and hand-drawn artwork

Extending

5. **Design a Photo Essay** Using "Spilling Open" as a model, create your own photo essay that expresses who you are and your basic values and views of life.

6. **Choose Appropriate Music** Select a song or a piece of instrumental music that you think captures the mood and message of "Spilling Open" or your own photo essay. Present it to a group and explain your choice.

> **PEER ASSESSMENT**
> - What did you think of other students' choice of music?
> - How well did they communicate the reasons for their choice of music?

7. **Use a Reference Book** Visit the library and find a dictionary of quotations. Look up five quotations that embody or express your own views on life. Share them with the class and explain your choices. (Be sure to note the source of the quotations and, if possible, find out who the person quoted is or was.)

Before you read, make a list of the best movies you have ever seen on the subject of being a teenager or coming of age.

As you read, note how the reviewer describes the main characters' objectives, the setting, the events, and situations of the movie.

October Sky
by Gary Johnson
Photographs by Universal Pictures

ON-LINE MOVIE REVIEW

Notes

Homer Hickam, Jr.: famous American rocket scientist

Sputnik: Russian satellite of the 1950s; first human-made object to orbit the Earth

genre: category of movie or literature

inevitable: fated to happen

oppression: feeling of heaviness or weariness; burden

poignancy: deeply touching or affecting

reconciliation: state of becoming friendly after a quarrel

redeeming: positively balancing

screenplay: script for a movie

sentimentality: false warm emotions

October Sky ventures into the well-familiar territory of the coming-of-age genre—a genre filled with potential pitfalls (such as a tendency for sticky sentimentality). However, director Joe Johnston, who directed the pleasant but unremarkable *The Rocketeer*, deftly avoids most of the genre's traps while creating an engaging and life-affirming portrait of life in a West Virginia coal mining town.

Based upon an autobiographical book by Homer Hickam, Jr., *October Sky* charts the growing conflict between a coal miner and his

son. John Hickam (Chris Cooper of *Lone Star*) has been a miner all of his adult life. It's what he knows. He expects his son, Homer (Jack Gyllenhaal), to follow in his footsteps. But one October evening, when the citizens of Coalwood look up into the skies for a glimpse of the Russian satellite Sputnik, Homer gets the fever for rockets. "I'm gonna build a rocket—like Sputnik," he says the next morning. His father can't comprehend what this means for the boy's future, so he forbids Homer to work on rockets on the mining company's property—and the mining company owns everything for miles. John Hickman assumes his son will then drop any interest in rockets. But Homer takes his father quite literally. Even though he and his friends (William Lee Scott, Chad Lindberg, and Chris Owen) must walk six miles to get off company property, they make this journey several times a week. They even set up their own launch site and work shed.

Unlike other movies that have mined this same father-vs.-son territory, such as *A Boy's Life*, the filmmakers resist the temptation to turn the father into a demon. Whereas the stepfather in *A Boy's Life* (played by Robert DeNiro) had virtually no redeeming characteristics, Homer's father is a more complex figure. We understand that his own lack of experiences outside of Coalwood has effectively fitted him with a pair of blinders. He sincerely loves his son, but rockets don't fit into any of his plans.

The screenplay sets up the conflict between the father and son in terms that are maybe a little too pat. The father is clearly the kind of guy who will eventually soften and accept his son's dreams of escaping the mining town. The movie's dramatic arc clearly points toward reconciliation, and thus the story's outcome is never in question (and thus any suspense is minimized). But *October Sky* is still a compelling movie because it gives itself completely to Homer's obsession with rocketry and allows us to experience the same sense of wonder (and disappointment) that he experiences when his rockets soar toward the clouds (or explode famously on the launch pad). Because rocketry also works as a wonderful metaphor for Homer's effort to escape his hometown and the bleak future that his father envisions for him, Homer's attempts acquire added poignancy. We experience disappointment when the rockets don't work, when the boys cower behind wooden barriers, waiting for the inevitable explosions. And we experience elation when the boys succeed and their rockets streak into the sky.

So that we can better understand coal mine work, director Joe Johnston takes us underground with the miners, where coal dust coats the lungs of the miners and frequent cave-ins threaten to end their lives. Johnston films these scenes so we are sure to notice the massive ceilings. The miners live in a world of constant claustrophobic oppression. By giving us access to the mines, we can better appreciate Homer's desire to soar free of restrictions. However, the filmmakers have respect for the work that miners do and the sacrifices that they make. That's what sets *October Sky* apart from other coming-of-age movies: it isn't about escaping one's background as much as it's about realizing one's own potential.

★★★

[rating 3 of 4 stars]

You take it from here ...

Responding

1. **Write a Précis**   Write a *précis* (brief summary) of the events and situations of the movie. Mention the main characters and setting as parts of your précis.

2. **Make Comparisons**   As a class, discuss what the review says about how this movie is different from *A Boy's Life*. Does this movie sound similar to or different from other movies about teenagers?

3. **Comment on Text and Purpose**   With a partner, discuss what the purpose of a movie review is. What types of information do movie reviews typically present? (Refer to this review for examples.)

4. **Discuss in a Group**   With two or three other students, consider the following:

   a) Do movie reviews affect your choice of movies to view? On what other bases do you decide whether or not to see a movie?
   b) Is *October Sky* a movie you would want to see? What sounds interesting, entertaining, or relevant about it? Is there anything mentioned about the movie that might make you decide not to see it? Explain.

   When you have finished discussing the above questions, share your answers with the class.

Extending

5. **View the Movie**   See the movie *October Sky* and make notes on your viewing experience compared with the reviewer's. Write a personal response commenting on the accuracy of the review. What did the review not mention? What aspects make the movie entertaining and engaging for teen audiences? What aspects, if any, did you not like? Explain your opinions.

   Look again at the Web site photos from the movie. Identify the characters and describe what is going on in those scenes of the movie.

6. **Write a Movie Review**   Using this review as a model, write your own movie review of a feature film about teenagers or coming of age.

> **TIPS**
> - Be sure to comment on the plot, conflicts, setting, characters, and actors' performances.
> - Indicate whether the movie presents a realistic or stereotypical view of teenagers overall. State whether the movie is upbeat or mostly serious. Also, comment on whether the ending is *optimistic* (hopeful, positive) or *pessimistic* (negative, unhopeful).

Before you read, discuss with the class the dangers in using the Web to talk to strangers.

As you read, note the key points made about Web safety.

Web Safety: Information for Parents and Kids
by the RCMP/GRC

WEB PAGE ARTICLE

PARENTS

1) Be aware that people may not be who they say they are on the Internet. An adult could pretend to be a child the same age as your child just to get to know your child. Sometimes they can do this over a long period of time to develop trust.

2) Be familiar with your children's use of the computer on-line. Get involved with your children and ask questions about what they're doing and how they're doing it.

3) Establish rules for use of the computer on-line. The rules should limit access time, duration, and type of use depending on the age and maturity of the child (e.g., surfing the net vs. chat rooms, etc.). Be sure that your children understand that they should not be sending personal information to people that they have only met over the Internet.

4) Keep the computer in a high-traffic, highly visible location in the house so that you can routinely walk by and see what your children are doing on the Internet. The child's

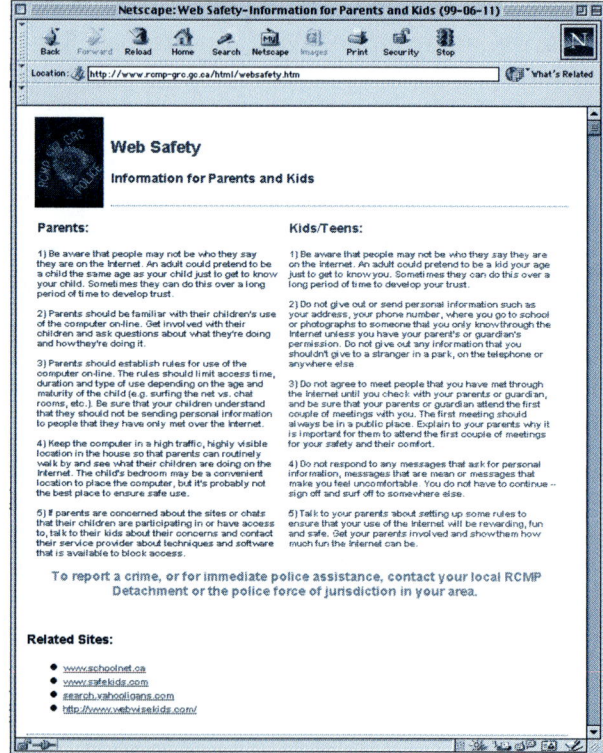

bedroom may be a convenient location to place the computer, but it's probably not the best place to ensure safe use.

5) If you are concerned about the sites or chats that your children are participating in or have access to, you should talk to your kids about your concerns and contact your service provider about techniques and software that is available to block access.

KIDS/TEENS

1) Be aware that people may not be who they say they are on the Internet. An adult could pretend to be a kid your age just to get to know you. Sometimes they can do this over a long period of time to develop your trust.

2) Do not give out or send personal information such as your address, your phone number, where you go to school, or photographs to someone that you only know through the Internet unless you have your parent's or guardian's permission. Do not give out any information that you shouldn't give to a stranger in a park, on the telephone, or anywhere else.

3) Do not agree to meet people that you have met through the Internet until you check with your parents or guardian, and be sure that your parents or guardian attend the first couple of meetings with you. The first meeting should always be in a public place. Explain to your parents why it is important for them to attend the first couple of meetings for your safety and their comfort.

4) Do not respond to any messages that ask for personal information, messages that are mean, or messages that make you feel uncomfortable. You do not have to continue—sign off and surf off to somewhere else.

5) Talk to your parents about setting up some rules to ensure that your use of the Internet will be rewarding, fun, and safe. Get your parents involved, and show them how much fun the Internet can be.

You take it from here ...

Responding

1. **Compare the Messages** In a group, discuss the information presented to parents and young people. Summarize the ideas that are presented to both groups. Then choose one of these ideas and discuss why the RCMP feels that the point needs to be made both to parents and children/teens.

2. **Evaluate the Information** With a partner, discuss whether or not you think the advice and concerns are valid. Is the advice useful? If so, for whom and why?

Extending

3. **Write an Advice Column** Compose two letters to a newspaper columnist who fields questions about netiquette (etiquette for the Internet) and Web safety. Write one from the point of view of a parent and the other from the point of view of a child or teen, raising issues and concerns related to the article. Then answer them in a positive way as such a columnist might, suggesting solutions and appropriate behaviour.

4. **Debate Censorship** As a class, conduct an open debate on whether the Internet should be regulated or policed and whether restrictions should be placed on sites accessed by teens and children.

5. **Research a Topic on the Internet** Type in the search word "RCMP" on an on-line search engine and find out more about public services available from Canada's highly respected police force. Choose one aspect of their work and present your findings in a format of your choice (e.g., a magazine article, a documentary script, a visual presentation).

Before you read, discuss as a class which news broadcasts you regularly watch, if any. Express your opinion on the way in which disasters and tragedies are reported on TV.

As you read, write a personal response to each of the six stanzas.

Notes

George Bowering is one of Canada's most prolific writers of short stories, novels, and poetry. He received the Governor General's Literary Award in 1969 for his poetry, and in 1980 for his novel *Burning Water*.

News

Poem by George Bowering

Every day I add an inch
to the pile of old newspapers
in the closet.

In that three foot pile now
a dozen airliner crashes,
one earthquake in Alaska,
seventeen American soldiers
face down in Asian mud.

I could go on enumerating
like newsprint—we record
violent death & hockey scores
& keep the front room neat.

In front of me, on the table
my empty coffee cup, somewhat melted
butter, carbon copy of an old poem,
familiar things, nothing unexpected.

A plane could crash into the kitchen—
a fissure could jag the floor open—
some olive faced paratrooper bash
his rifle butt thru the window—

It would be news, somewhere.

You take it from here ...

Responding

1. **Make a Chart**   Expand on the notes you took while reading the poem, and organize them in chart form.

Stanza	What the stanza describes	Personal reactions to descriptions
1		
2		
3		

2. **Discuss Irony and Juxtaposition**   As a class, take a second look at the poem and find examples of irony and *juxtaposition* (contrasting images side by side suggesting conflict). What points do the irony and juxtaposition make about human nature, mass media, and the world we live in today?

3. **Write a Personal Response**   In a journal response, compare your views with those presented in the poem. Do you think the poem accurately reflects the average person's response to media reports on disasters? Do you think people should be expected to respond differently?

4. **Refer to Prior Knowledge**   In a small group, discuss how television treats news about accidents, tragedies, and disasters. Is the reporting usually complete and impartial? Does TV present only sensational or dramatic moments that are not necessarily representative of actual events? What effects do negative stories have on TV audiences? Is there usually an attempt to balance the types of news stories presented?

> **PEER ASSESSMENT**
> - Assess one student's contribution to the discussion. What was his or her best point or example?

Extending

5. **View TV News Programs**   As research, do *one* of the following activities:

   a) Watch two or three TV news reports made by different networks on a common news story. Write an assessment in which you draw conclusions about the reporting. Does one broadcast have more information or balance than the other(s)? Which one seems more dramatic or sensational? Why? Support your opinion with examples.

   b) Watch one channel's reporting for three days. On a scale of 1 (poor) to 5 (strong), rate the quality of the news reporting based on the following criteria:
   - completeness
   - fairness
   - honesty
   - interest to viewer
   - types of reporting: studio interview, on-the-scene interviews or reporting, use of video footage with voiceover, etc.

6. **Present a Spoof**   A *spoof* is a "take-off" or humorous version of something serious. With a partner, perform a spoof of a "feel good" TV news broadcast for the class.

7. **Compose a Poem**   Scan a newspaper and, in your notebook, create a word list of images and phrases selected from the paper. Organize these words to create your own poem called either "News" or "Newspaper."

Before you read, survey the class to find out how many people are on-line at home, and how many use e-mail and chatlines.

As you read, jot down in your notebook abbreviations you use or would use on-line.

"It's the new lingo, it's the popular thing."

Chatline lingo catching on
by Michelle Macafee

NEWSPAPER ARTICLE

Chatline glossary

4ever: Forever

AFK: Away from keyboard

LOL: Laughing out loud

OMIK: Open mouth, insert keyboard

PMFJI: Pardon me for jumping in

TMI: Too much information

TEOTWAWKI: The end of the world as we know it

DGT: Don't go there

Source: www.netlingo.com

When 14-year-old Peter Lalonde was a computer newbie, he quickly realized getting connected was about more than learning how to log on to the Internet.

He also had to immerse himself in the language of e-mail and chat groups to truly feel part of the on-line in-crowd.

It's a world where a message that reads "AISI, it's TEOTWAWKI" might be met with the reply "IYSS." (That's "As I see it, it's the end of the world as we know it," followed by, "If you say so.")

To eliminate any potential misunderstanding about the tone of the exchange, the writer could also throw in a smiley face—also known as an emoticon.

Adding to the confusion, however, is the netiquette rule that says spelling out words in capital letters is equivalent to shouting, while it's the norm when using shorthand.

"At first, there was some stuff I just didn't get," said Lalonde, who spends about an hour a day on his family's home computer in Victoria.

"But then I just basically saw other people using it and I thought it was a lot shorter than writing it out. It saves quite a bit of time."

Such endorsements for computer-spawned slang delight Erin Jansen, co-founder of NetLingo Inc., an on-line company with a Web site (www.netlingo.com) that tracks the latest abbreviated catchphrases and emoticons.

The company soon plans to release a dictionary of about 2000 words and phrases.

While efficiency is the main motivator for many adults, Jansen says younger users have their own reasons for picking up the shorthand.

"They're wanting to be hip," Jansen, 33, said from Los Angeles. "It's the new lingo, it's the popular thing. It's not speed, it's more convenience—to be in with this new technology. It's a revolution."

"Short and fast is beautiful," said Herve Fischer, a philosophy professor who holds the Daniel Langlois chair of digital technologies and fine arts at Montreal's Concordia University.

"You find it in music, you find it in dance, in behaviour on skateboards, and so on."

Ian Foster equates it to stream of consciousness.

The 18-year-old university student from St. John's, Nfld., picked up the lingo while using the chatline program ICQ.

He finds the emoticons to be especially handy when sending messages to foreign friends.

"The smiley face is the best place to start," said Foster. "Even if you chat with someone around the block you can't tell their tone, so you can misinterpret and think someone is serious when they're joking."

You take it from here …

Responding

1. **Use Prior Knowledge**   In a group, brainstorm other abbreviations used by people in on-line communications.

2. **Develop Other Abbreviations**   Make up some new abbreviations that you could use in e-mail correspondence. Then try your abbreviations out on others and guess theirs. Examples:

   TTYS—talk to you soon   UWMA—until we meet again

3. **Define a Term**   Discuss with a partner what ICQ means. (If you are not familiar with the term, look it up in an on-line dictionary, or consult another source.) Write out the words for the pronunciation of ICQ. How does this pronunciation relate to its function?

Extending

4. **Use Chatline Lingo**   Visit the <www.netlingo.com> site mentioned in this article. What are some other terms that weren't mentioned in the article? Compile a list of terms that you find useful and use them to write an e-mail to a friend. Share the e-mail with a partner and explain any unfamiliar expressions.

5. **Design a Brochure**   Netiquette refers to rules for proper etiquette when using chatlines or e-mail. Find out more about it and make a brochure listing six do's and don'ts of netiquette.

Before you read, as a class, discuss the impact of modern audio technologies such as Walkmans, in-car stereos, and powerful home sound systems.

As you read, consider the phrase "Make the past the future." Does that seem like a good or bad idea to you?

Ear

She let the sounds wash over her, tumbling her in their waves, nearly drowning her.

Science-Fiction Story by Jane Yolen

Notes

Jane Yolen has written more than 150 books for children. She has been called the Hans Christian Andersen of America and the Aesop of the twentieth century.

Allusions made in this story …

- **"Swing!" "Low!":** humorous reference to a famous Black American spiritual hymn "Swing Low Sweet Chariot"

- **"Earless in Gaza":** a pun on *Eyeless in Gaza*, the title of a 1936 novel by Aldous Huxley about a weak-minded man behaving badly in a meaningless, valueless world

- **Townshend:** Peter Townshend, leader, songwriter, and singer-guitarist for The Who, an English rock band

Jily put on her Ear and sighed. The world went from awful silence to the pounding rhythms she loved. Without the Ear she was locked into her own thoughts and the few colours her eyes could pick out. But with the Ear she felt truly connected to the world.

"Bye, Ma!" she called in her thick voice, and waved.

Earless, her mother never looked up as Jily ran out the door.

The night was ablaze with sound and the winking of lights up and down the street. Everything was sending messages that she was never able to hear during the day in school when she was without her Ear. Jily touched the skin-coloured Ear and smiled.

Sanya and Feeny met her at the corner, under the sallow crooning light. Sanya's new Ear was a particularly odious shade of green, the hottest colour, but not good on her. Jily debated whether to say anything, then decided to keep silent. Sanya was too new a friend for her to chance honesty. Maybe later. Maybe when the music began. Maybe then she might have the nerve to tell Sanya how awful the green Ear was.

"Swing!" Jily called out to them.

"Low!" they returned. With their Ears, they could hear the greetings.

Arms linked, they walked down the noise-filled street.

The first club they came to, The Low Down, was too dark and too quiet for Jily's taste, but Sanya, with her new terrible green Ear, insisted on staying and sampling everything.

Showing off, Jily thought, but kept it to herself.

There was a grey bar in the corner, and the drinks sold were nonalkie of course, but with their Ears, they could pick up all the sub-lime messages, which made everything fine. The Olds were the only ones who still needed alkie to be high. And anyway, being *low* was the thing now.

202 Media/Technology Influences

Jily bent over and put her Ear near the drinks, grubbing on the sounds.

"Soooooo smooooth," whispered one of the drinks, its voice clear. "Soooooo smooooth."

The next glass bubbled. "Makes you smiiiiiile." By pushing the two glasses close together, Jily could hear them at the same time, a cheery duet. She ordered them both.

When she'd finished and looked up, Sanya was dancing slowly by herself on the tiny handkerchief-size dance floor, turning round and round, her arms spread wide. What she was hearing Jily didn't know because there was no band. *Maybe*, she thought, maybe the green Ear picks up something even lower. But she didn't ask. She didn't even want to mention the green Ear yet.

Feeny was standing at the other end of the grey bar staring at a couple of guys. They were Earless. Jily knew Earless never came into the clubs, just as Olds never did.

She walked over to Feeny and fitted her arm over Feeny's shoulder, whispering right into her Ear, something they had done ever since they had become best friends, turning twelve on the exact same day and getting their Ears together. "How *can* they?"

Feeny turned, whispered back, tickling Jily's Ear with her breath, the words coming out thick and thin, thick and thin, not at all clear like the voices from the drinks. "I heard about it at school. It's new. It's low. Coming out and grubbing Earless. It's called Kellering. And they have a sticker too. *Making the past the future*. Don't you think that's kind of cute?"

"I think that's kind of sick," Jily said. "And it's making them Old."

"Well, I think they're cute," Feeny said. "Let's ask them to dance."

"There's no band," Jily whispered furiously. "And even if there were, they couldn't hear without Ears."

Feeny shrugged and peeled away from Jily's imprisoning arm. She went up to one of the guys and pulled on his long straight black pigtail. Then she waggled her fingers. He nodded and they leaned forward, shoulders touching, to stare down at the floor, and slowly they began to dance The Slope. Even without music, he seemed to have rhythm, Jily thought. Even without an Ear.

Jily bit her lip. *Still—he was Earless! How could he!* She knew she'd just die at night on the street without her Ear. Just shrivel up and become an Old all at once. Being Earless meant being Ancient. Like in the far back days when no one had Ears and everyone was deaf from the loud music and the vid ads. Till the Townshend Law was passed, named after the old rocker who'd first admitted losing his hearing. And then everyone in junior high, everyone twelve years old, was issued an Ear to be worn only out of school. At night. On the streets. The Ears that gave new life and made the world real again. And low.

The other guy, redheaded with a star map of freckles across his nose, saw Jily. He waggled his fingers, an invitation to dance. She pointed at her Ear and shook her head, turning her back on him, refusing to sign properly because *she*, after all, was wearing an Ear.

When she glanced back over her shoulder, he was dancing with Sanya, not touching, fingertips apart, doing a dance Jily couldn't identify. Sanya's green Ear seemed almost alive. It was the colour of pond scum, the colour of bile. Jily's cat had sicked up something that colour once. Jily hated it and closed her eyes, trying to hear what Sanya was hearing. She heard feet scuffling and some low giggles from the corner and the coy whispering of the drinks lined up on the grey bar. *So smooooooth. Makes you smiiiiiiiile. Licking gooooooood.*

"I'm going!" she called, not even turning her face to her friends, an insult of the worst order, and she didn't even care. If they heard, they didn't bother to answer.

Outside, her Ear picked up every loud, comforting noise, grinding the messages into her skull. Trucks rattled by calling out *Heavy load, watch out!* The undergrounds grumbled ceaselessly, *Next stop Central*, when they were going north, *Next stop Market* when they were southbound. Chattering signs assailed her from the shops.

She found another club down the block, The Lower Depths, and turned in, somehow thankful to have the noise of the street muffled in the band's crankings. It was a dark club featuring a Cyber Band, with its

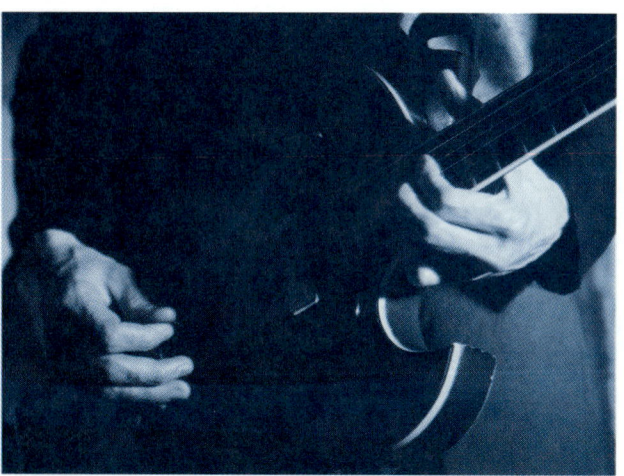

players fully chipped and plugged into their instruments. The only light was on the stage, and the bass player was really low, his hair looking as if it were electric itself, black and kinky, and standing up around his head like the rays of a black sun. The green plug lines were set into his forehead in their puckered sockets. It was the same green as Sanya's Ear, and for a moment Jily closed her eyes.

She moved forward onto the dance floor and to the right side of the stage to get as close to the band as possible. The lights on stage changed and she saw his plug lines weren't green at all, more a mellow yellow, and that made her smile. She let herself ground in his lows. She let the sounds wash over her, tumbling her in their waves, nearly drowning her. It was how she loved it most, leaving her no room to think, only room to feel. She didn't want to think anyway, about Sanya and Feeny back in the quiet club with the grey bar and its drinks whispering messages. Rather she would give herself up to the band's deep groundings, the great tidal pull of noise.

Someone tapped her on the shoulder. When she turned, swimming up from the music, she could see by the reflected light from the stage that it was the redheaded guy, the one without the Ear, only in the light his red hair looked almost orange, almost glowing. He cupped his hand to the side of his head, which meant he wanted to talk.

Jily shook her head, meaning *No talking. Not here. Not now. Not with the music still washing through me.*

But when he insisted, striking himself over the temples, the signal that no one was allowed to ignore, all her fifteen years of training punctured the wall of music and dragged her through. She nodded and followed him to the door. They'd speak outside where there was light to read the signs by, where she wouldn't be tempted by the music.

As she walked up the stairs, she called him names in her head. Horrible names, like derb and tweep. He was an Earless gink, she thought fiercely, making moves on her and forcing her up into the light. Still, by all the rules she grew up with, she knew she had to at least listen to him, if only for the time it took her to tell him to grub off.

Once they were outside, she took out her Ear and stuffed it into her jacket pocket.

"Grub off!" her hands shouted at him. "This is my Ear time. Leave me be, gink." The sign for *gink* was cramped and ugly.

He only grinned at the insult, and the constellations of freckles over his nose seemed to wink. His hands spoke quietly of a better sound, a lower sound, a sound they could share.

"You're an Earless gink," she retorted, her fingers picking at her ear and cramping again to show her utter disdain, though she did wonder how he could seem so happy despite not wearing an Ear. The Olds never really seemed happy Earless. You had to give up your Ear at thirty. Something to do with nerve damage and ruptured DNA or corrupted DNA. Something like that. She'd learned it at school. Or at least it was taught there.

He made the quiet sign again for lower sound and grinned.

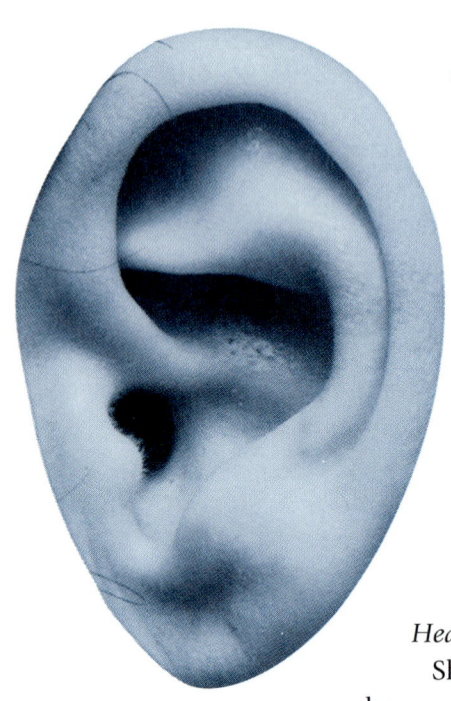

She might have asked him where, but just then she saw Sanya and Feeny out by another streetlight with the black-haired guy. The three of them were holding hands. Hand in hand in hand.

"Sanya!" she called out, and signed the name as well.

Sanya didn't respond, didn't even turn toward her. It was then she realized that the green Ear was gone.

"What have you done to them?" she signed furiously at the redhead. "Why are they Earless? Sanya's Ear was new. And even if it *was* an awful green, she'd never take it off. Not at night. Not the first night she had it on."

He only smiled and waggled back an innocuous, "Ask her yourself."

She flipped him the grub-off sign and pointedly took the Ear from her pocket, making a big fuss about putting it back in.

Just then a big truck barrelled by, rattling its monotonous *Heavy load* warning, and Jily turned away.

She went back down into The Lower Depths alone, leaving the two boys and her two best friends Earless in the street above. But somehow this time the sound in the club dragged her down. She'd lost the rhythm, lost the wonderful feeling of drowning in the sound. The bass player looked much older than she'd first thought. Maybe even closing in on thirty. Almost an Old. Of course he didn't need an Ear. He was a musician. He was chipped and plugged for as long as he lasted. Some even lasted to thirty-five before they died, before the Resurrection Men got their body parts. But they had sound all that time. And they never had to get Old and go Earless forever.

The drinks at the bar chittered away. The music ground on. But Jily couldn't stop thinking about Sanya and Feeny out on the street. Earless. After another twenty minutes, she left the club. But the street was empty. Sanya and Feeny and the two guys were long gone.

The next day at school both Sanya and Feeny were absent, and so Jily had no one to hand-chat with. She hung around the edges of a couple of the girl groups, and even sidled up to watch the flying fingers of one of the couples. But it was as if they were all signing some mysterious language she'd never learned.

Slowly she drifted back into the classroom, sat down at her desk, and booted up a favourite old novel. She was partway to scrolling the first chapter when the bell flashed and everyone returned, forcing her to dump the novel and get online with the teacher. After an hour, the phosphor words made her head ache. At school's end she had a raging migraine.

Walking home alone, she wondered if she should report Sanya and Feeny missing. Maybe she had been the last one to see them alive. *Maybe*, she thought suddenly, *maybe those weren't boys at all but murderers. Slavers. True, there was hardly any crime anymore, but ....*

∽

They were waiting for her at home, talking animatedly with her mother, finger on finger. Sanya wasn't wearing her bilious green Ear, but of course it was too early in the day for that.

"Where *were* you?" Jily signed frantically, not sure if she was angry with them, or relieved.

"They were Earless in Gaza," her mother spelled out.

What she said made no sense, but like many of the things her mother said, it probably referred to some book or other. Olds read *books*, not phosphor. *Figure Olds!* she thought savagely.

"We had our parents' permission," Sanya signed. "We didn't need yours."

Trying to soften Sanya's remarks, Feeny added, "We were at this *other* school. Where they read books. And discuss offline with real teachers. And ..."

Jily made a face. It all suddenly made terrible sense to her. Those two Earless ginks weren't just kids trying out a new style, looking for a new Low. They were part of that movement, that Kellering. And it wasn't just a fun thing! *Oh, no!* she thought. *They really do want to make the past the future.* She grimaced. *In the past, only the Olds had fun and the kids were Earless.*

"So you want to make the past the future!" she said to Sanya and Feeny suddenly, giving the extra little wrist twist that told them just what she *really* thought about the idea. Telling them without words, just motions, something signing did even better than the thick words, what ginks they both were. "Those guys were some kind of missionaries. Out to collect their quota of converts. And you two fell for it. Well, not me. I'm going to wear my Ear till the DNA twists!"

Sanya reached into her pocket and pulled out the bilious green Ear. "I don't want this anymore. And I don't know who else to give it to." Her fingers, snapping out the message, added a little pinkie flip that meant *or anyone else I'd do this to.*

"I don't want your cast-off," Jily shouted in her thick voice. "I don't want your stupid green sick-up colour Ear." And though no one could hear her, they all knew what she meant because she accompanied her words with a slap on Sanya's wrist that was so hard, the green Ear sailed into the air, spun over twice, and fell behind the couch.

Sanya held out her wrist, bright red from the slap, and showed it to Feeny, but she was smiling.

Feeny put her arm around Sanya's shoulder and turned her toward the door. They walked out that way, with Feeny's arm draped like a shawl around Sanya. The door closed silently behind them.

Jily sat the rest of the day in her room, refusing even to come out for dinner, refusing to do her homework, refusing even to turn on the computer. She let the silence, heavy as any noise, envelop her.

As night crept into her room on silent paws, she got up, patting the pocket where her Ear was waiting.

In the living room, she found the green Ear, covering it quickly with her hand so she didn't have to look at the colour.

Once in the street, she jammed the green Ear in her left, her own Ear in her right. The sudden noise of the street was so loud, she almost passed out.

Squaring her shoulders, she stared defiantly at a truck rattling by. "If it's too loud," she shouted in her thick voice, startling two pigeons off a garbage can, "then you're too old!"

Then with the pounding messages of trucks and stop lights and shop windows and subways growling into her from both Ears, drowning out her sorrow, drowning out her fear, drowning out the last of her thoughts, she danced and sang down the street into the ever-young night.

You take it from here …

Responding

1. **Review Jargon**   With a partner, define the following expressions as they are used in the story:

alkie	grey bar	Olds	Slavers
Ancient	hand-chat	phosphor	The Slope
Cyber band	low(s)	plug lines	Townshend Law
derb	Kellering	Resurrection	tweep
gink	Lower Depths	Men	vid ads

2. **Explore Contrasts** Set up a chart, noting differences between Jily and Sanya and Feeny. With a partner, assess which character(s) have the better, happier, freer life.

3. **Focus on a Symbol** As a class, review the references to Ears throughout the story. What does the Ear symbolize? How are the Ear people different from the Earless? What can you infer from this about the author's view of humans and their technology?

4. **Define Science Fiction** Look up *science fiction* in a dictionary and write down a definition in your notebook. In what ways is "Ear" science fiction?

Extending

5. **Write a Story** Consider new and current technology. Brainstorm with a partner the sorts of things that may be possible in the future. How might these affect humans? Then write your own short story based on the influence of technology on humans, especially with respect to human dependence upon technology as in "Ear." Run the story by your partner at the draft stage for feedback.

> **PEER ASSESSMENT**
> - Which of your partner's ideas in the brainstorming session did you think had the most potential for story development?
> - What improvements did you suggest to your partner at the draft stage?

6. **Audiotape a Presentation** A subtheme of this story has to do with humans' desire for increased sensitivity or heightened response to their environments. Record one to two minutes of different sounds from the world around you. Play the tape to the class and see how many sounds classmates can identify correctly.

7. **Compose Diary Entries** In the role of Jily, write three diary entries using jargon from the story.

Reflecting on the Unit

Responding

1. **Write a Summary**   What are five things that you learned from this unit about media and technology? Give examples from your reading and notebook to support each of the five things you mention.

2. **Create a Quiz**   Develop a quiz reviewing terms used in this unit. Include an answer key and then exchange with another student.

3. **Focus on a Selection**   Write a journal entry describing the selection that had the greatest impact on you. What new views and understandings did you gain from the selection?

Extending

4. **Prepare a Speech**   As a concerned citizen, present your opinions on how and why media and technology should be taught in schools.

5. **Present to the Class**   With a partner, present two tableaus based on moments from the unit selections. Invite the class to guess which moments and selections you are depicting. As an alternative, you can work with a partner to create a multimedia or visual statement about media and technology influences. It could take the form of a Web page, a collage, a cover for a book on the subject, a radio or TV documentary, etc. Present your work to the class.

> **SELF ASSESSMENT**
>
> Review what you have learned from this unit regarding
> - the ways in which the Internet can be used—and abused—as a tool for communication
> - the techniques used in advertising
> - the influence of television and recent computer technologies in terms of learning
> - the long-range effects of media and technology for current and future generations

UNIT 5

"Man's inhumanity to man
Makes countless thousands
mourn!"
–Robert Burns

"Toleration is the greatest gift of the mind; it requires the same effort of the brain that it takes to balance oneself on a bicycle."
–Helen Keller

"If we cannot end now our differences, at least we can help make the world safe for diversity."
–John F. Kennedy

Understanding and Acceptance

This unit is a study of what makes us unique and special, as well as of our universal human nature.

Scottish poet Robert Burns reminds us of the damage hatred and intolerance of difference has caused throughout history.

Helen Keller, who overcame blindness and deafness to achieve international respect for her writing and work on behalf of others, suggests that we must make an ongoing effort to be tolerant of each other.

Finally, the late U.S. president John F. Kennedy puts the whole unit in perspective, advocating diversity in a world too often dominated by conflict and disagreement.

As you read this unit, think about the following:

1) How do we define ourselves as individuals? In what ways are all people fundamentally the same?

2) What basic views are needed to create attitudes of understanding, acceptance, and appreciation of other people?

3) As Canadians, what are some things we can take pride in?

Before you read, in your journal, define yourself by your cultural background. What is unique about who you are, culturally speaking?

As you read, look up the words "conceiving" and "violation" in a dictionary.

Notes

Nigel Darbasie was born in Trinidad and moved to Canada in 1969, settling in Edmonton. His work has been widely published and broadcast in Canada.

Conceiving the Stranger

Poem by Nigel Darbasie

First define the tribal self
in skin colour, language
religion, culture.
Add to that
boundaries
of nation, city
village or street.
And there you are:
out of place
a foreigner
the strange other
a moving violation
of tribal differences.

You take it from here ...

Responding

1. **Discuss Meaning of Title and Poem** With a partner, and using the words you looked up while reading, explain what it means to "conceive the stranger." Who is "the stranger"? What must happen for someone to become "a foreigner" or "the strange other"?

2. **Make a List** Describe yourself in the poem's terms:

   skin colour   nation
   language   city or village
   religion   street or neighbourhood
   culture

   In your opinion, what is missing from this inventory of defining characteristics? Compare your list with another student's, then discuss things and interests you both have in common.

3. **Focus on a Section** Discuss with two other students what the poem is saying about how being unique or an outsider might lead to problems (i.e., a "moving violation of tribal differences"). How might one be in "violation"? In what sense might "tribal differences" cause a "violation"?

4. **Understand the Whole** As a class, discuss the following questions:
   - What are the poem's main ideas?
   - Does the poet suggest why misunderstandings, prejudice, and discrimination occur?
   - Being an outsider or someone who is "different" is something that can happen to anyone. With which word does the poet make this point?
   - Why is the poem called "*Conceiving* the Stranger"?

Extending

5. **Write from the Stranger's Experience** Imagine you have just moved to a different country and have completed your first day at school. Write a diary entry describing the experience. Write a second diary entry dated four months later, reviewing your first impressions and bringing them up to date.

6. **Make a Poster** The Immigration and Refugee Board is launching a campaign to make new Canadians feel welcome in this country. Create a poster for this purpose.

Before you read, look up the word "exclusion" in a dictionary. What does it mean to exclude somebody?

As you read, jot down notes about a time when you felt like the speaker of the poem.

Don't Give Me Looks

Poem by Maxine Tynes

Don't give me looks that put me in my place
that open my mail
that smell me coming and going, and see me everywhere.
Don't give me looks made of plastic smiles
reserved for co-workers who rush past
on a wave of caffeine and nicotine,
letting 'How are you!' drift and hang in the air.
You say, 'Fine!' neither hearing nor meaning it.
Don't give me those looks.
Don't give me looks full of hell and damn
and who cares? who cares?
that flap on the line like clothes in the wind
that ring and ring like a telephone in an empty room
that flicker white and snowy, like the telly at midnight
that are snowblind in August
that are full of all the rest of the world
and not me.

Notes

African-Canadian poet Maxine Tynes grew up in Dartmouth, Nova Scotia. Her first book, *Borrowed Beauty*, was published in 1987 and was followed by *Woman Talking Woman* (1990), *Save the World for Me* (1991), and *The Door of My Heart* (1993). Her work is characterized by an oral ebb and flow, rhythms she captures from the world around her. In another life, she also teaches at Auburn Drive High School in Dartmouth.

You take it from here ...

Responding

1. **Clarify First Impressions**   In a small group, reread the different looks described in the poem. What feelings are behind the looks the speaker gets? What does it mean to "give someone looks"? Share your group's answers with the rest of the class.

2. **Identify Purpose**   In a paragraph, present your views on why the poet wrote this poem. What did she want to protest?

3. **Focus on Images and Imagery**   *Imagery* is a pattern of *images* (words that create sense impressions). With a partner, discuss the effects on the reader of the following images:

   - [looks] "that open my mail"
   - "looks made of plastic smiles"
   - "co-workers who rush past on a wave of caffeine and nicotine"
   - "looks full of hell and damn"
   - [looks of] "who cares?"
   - [looks] "that flap on the line like clothes in the wind"
   - [looks] "that ring and ring like a telephone in an empty room"
   - [looks] "that flicker white and snowy, like the telly at midnight"
   - [looks] "that are snowblind in August."

   Which of these images are *similes* (indirect comparisons using "like" or "as")?

> **TIPS**
> - Review the definition of the word "exclusion."
> - Reread the last two lines to answer the question.

Extending

4. **Create a Collage**   Think about the looks the poet describes. Put together a collage of faces with a variety of expressions that might be of the sort described by the poem.

5. **Recall a Memory**   In a written response, tell about a time when you felt like an outsider in the company of others. Try to capture what it felt like to be the odd person out.

6. **Compose a Poem**   Imitating the *free verse* (rhythmical poems having no regular rhyme or structure) style of Maxine Tynes or Nigel Darbasie ("Conceiving the Stranger"), create your own poem about feelings of being "different."

Before you read, look up the words "prejudice" and "discrimination" in a dictionary. Then, as a class, go over what they mean.

As you read, record any circumstance that comes to mind in which you have had any first- or second-hand experience in the way of being discriminated against.

What might seem at first to be discrimination may be just a misunderstanding.

Filing a Complaint with the Canadian Human Rights Commission

by the Canadian Human Rights Commission

INSTRUCTIONS

The Canadian Human Rights Act gives each of us an equal opportunity to work and live without discrimination.

The Act applies to federal government departments, Crown corporations, and agencies, as well as to businesses under federal jurisdiction. These include such major employers as banks, airlines, railways, the CBC, and Canada Post.

The Canadian Human Rights Commission accepts complaints of discrimination in employment and in the provision of goods and services if the discrimination is because of your

- race
- national or ethnic origin
- colour
- religion
- age
- sex (including discrimination related to pregnancy and childbirth)
- marital status
- family status
- mental or physical disability (including previous or present drug or alcohol dependence)
- pardoned conviction
- sexual orientation

The Act also requires that women and men receive equal pay for work of equal value.

RECOGNIZING DISCRIMINATION

Sometimes discrimination is easy to spot. If a person comes right out and says you weren't hired for a job because of the colour of your skin or where you were born, you know that is discrimination.

But discrimination is not always so direct. An employer might not mention your age, sex, race, or disability, but could say you didn't get a job because you wouldn't "fit in." Or someone might stare at you or touch you in a way that makes you uncomfortable.

216 Understanding and Acceptance

In other cases, a longstanding practice or policy could unintentionally discriminate against members of a particular group. For example, at one time police forces had height requirements that excluded most women and people of certain races.

If you believe you are being discriminated against, you can do something about it. When the discrimination is based on any ground covered by the Canadian Human Rights Act, the Canadian Human Rights Commission is there to help.

SHOULD YOU FILE A COMPLAINT?

In many cases, unpleasant situations can be resolved easily and quickly right on the spot. If you are treated in a way that you feel is unfair, speak to the people involved. What might seem at first to be discrimination may be just a misunderstanding.

Many employers have policies against discrimination and harassment; these policies often identify a specific person you can contact if you have a problem. Or there might be a union or company grievance procedure you can follow. Similarly, if you are refused a service, you could complain to the manager.

FILING A COMPLAINT

If these steps don't get results, you can contact the Canadian Human Rights Commission. Sometimes we can help resolve the situation simply by talking to the people involved. If that doesn't work, you can file a complaint and initiate an investigation. You should file your complaint within one year of when the discrimination took place.

A human rights investigation is a serious matter in which you have an important role. There are several things you can do that will help you to present your case as clearly and as forcefully as possible.

Be sure to

- **Be specific.**

When you file a complaint, be as specific as possible about what happened. The exact words, gestures, or other details help. You must have good reason to believe you were discriminated against because of your sex, disability, race, religion, or any of the other grounds covered by the Canadian Human Rights Act.

- **Keep a diary.**

Write down any incident you believe might be related to your complaint. Because memories can be vague, you should write down details about the incident, such as the date, time, and place, while they're still fresh. A diary can be useful in another way, too. An unpleasant incident may not look like discrimination in and of itself, but may fit into a pattern of discriminatory behaviour that shows up over time. A diary will help the investigator identify any such pattern. It is also important to write down what you have done to try to resolve the situation.

- **List all possible witnesses.**

A witness can be someone you believe saw or heard the incident take place. A witness also can be someone who heard other people talking about the incident or someone who experienced the same kind of discrimination or harassment. Writing down the names of possible witnesses will help the human rights investigator gather evidence.

- **Save all physical evidence.**

Keeping physical evidence of discrimination, such as memos, notes, reports, or offensive cartoons, is just as important as writing down the incidents. Such material is valuable evidence and could help prove your complaint. Be sure to save it.

WHAT HAPPENS TO YOUR COMPLAINT?

When you file a complaint with the Canadian Human Rights Commission, an investigation will be conducted. A human rights investigator will ask you for evidence to support your complaint. The investigator may also gather more evidence from your colleagues or others who could shed light on the case.

Even while the investigation is going on, we will try to settle your complaint. Sometimes, the employer, service provider, or individual you are complaining about will offer to make amends. If that happens and you are satisfied, your complaint will be settled, the investigation will end, and the matter will be considered resolved.

If your complaint is not settled, the investigator will put the evidence in a report that will go to members of the Commission for a decision. At this point, the Commissioners could:

- appoint a conciliator to resolve the complaint;
- refer the complaint to the Canadian Human Rights Tribunal; or
- dismiss the complaint if there is not enough evidence of discrimination.

PROTECTION AGAINST RETALIATION

You should not be afraid of someone getting back at you if you file a complaint or act as a witness in an investigation. The Commission can investigate and deal with complaints of retaliation against persons who file a complaint. It may also be a criminal offence for anyone to threaten, intimidate, or discriminate against a complainant or witness.

You take it from here ...

Responding

1. **Discuss in a Group**   Review the article's main points and understand what it is saying. Explain each of the 11 ways that the Human Rights Commission states a person can be discriminated against.

    - Which ones surprised you?
    - What are some instances of discrimination mentioned in the article?
    - What happens after a person has filed a complaint?
    - Is a person making a complaint protected by the commission?

2. **Refer to Personal Experience**   In a class discussion, tell *anecdotes* (short interesting story-incidents) about cases of harassment or discrimination that you have observed or heard of. For each one, tell how the problem was addressed or resolved.

3. **Discuss Text, Audience, and Purpose**   Write a paragraph explaining the following:
   - Where does this article originate? Where else could this information be found?
   - Who is the potential audience of this piece? Are there people who would especially benefit from it?
   - What is the purpose of the article? In your opinion, is it necessary?

Extending

4. **Discuss on a Talk Show**   In groups of three or four, conduct a radio call-in show in which callers describe their own experiences of discrimination. Take turns hosting the show and offering an opinion or advice for each caller. Choose from the following scenarios or create some of your own.
   - a new immigrant experiences discrimination when applying for a constable job
   - a 66-year-old female professor wishes to continue teaching but is told by a department head that she's past the mandatory retirement age
   - a homosexual person goes for a job interview as a child care worker
   - a man recently released from jail applies for a custodial job after-hours at a bank
   - a woman with a physical disability applies for a job as a girls' volleyball team coach
   - a man complains about a female boss who is sexually harassing him

5. **Create a Web Page**   Design a Web page to provide advice and information to the public about discrimination and harassment on the job.

> **TIPS**
> - You can either create your Web page on computer or design it on paper.
> - Include links to relevant Web sites.
> - Suggest positive solutions for dealing with various kinds of problems.

Before you read, as a class, discuss how you felt during a family event attended by people you hadn't seen for a long time.

As you read, sketch a moment from the poem.

Notes

Marisa Anlin Alps is of Chinese and Dutch descent. She was born in 1970 and raised on Quadra Island, BC. She currently lives on BC's Sunshine Coast.

dim sum: Chinese meal offering a variety of delicacies

emulate: try to equal or imitate

tripe: food made from the first two stomachs of an ox

After the Wedding

Poem by Marisa Anlin Alps

The first time I realized I was Chinese
I was seventeen, travelled east
to Toronto to celebrate my cousin's
marriage, the sole relation
from my branch of the family tree.
I'd never seen so many of my relatives
in one place, their unknown
faces swirling before me
and everyone there was Chinese.

Suddenly it hit me and I knew
I was too (or at least half)
a surprise since I've been everything else
for so long.

My mother says she feels more Canadian
than anything else, but perhaps we moved
to the island pockets of the west
coast to emulate her island childhood, a hint
of possibility in the Caribbean accents
slipping so easily around me, a little
like those split leaf plants
my grandmother smuggled into Trinidad,
the ones that grew, flourished
took over a whole corner of her lovely
garden and yet, I felt white
for the first time in my life, different
still from everyone around me, especially
during dim sum in Toronto's Chinatown
an intense experience with tripe and
chicken feet and the wonder
of what was not said.

220   Understanding and Acceptance

After the wedding, long and noisy tables
filled the banquet hall like sunflowers
pushing toward the centre of the dance
floor, couples whirling around the chairs.
My cousin asked me to dance but I was shy,
eyes downcast. *How did he see me?*
The flowers scented the air like wine,
voices like music, while others
flew I sat there on the edge, wonder pouring
from me, distant from the centre
I did not feel much, but I thought
I am Chinese
horizons shrinking
and changing before my eyes
a second wedding taking place
within me, two
inheritances exchanging vows.

You take it from here ...

Responding

1. **Paraphrase the Events**   Write a paragraph describing the speaker's experience and moods before, during, and after the wedding.

2. **Analyze Key Lines**   As a class, explain what the following lines and phrases mean:

   - "I knew I was too (…) a surprise since I've been everything else for so long."
   - "the wonder of what was not said."
   - "I sat there on the edge, wonder pouring from me, distant from the centre"
   - "horizons shrinking and changing before my eyes"
   - "a second wedding taking place within me, two inheritances exchanging vows."

3. **Explain Poetic Devices** This poem is special and powerful because of its use of poetic devices. With a partner, locate examples of the following:

Poetic device	Definition	Quoted example
image word(s)	words that create a sense impression	
alliteration	use of repeated consonant sounds, especially at beginnings of words	
assonance	repetition of vowel sounds	
simile	indirect comparison using "like" or "as"	
metaphor	direct comparison between two unlike things	
symbol	something that stands for something else	

Extending

4. **Compose Dialogue** Imagine and write a conversation between mother and daughter after the wedding.

5. **Experience Chinese Culture** One way to explore Chinese culture is to try the cuisine. Go to a restaurant that serves dim sum, and share your impressions about the experience in class. As an alternative, find some information about authentic Chinese cuisine, including some dim sum recipes. Try some out and share your impressions (or even samples) with the class.

6. **Write a Thank-You Letter** Imagine and write the letter the speaker of the poem might have sent to her "new family" after the wedding party.

Before you read, write about what it would be like to be a young person going to a far-away country. Share your response with the class.

As you read, ask yourself questions: Who is Michael? Where has the speaker moved to? How is she different from the people of this culture?

It's a terrible thing: to stand in the midst of almost three thousand singing, praying people when you have nothing to sing or pray yourself.

Touch the Dragon
by Karen Connelly

DIARY ENTRY

Notes

Touch the Dragon is a book of diary entries by a young Alberta poet who travelled to Thailand for a one-year exchange. For this book, Karen Connelly won the 1993 Governor General's Award for Non-Fiction—at 24, she was the youngest writer ever to receive this honour.

September 9

I've had the same dream for three nights now. It's a winter dream, beginning with a man walking down a road into the dark. I see him from a height, behind a window; I watch the snow blur cold and silver through the columned light of streetlamps, and the glass of my window is too cold to touch. Or maybe it's too hot—in the dream I know that if I touch it, I'll burn myself. I only stand and watch the man walk away, and he will not turn around to look at me. The soft thud of his feet in the snow is the dream's only sound. It gets louder as the distance between us grows. Somehow I know that if I push on the window long and hard enough, it will part smoothly under my hands, melt, and I'll be able to get out. But I don't even touch it because of the heat (or coldness). If I pressed my lips to the window for just a moment, the man would come back, but out of fear I don't do it. Instead, I shout his name and wake up.

Michael.

Even when I don't dream I wake at night to turn off the overhead fan. During the days it's sticky and hot; during the nights it's sticky and cool. The breeze from the fan gets under the sheet and shivers me awake. Outside, Denchai sleeps, though a dogfight in the field has torn away a corner of silence. The quiet returns, lies smooth beneath a whirr of insects and frogs. I want to stay awake for this wordlessness. If I cannot have English, let me have this instead. I can understand the silence of sleep, whole in itself, complete.

The days themselves are not whole. They are made of half-eaten words, words left behind, nibbled words too long and strange to get in my mouth or ears. Everything is the wrong size here. My bones are too big, my mind is too small. I never thought words could fail me, but here they're not even words. They're useless noises, wholly unreliable. Meh, Pree-Moi, Koon Yiy, the children all blink innocently at me,

smile, shake their heads. It would not matter how very slowly I said, "Please leave me alone in my room for just five minutes." They would not understand. They've lived within fifteen feet of each other for most of their lives. They're afraid to leave me alone.

I write out of tiredness, loneliness, longing. The danger is not that I'll forget anything I left in Canada, but that I'll remember it too sharply. Loneliness is so ironic when I'm surrounded constantly with new people and their lives. The bicycle-rickshaw drivers are anxious to teach me Thai, the children in Nareerat lean over the green terraces and call my Thai names, Kanikaa, Ploy. They're still very shy but sometimes when I'm sitting in the little pavilion under the tamarind tree, they appear quietly, cautious as fawns. If I sing something for them, they will sing the morning assembly songs for me, which I want very much to learn.

It's a terrible thing: to stand in the midst of almost three thousand singing, praying people when you have nothing to sing or pray yourself. I sway in the waves of so much lucent music, but they wash around me instead of through me because I haven't the key, the language, to let them in. The children are teaching me, and they bring roses to the English room, paper bags of sugared fruit and sweet rice. They are very shy, with black-lashed eyes and a velvet cover over their bones. I'm a rare specimen here: the blonde hairs on my arms astound them because my eyebrows are so black. My long Caucasian nose is an absolute mystery. After touching my skin they touch their own, trying to name the differences between us. We understand each other primarily through laughter.

But laughter is too simple a language for me. If I am happy, I am also miserable, prone to emotion, impatience, self-pity. The place and pace of my life have changed so quickly; it's difficult to recognize all this newness as my own life. I've been made into something completely different in less than a month, just because of a long day and night in a plane. In the English room, one of the children's storybooks has figures which unfold upward when the book is opened. (The kids are fascinated by it—Ajahn Champa brought it from England.) I cannot get that image out of my mind, the flat book flipping open, its magical characters rising straight off the page, the scurry of Thai fingers wanting to touch. Thailand itself has opened

224 Understanding and Acceptance

like that for me, gone from picture books to tangible form, and I am still surprised. The only trick that isn't available is the one that would unfold Canada into three dimensions.

Sometimes I forget this was my choice; I wanted to come here despite what I would leave behind. Apparently (it's on file somewhere) I came here to live and learn in a new culture, to adapt myself to a country very distinct from my own. At the moment, this seems just short of impossible. Even things I know (sunlight on water, fog caught in trees, a long expanse of green) leave me breathless, as though I've never seen colour before. The stars and planets confuse me when I sneak out to the field at night. I turn around and around slowly, testing angles, trying to chalk together a constellation I can recognize. I want an old image. Instead, what I never expected is suddenly there; I see it or am seen by it, caught. Yesterday, I spotted a praying mantis clinging to one of the outer folds of my green curtain, gazing in my direction with the focused concentration of a tiny silk-green cat.

At night, one sheet sleeps over me and mosquitoes light on my skin. Nothing else, no one, touches me here. After my strange empty dream of snow and hot glass, I don't return easily to sleep. In a place where there is nothing for you, no prayers or songs or even stars, you turn blindly to your body, hug your shoulders in the dark, and touch your own pale arms, amazed. This is how I know I'm alone. My own skin surprises me.

You take it from here ...

Responding

1. **Focus on Character**   In a small group, analyze the speaker.
    a) Who is she? Why has she gone to Thailand?
    b) Has she left her Western culture and memories behind? Comment.
    c) Does she feel part of her new adopted culture? Is she comfortable?
    d) How do Thai people react to her?
    e) Has she achieved her goal? What has she learned so far?

2. **Explain a Section**   With another student, analyze the meaning of the dream that starts the entry. Compare your opinions with those of another pair of students.

Extending

3. **Make a Diary Entry**   Recall a place that you have travelled to that was distinctly different from your home area. Using vivid descriptive images, recreate the experience of what it was like to be in this new place.

4. **Sketch a Scene**   Find one section of the selection you think might lead to a good line drawing. Create your own visual impression of that particular scene.

Before you read, discuss the following in class: Are Aboriginal peoples in danger of losing their culture in the twenty-first century?

As you read, write down your reactions to the way Grandma Weaver was treated by the visitors.

Grandma Weaver's Last Arrow

Wouldn't this old woman ever start speaking English?

Short Story by Rosemary M. Huggins

Notes

Rosemary M. Huggins is an American Native of the Tlingit tribe.

Grandma Weaver was 110 years old when the social scientists came to interview her. They came from the universities all over the United States—Yale, Harvard, Princeton, UCLA, and UW. There were thirty of them and they had come to southeast Alaska to help us find our lost Indian culture. Since we hadn't known it was lost we didn't know how to answer their questions, but we did tell them about the oldest member of the tribe. When they heard of Grandma Weaver they rushed to interview her with renewed hope and enthusiasm shining from their eyes, hopeful of capturing their elusive quarry.

All thirty of them trooped into her bedroom. Some of them immediately took out 35-mm cameras and started snapping away—all the flashbulbs flashing looked like a mini-thunderstorm occurring only in Grandma Weaver's room. The other social scientists gathered around her bed, pens and pads poised. They looked like giant birds of prey, dressed in three-piece suits, hovering over her as if to pluck morsels of knowledge from her mind. Grandma Weaver looked even more like an undernourished six-year-old as she sat huddled in the middle of her bed, frightened and alone. Were these strange noises caused by the *Kushtica*—evil spirits—come to take her away?

They took pictures of everything in her room—the dance masks sharply defined against the stark white walls, the reeds (soaking in the sink) needed for basket weaving, even her panties folded neatly in a drawer. Grandma Weaver ignored the cameras and notebooks and started weaving a new basket as she sat there, muttering away to herself in Tsimsian, the only language she spoke.

As each day passed the social scientists became more worried, as if their last hope was disappearing. Wouldn't this old woman ever start speaking English?

226 Understanding and Acceptance

Finally the social scientists held a whispered conference, packed up their 35-mm cameras, stuffed their pens and pads into bulging black briefcases, and left.

The next day they returned, but this time armed with moving-picture cameras and tape recorders, the reels of which they could send to the experts at the University of Alaska's Indian Museum for translation. Moving swiftly, they set all their modern equipment around her bed. Grandma Weaver, hearing all these strange new noises, sat up, her blind eyes darting from side to side as if she was trying to see what was going on around her. Muttering to herself in Tsimsian, she picked up her unfinished reed basket as if seeking comfort from the familiar act of weaving. Cameras and tape recorders clicked on and later it was said that the sound of the machines almost drowned out Grandma Weaver's voice.

When the social scientists got their films developed and the tapes translated, they invited some of the Indian community to share their triumph. Silently everyone waited with hushed expectancy; finally the movie started and there was Grandma Weaver on the screen, with a voice-over reading the translation of her Tsimsian. Except for the occasional muffled laughter of Indians, the group remained silent as the social scientists digested the translation. Interspersed with comments about walking across rivers on the backs of fish, about owning slaves and what tribes they were from, about which of her three or four husbands she had liked best, there were comments about these foreigners who came disrupting her peace. Would they like it if her grandsons went to their homes and disturbed their grandmothers? Why were these rude foreigners here, talking in a heathen tongue that no decent person would speak? Didn't these strange men know she was too old for all that? Maybe they were sent from the *Kushtica*—the evil spirits—to take her away.

After the show was over some of the social scientists packed up their equipment quietly, their faces red as if they knew they had failed and were embarrassed at their part in the fiasco. The others were jubilant, talking loudly about the great dissertations they could write about their important discoveries. They said the films could be put on our VCRs and the tapes on computers for future social scientists. As they filed out, one ran back to retrieve Grandma Weaver's unfinished reed basket—their proof that they had successfully captured the essence of an almost lost culture.

Grandma Weaver started murmuring to herself about these *cheechakos*—strangers—who didn't know that an unfinished basket had no value. Calmly she reached out for her reeds and began weaving a new basket.

Grandma Weaver's Last Arrow **227**

You take it from here ...

Responding

1. **Focus on Conflict** With a classmate, discuss who or what is in conflict in the story. Which side came out victorious? Why?

2. **Write about Humour** In this story, social scientists and the media are ridiculed. In your notebook, jot down sentences that make fun of the modern invasion into Grandma Weaver's life.

3. **Examine Title and Symbol** With another student, review the significance of the title. Then write a paragraph explaining what Grandma Weaver's "last arrow" was.

4. **Have a Class Discussion** Look up the word "expropriation." Periodically, we hear of the *expropriation* of one culture by another. What does that mean? How is that true in this story? Do the social scientists understand or appreciate the old woman's culture? Have they captured its message and meaning? What are your own feelings about the process of larger or more dominant cultures trying to "capture" or preserve minority cultures?

Extending

5. **Write a Report** Imagine and write the report that one of the social scientists submitted after meeting Grandma Weaver.

6. **Investigate Another Culture** Choose a different culture from your own to research. Report your findings to the class.

> **TIPS**
> - Use a map to show where the culture originates.
> - Tell about some of the myths or stories of the culture.
> - Identify basic values and lifestyles of the culture.
> - Use artifacts, photographs, or video clips to add visual interest.

Understanding and Acceptance

> **Before you read,** as a class, discuss what unites all races and cultures. How are all people the same?
>
> **As you read,** think about how life would be different if all races could realize the vision offered by this poem.

To Human Race

Poem by Syeda Nuzhat Siddiqui
(Translated by Saleem Siddiqui)

Even though our colours and our names
are not the same
even though our lands
lay asunder
and the space above us
is victim
of plunder
we still are of the one
human clan

Our beginning, the same
our end is the same
our short lives
full of strives
our hopes, our illusions
and our dreams
are the same

The pangs of birth
the giggly laughter of children's mirth
our pleasures, our pains
our dreams are the same
we all belong to the same
domain

All children
of mother Earth
all drenched
in heavenly light
of sound and sight
we share the same seasons
sun, moon, storms

Notes

Syeda Nuzhat Siddiqui is a poet, writer, and educator. Born in Pakistan, she currently lives in Toronto. She is a co-founder of World University Peace in Toronto and, in 1987, won the Aalami Urdu Award in Delhi, India.

and their flight
we have the same
home and hearth

We are the same
but who did play
this cruel game
of encircling us
with a wall of pain
we are still alive
but who did try
to choke our breath
and to entangle us
in the cobweb of death

Our hearts were clean
and who is the one
who put dust
of mistrust
our minds were
like a star
giving light
near and far
who did play
this cruel game
of turning into smoke
this light and flame

The answer to these questions
is the same
as history of torture
and violence
is the same

Dreams of peace, truth and love
of breaking shackles
spreading our wings
soaring high
in the sky
our dreams are the same

As we are one
we stand
hand in hand
we will then break
the wall of pain
and start again
from the point
where we were
one
belonging to the one human clan

You take it from here ...

Responding

1. **Discuss Relevance**   In a group, tell about what you thought of the poem. What is the poem's message? Is it a good or necessary one for our world today? What would be necessary to achieve its vision?

2. **Paraphrase the Stanzas**   With another student, put the meaning of each stanza into your own words. Then share your views on the poem in a class discussion.

3. **Consider Form**   Does the poem rhyme or is it purely free verse? (Try reading it aloud.) How do the shape and the sound of the poem affect how a reader responds to the message?

Extending

4. **Role-Play a Talk Show**   With two or three other students, act out a TV talk show that features guests from various cultures exchanging ideas about promoting international cooperation on a particular issue (for example, working for peace among warring nations, working together on an environmental issue, etc.). Rehearse and present the show to the class.

5. **Create a Magazine Ad**   Make an ad promoting the idea of world peace and global harmony.

Before you read, as a class, discuss the two lines above the title. What makes Canada a great country to live in?

As you read, make notes on why the author thinks Canada is a great country.

For six years in a row now the United Nations has designated Canada the No. 1 country in which to live.

Canada, My Canada
by Tomson Highway

PERSONAL ESSAY

Notes

Tomson Highway is Cree, born in northwest Manitoba in 1951. He is a musician and an award-winning playwright. His best-known plays include *The Rez Sisters* and *Dry Lips Oughta Move to Kapuskasing*, which deal with life on the reservation.

Three summers back, a friend and I were being hurtled by bus through the heart of Australia, the desert flashing pink and red before our disbelieving eyes. It seemed never to end, this desert, so flat, so dry. The landscape was very unlike ours—scrub growth with some exotic cacti, no lakes, no rivers, just sand and rock forever. Beautiful, haunting even—*what the surface of the moon must look like*, I thought as I sat in the dusk in that almost empty bus.

I turned to look out the front of the bus and was suddenly taken completely by surprise. Screaming out at me in great black lettering were the words CANADA NO. 1 COUNTRY IN THE WORLD. My eyes lit up, my heart gave a heave, and I felt a pang of homesickness so acute I actually almost hurt. It was all I could do to keep myself from leaping out of my seat and grabbing the newspaper from its owner.

As I learned within minutes (I did indeed beg to borrow the paper), this pronouncement was based on information collected by the United Nations from studies comparing standards of living for 174 nations of the world. Some people may have doubted the finding, but I didn't, not for an instant.

Where else in the world can you travel by bus, automobile, or train (and the odd ferry) for ten, 12, or 14 days straight and see a landscape that changes so spectacularly: the Newfoundland coast with its white foam and roar; the red sand beaches of Prince Edward Island; the graceful curves and slopes of Cape Breton's Cabot Trail; the rolling dairy land of south-shore Quebec; the maple-bordered lakes of Ontario; the haunting north shore of Lake Superior; the wheat fields of Manitoba and Saskatchewan; the ranch land of Alberta; the mountain ranges and lush rain forests of the West Coast. The list could go on for pages and still cover only the southern section of the country, a sliver of land compared with the North, the immensity of which is almost unimaginable.

For six years in a row now the United Nations has designated Canada the No. 1 country in which to live.

We are so fortunate. We are water wealthy and forest rich. Minerals, fertile land, wild animals, plant life, the rhythm of four distinct, undeniable seasons—we have it all.

Of course, Canada has its problems. We'd like to lower the crime rate, but ours is a relatively safe country. We struggle with our healthcare system, trying to find a balance between universality and affordability, but no person in this country is denied medical care for lack of money. Yes, we have our concerns, but in the global scheme of things we are well off.

Think of our history. For the greater part, the pain and violence, tragedy, horror, and evil that have scarred forever the history of too many countries are largely absent from our past. There's no denying we've had our trials, but they pale by comparison with events that have shaped many other nations.

Our cities are gems. Take Toronto, where I have chosen to live. My adopted city never fails to thrill me with its racial, linguistic, and cultural diversity. On any ordinary day on the city's streets and subway, in stores and restaurants, I can hear the muted ebb and flow of 20 different tongues. I can feast on food from different continents, from Greek souvlaki to Thai mango salad, from Italian prosciutto to Jamaican jerk chicken, from Indian lamb curry to Chinese lobster.

And do all these people get along? Well, they all enjoy a life of relative harmony, cooperation, and peace. They certainly aren't terrorizing, torturing, and massacring one another. They're not igniting pubs, cars, and schools with explosives that blind, cripple, and maim. And they're not killing children with machetes, cleavers, and axes. Dislike—rancour, even—may exist here and there, but not, I believe, hatred of the blistering intensity we see elsewhere.

Is Canada a successful experiment in racial harmony and peaceful coexistence? Yes, I would say so—and proudly.

When I, as an Aboriginal citizen of this country, find myself thinking about all the people we've received into this beautiful homeland of mine, when I think of the millions to whom we've given safe haven, following agony, terror, hunger, and great sadness in their own home countries, well, my little Cree heart just puffs up with pride. And I walk the streets of Canada, the streets of my home, feeling tall as a maple.

You take it from here ...

Responding

1. **Write Paragraphs** Write a paragraph listing five reasons why the author thinks Canada is a great country to live in. Then, in a separate paragraph, respond to his position, agreeing or disagreeing, or both.

2. **Reflect about the Author** What is the cultural heritage of the author? Why do you think he feels as "tall as a maple"? In what way could he be considered a goodwill ambassador for our country? Share your views with a partner.

3. **Examine Setting** With a partner, compare the "heart of Australia" that Tomson Highway experienced with his description of Canada. In what ways are Canada's regions diverse? In what sense do "we have it all"?

4. **Focus on Diction** Write five sentences or phrases that are especially effective in presenting certain ideas of the author. Then, beside each quotation, express the ideas in your own words.

Example of effective diction	Ideas suggested by words
"They're not igniting pubs, cars, and schools with explosives that blind, cripple, and maim."	unlike some peoples, Canadians are respectful and not violent

Extending

5. **Describe a Place** Using Tomson Highway's descriptive style to create a mood, write a description of a town, city, or region of Canada you especially like.

6. **Conduct a Survey** Interview five to eight people about what they like about Canada. Report your findings to the class.

7. **Draft a Thank-You Letter** Write a first draft for a letter thanking the author for opening your eyes to the advantages of living in Canada.

Before you read, tell the class about a neighbour you consider or once considered to be odd or strange.

As you read, sketch a scene or moment from the story.

Arctic Plums

Most of the neighbourhood kids believed Gladys was a witch.

Memoir by Brian Fawcett

Notes

Brian Fawcett was born in Prince George, BC. He was a community organizer and urban planner in Vancouver until 1985, and he taught in maximum security federal prisons. He currently lives in Toronto.

When I was a kid, a woman named Gladys Snow lived in a small white house with a big yard a couple of blocks away from my house. She died a short time ago, and that's what made me think of her. I never thought of her as a friend, and the only time I ever spoke to her was when I used to collect money for the local newspaper, and even then we had little to say to each other; a bad-tempered old lady and a barely curious young boy.

The only questions I might have wanted to ask her would have been about her garden, and why it was so odd. There were things in her garden no one else in town had, and I was curious about them. Most of the neighbourhood kids believed Gladys was a witch, and my older sisters claimed that every plant in her garden was poisonous—that was why so many of them were always withered and dead, even in the middle of summer.

Neither of these stories was true. I knew that because I got to walk though the garden twice a week to deliver the paper, which meant that I got as close to the plants as any neighbourhood kid ever did, and I was the only one who had time to look. Most of the plants in her garden I knew from helping my mother in our own family garden. I'd even have known what most of the dead ones were and where they came from if I'd bothered to think about it.

Each spring a delivery truck arrived at Gladys's house and unloaded boxes of plants. Most of the boxes came from the States, and a few of them, the smaller ones, came from England. Some of the plants she got were roses. I knew that because my father grew roses too, or tried to. Every year he ordered plants from the catalogue, every spring they arrived and were planted, and every winter they died. I never asked my father why he kept on planting roses every year, and it's too bad I didn't. If I'd asked, he might have given me a clue to what was going on in Gladys Snow's garden.

But, as I said, I didn't ask him. I assumed that my father had a good reason for what he did, even though each spring he would let fly with

some truly eloquent curses as he pulled up the previous year's dead roses. He cursed the roses, the company that sold them, and he cursed the bitterness of the climate, and for all I know he might have cursed Luther Burbank himself. But since he cursed at a lot of other things too, I didn't see anything special about his maledictions over the dead roses.

If I'd been paying attention, I'd have noticed that the dead plants in Gladys Snow's garden were the plants that had come in the boxes from England and the States. Nearly all of them died: spindly little vines, misshapen saplings, even the seedlings she set out from the pots that littered the windowsills of her front porch each spring. The late frosts killed some of them right away, the early frosts killed others in late summer, and in the hottest months the mid-summer frosts killed still others. And those few saplings that survived died during the winter, despite the piles of leaves Gladys heaped around them. Eventually almost all of them ended up in the huge, stinking compost heap she kept at the bottom of her garden. She put so many things in that compost heap that it would sometimes stay active all year, and more than once I saw, in the dead of winter, small plumes of steam percolating up through the snow.

Nothing exotic lived long in her garden, except for one small fruit tree. It had been planted before I could remember, and each spring it flowered profusely, and the white blossoms were succeeded in turn by masses of poisonous blue-black plums no bigger than cherries, and as hard as rocks.

Every kid in the neighbourhood knew the plums were poisonous. There were stories about those who had tasted them years ago, and how they'd sickened and died, or been sent away to the loony bin where they were said to languish still, dull, drooling, and idiotic. Notwithstanding, Gladys never got to harvest her poisonous plums. Partly to make sure she wouldn't use them against us in some evil spell, and partly in the pure spirit of gleeful juvenile vandalism, each autumn one group of kids or another always succeeded in stripping the tree. The climate was too cold for horse chestnuts, and we needed something moderately lethal to throw at one another during harvest time. The plums were ideal. It was probably the reason Gladys seemed to hate us all so much—for weeks after the tree was stripped she was even more grumpy than usual, staring me in the eye for long seconds when I collected for the newspaper, no doubt having decided I was the villain. But she never came right out and accused me of anything, even though a few times I'd been among the culprits.

I don't remember the little tree growing much. Maybe we kids broke too many branches pulling the plums off, or maybe the tree grew taller as I grew and I didn't notice.

All of that was years ago. As soon as I grew large enough I left town. I hated that cold climate and I didn't want to die there, killed off like Gladys's exotic plants, or grown small and hard and poisonous like the plums.

I heard about her death while I was back there visiting friends. It seems that Gladys had a son nobody knew about until he came to live with her ten years ago. My friends had bought the house right next door to her place, and they had a ringside seat for what happened.

The son was nearly fifty, and he turned out to be a hopeless drunk. He couldn't keep a job, and he couldn't get along with anyone, least of all old Gladys. He'd come home dead drunk one night in the middle of a snowstorm, and Gladys threw him out of the house after an argument. He disappeared into the night and didn't come back. It snowed more than a foot that night, and the snowstorm continued unabated for several more days. After that, it turned bitterly cold. The snowpack was deep that year, more than six feet, and after a desultory search, and a lot of matter-of-fact tsk-tsking and shaking of heads, people quickly lost interest in what had become of Gladys's son. It was cold, and most people assumed that he was either dead or that he'd left town on the bus the next day.

Well, he turned up right in Gladys's garden, underneath all her dead plants in the compost pile. It seems he'd burrowed his way under them, thinking, in his drunken stupor, to keep warm. They didn't find him until most of the snow had gone the next spring.

I heard all this while I was sitting on my friend's back porch, looking across into Gladys's garden.

"What happened to the old lady after that?" I asked my friend.

"Nothing much. She was pretty rickety by that time, and about the only change we noticed was that she started letting the garden go to hell."

I looked back into the garden. The plum tree was about fifteen feet tall now, and it was full of small blue-black plums.

"Crazy the way old Gladys gardened, eh?" I laughed. "The only thing that really worked in her whole garden was that plum tree, and all it every produced were inedible plums."

"Those plums aren't inedible," my friend said mildly.

"Sure they are," I insisted. "We used to think they were poisonous."

My friend got out of his chair, leaped over the short fence into Gladys's overgrown yard and picked a half-dozen plums.

"We've been making jam out of them ever since Gladys stopped gardening," he said. "She told us to take them. As a matter of fact you had some of the jam at breakfast."

Arctic Plums **237**

He tossed a plum across the fence. I caught it and rolled it around in my hand. It was no bigger than I remembered, but much softer. Then I bit into it, and let the nectar of the sweetest plum I've ever tasted roll across my tongue and into my throat.

You take it from here ...

Responding

1. **Consider Reader Response**   Think about what you have just read. Write down the answers to the following questions:
   - Did the memoir bring to mind any memories from your own childhood? Have you ever known anyone like Gladys?
   - Is the ending a good one? How is it different from what the narrator expected? Were you surprised? Why or why not?

2. **Analyze Theme**   Write a paragraph comparing the narrator's childhood impressions of Gladys with his new understanding as an adult. Illustrate your points with examples.

3. **Work in a Group**   Exchange views with two or three other students about the following questions. Then report your conclusions in a class discussion.
   - How did Gladys get her reputation as a witch?
   - Why did her plants die?
   - Did Gladys lead a happy life?
   - When did she take a turn for the worse?
   - Do you think there were any other reasons why she was regarded as an outsider?

Extending

4. **Compose Diary Entries**   Record three diary entries written by Gladys. One of them should be about the night her son came home drunk.

5. **Write a Poem**   Think about a person you know of who is an outsider. Write a poem describing this person either from "outside" as others see her or him, or from "inside"—from the person's own point of view.

6. **Write a Profile**   Create a character who is an "outsider." Include a physical description, a personality profile, and some background information on the character's life and circumstances. Identify why the person does not fit in and perhaps what might have to happen to change that.

Before you read, look up "alienation" in a dictionary. Think about a time when you have felt alienated.

As you read, think about how "alienation" applies to Jamie.

Notes

Elizabeth Brewster was born in Chipman, NB. She taught English at the University of Saskatchewan and worked as a librarian and cataloguer in New Brunswick, Ontario, Alberta, and British Columbia. She is best known for her stories and poetry.

Jamie

Poem by Elizabeth Brewster

When Jamie was sixteen,
Suddenly he was deaf. There were no songs,
No voices any more.
He walked about stunned by the terrible silence.
Kicking a stick, rapping his knuckles on doors,
He felt a spell of silence all about him,
So loud it made a whirring in his ears.
People moved mouths without a sound escaping:
He shuddered at the straining of their throats.
And suddenly he watched them with suspicion,
Wondering if they were talking of his faults,
Were pitying him or seeing him with scorn.
He dived into their eyes and dragged up sneers,
And sauntering the streets, imagined laughter behind him.
Working at odd jobs, ploughing, picking potatoes,
Chopping trees in the lumber woods in winter,
He became accustomed to an aimless and lonely labour.
He was solitary and unloquacious as a stone,
And silence grew over him like moss on an old stump.
But sometimes, going to town,
He was sore with the hunger for company among the people,
And, getting drunk, would shout at them for friendship,
Laughing aloud in the streets.
He returned to the woods,
And dreaming at night of a shining cowboy heaven
Where guns crashed through his deafness, woke morose,
And chopped the necks of pine trees in his anger.

You take it from here ...

Responding

1. **Focus on Diction**   With a partner, write down words and phrases that reflect Jamie's views of, and responses to, his disability. Look up the following words and explain what they reveal in the poem: "scorn," "sneers," "[un]loquacious," "morose."

2. **Understand Poetic Techniques**   Find examples of the following poetic devices in the poem:
   a) alliteration (repetition of consonant sounds especially at the beginnings of words)
   b) onomatopoeia (words that imitate sounds)
   c) metaphor (direct comparison of unlike things)
   d) simile (indirect comparison using "like" or "as")
   e) symbol (something that stands for something else)

3. **Offer a Personal Response**   What advice would you offer Jamie? How might he have had a better life if he had been able to get the kind of counselling and support available in our society today?

Extending

4. **Compose a Stream-of-Consciousness**   From Jamie's perspective, write a description of your thoughts and feelings for three or four different situations typically experienced by teenagers (e.g., sitting in a classroom, talking in a busy cafeteria, going to a dance, watching television or a movie).

5. **Research and Experience Sign Language**   Look up information on American Sign Language (ASL). With a partner, incorporate some of the signs from the ASL alphabet into a brief dialogue for the class. After the presentations, discuss as a class the emotions you experienced while communicating in this manner (e.g., frustration, pressure, the joys of success and understanding).

Before you read, as a class, define and discuss the following terms: sexism, gender, chauvinism, subservience, feminism.

As you read, make a simple chart with two sides, one for the men and one for the women. List the activities, roles, and feelings for each side.

Notes

Paulette Jiles has written several books of poetry, including her 1984 Governor General's Literary Award–winning *Celestial Navigation*. She spent a lot of time working with Native communications groups in the Canadian North, and much of her work celebrates the Arctic landscape.

Paper Matches

Poem by Paulette Jiles

My aunts washed dishes while the uncles
squirted each other on the lawn with
    garden hoses. Why are we in here,
I said, and they are out there?
    That's the way it is,
    said Aunt Hetty, the shrivelled-up one.

I have the rages that small animals have,
being small, being animal.
    Written on me was a message,
'At Your Service,' like a book of
paper matches. One by one we were
taken out and struck.
    We come bearing supper,
our heads on fire.

You take it from here ...

Responding

1. **Analyze Conflict** With a partner, discuss the following:
    a) the conflict in the first stanza
    b) why Aunt Hetty may be "shrivelled-up"
    c) why the speaker mentions "small animals" and their "rages"
    d) the simile of the matchbook—how the women are like matches
    e) the two different uses of water

2. **Give a Personal Response** If you were given a chance, what would you say to the men and women of this poem? What advice might you have for the women? How might the conflict be resolved?

3. **Consider Purpose** In a paragraph, explain why the author has written this poem. Does the author accomplish her purpose?

4. **Comment on Relevance** Do you think the poem's scenario is typical in today's society? With two or three other students, discuss and compare both first- and second-hand knowledge about how household tasks are divided in most homes today. Do you think, overall, that household tasks are more fairly divided among family members now than they were in the past? Explain.

Extending

5. **Write an Essay** Take another look at the poem and write a brief essay analyzing the symbols. Explain how these develop the theme.

6. **Rewrite the Poem** Present the point of view of one of the uncles in poetic form. There should be two stanzas (much like the original poem)—one focused on the women, then one on the men.

7. **Script Dialogue** With a partner, write a conversation that one of the women might have had with one of the men. Then present your scripted conversation to the class. You might choose to work in a group of four and create your script based on the number of males and females there are in your group.

Before you read, with a partner, recall and recite the nursery rhyme "Little Bo Peep" and one other Mother Goose poem.

As you read, before you look at the last frame of the cartoon, cover it and predict what it will be about.

Doonesbury

Cartoon by G.B. Trudeau

Doonesbury 243

You take it from here ...

Responding

1. **Discuss a Concept**   As a class, discuss the concept of political correctness. Is Peter a "sexist porker" in your opinion? In what ways might the cartoon itself be considered offensive? To whom and why?

2. **Understand Theme**   Look at the last frame of the cartoon. What ideas are being presented about a) how fairy tales may be interpreted, b) how parents influence children, c) what children understand of fairy tales and of what their parents tell them?

3. **Describe Style**   Two things that influence the reader's response to this cartoon are the words and images. Which words and images did you find amusing? How can a reader tell that the author's intention is deliberately humorous and thought-provoking?

Extending

4. **Rewrite a Poem**   Choose one of the famous Mother Goose nursery rhymes to rewrite in a politically correct fashion.

5. **Analyze Texts**   Find two other Mother Goose rhymes that might be considered sexist or violent from today's perspective. For each one, write a paragraph explaining how it might be seen as sexist or violent.

6. **Draft a Children's Book**   Plan a book of modern nursery rhymes. What topics would you cover? Write and illustrate at least two of these modern nursery rhymes.

Before you read, as a class, recall the events in the original fairy tale *Little Red Riding Hood*. Are there different endings?

As you read, look up the following words: engender, forbidding, intimidate, accosted, adherence, linear, matriarch, melee, Neanderthal, mutual.

Little Red Riding Hood

Red Riding Hood said, "I find your sexist remark offensive in the extreme."

Fairy Tale Spoof by James Finn Garner

Notes

James Finn Garner is a writer and performer living in Chicago. He has written several collections of "politically correct" stories, including *Once Upon a More Enlightened Time* and *Politically Correct Holiday Stories*.

Freudian imagery: sense impressions suggesting sex(uality). Sigmund Freud was a twentieth-century psychoanalyst famous for his views about sexual subconsciousness in human beings, including children.

womyn: a radical feminist spelling of "woman," considered politically correct because it does not use "man" as the root word

There once was a young person named Red Riding Hood who lived with her mother on the edge of a large wood. One day her mother asked her to take a basket of fresh fruit and mineral water to her grandmother's house—not because this was womyn's work, mind you, but because the deed was generous and helped engender a feeling of community. Furthermore, her grandmother was *not* sick, but rather was in full physical and mental health and was fully capable of taking care of herself as a mature adult.

So Red Riding Hood set off with her basket through the woods. Many people believed that the forest was a foreboding and dangerous place and never set foot in it. Red Riding Hood, however, was confident enough in her own budding sexuality that such obvious Freudian imagery did not intimidate her.

On the way to Grandma's house, Red Riding Hood was accosted by a wolf, who asked her what was in her basket. She replied, "Some healthful snacks for my grandmother, who is certainly capable of taking care of herself as a mature adult."

The wolf said, "You know, my dear, it isn't safe for a little girl to walk through these woods alone."

Red Riding Hood said, "I find your sexist remark offensive in the extreme, but I will ignore it because of your traditional status as an outcast from society, the stress of which has caused you to develop your own, entirely valid, worldview. Now, if you'll excuse me, I must be on my way."

Red Riding Hood walked on along the main path. But, because his status outside society had freed him from slavish adherence to linear, Western-style thought, the wolf knew a quicker route to Grandma's house. He burst into the house and ate Grandma, an entirely valid course of action for a carnivore such as himself. Then, unhampered by rigid, traditionalist notions of what was masculine or feminine, he put on Grandma's nightclothes and crawled into bed.

Red Riding Hood entered the cottage and said, "Grandma, I have brought you some fat-free, sodium-free snacks to salute you in your role of a wise and nurturing matriarch."

From the bed, the wolf said softly, "Come closer, child, so that I might see you."

Red Riding Hood said, "Oh, I forgot you are as optically challenged as a bat. Grandma, what big eyes you have!"

"They have seen much, and forgiven much, my dear."

"Grandma, what a big nose you have—only relatively, of course, and certainly attractive in its own way."

"It has smelled much, and forgiven much, my dear."

"Grandma, what big teeth you have!"

The wolf said, "I am happy with *who* I am and *what* I am," and leaped out of bed. He grabbed Red Riding Hood in his claws, intent on devouring her. Red Riding Hood screamed, not out of alarm at the wolf's apparent tendency toward cross-dressing, but because of his willful invasion of her personal space.

Her screams were heard by a passing woodchopper-person (or log-fuel technician, as he preferred to be called). When he burst into the cottage, he saw the melee and tried to intervene. But as he raised his axe, Red Riding Hood and the wolf both stopped.

"And just what do you think you're doing?" asked Red Riding Hood.

The woodchopper-person blinked and tried to answer, but no words came to him.

"Bursting in here like a Neanderthal, trusting your weapon to do your thinking for you!" she exclaimed. "Sexist! Speciesist! How dare you assume that womyn and wolves can't solve their own problems without a man's help!"

When she heard Red Riding Hood's impassioned speech, Grandma jumped out of the wolf's mouth, seized the woodchopper-person's axe, and cut his head off. After this ordeal, Red Riding Hood, Grandma, and the wolf felt a certain commonality of purpose. They decided to set up an alternative household based on mutual respect and cooperation, and they lived together in the woods happily ever after.

You take it from here ...

Responding

1. **Consider Choices Related to Purpose**   The purpose of a politically correct fairy tale would be to avoid giving offence and to promote good, healthful lifestyles. Review the story and list as many "politically correct" words as you can; beside each, write the "politically incorrect" version.

2. **Discuss Audience**   As a class, decide what type of audience this fairy tale would be appropriate for. How does this audience compare with the typical audience for fairy tales? What aspects of this version of "Little Red Riding Hood" helped you decide?

3. **Identify Theme**   With a partner, write down three key ideas presented in the story. Share these with the class and, together, decide on the story's theme.

Extending

4. **Rewrite a Fairy Tale**   Using Garner's spoof as a model, create your own politically correct fairy tale based on another well-known story.

5. **Create Trading Cards**   Using five to seven characters from different fairy tales, make politically correct trading cards and display them in the classroom.

6. **Put on a Puppet Show**   Present to the class a puppet show of "Little Red Riding Hood" or another of James Finn Garner's fairy tales from his *Politically Correct Bedtime Stories*.

Reflecting on the Unit

Responding

1. **Write an Essay**   Using one of the quotations from the unit introduction, write a response referring to lessons you learned from specific unit selections.

2. **Present Orally**   Which selection influenced you the most in this unit? In a two-minute speech, explain why you picked that particular selection.

3. **Compare and Contrast**   Take one of the following pairs of selections and discuss similarities and differences between them in a written response.
   - "Conceiving the Stranger" and "After the Wedding"
   - "Touch the Dragon" and "Grandma Weaver's Last Arrow"
   - "Arctic Plums" and "Jamie"
   - "Doonesbury" and "Little Red Riding Hood."

Extending

4. **Write a Letter**   In the role of one of the characters of this unit, write a letter to another character for one of the following purposes:
   - apology
   - complaint
   - invitation
   - congratulations
   - thank you

5. **Review a Movie**   Have a class discussion on movies with themes of promoting understanding and acceptance, and create a class list of recommended ones. Choose one from the list to view, and write a review of it to be posted on the bulletin board.

> **SELF ASSESSMENT**
> Review what you have learned from this unit regarding
> - accessing previous knowledge
> - vocabulary development
> - poetry devices
> - audience, purpose, and context
> - creating new texts based on readings

UNIT 6

"I don't believe in things. I believe in relationships."
–Georges Braque

"Having someone wonder where you are when you don't come home at night is a very old human need."
–Margaret Mead

"A relationship isn't meant to be an insurance policy, a life preserver, or a security blanket."
–Diane Crowley

Relationships

Relationships bring meaning to our lives. In an age of increasing materialism, the quotation by French artist Georges Braque is a reminder that the best things are the "ties that bind." Things can never replace relationships!

Anthropologist Margaret Mead highlights the fundamental human need to be cared for by someone else, and advice columnist Diane Crowley reminds us that it is important to be in a relationship for the right reasons.

The selections in this unit present many different kinds of relationships, as well as some insights into how our human need for each other plays out in the different stages of our lives.

As you read this unit, think about the following:

1) How do the bonds between children and parents change over time?
2) What drives our quest for "significant others"?
3) How do others make our lives richer and more meaningful?

Before you view, tell a partner about one of your special childhood friends.

As you view, jot down notes on your interpretation of the photograph's title.

The Walk to Paradise Garden

Photograph by W. Eugene Smith

Notes

Gene Smith saw his work as basically affirmative, saying "I like pictures that surmount the darkness." This memorable, moving picture reflects his belief that the photographer should become a participant in his own work. The subjects of this famous 1946 image taken in Croton, New York, are the photographer's children, Patrick and Juanita Smith.

You take it from here ...

Responding

1. **Share a Memory** In a written response, tell about a childhood memory that the picture brings to mind.

2. **Discuss Photograph Elements** In a small group, answer the following questions, making comments about the photographer's choices:

    a) How old are the children? What is their relationship? What can you tell from their "body language"?
    b) Where are they going? What is behind and ahead of them? Why do you think the photographer took the picture from behind them?
    c) What use is made of light and darkness? How do these choices help the viewer to imagine a context or story?
    d) What is the mood created by the photograph? Does the picture reveal a positive or negative *tone* (photographer's attitude toward the scene and the children)?

3. **Comment on Purpose and Theme** Look at the title of the photograph again. What does it tell us about the author's purpose and the idea behind the photo? Write your answer in a paragraph.

Extending

4. **Create Dialogue** What might the children be saying to each other? Imagine and write the conversation they are having.

5. **Write a Children's Story** Imagine events that led up to the moment in the picture. Using the title of the photograph, write a short story for children aged four to six.

6. **Snap a Photograph** Take a picture of an intriguing moment or scene in your day. Using this selection as an example, do something interesting with your subject. Try also to create a mood with your picture. Share your photo with your classmates and invite their responses.

> **PEER ASSESSMENT**
> - As you view others' photos, do you understand what they were trying to convey? What ideas did you get from other students' photos?

Before you read, with a partner, share a special memory about a favourite grandparent or older relative.

As you read, write down in your notebook how you think Michael feels about his grandfather's illness.

The Sea Shell

His grandfather had tried to teach him how to swim.

Short Story by Ed Kleiman

Notes

Ed Kleiman is a Winnipeg author who teaches English at the University of Manitoba. He has published three collections of short stories, *The Immortals* (1980), *A New Found Ecstasy* (1988), and *The World Beaters* (1998).

It was growing dark when Abe Buchalter, his wife, Rosa, and their son, Michael, left their apartment behind the family bakery on Selkirk Avenue and walked toward the car parked in the side driveway.

"Come on, Michael. Hurry up."

There was a note of urgency in the voice which Michael refused to recognize. "I'll come later," he replied.

"But your grandfather wants to see you," his mother explained.

"It's not that far. I'll walk."

The look on his father's face showed his impatience as he backed the car carefully along the driveway, turned onto the street, and then headed toward Michael's grandfather's home in Elmwood.

Slowly Michael began walking toward Main Street. The night was cold, as it often is in spring, no matter how warm the days had become, and no one had reminded Michael to bring a jacket. Worse than the cold was the damp, and though the street lights had been turned on, they only made Michael more aware of the mist descending about him. Few people passed by, and he became aware of the dull sound of his shoes echoing about him as he approached the corner.

On Main Street, he found the lights and noise startling after the relative silence and darkness of the side street, and he began walking more quickly toward the Redwood Bridge, which led into Elmwood and to his grandfather's home. It was Saturday and he noticed many families driving downtown; then, as he crossed the street and approached the bridge, the noise and almost overpowering movement of Main Street faded behind him ....

It seemed like a long time ago now, though it was only that morning they had received the phone call. Michael had thought his grandmother's voice sounded awkward and hesitant as she explained that his grandfather was very sick and wanted to see them. But Michael's father could not leave the bakery, and his mother, who may have thought that

252 Relationships

her father-in-law's sudden illness was being dramatized a little, had delayed going over till early that afternoon.

When they arrived at his grandparents' place, however, Michael realized, from the moment he entered the house, that the phone call, if anything, had understated the seriousness of what was happening. He would soon be thirteen—almost grown up now—and he knew that his grandfather would die that day. No one had to tell him; he knew. He could feel it about him. His grandparents' wedding picture over the piano, the furniture arranged neatly about the house, the windows clear, the curtains limp, the second hand of the kitchen clock turning—they were all part of a despair that filled the house with a helpless feeling.

His grandfather lay asleep in the bedroom. He was a tall man with light grey hair and a thin face. Michael longed for the warmth of his eyes and voice and stayed with him all afternoon, hoping that he would awaken. But he was still asleep when, toward evening, Michael had had to go home for supper.

His father looked more worried now and kept asking, over and over again, what exactly had the doctor said? Then, impatient with the answers, he telephoned the doctor himself. It was only a short while later, when supper was finally over, that they had gotten into the car and driven off, upset that Michael would not come with them.

He was walking on the bridge now and could feel the dark water moving below him, but the mist and the night hid it from view. Only the tiny bubbling sounds of the water lapping against the riverbanks told him of its presence; yet he realized that even without this sign he would have known the river was there, just as he knew that a short distance away his grandfather was dying: his grandfather, whose strength to him had once seemed that of a god.

When he was six and had been taken to Winnipeg Beach by his parents, his grandfather had tried to teach him how to swim. He hadn't learned easily, and, angry and sick from swallowing too many mouthfuls of lake water, he had dared his grandfather to do better. Michael had watched in amazement as his grandfather started out with long, mighty strokes that carried him effortlessly through the water, which even now, as he remembered it, seemed to have been almost white. His grandfather had swum further and further away until he was only a tiny speck, and then not even that.

Michael had run, frightened, to his parents, but they had assured him that his grandfather would soon be back. Sure enough, an hour later he returned, bringing with him a large sea shell. When Michael asked him

where he got the shell, his grandfather pointed toward the lake, but his parents later told him that he had probably swum further down the beach and bought it at a souvenir stand with some money borrowed from a friend nearby.

By putting the shell to his ear, Michael could hear winds and storms and movements vaster even than that of the lake he looked upon, vaster even than that of the sea. His grandfather had offered to give him the shell, but he refused, feeling that there was something alien about the object which had been brought from beneath water he had never seen.

"I'll keep it for you until you want it, then," his grandfather had said. "Perhaps for your Bar Mitzvah," he laughed.

Now, hearing the murmur of the river passing beneath him, Michael remembered the sound of the sea shell. His grandfather was waiting for him; he must hurry. Looking back toward Main Street and seeing the lights, he felt an aching despair well up within him. He began running, suddenly frightened, as the sound of the river grew in intensity. Then he knew it was the sound of the shell he was hearing and running toward.

When he arrived at the house, he could see only the porch light burning, for the blinds at the front of the house were drawn. He pressed the doorbell and heard the ringing within. The sound seemed so tiny and the house so very empty that he was a little surprised when his grandmother came to the door. She was very pale, and the light from the small lamp in the hall fell just as palely upon her white face. He could barely hear her voice when she asked him in.

Several of the other relatives were there now, moving slowly, their voices quiet, their eyes filled with sorrow. He felt a shadow of disappointment fall from his father's face toward him. In the bedroom his grandfather lay still, his hands not folded together but at his sides. Michael looked at him and remembered the day he had swum out into the lake, his arms moving strongly through the white water.

Suddenly he became aware that his mother was standing beside him.

"He wanted to see you, Michael," she said.

Michael said nothing, but continued watching his grandfather as if believing that there was still time for him to speak.

"He was sorry you weren't here," she said, "but he wasn't cross. He said, 'Michael is growing up; that's all. A boy only twelve. He's just growing up.'"

Michael tried to imagine the way his grandfather would speak the words: slowly and gently, very softly.

"He was saying how scared we all looked; he wasn't frightened at all, just lying there, talking in his calm, steady voice. We could hardly look at him and he just kept on smiling and talking as if we were the ones who needed reassuring, saying things we had all heard him speak about before. But now they sounded different, as if we were understanding him for the first time."

As his mother spoke, Michael thought he could hear the wind rushing over the lake, the dark river flowing quietly under the bridge. But it was a salt spray that brushed his face and lips, when, through a mist, he saw his grandfather moving through the white water—those strong arms, that effortless movement—bringing the shell as if from the depths of the ocean he had once crossed and offering to Michael so that he, too, could hear the roar and swell of the sea.

You take it from here …

Responding

1. **Make a Connection**   With another student, discuss the boy's relationship with his grandfather. Why does he connect the sea shell with his grandfather?

2. **Understand Epiphany**   An *epiphany* is a sudden realization that the protagonist has at the end of a story. Review the last paragraph. What insight does Michael have? How does this change him?

3. **Find Literary Devices**   With a partner, review the story and find examples of the following devices used in fiction. Record the examples in a chart.

complicating incident	event that starts the conflict
suspense	feeling of uncertainty about the outcome of events
flashback	imagined past action or memory of a protagonist
atmosphere	details in the story that create mood in the reader
symbol	something that represents or stands for something else
climax	emotional high point in the narrative
denouement	resolution or "unknotting" of the conflict

Extending

4. **Write a Stream-of-Consciousness**   What might Michael be thinking about after the story ends? In your notebook, write what you think he would like to have said to his grandfather.

5. **Draft a Proposal**   As an aspiring director, you want to make a short film for TV based on this story. What elements of the story would make an interesting film? Put together a proposal indicating how you would shoot the film, and explain your choices.

Before you read, as a class, discuss why some parents give up their children to be adopted.

As you read, write in your notebook how you would feel if you were Michelle at the different stages of tracking her birth parents.

At 28 years old, who needs new parents?

One Woman's Story
by Michelle McColm

ESSAY

Notes

Michelle McColm lives in Toronto and is the author of a nonfiction book, *Adoption Reunions*.

At 15, I had a favourite tree by the river across the road from my family's home. After school, I'd sit on a branch for hours, listening to my transistor radio. Sometimes I'd cry as I pondered the reflection in the water below. Who was this person?

My first storybook, read to me by my parents, was about adoption. It reinforced how loved and wanted I was by my adoptive family. And yet, even as a child of 6, I knew that something was missing from the story. What happened to my first mommy? I felt I must have done something really horrible for my *own mother* to have given me away.

I was four months old in 1959 when a Toronto family adopted me. My sister was born to my adoptive parents two years after. While she grew up hearing about her "breech birth," I was "brought home from the agency." I concluded that I was an alien—hatched, not born.

The others were sure of their origins. They took pride in their Scottish ancestry, bagpipes attended weddings and funerals, genealogy books were pored over at holiday gatherings, and a huge embroidered family tree adorned my cousins' living room. That I was grafted onto that tree, and somewhere had a line of my own, went unacknowledged during these occasions. I felt isolated and depressed, and guilty for having these feelings. My family took it for granted that I was "one of them." But *my* history was important to me, too.

Until recently, families regarded adoption as a source not only of joy but of embarrassment. Adoptees were, after all, "illegitimate" children. Although I didn't know the word, I experienced its implications through tauntings at school, comments from neighbours, trips to the doctor. I remember sitting on the examining table as my mother blushed and lowered her eyes when asked: "Does this illness run in your family?"

"I don't know," she'd reply. "She was adopted."

My parents shared with me what they'd been told about my past: I was of German ancestry. My birth mother was young, unmarried, and loved me; her father pressured her into giving me up. He made her give up my birth father, as well, although they had planned to marry.

Once my adoptive dad told me I could see my "papers" anytime I wished. My mom, on the other hand, felt hurt and threatened by my interest. I stopped asking for a while.

A year later, when I was 17, my adoptive mother stood at the threshold of my room and tearfully proffered a wooden box. "This was given to us by our social worker when we adopted you," she said. "It's from your birth mother." As I touched the satiny wood, held the tiny carved deer and necklace inside, my mom explained that these gifts had originally belonged to three generations of women: mother, grandmother, great-grandmother. For the first time in my life, I knew, unequivocally, that I hadn't been callously "rejected." I came from a thoughtful, loving woman.

My adoptive mother died in 1986. A year later, I decided to search for my roots, knowing that she could no longer be hurt by this decision. I had my father's blessings, but evoked the shock of others. Why was I looking for my parents? I wasn't. At 28 years old, who needs new parents? They also worried that I would "disrupt" my birth mother's life. Yet my own life had been profoundly disrupted the day I was separated from my mother, my kin, and my past, and placed into the hands of strangers: nurses, social workers, foster parents, and, finally, my adoptive parents. But what about the risk of discovering the strangers who were my birth family? To me, any gains were worth the risks.

I sent my application to Ontario's Adoption Disclosure Registry. Two months later, I received a letter stating that my birth mother had also registered. Initially, we exchanged photos and letters. Her pictures revealed the same unruly hair, the same bump on the nose and familiar curves of arm and leg—me! My sense of belonging was immediate. Even more surprising than the physical resemblance were her letters. Several friends incredulously commented that she sounded like me: her love of nature, her descriptive style.

The day before our meeting, I considered bringing her a rose. Frightened, I decided against it. I didn't even know this woman, why should I bring her anything?

When we met, we embraced wordlessly, tears flowing. Then, she handed me a long-stemmed red rose. When she learned of my original intent, she said, "We'll share this one."

My birth mother welcomed me with open arms, as did her husband and two young sons. I later met my birth father and his son and daughter, widening the circle.

Not all responses were positive, however. During a party, my birth mother introduced me to many of her acquaintances, who knew nothing of my existence. Pointing an accusatory finger at me, one of them exclaimed: "You're not her daughter. She doesn't have a daughter." The rest of them easily accepted me.

I believed my reunion would answer all the questions my childhood storybook had

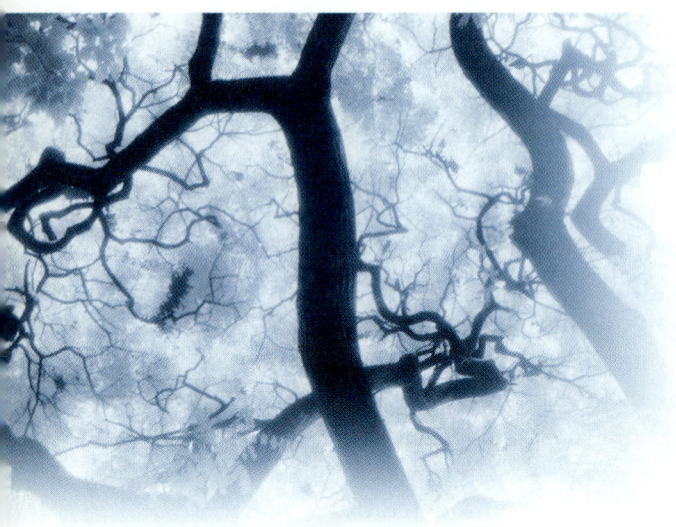

neglected. Yet my mother had forgotten the details of my birth, saying the trauma of giving up her child had made them too painful to remember. Long ago, she destroyed the first photos of me as an infant, trying to do as she was told, to get on with her life. After all, we were never to meet again.

We not only met but travelled to Europe together the following year. There, I visited relatives I could not speak with. But I gazed into their eyes, heard their laughter and saw my ancestors' homeland. I reclaimed my history.

I continue to visit my birth family, and sometimes they gather with me and my adoptive family. We're still all getting to know each other; there's a lot to catch up on.

Recently, my husband and I went walking on a brisk fall afternoon. I showed him that tree by the river where I had cried and wondered who I was. Only this time, the pain had lessened, giving way to the peace of knowing where I come from, and who I am. I now feel both loved *and* whole.

You take it from here ...

Responding

1. **Write a Personal Response**   In your journal, write your feelings about Michelle's quest to find her birth parents. Was she right to do this? Would you have done the same? Why or why not? Is her story touching? Did it have a happy ending? What insights does it give about relationships?

2. **Identify Audience**   With another student, discuss who you think this story was written for. Is it a piece that has something to offer people who are not adoptees? Explain.

3. **Focus on Motivation**   In a paragraph, explain Michelle's motivation for her quest. What are some reasons why she sought the identity of her biological parents?

Extending

4. **Debate an Issue**   Discuss in a group whether children have the right to know they are adopted and who their biological parents are. Do you think all adoptive children should be allowed or even helped to contact their birth parents? What possible risks and benefits are involved for all parties?

> **GROUP ASSESSMENT**
> - On which points did your group come to agreement?
> - Did your group try to involve everyone in the discussion?

5. **Create a Poster**   Create a poster advertising a registration service to help birth parents and adopted children locate each other. As an alternative, you can address your poster to parents looking to adopt children. Be sure to address this topic with sensitivity.

6. **Improvise Dialogue**   With a partner, act out the meeting between an adopted child and a birth parent. What would they say to one another? Report to the class on how your improvisation went.

Before you read, have a class discussion about dreams. Can they foretell the future?

As you read, make notes on why Ken was so special to the narrator.

Jamaican Dreams

Birthdays always brought a special gift from Ken.

Memoir by Cynthia Reyes

Notes

Cynthia Reyes moved to Canada from Jamaica in 1974 to study journalism at Ryerson University. She went on to become an award-winning broadcaster and executive producer at CBC.

I have lived in this country for half of my life. I came here a Jamaican. But with each passing year I have become more and more Canadian, less and less Jamaican. If you were to ask me, I would probably say I am now mostly Canadian. That is how I see myself, most of the time. But my past has a way of tripping me up. One night about four years ago, I had a worrisome dream. I dreamed that all my teeth had fallen out.

My friend, born and raised in Canada, blamed my dream on indigestion. "Upset stomach," she declared. "Gives you nightmares." My husband, also raised in Canada, had another explanation: "You forgot to brush your teeth before going to bed. That's what your subconscious was trying to tell you." I laughed out loud, not bothering to remind him that I never forget to brush my teeth before going to bed.

A feeling of unease gnawed at me.

I called Pat, my older sister, who also lives in Toronto. My sister has managed to become a Canadian without rejecting Jamaican traditions, cures, and dream interpretations. "I dreamed that my teeth fell out," I told her.

"Uh-oh," she said. "You know that means death."

"Well, I know it means death if you live in Jamaica. But does it mean the same if you live in Canada?" I made a feeble attempt at laughter. My sister didn't laugh back. I hung up and reminded myself that the last time my sister dreamed about fish, no one she knew became pregnant. It's a Jamaican belief that if you dream of fish, someone you know will get pregnant.

I tried to keep my thoughts away from the dream, but my mind kept shifting gears on its own. I called my sister again: "You heard from home?"

"Not since Momma phoned," she replied. "That was three weeks ago. She sounded great, and said everyone was fine. Try not to worry yourself."

If I were as Canadian as I claimed, if I had really dismissed those Jamaican beliefs, I would have dropped the whole thing right then. But I didn't. As I folded the laundry, another thought popped into my head. Why had our mother phoned? She had only phoned me once in all the time I'd been in Canada. That was right after she received my letter telling her I was pregnant with my first child. My mother didn't even have a telephone in her house. She lived on top of a hill outside the town, and the telephone company had said it was "not economically feasible" for them to run a line that far. So why had my mother walked all the way to town to call us? She told Pat she had tried to reach me first, but I was out. Just to say everything was fine? Or had she also been dreaming of death?

Maybe it's time to go home, I thought. But then, the automatic reply: you can't afford to. They need you at work. It's just cost a thousand dollars to fix the car. Now the insurance is due.

It didn't occur to me to pay for the trip with my credit card. Mounting debts have the same effect on me as a cross reputedly has on a vampire. This problem had once been diagnosed by a friend as an immigrant condition. "You don't feel secure enough to go heavily into debt," she said knowingly.

"Nonsense," I replied. "I took out a mortgage. I bought a car. Now that's a lot of debt."

But it just didn't feel right to leave for Jamaica then. For one thing, you can't show up in your hometown with your "two empty hands"—when you go home you feel compelled to bring gifts for every relative, friend, and kindly neighbour. Going home is not as simple as it sounds. Every logical bone in my body said there was no reason to visit Jamaica. But, like the atheist who half-believes in God at night, I was unable to shake the dream of my teeth falling out: What if the Jamaican interpretation of my dream was a warning from up above?

An unbidden memory kept creeping to the edges of my mind. Another time, another dream, another justification for not going home. Something terrible had happened.

The person at the heart of that memory was Ken, my mother's younger cousin. He was tall, handsome, and stylish. He was also a bright, well-read man who challenged me with provocative arguments. Ken told me wonderful stories about our multiracial, multiclass, multireligious family. With a hint of pride and great relish, he would divulge the details of ancient family scandals. He would give a hilarious twist to tales our family elders had tried so hard to keep secret.

There was no question that of all the people in our huge family conglomerate, Ken and I were each other's favourite. One anecdote said

Ken had fallen in love with me when I was barely 2 and he was 21. It happened the night he accidentally got me drunk by leaving his wineglass within my reach. Ken loved to tell the story of the drunken 2-year-old who staggered around repeating something that sounded suspiciously like a Jamaican cuss-word.

As I grew older, there seemed another reason why Ken and I got along so well. We were both oddities in our family. Ken belonged to the mostly Chinese branch of the family, but unlike his parents and many of his siblings, he had light-brown hair streaked with blond. I too differed from my parents and siblings. I had brown hair streaked with a coppery red. Our looks were easily explained as a product of our extended family's racial confusion. But we stood out nonetheless.

Ken and I shared something else. We dared to dream of things way beyond the scope of our small-town upbringing. We dared to ask questions of things that current wisdom deemed unquestionable. Together we would debate politics, the authenticity of the Bible, even the existence of God. Together we dreamed of travelling the unknown of foreign lands, of writing the great family chronicle.

Birthdays always brought a special gift from Ken. My first camera. My first set of dangling gold earrings. My first pair of sling-back shoes with a matching handbag, both in yellow patent leather.

But on my fifteenth birthday, Ken showed up mysteriously empty-handed. "Get dressed," he said. "We're going into town." And so we did. He pulled up in front of the local branch of the Royal Bank of Canada in nearby Mandeville. Once inside the doors, Ken stopped and turned to me. "In a couple of months you will be graduating from high school," he said. "Every young lady should have a bank account." Then he entered the bank manager's office and started an account in my name. Initial deposit: $1000. It was a small fortune, as the Jamaican dollar in the late sixties was worth about $1.25 (U.S.). Around Ken I had always been a chatterbox, but now I was silent. My gratitude choked me up.

"Use your money wisely," was all Ken said as we left the bank.

Suddenly, the day seemed shiny and bright with promise. To a 15-year-old girl feeling trapped in a small town, a thousand dollars buys a lot of hope. And now my dreams of going abroad to study didn't seem so impossible.

I brought that money, plus interest, with me when I left for Canada in 1974. It would help send me to journalism school at Ryerson.

I left Ken behind in Jamaica with a promise that I would "do something meaningful" with my life. I made another solemn promise: that I would return to help him write that book about "our crazy family."

I would, to some extent, keep the first promise to Ken. I got my degree and became a television news reporter with the CBC. I did voluntary work on behalf of immigrant and minority children. But the second promise lay in the recesses of my mind, almost forgotten. I had originally planned to go home and work on the book with Ken right after graduation. But schooling expenses had worn me out. The CBC job offer came just in time.

It seemed there was always a commitment, always an expense preventing me from going home to keep my second promise. And, to tell the truth, I was getting caught up in my own obligations. I had already started a family. I thought less and less about Ken.

Then, one day while I was preparing a story for the late news, the phone rang. It was my husband.

"Call your sister in Jamaica," he said. "Something about Ken."

I called right away. "What about Ken?"

"He's sick. All of a sudden, he lost the use of his legs. The doctors say they've never seen anything like it."

I was in Jamaica within two days. The trip took all my savings, but that didn't matter at all. By the time I got there, Ken had been moved to the University Hospital in Kingston. He squinted at me as I approached his bed in the intensive care ward. I rushed to hug him. He didn't hug back. Within minutes I realized he had lost the use of his arms too. "Scratch the top of my head for me," he asked in a weak voice. I scratched his head and dampened his soft hair with my tears. Huge, unstoppable tears that burned my eyes and cheeks.

Ken had never been sick in all the time I'd known him. Or perhaps he had, but he'd never let me see him when he was ill. He was the most fiercely independent person I had ever met. I knew without being told that Ken would sooner die than not be able to care for himself. These thoughts went around and around, even as I held Ken's useless hand between my own hands.

The doctors had still not diagnosed his illness. But whatever it was, this disease moved swiftly, mercilessly.

Then, one week later, Ken started to improve. He was still in bed, but he could sit up. His colour came back. He spoke clearly now. His sisters and brothers who had flown home from other countries were delighted with the improvement. There were so many other relatives around that I felt sure Ken wouldn't miss me if I returned to Toronto.

As I said goodbye, I promised Ken I'd return. But this time I put a deadline on it: six months, a year at most.

I told Ken I was sorry I couldn't afford to stay. He remarked, without bitterness, that "now would have been perfect. I'm not going anywhere in this condition."

But he did. Ken did not last a year. He didn't even last six months.

On a Sunday morning in the spring, the phone rang. It was Ken's sister Glenor, who had stood with me beside Ken's hospital bed.

"Hya?" she called me by my Jamaican pet name in her unmistakably Jamaican lilt.

"Don't say anything, Glenor," I whispered. "I don't want to hear."

"I'm really sorry," was all she said.

"I promised to go back, Glenor. I thought we had time." I was babbling on, but unable to cry.

I had a lot of time for memories on that four-hour flight to Kingston. Sweet memories of Ken. But one memory belonged to a much more recent past. A memory of a dream I'd had just one week earlier. In that dream, I was in my mother's garden. I was picking green fruit from my mother's orange tree and digging up yams from the ground. Jamaicans will tell you that such a dream warns of great disappointment and death. My sophisticated Canadian self had told me to ignore it.

The funeral went the way of Jamaican funerals. People wore their most dignified black or purple clothes. Everywhere you looked, there were sombre, tear-stained faces. A priest stood at the altar and said wonderful things about the "dearly departed," in this case a man he barely knew, since Ken never went to church.

At a get-together after the funeral, people swapped warm memories of Ken's life, and shared dreams that had foretold Ken's death. I could hardly bear to share my memories, and I didn't share my dreams. I returned to Toronto racked with guilt.

Then, one day, a chat with a neighbour turned into a discussion about what it means to live so far from your family. My neighbour had come to Canada from Italy many years before. Year after year, she saved a bit of money toward her planned trip home. Finally, she had saved enough. She could hardly wait to see her parents. But just two weeks before her planned visit, the phone rang. Her mother was dead.

"It is the curse of being an immigrant," said a Scottish-born neighbour who had joined us. "You never have enough money to go home. Then someone dies and somehow you find the money. I have been home only twice. Each time it was to bury somebody."

I vowed then I would visit my family frequently. And I meant it. But once again the demands of my own life got in the way, and I forgot my vow.

Then, several years later, came the dream about losing teeth.

I told myself I didn't really believe in dreams. I told myself the dream had only served to remind me of my promise to return home. Still, I took some overdue vacation, booked a flight, and started packing. Whatever was scarce in Jamaica could be found in my bulging suitcases: rice, soap powder, garlic, running shoes, money.

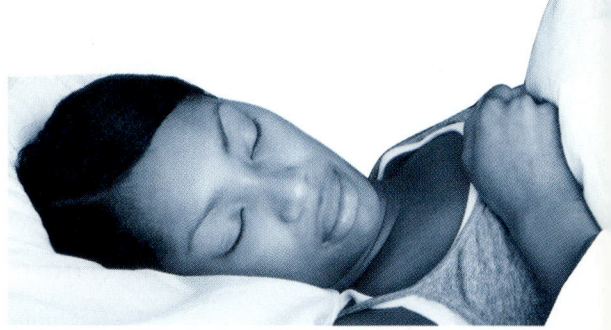

Once there, I scrutinized everyone with a worried eye. My mother seemed a little shorter, a little older, her hair a little more grey. But her smooth brown skin was radiant, and she seemed strong and healthy. My stepfather looked exactly the way I had left him. His dark-brown face seemed to glow with good health. No one seemed ill or in danger of imminent death. It was wonderful to be home.

By the time I returned to Toronto, the bad dream was forgotten. I was so broke I didn't even have enough money to buy gas for my car. But going home had recharged me. My mother, as usual, had loved and inspired me.

They say superstition is born from people's deepest fears. Bad dreams, I think, must come from the same place. My deepest fear about my loved ones in Jamaica is that they will die suddenly, giving me no opportunity to say goodbye, no opportunity to fully repay debts of kindness. Perhaps that is why today, even while I shrug off many of the beliefs with which I was raised, there are some dreams that have the power to shake up my new life and remind me of the life I left behind.

These days, I have started to see the dreams in a different light. I see now they give me an occasion to linger awhile in memories of the life I left behind. They remind me to cherish the people and places in my younger life who helped make me what I am. And they remind me to write home more often.

You take it from here ...

Responding

1. Discuss Context

   a) As a class, discuss the following cultural references:
      - the "immigrant condition"
      - the "curse of being an immigrant"
   b) What makes it difficult for immigrants to retain close connections to their homelands?
   c) What Jamaican dream interpretations does the narrator describe? To what extent is she superstitious?

2. **Write a Character Sketch**   Using adjectives and examples, analyze the character of Ken. How was he unique? What were his outstanding qualities as a person?

3. **Analyze the Title**   "Jamaican Dreams" refers to more than the narrator's premonitions. Tell about a deeper figurative meaning for the title in a paragraph response.

Extending

4. **Role-Play a Talk Show**   With two or three other students, role-play a radio phone-in show called "Dream Doctor," in which people call in with their dreams and ask for interpretation. Choose the most interesting dream/interpretation you came up with and perform it for the class.

> **PEER ASSESSMENT**
> - What did you think of others' presentations?
> - Were the dreams and interpretations presented clearly?

5. **Recall a Family Reunion**   Write about a memorable get-together of your extended family. (Include photos if you took some, or draw a picture to illustrate a moment at the reunion.)

> **Before you read,** as a class, discuss the purpose of writing letters to family members and friends.
>
> **As you read,** think about why the author has written this letter.

It would be nice if I could just pick up the phone and talk to you.

Thanks for being out there, brother

Letter by Jennifer Champion

Notes

Jennifer Champion is an Edmonton writer. She wrote this letter in response to a newspaper's call for personal stories that would "touch others."

Dear Brother:
It will be five years this November since you left this earth, and I just wanted to tell you that I miss you.

Mom was just here for a visit. She and Dad live in Nova Scotia now, not far from where they buried you.

Remember Lockerbys? Remember how you thought it was a nice cemetery because it is built on a hill, enabling people passing by to see all the tombstones? That's where your remains are. Right beside your great-grandfather. Mom and Dad bought the plot next to you for when it is their turn to pass on.

So much has happened since you've left. There are days, now, when I laugh as I remember the fun things we did as children, such as tobogganing in the winter and going to the Q-Mart during the summer. Then there are days like today when I cry because I miss you and wish you were here.

I'm married now. It will be four years this September. Too bad you never got to meet my husband. I think you would have liked him. He's not weird and demented like the guys you tried to protect me from when I was in high school.

I'm going to have a baby in November. This is baby number two. Do you believe that I have a daughter who's two years old? Her name is Julianne. She has curly blond hair and big blue eyes.

I wish you could see her. When she's old enough, I will tell her about her uncle who was diagnosed with cancer when he was 16 years old. I will tell her about your countless surgeries, your radiation treatments, and how you were in a wheelchair for a year before you could get enough strength to walk using a cane and a brace on your right leg.

I will tell her about your 3 a.m. walks, and Dad fixing your car so you could drive using your left foot. I will tell her about how much you loved history and politics and talking. She likes to talk, too.

Sometimes I get lonely. Mom and Dad are clear across the country while you're off in another realm of existence. My in-laws are good to me, but it's not the same as having the family that I grew up in nearby. It would be nice if I could just pick up the phone and talk to you.

I graduated from university a couple of weeks ago. That's why Mom was here. Dad couldn't make it because he is lobster fishing. Can you believe it? Right after I got married, Mom and Dad sold their company, their house, and most of their possessions so they could buy a sailboat. They sailed from Vancouver, down through the Panama Canal and up the east coast where they have settled down.

I graduated with a liberal arts degree. I know you thought I was flaky when I chose to go into arts instead of nursing, but it was a good experience for me. If you were here, we'd have so much more that we could talk about. You're right about me being unemployed when getting out of school, but that's only because I haven't been looking hard

enough for work. It's nice being able to spend time with Julianne. And, with all the health-care cuts in the province, there is no way I would have been able to find a nursing job here.

Ross, my husband, is landscaping for the summer. He has one more semester of university and we are doing everything in our power to make sure he is employed come January. I refuse to starve anymore. You know how I was always, to use your words, "well built" as a teenager? By Christmas, I weighed as much as I did when I was 12 years old. My cheeks were sunken in and my ribs were sticking out. Now, I wasn't anorexic. It was partly due to my sacrificing food so Julianne could eat properly, and partly due to being on the go too much.

Ross and I both went to school full time and we arranged our schedules around one another so we could avoid having Julianne raised in a daycare or by babysitters. My days would start at 6 a.m. and end at 1 or 2 a.m. if I was lucky.

I know that if you were alive you would have thought I was insane for getting married and having a baby while in school, but my hard work did pay off and I am happy to say that I get at least eight hours of sleep a night these days, and Ross is making enough money this summer so we can all eat properly.

Thanks for being out there somewhere. I don't know where you are exactly, but there are times when I feel you near.

And there are times when I see you in my daughter. There are times when I even see you in myself. And I am sure I will see you in the new baby. I still miss you, nothing can change that. Just know that I love you and next time I won't take so long to write.

Love,
Your sister.

You take it from here ...

Responding

1. **Discuss Purpose and Context**   With another student, discuss why the author is writing her deceased brother. Why has she chosen the letter form to communicate with him? (Note: This letter appeared in a newspaper feature that invites readers to "touch others" with their personal stories.) Do you think Jennifer Champion has succeeded in accomplishing this purpose?

2. **Draw Conclusions**   Make a list of the things we learn about the author's life. Does she have a sense of humour? Does she miss Nova Scotia? What is her educational background? Does she sound like a good mother? Describe the lifestyle of Jennifer and her husband.

3. **Explore Personal Feelings**   How can you tell that the brother was an inspiration to his sister? What else does she miss about him? What are some sentences in the letter that reveal her love and respect for him?

Extending

4. **Answer the Letter**   Imagine and write the letter Jennifer's brother might have written to tell her he is proud of the way she turned out.

5. **Write a Personal Response**   Who are three people who have had the most influence on your life? Write an essay with a body paragraph on each person, explaining why they are significant influences on your life.

> **SELF ASSESSMENT**
> - As you did this activity, did you proofread what you wrote?
> - Did you find that one person influenced you more than the others overall?

6. **Do a Personal Inventory**   What are your own special and unique qualities? What values and beliefs do you hold that guide your life? Is there something that many people don't know about you? Write about how you have tried to affect others positively, much like Jennifer and her brother.

Before you read, predict what the memoir will be about based on its title.

As you read, sketch one of the key scenes of the selection.

First Kiss— First Lesson

"You're untrustworthy, you're irresponsible, and you're a disappointment."

Notes

Jennifer Braunschweiger is a journalist whose articles and reviews have appeared in *Mademoiselle*, *Book Magazine*, and *MTV Online*.

Memoir by Jennifer Braunschweiger

It's all right letting yourself go, as long as you can get yourself back.
—Mick Jagger

The night of my first real kiss was also the night of the worst fight I ever had with my mother. I'd had my eye on Jon Glass forever, and suddenly out of nowhere I spied him at the party that my best friend, Lara, and I had finally gathered the courage to stop by. The guy throwing the party lived in a skinny brick house on a crazy steep hill in San Francisco. Light from the kitchen and a streetlight down the block spilled into the little backyard garden, not quite reaching the corner where Jon was standing in a cluster of people. I was wearing my favourite pink shirt and Levi's with patches I'd sewn onto the knees. Lara smoothed my hair and told me to smile and pushed me out the door of the kitchen and into the garden. The next thing I knew, Jon and I were talking and then we were the only people still in the garden and then we were leaving the party together and walking hand in hand up and up the steep street and then we kissed and I felt like I was living someone else's life, I was so happy.

The party was only a couple of blocks from my school, so I knew the streets we walked along as well as I knew the ones in my own neighbourhood. But as I held Jon's hand and we walked and stopped and kissed, I felt like I was seeing the houses and the trees and the world for the first time. In a way I felt as if I were seeing Jon for the first time. Like, before he was just this guy—okay, a very nice guy with amazing pale blue eyes who helped me with my calculus homework and played soccer as if he were born with cleats on his feet—but now here he was picking me a flower off a tree in someone's front yard. We meandered to a nearby park and sat on the swings and looked at the stars. Of course I lost track of time as we roamed around, and when Jon finally dropped me off at my house, the sky was starting to turn light blue and pink with the dawn.

My key had barely hit the lock on the front door when my mother pulled it open and said in her most dangerous and quiet voice, "Where is

he?" Just like that—deadpan. Each word equally weighted, equally heavy: "Where is he?" I stood on the stoop in the early-morning spring cold, yearning to bolt the 10 feet—so close, so far—between me and the safety of my room.

I tried to play dumb. "Who are you talking about, Mom?"

But she just stood there blocking the doorway—hands on hips, face contorted with anger—and said, "You're untrustworthy, you're irresponsible, and you're a disappointment."

Later that day, Lara told me my mom had freaked out and called her at home in the middle of the night. Lara didn't have any idea where I'd gone after I left the party, but she tried to cover for me by saying she was sure I was fine; after all, I was just hanging out with Jon. But that just made my mother worry more ("Jon? Who is Jon?"), and by the time I got home, her worry and stress and churning imagination—combined with her fatigue and relief that I was home safely (no longer wandering the streets in the middle of the night with some strange boy)—finally boiled over, and she exploded at me. I was so shocked at her harsh reaction—shouldn't she be happy that I was actually safe and would no longer have to cope with the shame of never having kissed a boy?—that I screamed right back at her and, after she let me in off the stoop, I slammed my door and flung myself face down on my bed and cried and cried at the grand injustice that was my life.

The next morning at breakfast, I could barely eat. My mom didn't yell anymore—she just told me I couldn't go to the formal citywide dance I'd been looking forward to for months. So I didn't yell anymore either. I just got up from the table and went to my room and called Lara and made plans to have her pick me up for the dance at 7 p.m. that Friday. I didn't care what my mother said, I was going anyway.

The week passed perfectly pleasantly. I went to school, I raced home in time to see *Days of Our Lives*, I fussed around pretending to study, my mom got home late from work, we ate spaghetti and salad, and I silently cleared the table without her asking. When Friday night rolled around, I gathered my formal dress and my favourite heels and my stockings and shoved them into a bag. Then, as soon as the headlights from Lara's car swept into my window as she swung into the driveway, I slipped out the front door and softly pulled it closed behind me. Free.

Jon didn't show up at the dance, but some other cute boys did, and a couple of them talked to me and I was complimented on my purple silk dress and my purple suede shoes and I made sure to stand next to Lara, who looked stunning in something backless and red and short. But I was so racked with guilt for having taken it out on my mother that I just couldn't have the time of my life like I'd anticipated. Afterward, I was scared to go home and face the music, so Lara and I just drove the dark streets of San Francisco aimlessly, with the radio on way too loud, and ended up eating slightly stale muffins at Dunkin' Donuts with a couple of worn-out cops who looked at us like we were crazy delinquents for not being home in bed at such a late hour.

I finally went home and crept under the covers, and in the morning my mother looked upset and didn't really talk to me. In fact, she hadn't really talked to me since our big fight. I guess she didn't know what to do, so she put me on the phone with my father, who was living in Los Angeles at the time. He didn't lose his temper. He just asked, "Why didn't you talk to her about it? Ask her again if you could go to the dance? Tell her you were sorry you were late? Call when you knew you'd be out with Jon?" In other words, why didn't I just think about what I was doing and realize my actions affected other people?

Uh, good question. And I wish I could say that I had a big talk with my mother right after I got off the phone with my father, but I didn't. And the situation got worse before it got better.

The next time I saw Jon outside of school was when I walked into a party just in time to see him disappear into a bedroom with another girl. Her name was Michele, and she was a year younger than me and had a reputation for going too far with too many people. Standing there in the middle of some stranger's sunken living room where people were dancing, I started crying. In a burst of boldness, Lara tried the door of the room Jon and Michele occupied ("I'll interrupt them, and then he'll feel bad and come out," she promised)—but the door was locked. I had lost him. I had never had him.

While I sat in another bedroom and cried and imagined what the two of them were doing together, girls from the party came in and sat with me and told me raunchy men-are-jerks jokes. ("A man asked a genie to make him a billion times smarter than any other man on earth. The genie turned him into a woman.") Eventually, after Jon had finally emerged from the locked bedroom, I confronted him by a swing set in the backyard and made him tell me to my face that he was sorry.

I listened to him say that he didn't want a girlfriend and had a problem with commitment, and I listened to the litany of crimes against his soul: his parents' divorce, the death of his dog, the difficulty of his chemistry class, living in the shadow of his older brother. All the excuses he used seemed pretty lame and beside the point, to tell the truth. In fact, what he offered wasn't an apology at all, and it didn't make me feel any better because nothing really could. (Although, I must admit, I was not unhappy the next week at school when all the girls snubbed Jon because they knew everything that had happened. And I was willing to

listen when his cousin cornered me in an empty classroom and told me that she thought I was too cool for him anyway.)

So things with Jon obviously didn't end perfectly or even anywhere near how I would have liked, but at least I tried to settle things with him and gave him the benefit of listening to his side of the story. It kills me that I cornered Jon—who had betrayed me—and made him talk to me, but I never even gave my mom that chance. So how could I expect her to understand what was at stake for me in staying out late that night, in going to the dance? I owed her—and she owed me—a conversation. But that meant we each would have to articulate what we wanted, we each would have to deal with the other person's needs, and at the time I thought I couldn't deal.

A conversation is a slippery creature. A conversation is a risk. A real conversation changes the people who have it. It's about exchanging ideas, considering other opinions, shifting positions. That's why conversations are so difficult: You risk changing yourself, admitting you were wrong, coming to appreciate the other person's perspective. My mother and I were afraid to have an honest conversation because then she would have to admit her daughter was no longer a baby, was old enough to kiss a boy, wanted to kiss boys. And I would have to admit I was wrong not to call. That I was way later coming home than I'd ever been before. That even though I wanted to kiss boys, I still needed my mom.

Sometimes the whole story replays in my mind like a movie, and I know exactly what to do. Outside by the swing set, I calmly tell Jon how hurt I am, how I feel that he misled and betrayed me, and that I'm sorry about all the stuff he's been through in his life, but it's really no excuse for the way he acted. And instead of being silent at breakfast, I tell my mom how sorry I am to make her worry, but I also tell her why I like Jon so much. I describe how he sits next to me in history class and leans over and doodles on the edge of my notebook and how his shoes are always scuffed and his socks almost never match, and my mom and I laugh together. I mean, what mom's heart isn't going to melt when you tell her about a guy who saves you a seat in class and waves as the boys' soccer team runs by the girls' practice field? And in the new movie, I listen to my mom's side of the story and try to see the situation from her point of view.

It's not like I just settle for everything she tells me, either. When she says that I can't go to the dance, I persist. Ask again. Think about why she says I can't go, reevaluate the situation using my new understanding of where she's coming from, revise my approach, and ask again. When it comes out in our conversation that she doesn't think I deserve to go out because I rarely help out around the house, I do extra chores and ask again. Bring home an A on a tough test and ask again.

What I really wanted in the end wasn't Jon, specifically—obviously, he turned out to be a jerk—but the kind of life where Jon was possible, where my mom wouldn't freak out when I missed curfew, where I could go out with boys without causing a major crisis. And what my mother ultimately wanted wasn't a slave daughter who blindly obeyed her every rule, but a daughter she could rely on and trust and not stay up half the night worrying about. And what I know now is this: If my mom and I had done that deceptively simple thing, talking, negotiating, compromising until we agreed on a set of privileges, then we both would have gotten something we wanted.

You take it from here ...

Responding

1. **Discuss Relevance**   With a classmate, discuss the relevance of this memoir to students today.

2. **Focus on Conflict**   In a group, define the term "generation gap."
   - What are some examples of the generation gap in this selection?
   - What caused the narrator's fight with her mother?
   - Is the conflict finally resolved?
   - What would the narrator have done differently if she could relive the experience?

3. **Write a Moral**   In your notebook, write down a moral (lesson) for the story. Compare your moral with those of a couple of other classmates.

Extending

4. **Compare Two Situations**   In a written response, compare your own experiences with those of the narrator. What agreements or rules, if any, have you had with your parents or guardians to avoid the kind of misunderstanding she describes? How have your actions, by building or breaking trust, affected these agreements?

5. **Design a Brochure**   Create a brochure about first dates for a junior high-school guidance counsellor's office.

6. **Write a Memoir**   Assume a teen magazine is having a writing contest. Write on one of their topics: "My Date from Hell," "I Was So Embarrassed," or "A Party to Remember."

Before you read, tell a partner about the most embarrassing moment you have ever had in public or with your friends in the company of adults.

As you read, write down three details that make the cartoon funny.

First Date

Cartoon by John McPherson

"Oh, look at this! Our little girl coming home from her first date! You kids just go ahead and say good night as though we're not even here!"

You take it from here ...

Responding

1. **Imagine Emotions**   Write a brief paragraph describing the feelings and thoughts of the boy and girl in the cartoon. What would you be feeling in their situation? What feelings do the parents have? What tone of voice would the mother have?

2. **Discuss with a Partner**   With another student, comment on the parents' behaviour and remarks. Are they too involved in their daughter's life? Are they having a negative effect on their daughter and her date? Is there any way these teenagers could pretend the parents aren't there?

3. **Make Predictions**   What do you think will happen next? Do you think the parents' behaviour will affect the daughter's behaviour and choices in the future?

Extending

4. **Give Advice**   As the daughter, write to advice columnist Ann Landers outlining your problem. Then write a reply.

5. **Script Conversation**   Write dialogue for the next meeting between the boy and the girl in the school cafeteria.

6. **Draw a Cartoon**   Make your own cartoon about some aspect of the generation gap.

Before you read, make a list of the qualities you would look for in a mate.

As you read, write in your notebook a list of qualities describing the kind of person you think the author is looking for.

Notes

Allison Mitcham is an author and professor of Canadian, English, and American literature at the Université de Moncton. In 1994 she received the British Columbia Lieutenant Governor's Medal for her book *Taku*.

Berrypicking

Poem by Allison Mitcham

Before choosing a mate
I would need to have him
as my berrypicking companion
all one summer
from the time
of the first wild strawberries
till the cranberries and blackberries
were frost-finished

Then I would know
all about his character

Whether he persevered
despite blackflies and sunburn

    Whether he picked
    the berries clean
    or carelessly
    tore off the leaves as well

    Whether he stayed
    to fill the pail
    or bored
    by the buzzing loneliness
    of field or wood
    left it half-filled
    and went off
    to join the others
    in the house

Whether he worked
with ease and pleasure
at my side
or angry
one day
that I had almost filled my pail
and he had not
pushed my hand
so that my berries
spilled upon the ground
were trampled underfoot

Should he pass
all these natural tests
of berrypicking
I would know
he was just right for me

You take it from here …

Responding

1. **Discuss the Metaphor**   Make a chart relating berrypicking to a person's overall attitudes and behaviour.

Berrypicking reference	What this shows about a person
"Whether he persevered / despite blackflies and sunburn"	can the person be patient and put up with minor difficulties or personal inconvenience?
⌇	⌇

2. **Respond Personally**   In a paragraph, discuss whether you think berrypicking would be a good test of character. Include a comment on the last stanza.

3. **Comment on Structure**   There are three main parts to the poem. With a partner, go over what they are. Does the conclusion logically follow the previous stanzas? Explain.

Extending

4. **Think Metaphorically**   Write a poem based on another metaphor that could be used for assessing the suitability of a partner (e.g., driving a car, painting a fence, using a toothpaste tube, shopping for groceries, bowling).

5. **Design a Report Card**   With a partner, create a report card that could be completed and given to a significant other one month into a relationship.

6. **Conduct a Survey**   Interview several people about the ideal qualities of a mate. What aspects are most important? How relevant are basic values, beliefs, and attitudes? Compile your results and report back to the class.

Before you read, in a group, brainstorm the elements of a good love story.

As you read, make predictions at various points as to what will happen next. What does Newt really want? Will Catharine accept him?

Long Walk to Forever

"What a crazy time to tell me you love me," she said.

Short Story by Kurt Vonnegut, Jr.

Notes

Kurt Vonnegut, Jr., is an American author who is famous for his humour and wit. One of his best-known books is *Slaughterhouse Five* (1969).

A.W.O.L.: absent without leave (a military term)

furlough: approved leave from the military

Scarlett O'Hara: flirtatious heroine of the famous romantic novel and movie *Gone With the Wind*

They had grown up next door to each other, on the fringe of a city, near fields and woods and orchards, within sight of a lovely bell tower that belonged to a school for the blind.

Now they were twenty, had not seen each other for nearly a year. There had always been playful, comfortable warmth between them, but never any talk of love.

His name was Newt. Her name was Catharine. In the early afternoon, Newt knocked on Catharine's front door.

Catharine came to the door. She was carrying a fat, glossy magazine she had been reading. The magazine was devoted entirely to brides. "Newt!" she said. She was surprised to see him.

"Could you come for a walk?" he said. He was a shy person, even with Catharine. He covered his shyness by speaking absently, as though what really concerned him were far away—as though he were a secret agent pausing briefly on a mission between beautiful, distant, and sinister points. This manner of speaking had always been Newt's style, even in matters that concerned him desperately.

"A walk?" said Catharine.

"One foot in front of the other," said Newt, "through leaves, over bridges—"

"I had no idea you were in town," she said.

"Just this minute got in," he said.

"Still in the Army, I see," she said.

"Seven more months to go," he said. He was a private first class in the Artillery. His uniform was rumpled. His shoes were dusty. He needed a shave. He held out his hand for the magazine. "Let's see the pretty book," he said.

She gave it to him. "I'm getting married, Newt," she said.

"I know," he said. "Let's go for a walk."

"I'm awfully busy, Newt," she said. "The wedding is only a week away."

"If we go for a walk," he said, "it will make you rosy. It will make you a rosy bride." He turned the pages of the magazine. "A rosy bride like her—like her—like her," he said, showing her rosy brides.

Catharine turned rosy, thinking about rosy brides.

"That will be my present to Henry Stewart Chasens," said Newt. "By taking you for a walk, I'll be giving him a rosy bride."

"You know his name?" said Catharine.

"Mother wrote," he said. "From Pittsburgh?"

"Yes," she said. "You'd like him."

"Maybe," he said.

"Can—can you come to the wedding, Newt?" she said.

"That I doubt," he said.

"Your furlough isn't for long enough?" she said.

"Furlough?" said Newt. He was studying a two-page ad for flat silver. "I'm not on furlough," he said.

"Oh?" she said.

"I'm what they call A.W.O.L.," said Newt.

"Oh, Newt! You're not!" she said.

"Sure I am," he said, still looking at the magazine.

"Why, Newt?" she said.

"I had to find out what your silver pattern is," he said. He read names of silver patterns from the magazine. "Albemarle? Heather?" he said. "Legend? Rambler Rose?" He looked up, smiled. "I plan to give you and your husband a spoon," he said.

"Newt, Newt—tell me really," she said.

"I want to go for a walk," he said.

She wrung her hands in sisterly anguish. "Oh, Newt—you're fooling me about being A.W.O.L.," she said.

Newt imitated a police siren softly, raised his eyebrows.

"Where—where from?" she said.

"Fort Bragg," he said.

"North Carolina?" she said.

"That's right," he said. "Near Fayetteville—where Scarlett O'Hara went to school."

"How did you get here, Newt?" she said.

He raised his thumb, jerked it in a hitch-hike gesture. "Two days," he said.

"Does your mother know?" she said.

"I didn't come to see my mother," he told her.

"Who did you come to see?" she said.

"You," he said.

"Why me?" she said.

"Because I love you," he said. "Now can we take a walk?" he said. "One foot in front of the other—through leaves, over bridges—"

They were taking the walk now, were in a woods with a brown-leaf floor.

Catharine was angry and rattled, close to tears. "Newt," she said, "this is absolutely crazy."

"How so?" said Newt.

"What a crazy time to tell me you love me," she said. "You never talked that way before." She stopped walking.

"Let's keep walking," he said.

"No," she said. "So far, no farther. I shouldn't have come out with you at all," she said.

"You did," he said.

"To get you out of the house," she said. "If somebody walked in and heard you talking to me that way, a week before the wedding—"

"What would they think?" he said.

"They'd think you were crazy," she said.

"Why?" he said.

Catharine took a deep breath, made a speech. "Let me say that I'm deeply honoured by this crazy thing you've done," she said. "I can't

believe you're really A.W.O.L., but maybe you are. I can't believe you really love me, but maybe you do. But—"

"I do," said Newt.

"Well, I'm deeply honoured," said Catharine, "and I'm very fond of you as a friend, Newt, extremely fond—but it's just too late." She took a step away from him. "You've never even kissed me," she said, and she protected herself with her hands. "I don't mean you should do it now. I just mean this is all so unexpected. I haven't got the remotest idea of how to respond."

"Just walk some more," he said. "Have a nice time."

They started walking again.

"How did you expect me to react?" she said.

"How would I know what to expect?" he said. "I've never done anything like this before."

"Did you think I would throw myself into your arms?" she said.

"Maybe," he said.

"I'm sorry to disappoint you," she said.

"I'm not disappointed," he said. "I wasn't counting on it. This is very nice, just walking."

Catharine stopped again. "You know what happens next?" she said.

"Nope," he said.

"We shake hands," she said. "We shake hands and part friends," she said. "That's what happens next."

Newt nodded. "All right," he said. "Remember me from time to time. Remember how much I loved you."

Involuntarily, Catharine burst into tears. She turned her back to Newt, looked into the infinite colonnade of the woods.

"What does that mean?" said Newt.

"Rage!" said Catharine. She clenched her hands. "You have no right—"

"I had to find out," he said.

"If I'd loved you," she said, "I would have let you know before now."

"You would?" he said.

"Yes," she said. She faced him, looked up at him, her face quite red. "You would have known," she said.

"How?" he said.

"You would have seen it," she said. "Women aren't very clever at hiding it."

Newt looked closely at Catharine's face now. To her consternation, she realized that what she had said was true, that a woman couldn't hide love.

Newt was seeing love now.

And he did what he had to do. He kissed her.

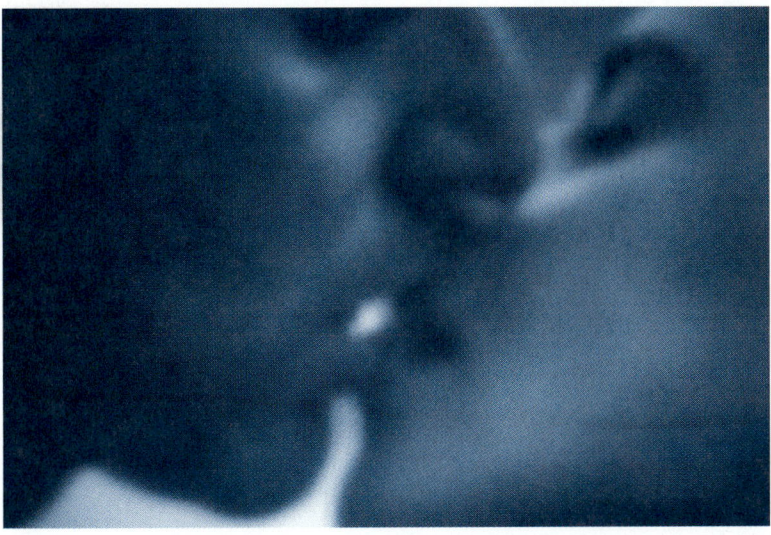

"You're hell to get along with!" she said when Newt let her go.

"I am?" said Newt.

"You shouldn't have done that," she said.

"You didn't like it?" he said.

"What did you expect," she said—"wild, abandoned passion?"

"I keep telling you," he said, "I never know what's going to happen next."

"We say goodbye," she said.

He frowned slightly. "All right," he said.

She made another speech. "I'm not sorry we kissed," she said. "That was sweet. We should have kissed, we've been so close. I'll always remember you, Newt, and good luck."

"You too," he said.

"Thank you, Newt," she said.

"Thirty days," he said.

"What?" she said.

"Thirty days in the stockade," he said—"that's what one kiss will cost me."

"I—I'm sorry," she said, "but I didn't ask you to go A.W.O.L."

"I know," he said.

"You certainly don't deserve any hero's reward for doing something as foolish as that," she said.

"Must be nice to be a hero," said Newt. "Is Henry Stewart Chasens a hero?"

"He might be, if he got the chance," said Catharine. She noted uneasily that they had begun to walk again. The farewell had been forgotten.

"You really love him?" he said.

"Certainly I love him!" she said hotly. "I wouldn't marry him if I didn't love him!"

"What's good about him?" said Newt.

"Honestly!" she cried, stopping again. "Do you have any idea how offensive you're being? Many, many, many things are good about Henry! Yes," she said, "and many, many, many things are probably bad too. But that isn't any of your business. I love Henry, and I don't have to argue his merits with you!"

"Sorry," said Newt.

"Honestly!" said Catharine.

Newt kissed her again. He kissed her again because she wanted him to.

They were now in a large orchard.

"How did we get so far from home, Newt?" said Catharine.

"One foot in front of the other—through leaves, over bridges," said Newt.

"They add up—the steps," she said.

Bells rang in the tower of the school for the blind nearby.

"School for the blind," said Newt.

"School for the blind," said Catharine. She shook her head in drowsy wonder. "I've got to go back now," she said.

"Say goodbye," said Newt.

"Every time I do," said Catharine, "I seem to get kissed."

Newt sat down on the close-cropped grass under an apple tree. "Sit down," he said.

"No," she said.

"I won't touch you," he said.

"I don't believe you," she said.

She sat down under another tree, twenty feet away from him. She closed her eyes.

"Dream of Henry Stewart Chasens," he said.

"What?" she said.

"Dream of your wonderful husband-to-be," he said.

"All right, I will," she said. She closed her eyes tighter, caught glimpses of her husband-to-be.

Newt yawned.

The bees were humming in the trees, and Catharine almost fell asleep. When she opened her eyes she saw that Newt really was asleep.

He began to snore softly.

Catharine let Newt sleep for an hour, and while he slept she adored him with all her heart.

The shadows of the apple trees grew to the east. The bells in the tower of the school for the blind rang again.

"*Chick-a-dee-dee-dee,*" went a chickadee.

Somewhere far away an automobile starter nagged and failed, nagged and failed, fell still.

Catharine came out from under her tree, knelt by Newt.

"Newt?" she said.

"H'm?" he said. He opened his eyes.

"Late," she said.

"Hello, Catharine," he said.

"Hello, Newt," she said.

"I love you," he said.

"I know," she said.

"Too late," he said.

"Too late," she said.

He stood, stretched groaningly. "A very nice walk," he said.

"I thought so," she said.

"Part company here?" he said.

"Where will you go?" she said.

"Hitch into town, turn myself in," he said.

"Good luck," she said.

"You, too," he said. "Marry me, Catharine?"

"No," she said.

He smiled, stared at her hard for a moment, then walked away quickly.

Catharine watched him grow smaller in the long perspective of shadows and trees, knew that if he stopped and turned now, if he called to her, she would run to him. She would have no choice.

Newt did stop. He did turn. He did call. "Catharine," he called.

She ran to him, put her arms around him, could not speak.

You take it from here ...

Responding

1. **Establish Criteria** As a class, discuss how true love might be defined. Do Catharine and Newt experience true love? Comment.

2. **Discuss Conventions** In a small group, identify some *conventions* (rules or typical features) of a love story. Does this story conform to the conventions or does it "break the rules"? Discuss with references to dialogue and behaviour in the story.

3. **Explain Motivation** In a paragraph, review character motivation.
   - Why has Newt come to see Catharine at this time? What is his goal?
   - Why does Catharine go walking with Newt? Why does she run to him at the end of the story?
   - How does Newt convince Catharine that he really loves her?

4. **Evaluate a Decision** In a class discussion, consider whether or not Catharine makes the right decision. Give reasons to back up your opinion. If you were Catharine, would you have made the same choice?

5. **Interpret the Title** With another student, discuss the author's choice of title. What does it mean? How does it relate to the story's events?

Extending

6. **Write an Announcement** Draft a list of information that is found on a typical wedding announcement. Using your list as a guide, write a newspaper announcement for the wedding of Catharine and Newt.

7. **Improvise a Conversation** Imagine that Catharine and Newt return home to find her fiancé, Henry, and Catharine's mother waiting for them. In groups of four, improvise a conversation among them. Be creative when generating your dialogue.

> **PEER ASSESSMENT**
> - What did you think of the improv?
> - What did you think of the group's performance? Were they convincing?

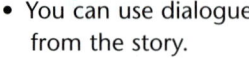

TIP
- You can use dialogue from the story.

8. **Create a Storyboard** Consider how you would present this story as a movie. Draw at least three frames showing one of the scenes.

Before you read, as a class, discuss the different ways in which people can express their love for another person.

As you read, paraphrase what the poem says.

"How do I love thee?"

Poem by Elizabeth Barrett Browning

Notes

Elizabeth Barrett Browning (1806–1861) was a famous English Victorian poet who was married to an equally famous poet, Robert Browning. In her youth, Elizabeth was an invalid because of a spinal injury and was kept secluded from the world by her possessive father. Robert met her in 1845, and for both it was "love at first sight." They both realized, however, that her father would never accept their relationship, so they eloped, married, and settled in Italy.

"How do I love thee?" is Sonnet 43 in the series know as *Sonnets from the Portuguese*.

How do I love thee? Let me count the ways.
I love thee to the depth and breadth and height
My soul can reach, when feeling out of sight
For the ends of Being and ideal Grace.
I love thee to the level of everyday's
Most quiet need, by sun and candlelight.
I love thee freely, as men strive for Right;
I love thee purely, as they turn from Praise.
I love thee with the passion put to use
In my old griefs, and with my childhood's faith.
I love thee with a love I seemed to lose
With my lost saints,—I love thee with the breath,
Smiles, tears, of all my life!—and, if God choose,
I shall but love thee better after death.

You take it from here ...

Responding

1. **Understand the Purpose**   Read the sidebar information about the poet. Why do you think she wrote the poem? Compare observations with another student.

2. **Analyze Form**   A sonnet is a 14-line *lyric* poem (lyric poems express deep feelings). There are two common forms of sonnets:

   a) *Elizabethan (Shakespearean)*: with end-line rhymes AB-AB-CD-CD-EF-EF-GG. The last two lines are called a rhyming couplet.
   b) *Italian (Petrarchan)*: with end-line rhymes ABBA-ABBA-CDE-CDE.

   Which of the two forms does this poem most closely resemble? Why do you think Browning changed the pattern in the second half? Why is the sonnet a good choice for a serious, reflective love poem? Discuss with a partner.

3. **Discuss Poem's Relevance**   With a partner, consider whether this poem from the nineteenth century is still relevant to us in the twenty-first century. Do you think this poem would be appropriate to read at a modern wedding ceremony? Explain.

Extending

4. **Assemble an Anthology**   Find and copy several poems or song lyrics that "speak to you" about the meaning of love. Assemble them into an illustrated collection.

5. **Research an Author**   Find out more about Elizabeth Barrett Browning. What was her life like? How did Robert court her? Why did she elope and move to Italy? Was her marriage a happy one? Share your findings with the class.

6. **Illustrate the Poem**   Responding to the images in the poem, draw a picture suitable for an anthology like this one.

> **TIP**
> - Illustrate your collection with your own artwork, or use images from magazines or a computer clip art collection.

Before you read, look up the word "parody." Write a definition of it in your notebook.

As you read, jot down your thoughts about how Snoopy's poem is a parody.

Peanuts

Cartoon by Charles M. Schulz

Notes

Charles M. Schulz (1922–2000) was the most famous and beloved American cartoonist. His comic strip, *Peanuts*, ran for almost 50 years.

You take it from here ...

Responding

1. **Discuss Purpose and Audience** Exchange views with a partner about why Schulz drew this cartoon. To which audience do you think it would appeal?

2. **Explain the Humour** In a paragraph, explain why the cartoon is funny. Refer to both the visuals and the language.

3. **Continue the Cartoon** Add another frame or two to the cartoon, or write a humorous reply from the Ex-Sweetheart.

Extending

4. **Create Your Own Parody** Write your own "take-off" of "How do I love thee" or another famous poem such as William Carlos Williams' "The Red Wheelbarrow" ("So much depends upon ...") or Joyce Kilmer's "Trees" ("I think that I shall never see ...").

5. **Listen to a Song** Many songs have been written on the theme of saying goodbye to a loved one. Find and listen to Paul Simon's "Fifty Ways to Leave Your Lover." What different ways to "say goodbye" does Simon include in his song? Has he missed any?

6. **Make a Video** Work in groups to shoot a video based on Browning's poem, or write your own extended version of Snoopy's poem in the cartoon, and then make the video.

> **GROUP ASSESSMENT**
> - Discuss what it was like to work on this project. What things would you have changed had you more time?

Before you read, identify who Tracy Chapman is. What are some of her famous songs?

As you read, think about the title. Why does the song repeatedly refer to a fast car?

Notes

Tracy Chapman is a Black American singer and songwriter. Her first album debuted in 1988 to critical acclaim. Her album, *Telling Stories*, was released in 2000.

Fast Car

Lyrics by Tracy Chapman

You got a fast car
I want a ticket to anywhere
Maybe we make a deal
Maybe together we can get somewhere
Anyplace is better
Starting from zero got nothing to lose
Maybe we'll make something
But me myself I got nothing to prove

You got a fast car
And I got a plan to get us out of here
I been working at the convenience store
Managed to save just a little bit of money
We won't have to drive too far
Just 'cross the border and into the city
You and I can both get jobs
And finally see what it means to be living

You see my old man's got a problem
He lives with the bottle that's the way it is
He says his body's too old for working
I say his body's too young to look like his
My mama went off and left him
She wanted more from life than he could give
I said somebody's got to take care of him
So I quit school and that's what I did

Fast Car **293**

You got a fast car
But is it fast enough so we can fly away
We gotta make a decision
We leave tonight or live and die this way

I remember we were driving, driving in your car
The speed so fast I felt like I was drunk
City lights lay out before us
And your arm felt nice wrapped 'round my shoulder
And I had a feeling that I belonged
And I had a feeling I could be someone, be someone, be someone

You got a fast car
And we go cruising to entertain ourselves
You still ain't got a job
And I work in a market as a checkout girl
I know things will get better
You'll find work and I'll get promoted
We'll move out of the shelter
Buy a big house and live in the suburbs

You got a fast car
And I got a job that pays all our bills
You stay out drinking late at the bar
See more of your friends than you do of your kids
I'd always hoped for better
Thought maybe together you and me would find it
I got no plans I ain't going nowhere
So take your fast car and keep on driving

You got a fast car
But is it fast enough so you can fly away
You gotta make a decision
You leave tonight or live and die this way

You take it from here ...

Responding

1. **Discuss Conflict**   As a class, consider the following:
   a) Is the relationship between this young couple realistic? What problems do they have? What circumstances limit them?
   b) What were the original goals and plans of the speaker? How have these been frustrated?
   c) What problems does the speaker have with her partner? What does she want him to do?

2. **Explain the Title**   In a paragraph, analyze the title, referring to the conflicts in the speaker's life. What does the fast car symbolize to her?

3. **Respond to the Speaker**   Discuss with a partner what the speaker's life has been like. Is she to be pitied or admired? Do you think she will achieve her goal? Why or why not?

4. **Consider Relevance**   This song is about achieving one's dreams and hopes for a better life. What sort of dreams do you have? In 10 years, what do you see yourself as having accomplished? What action will you have to take to achieve these dreams? Write your response in your journal.

Extending

5. **Write a Letter**   Assume that the speaker finally breaks down and leaves home with the children. Write the letter she leaves for her partner.

6. **Create a Collage**   Using cut-out pictures from magazines, make a collage to illustrate the conflicts in this song.

7. **Script a Video of the Song**   Plan a video version of "Fast Car," making a chart first to organize your thoughts on the video.

Lines from song	*Visual images to illustrate the lines*

Before you read, tell the class about couples you know who have been married for many years. Why do you suppose their marriages have lasted so long?

As you read, form an impression of what Frank's problems are.

Remember Africa?

"We've sure had a good life together."

Narrative Essay by Jo Beth McDaniel

Notes

Jo Beth McDaniel is a journalist and author living in Long Beach, California. Ruth and Frank are her great aunt and great uncle.

"Who are you?" Frank demanded when Ruth walked into the room. She sighed and eased gently down on the bed next to him, folding his age-shrunken hand in hers. He recoiled from her uncertainly, fear widening his eyes.

"I'm Ruth, your wife," she said, forcing a polite smile and patting his hand.

His eyebrows shot upward as he bolted upright in bed. "Wife?"

"We've been married forty years, Frank."

"No." Frank shook his head vigorously. "No. I don't remember you."

Ruth nodded and closed her eyes. It was a conversation they had had nearly every day during the past few months. The illness had not much weakened Frank's body, but his mind faded, day to day, like colour from an oft-washed cloth.

"That's okay, dear," Ruth answered. "I love you whether you know me or not." She adjusted the pillow between his back and the wooden headboard, then straightened the covers around his waist. "Oh Frank, we've had so many wonderful years. We've sure had a good life together."

He smiled back at her tentatively, eyes still clouded in confusion.

"Was I a good husband?"

She chuckled. "You devil," she said, pinching his cheek softly. "The best. You were always kind and gentle and lots of fun. Even now, you try, don't you?"

He nodded. Her words seemed to reassure him. He looked around the room, as if desperately searching for clues. "Our family …?"

Ruth hesitated. "We never had children, Frank. We tried, but we couldn't. But we have so many friends and loved ones. You've lived eighty-two good, long years now. People have always loved you, Frank. And you've touched so many lives."

"Hmmm."

296 Relationships

He nodded, but his eyes kept that faraway gaze, unable to connect with any familiar faces. "Well, what did we do?"

"Well, mister, we worked. We worked hard and we built up your family business and we went to church and we enjoyed ourselves just fine. And we travelled all over the world."

"Oh?" His eyes danced, just a flicker of light. "Where?"

"Everywhere, Frank. We went to so many beautiful places. Do you remember Edinburgh, Frank? The castles and the countryside of Scotland? You loved how green it was, even when we were freezing. And you wore this silly plaid cap that made me laugh." She searched his eyes, but the light had passed.

Frank slipped back down on the pillow and stared at the ceiling. His profile was nearly the same as her first sight of him forty years earlier, as he stood in her doorway, coming to pick her up for a ride to church camp. When she opened that door, his eyes had grown wide with interest, and he gave her that devilish grin she'd come to love so much. Now his mouth was drawn tight, grim with irritation.

"And Japan. Remember Tokyo, Frank? Remember the lights and those crowded streets, and the temples? How you bought all those tiny mechanical toys, and the radio as small as your fingernail?"

She held up his hand to show him, but his eyes were squeezed tight, his mind fruitlessly searching for his memories. He shook his head, a frown deepening on his face.

A moment passed. He blinked and stared at her again, at the face he had awakened to every morning for forty years.

His eyes narrowed. "Who are you?" he asked, his voice edged with fear.

She drew a long, steady breath, looking into his bewildered eyes. "Africa, Frank," she said slowly. She took his hand back, gripping it tightly. "Do you remember our travels through Africa?"

"Africa ..." he repeated quietly.

"We saw animals ..." she ventured softly.

"Lions ..." he answered. She sat silently, waiting.

"We saw lions," he said, pulling himself up slowly beside her. "We sat in the Land Rover and the lions were surrounding us, coming right up to us. And there were elephants, and a huge one with the huge tusk that came crashing out of the bush right at us ..."

Ruth nodded, smiling back at him.

"You were there with me. You were sitting next to me." His eyes were clearing, shining: she could feel the tears begin to well in her own.

"And the flamingoes," he said, his voice rising. "We stood at the edge of the lake and watched them fly. There were so many of them, it was just like a pink cloud rising up from the water."

His words slowed, and his eyes closed.

"Frank ..." she said, and he sat still, not moving, not answering.

"Frank, remember the night in Uganda, when the children sang to us? We were in that little village near the river ..."

"The children! Yes," he said, opening his eyes again. "They were so young, so sweet ..."

"And their round little faces all lit up ..."

"... they were all holding candles! And afterward, we ate in that man's home, with the dirt floor. We sat in the candlelight, and they brought us the food in those huge black bowls ..."

"Remember how strange that food looked?"

Frank laughed, then groaned. "We didn't know if it was raw, or worms, or what. And, and ... were we with missionaries?"

She nodded. "Yes, we were visiting missionaries who had a church in the village."

"Yes, yes," he said. "I can see them now. And the missionary told us how he prayed before he ate. He prayed, 'Lord, I'll put it down if you keep it down!'"

As they laughed, she took in every detail—the blueness of his eyes, the curve of his cheekbones, the wrinkles surrounding his smile.

Then Frank looked toward the window, where sunlight streamed in through a crack in the curtains. "Ruth," he asked worriedly. "Why am I in bed so late this morning?"

"You're not well today, Frank."

"I am feeling tired," he said, yawning. He slid back down onto his pillow, smiling dreamily up at her. "Ruth, what were those waterfalls?"

"Victoria Falls?"

"Yes. Victoria Falls. Ruth, I remember standing there, feeling the spray from the falls, and you were scared and holding onto my arm so tight. And you said it was the most beautiful sight you had ever seen. And I told you no, you were still more beautiful to me."

He curled up and kissed her softly on the cheek. She was shaking, holding as tight to his arm as she had at the edge of the falls.

"And you still are beautiful."

"You are something else, mister," she laughed.

"I love you, Ruth."

"And I love you, Frank."

His eyes were blinking, fading.

"Why don't you dream about those waterfalls?" Ruth said. "I'll be right here."

With that, he gave a sigh and relaxed, his sparse grey hair flattening against the pillow.

Ruth pulled the covers up around his chest and kissed him, listening to his breath rise and fall. His mind was drifting back in the fog, away from her and the world they had shared. When he woke, he would again recoil from her. And she knew the sight of his face and the warmth of his skin were a gift, a brief glimpse too soon lost to memory. Someday, even the vast continent would not have the power to bring him back to her.

You take it from here ...

Responding

1. **Describe a Relationship**   With a partner, review the essential facts of Ruth and Frank's marriage. Why does Ruth continue to encourage Frank? How has Frank remained the same despite his problems? Does Frank remember anything of the past? What is special and remarkable about their relationship?

2. **Focus on Theme and Purpose**   As a class, discuss the main idea presented by the selection. Then, think about why the writer chose to write about her Aunt Ruth and Uncle Frank.

3. **Tell about a Favourite Moment**   Quote a passage that you found moving or humorous. In a brief written response, tell why you liked the passage. What does it reveal about human nature or the human spirit?

Extending

4. **Research a Topic**   Find out what you can about human memory and related topics, for example, Alzheimer's disease, or how to improve memory. Then share your findings with the class in the form of an illustrated article or an oral presentation.

5. **Conduct an Interview**   Talk to an elderly person about his or her favourite memory, and retell the story for the class.

6. **Recall a Memory**   Write about your own favourite moment or relationship from the past.

> **SELF ASSESSMENT**
> - Check the sentences in your memoir. Did you use a variety of sentences? Are there any sentences that can be clarified or made less awkward?

Reflecting on the Unit

Responding

1. **Give a Speech**   Review the selections in this unit and notice the different views on the family that are presented. Look up a quotation about the family in a dictionary of quotations. Use that quotation as your introduction in an oral presentation titled "The Importance of Family Today."

2. **Write a Letter**   Write to the editors of this anthology telling what you thought about the relationships included in this unit. Were there any that you feel were omitted and should be included in a next edition?

Extending

> **TIPS**
> - Decide who they will write to.
> - Use information from the selection in which the characters appear for clues on what they would talk about.

3. **Make Postcards**   Create two postcards from different characters in the unit selections.

4. **Design a Guide**   Put together a guide identifying the key steps to creating and enjoying positive relationships. Present the information as a talk show, a how-to manual or brochure, a magazine article, or another format of your choice.

> **SELF ASSESSMENT**
>
> Review what you have learned from this unit regarding
> - speaking, listening, and representing skills
> - how to use specific evidence to back up points or ideas
> - how to interact positively with others in group situations
> - how to make choices to get an assignment or task done
> - how to access, select, and organize information relevant to research
> - how to respond critically to a variety of texts

UNIT 7

"Youth comes but once in a lifetime."
–Henry Wadsworth Longfellow

"People are always talking about the joys of youth—but, oh, how youth can suffer!"
–Willa Cather

"Youth is, after all, just for a moment, but it is the moment, the spark that you always carry in your heart."
–Raisa M. Gorbachev

Youth—the Awakening Years

This unit focuses on coming of age and the experiences of adolescence.

American poet Henry Wadsworth Longfellow's words set the tone by observing that youth is a temporary time of life—intense, memorable, and relatively brief.

Author Willa Cather reminds us that youth is a time of limitations as well as limitless possibilities. To be young is not to be without problems; teenagers are not immune to the stresses and obstacles faced by adults.

The last word goes to Raisa Gorbachev, former First Lady of the Soviet Union, who reminds us of the importance of keeping the vitality, curiosity, and enthusiasm of youth alive all through life.

As you read this unit, think about the following:

1) What are the basic values, beliefs, and ideals of youth today?
2) What are the experiences that make youth so special and exciting?
3) What are the problems and concerns of youth today?
4) What influences are exerted by parents, adults, and elders?
5) What goals and ideals are worth striving for and celebrating?

> **Before you read,** as a class, discuss the basic values, beliefs, and goals of teenagers today.
>
> **As you read,** write down three points or observations that reflect how you feel about the world. Add three more of your own.

It is the best of times to be a young teenager. And the most difficult of times.

Designer Teens
by Ian Haysom

NEWSPAPER ARTICLE

The three 13-year-old boys are huddled around a video game in an arcade in a suburban bowling alley, their eyes glued to the screen as characters in army fatigues battle one another with kicks, punches, machetes, machine guns, and rocket launchers.

"Kill him, kill him," cries one of the three, a gangly red-haired boy in a Nike sweatshirt, as a yellow-clad opponent tries to flatten the action hero. The smallest of the three boys, the one at the game's controls, coolly dispatches the enemy with an axe.

"I kicked his butt," he says, unsmiling. "I really HATE that jerk."

A similar scene is playing around the arcade, in other arcades, in front of home computers and on TV screens across Canada. Today's pre-pubescent boys get some of their biggest kicks blowing up enemies in such war games as Doom, Die Hard, Command and Conquer, and Mech Warrior 2 that horrify parents.

The blurb on the cover of Mech Warrior 2 is especially disquieting to any baby-boomer parent who grew up in a peace and love era: War is Life. And Death is the only True Peace.

Later, when the boys are asked why they play the game, they offer few profound insights. "It's neat." "It's fun." "It's challenging." Do their parents like them playing the games? All three roll their eyes. Like, who cares?

We have never seen anything like the teens and pre-teens of today. If the 1950s created the teenage phenomenon, complete with its own language—square, daddy-o, far out, cool, and creep—its own music and its anti-anything-adult philosophy, the 1990s have brought us an increasingly sophisticated, savvy, high-tech, designer-dressed, and independent form of the species.

Today's young people possess some of the most sophisticated consumer skills in the country, care passionately about clothes and about their body image, and fret about their self-esteem. They yearn for $120 Nike Air shoes, insist on such designer labels as Tommy Hilfiger, Calvin Klein, Nautica, DKNY, and Polo. The girls want to be skinny. The boys want to muscle up.

They play video games, mostly violent, preferably on Sony Playstations, watch *The X-Files*, *Fresh Prince of Bel Air*, and *The Simpsons* on TV, and Jim Carrey, Arnold Schwarzenegger, and Demi Moore in the movies. The average Canadian teenager sees 30 000 TV commercials a year.

They use computers and access the Internet with consummate ease. They listen to the Beastie Boys, the angst of Alanis Morissette and PJ Harvey, gangsta rap, and by the age of 15 have usually travelled to at least one exotic holiday destination.

They want stuff. Lots of stuff. Lots of brand new stuff. In the 1960s, teenagers rebelled against materialism. Today, their kids are embracing it with a passion.

It is the best of times to be a young teenager. And the most difficult of times.

Today's pre-pubescents are confronted with the most challenging problems of any teenage generation in the last 40 years: AIDS, drugs, violence, abortion, urban crime, broken families, pollution. And, perhaps, the scariest of them all, fear of an uncertain future.

In the 1960s, few teens worried about getting jobs. Today, it has become an obsession. Where will they work? Will they work? Twenty years ago, nobody talked about teenage suicide or teenage self-esteem as pressing social issues. Today, they are part of the fabric of growing up. Everything's bad for you.

Diane O'Connor, a psychologist with the [Toronto] Board of Education, says today's teenage society has more stress and less meaning than ever before.

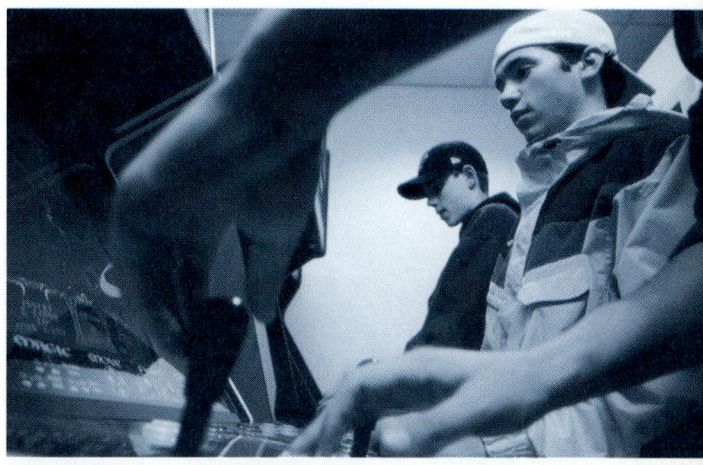

"It worries me what we're doing to young people. There are very few places for them to go except in front of a TV or a video screen, where they're exposed to increasingly violent images, where materialism is the most important value that they are continually presented with.

"I think that we have to look at our overall values in respect to teenagers. We have told them that $100 Nike running shoes are the norm. We have allowed violence to pervade TV screens.

"We have removed the relaxing atmosphere from life. We give our children very little peace, very little simplicity. We just keep giving them more and more. I think it's time we started looking at our values as a society when it comes to teenagers. We've let it get out of hand."

Alan Reynar, director of Active Parenting, a Medicine Hat–based national parenting program, agrees. Too many teens and preteens are raising themselves, he says, with diminishing parental involvement. Two parents working and single-parent families—another phenomenon almost unheard of 30 years ago—have put enormous pressures on today's teens, he says.

"Parents have to get involved in their children's lives again. We have to help them make realistic, wise choices. Nowadays,

teenagers' friends have a greater influence than any parent."

Reynar echoes the disquiet many parents feel about today's teenage trends: the obsession with body image; the massive importance of fashion; the increasingly violent and sexual TV and video images; increased drug and alcohol use; the questionable content on the Internet; the increasing materialism that is creating what he calls "the designer child."

"We are not allowing children to be children any longer," he says. "Kids are growing up more quickly now than at any time in recent history. Too many parents are allowing young minds to become endangered without setting guidelines, without giving some kind of perspective.

"I find the present situation scary. I think society has to take a major step back and examine what we're doing to our children."

Yet today's teens have inherited some of their parents' social activism. Widespread vegetarianism among teens is a phenomenon of this decade. While the commonplace 1990s teenage stereotype may suggest a high-tech, fashion-and-money obsessed cyberteen, thousands of young Canadians are going to youth workshops, participating in environmental cleanups, joining music and drama groups, working hard at school and on weekend jobs at shopping malls and service stations.

The discomfort many of today's parents feel about their kids may just be part of the nature of things. Didn't 1950s parents worry about boys on motorbikes and 1960s parents worry about girls on the pill? Every generation has its challenges and its generation gaps.

Deborah Senior, coordinator of the Youth Action Network, a Toronto-based national youth organization, says, for instance, that tens of thousands of teens will participate in 1500 events—from highway cleanups to human rights youth conferences—in Youth Week across Canada this May.

Young people, she says, are more informed than any of their predecessors but have a growing mistrust of the systems and processes in Canada.

"Many of them are worried about getting meaningful work in the future. That's probably the biggest concern of all."

Senior says that the current obsession for materialism is understandable "because that's where many teenagers feel a sense of validation. It's an escape.

"For us, the challenge now is to get teenagers to think of themselves as global citizens, as having a role to play in the future, not just about the here and now."

Opreek Kang, a 19-year-old student who sits on a youth advisory council for the McCreary Centre Society, a Vancouver-based youth health organization, says today's teenagers are living through a much more difficult period than their parents imagine. They are given little respect. And they feel they're not an important part of society's agenda.

"Youth doesn't fit into one overall stereotype. There are many subcultures now. Mainstream youth. Gay youth. Immigrant youth. But all youth, to some extent, feel discriminated against, mistrusted."

For instance, she says, few young people can go into a mall today without feeling that they're instant shoplifting suspects. Her advisory council has prepared pamphlets it will give to store operators that ask them to treat teens with respect.

"Nowadays, teenagers have plenty of concerns their parents didn't have to worry about. They have major job concerns. They worry about safety, about getting from one place to another without being harmed.

"They worry about body image. Girls are encouraged, almost forced, to look incredibly slim by the images on TV and in magazines. Boys have to head for the gym to get big muscles.

"Teens are also part of an increasingly wealthy society. They expect to wear name brands, expect to have their own cars when they're 16. There's nowhere for them to hang out, very few places that offer safe fun."

For all that, she says, youth are having a good time. "I can't honestly say it's an overwhelmingly bad time. It's just more difficult than it's ever been before."

Forty years ago, teenagers worried about acne. Today's kids should be so lucky.

"You're always pressured to get the new clothes," says 13-year-old Tomas Bush of Vancouver, sporting a Nike track suit.

"You're kind of a geek if you aren't wearing the latest trend. You've kind of got to fit in. That's what it's all about, isn't it?"

You take it from here ...

Responding

1. **Make Connections** In a small group, share the observations you noted while reading. Arrive at a consensus of five key values, beliefs, and goals of teens today. Share these with the rest of the class.

2. **Discuss Advertising and Marketing Influences** With a classmate, discuss specific brands referred to in this selection. What are some other ones that are popular with young people today? In what way are brand names or designer labels status symbols? Can you tell what a person is like by the logo on her or his shirt, jeans, or shoes? Comment.

3. **Focus on Context**   In a small group, discuss the following questions:
   a) According to the article, how are young people today different from the 1960s generation?
   b) What are some social and ecological problems that need to be addressed? What are some positive steps being taken?
   c) According to Diane O'Connor, is our society becoming too violent? Is violence having a negative impact on youth today?
   d) According to Alan Reynar, what pressures are put on teens?
   e) Summarize Deborah Senior's opinions on youth.
   f) How do Opreek Kang's views on young people differ from those of the other people interviewed? In what ways does she speak on behalf of teens?

> **GROUP ASSESSMENT**
> - What did your group learn about using support from the text to back up opinions?
> - How did the group stay on task when a disagreement occurred?

Extending

4. **Have a Panel Discussion**   With two or three other students, prepare a panel presentation to the class on the main problems facing youth today, and suggest some solutions.

5. **Compose a Poem**   Write a poem or lyrics expressing your own views and feelings about what it means to be a teenager today.

6. **Draft a Letter to the Editor**   This selection originally appeared in a newspaper. Draft a letter responding to the article for the newspaper's Letters to the Editor page.

Before you read, tell the class about a time you overcame fear to do something challenging or risky.

As you read, sketch a picture of a scene described in the poem.

Cooks Brook

Poem by Al Pittman

At the pool where we used to swim
in Cooks Brook
not everyone had guts enough
to dive from the top ledge

not that it would have been
a difficult dive
except for the shelf of rock
that lay two feet below the surface
and reached quarter of the way out
into the width of the pool

one by one the brave few of us
would climb the cliff to the ledge
and stand poised
ready to plunge headfirst
into the dark water below
and always there was that moment
of terror
when you'd doubt that you could
clear the shelf
knowing full well
it would be better to die
skull smashed open in the water
than it would be to climb
backwards down to the beach

Notes

Al Pittman, born in St. Leonard's, Placentia Bay, Newfoundland, is an author of plays, children's books, stories, and poems. A retired teacher, he lives in Corner Brook, Newfoundland, and he has been inducted into the Newfoundland and Labrador Arts Council's Hall of Honour.

so always there was that moment
when you prayed for wings
then sailed arms outspread into the buoyant air
what you feel is something
impossible to describe
as the water parts like a wound
to engulf you
then closes just as quickly
in a white scar where you entered

and you are surprised always
to find yourself alive
following the streaks of sunlight
that lead you gasping to the surface
where you make your way
leisurely to shore
as though there had been nothing to it
as though it was every day of the week
you daringly defied the demons
who lived so terribly
in the haunted hours of your sleep

You take it from here …

Responding

1. **Review Conflicts** With a partner, discuss
   - why "it would be better to die / skull smashed open in the water / than it would be to climb / backwards down to the beach"
   - the role peer pressure plays in making teens take risks
   - the inner conflicts the diver would have

   > **PEER ASSESSMENT**
   > - What do you think of your partner's interpretations?
   > - Did you and your partner make the same connections between different parts of the poem?

2. **Think about Point of View** The poet uses the second person ("you") rather than the first person ("I") or the third ("he"). Why is that an effective choice in this poem? What difference does it make to the reader's response to the poem? Discuss in a paragraph.

3. **Locate Poetic Devices** With a partner, find an example of a simile in stanza 4 and an example of *personification* (giving human characteristics to something abstract or non-human) in stanza 5.

4. **Establish Relevance** In a paragraph, discuss how this poem is relevant to the experience of teenagers today.

Extending

5. **Search for Information** Look up Cooks Brook (Newfoundland) in an atlas. Where is it located? Does this information affect your experience of the poem?

6. **Compose a Poem** Create your own poem about another outdoor activity or sport. As in "Cooks Brook," try to create a sense of immediacy and bring the experience to life.

7. **Remember an Experience** Write a narrative essay about a memorable experience you have had with your friends or siblings.

Before you read, in a small group, discuss different ways in which young people come of age. What is the role of elders, mentors, or teachers in this process?

As you read, write down in your notebook your impressions of what Shamaya means.

Notes

"Shamaya" records the tradition of the hunt, an important part of male Inuit coming-of-age experiences. The Shamaya is a celebration song sung when a male hunter catches the five largest sea mammals.

Susan Aglukark was born in the early 1970s in Churchill, Manitoba. She grew up in the Northwest Territories, later moving to Ottawa to work as a linguist for the Inuit Tapirisat (Brotherhood) of Canada. Her musical career started in 1992 and "Shamaya" is a song from her breakthrough album, *This Child*.

Shamaya

Lyrics by Susan Aglukark

Deep in time a hunt took place
That made the boy a man
A song was sung to celebrate
And welcome each new hand
The story of Shamaya
The song that brings to life
The hunt that each boy has to face
The hunt of joy or strife
And he knows, there he goes
Shamaya, shamaya

So they paddle down the water's edge
A journey of first rites
His trembling hands are clenching tight
Excitement in his eyes
The old man starts to tell him
Of a journey just like this
When forty years before he'd lost himself
In this same myth
And the boy became a man
Shamaya, shamaya

He hunts with such a vengeance
The pattern turns to pride
The hunt no longer born of need
But fuelled by his desire
Shamaya's not a myth he learns
It's a parable of life
So when you know your need's too great
You should put out the fire
And journey on, journey on
Shamaya, shamaya

You take it from here ...

Responding

1. **Place Poem in Context**   As a class, discuss the *context* (situation, cultural setting) of the poem. What role does hunting play in the lives of Northern peoples? How does knowing that Aglukark is Inuit influence your understanding of the lyrics?

2. **Analyze Lines**   With a partner, go over the meanings of the following lines:
    a) "The hunt that each boy has to face"
    b) "A journey of first rites"
    c) "He hunts with such a vengeance / The pattern turns to pride"
    d) "So when you know your need's too great / You should put out the fire"

3. **Understand a Myth**   In a group, discuss the following questions:
    a) What is the purpose of the hunt?
    b) Why is the journey so important to the old man?
    c) How and why might the goal or purpose of the hunt change over time?
    d) How is Shamaya a "parable of life"?

Extending

4. **Discover a Canadian Talent**   Using the Internet and library sources, find out more about Susan Aglukark, her music, songwriting, and beliefs. Choose one aspect of her life and work to research in greater depth, and share your findings with the class. Include a brief assessment of your information sources, identifying the ones you found most useful.

5. **Research Cultural Traditions**   Working with a partner, research coming-of-age traditions and ceremonies in various cultures, and present your findings as a feature article for a magazine.

> **TIPS**
> - Start with a general definition of "coming of age" that applies to all cultures.
> - Include pictures and illustrations.
> - Consider placing detailed definitions and descriptions in sidebars.

Before you read, share some memories with the class about travelling in a snowstorm or other bad weather.

As you read, predict what will happen at the following points: a) when the trooper pulls the car over and b) when the boy and his father return to the barricade.

Powder

"Your mother will never forgive me for this," he said.

Short Story by Tobias Wolff

Notes

Tobias Wolff is an award-winning American novelist and writer of short stories and nonfiction. His memoir of growing up in the 1950s, *This Boy's Life*, was published in 1989, and a movie version was produced in 1993 starring Ellen Barkin, Robert DeNiro, and Leonardo DiCaprio.

Just before Christmas my father took me skiing at Mount Baker. He'd had to fight for the privilege of my company because my mother was still angry with him for sneaking me into a nightclub during his last visit, to see Thelonious Monk.

He wouldn't give up. He promised, hand on heart, to take good care of me and have me home for dinner on Christmas Eve, and she relented. But as we were checking out of the lodge that morning it began to snow, and in this snow he observed some rare quality that made it necessary for us to get in one last run. We got in several last runs. He was indifferent to my fretting. Snow whirled around us in bitter, blinding squalls, hissing like sand, and still we skied. As the lift bore us to the peak yet again, my father looked at his watch and said, "Criminy. This'll have to be a fast one."

By now I couldn't see the trail. There was no point in trying. I stuck to him like white on rice and did what he did and somehow made it to the bottom without sailing off a cliff. We returned our skis and my father put chains on the Austin-Healey while I swayed from foot to foot, clapping my mittens and wishing I was home. I could see everything. The green tablecloth, the plates with the holly pattern, the red candles waiting to be lit.

We passed a diner on our way out. "You want some soup?" my father asked. I shook my head. "Buck up," he said. "I'll get you there. Right, doctor?"

I was supposed to say, "Right, doctor," but I didn't say anything.

A state trooper waved us down outside the resort. A pair of sawhorses were blocking the road. The trooper came up to

312   Youth—The Awakening Years

our car and bent down to my father's window. His face was bleached by the cold. Snowflakes clung to his eyebrows and to the fur trim of his jacket and cap.

"Don't tell me," my father said.

The trooper told him. The road was closed. It might get cleared, it might not. Storm took everyone by surprise. So much, so fast. Hard to get people moving. Christmas Eve. What can you do.

My father said, "Look. We're talking about five, six inches. I've taken this car through worse than that."

The trooper straightened up. His face was out of sight but I could hear him. "The road is closed."

My father sat with both hands on the wheel, rubbing the wood with his thumbs. He looked at the barricade for a long time. He seemed to be trying to master the idea of it. Then he thanked the trooper, and with a weird, old-maidy show of caution turned the car around. "Your mother will never forgive me for this," he said.

"We should have left before," I said. "Doctor."

He didn't speak to me again until we were in a booth at the diner, waiting for our burgers. "She won't forgive me," he said. "Do you understand? Never."

"I guess," I said, but no guesswork was required; she wouldn't forgive him.

"I can't let that happen." He bent toward me. "I'll tell you what I want. I want us all to be together again. Is that what you want?"

"Yes, sir."

He bumped my chin with his knuckles. "That's all I needed to hear."

When we finished eating he went to the pay phone in the back of the diner, then joined me in the booth again. I figured he'd called my mother, but he didn't give a report. He sipped at his coffee and stared out the window at the empty road. "Come on, come on," he said, though not to me. A little while later he said it again. When the trooper's car went past, lights flashing, he got up and dropped some money on the check. "Okay. Vamanos."

The wind had died. The snow was falling straight down, less of it now and lighter. We drove away from the resort, right up to the barricade. "Move it," my father told me. When I looked at him he said, "What are you waiting for?" I got out and dragged one of the sawhorses aside, then put it back after he drove through. He pushed the door open for me. "Now you're an accomplice," he said. "We go down together." He put the car into gear and gave me a look. "Joke, son."

Down the first long stretch I watched the road behind us to see if the trooper was on our tail. The barricade vanished. Then there was nothing

but snow: snow on the road, snow kicking up from the chains, snow on the trees, snow in the sky; and our trail in the snow. Then I faced forward and had a shock. The lay of the road behind us had been marked by our own tracks, but there were no tracks ahead of us. My father was breaking virgin snow between a line of tall trees. He was humming "Stars Fell on Alabama." I felt snow brush along the floorboards under my feet. To keep my hands from shaking I clamped them between my knees.

My father grunted in a thoughtful way and said, "Don't ever try this yourself."

"I won't."

"That's what you say now, but someday you'll get your licence and then you'll think you can do anything. Only you won't be able to do this. You need, I don't know—a certain instinct."

"Maybe I have it."

"You don't. You have your strong points, but not this. I only mention it because I don't want you to get the idea this is something just anybody can do. I'm a great driver. That's not a virtue, okay? It's just a fact, and one you should be aware of. Of course you have to give the old heap some credit, too. There aren't many cars I'd try this with. Listen!"

I did listen. I heard the slap of the chains, the stiff, jerky rasp of the wipers, the purr of the engine. It really did purr. The old heap was almost new. My father couldn't afford it, and kept promising to sell it, but here it was.

I said, "Where do you think that policeman went to?"

"Are you warm enough?" He reached over and cranked up the blower. Then he turned off the wipers. We didn't need them. The clouds had brightened. A few sparse, feathery flakes drifted into our slipstream and were swept away. We left the trees and entered a broad field of snow that ran level for a while and then tilted sharply downward. Orange stakes had been planted at intervals in two parallel lines and my father steered a course between them, though they were far enough apart to leave considerable doubt in my mind as to exactly where the road lay. He was humming again, doing little scat riffs around the melody.

"Okay then. What are my strong points?"

"Don't get me started," he said. "It'd take all day."

"Oh, right. Name one."

"Easy. You always think ahead."

True. I always thought ahead. I was a boy who kept his clothes on numbered hangers to insure proper rotation. I bothered my teachers for homework assignments far ahead of their due dates so I could draw up schedules. I thought ahead, and that was why I knew that there would be other troopers waiting for us at the end of our ride, if we even got there. What I did not know was that my father would wheedle and plead his way past them—he didn't sing "O Tannenbaum," but just about—and get me home for dinner, buying a little more time before my mother decided to make the split final. I knew we'd get caught; I was resigned to it. And maybe for this reason I stopped moping and began to enjoy myself.

   Why not? This was one for the books. Like being in a speedboat, only better. You can't go downhill in a boat. And it was all ours. And it kept coming, the laden trees, the unbroken surface of snow, the sudden white vistas. Here and there I saw hints of the road, ditches, fences, stakes, but not so many that I could have found my way. But then I didn't have to. My father was driving. My father in his forty-eighth year, rumpled, kind, bankrupt of honour, flushed with certainty. He was a great driver. All persuasion, no coercion. Such subtlety at the wheel, such tactful pedalwork. I actually trusted him. And the best was yet to come—switchbacks and hairpins impossible to describe. Except maybe to say this: if you haven't driven fresh powder, you haven't driven.

You take it from here ...

Responding

1. **Follow up on Predictions**   Did you correctly predict the outcome for either situation mentioned in the "As you read" activity? What surprised you about the father and the outcome of the story? Discuss with another student.

2. **Focus on Ideas**   With a classmate, go over the following subtopics mentioned in the story. Then pick one and write your own personal response about it.

   - cars and relationships
   - special bonds between parents and teenagers
   - parents as role models
   - effects of divorce or separation
   - risk taking
   - safe driving

3. **Write a Character Sketch**   Look at how the father responds to different situations in the story. Write down some adjectives to describe his personality. Then write a character analysis of him using examples to back up your adjectives.

4. **Discuss Realism**   What makes this story believable? What details impressed you with their *verisimilitude* (life-likeness)? How are the father and son "real people"? Write a paragraph response, then compare ideas with a partner.

Extending

5. **Recall a Memory**   "Powder" is about a special memory of a parent and role model. Write about a special moment or episode you shared with a parent, grandparent, guardian, teacher, or coach.

6. **Write a Sequel**   Continue the story of the boy's ride with his father. Imitate the style of the original story.

7. **Sketch a Scene**   Pick one moment from the story to illustrate.

Before you read, as a class, discuss what an eating disorder is. Why might some teens be prone to eating disorders?

As you read, notice what point of view is used to present the poem's experiences.

In the Past

Poem by Lesley-Anne Bourne

Notes

Lesley-Anne Bourne grew up in North Bay, ON, currently lives in Charlottetown, and teaches at the University of Prince Edward Island. Among the awards she has won for her writing are the Bliss Carman Award, the Air Nova Poetry Award, and the Air Canada Award.

anorexia nervosa: emotional disorder in which the person refuses to eat. It leads to malnutrition, excessive weight loss, and sometimes death.

bulimia: eating disorder in which the person alternately binges, then purges or vomits

ten years her father's seen her die
almost. He still asks why
did she starve so long?
How? Under the hospital window
he thought she couldn't hear

*When can I trust
her again?* The nights
he'd sign her out for baseball
games in Lee Park, returning
at ten to the fourth floor

as if normal. His heart
breaking each time they passed
icecream stands. Or lunch hours
he walked from the office
to watch her not eat. In the past

ten years she's come back
a pound at a time.
He pretends not to count.
Playing catch in the yard
when she visits, they throw

fast balls and curves
without effort or hurting
each other that bad.

You take it from here ...

Responding

1. **Take a Second Look**   With another student, answer the following questions:

    a) Does the father blame himself for his daughter's illness?
    b) Does he know that she knows what he thinks?
    c) Why is she in hospital?
    d) What is significant about the way they play baseball?
    e) Would you do anything different if you were the father? Explain.

2. **Analyze a Relationship**   In a paragraph, first analyze whether, in your opinion, the man is a good father. Then comment on the words in italics (stanza 2) and the reference to playing baseball (last stanza).

3. **Discuss Purpose and Title**   What do you see as the purpose of the poem? How does the title relate to the purpose? Does the poem shed light on the problems of teenagers? Exchange ideas with a classmate.

Extending

4. **Compose Dialogue**   Script a conversation between the daughter and her therapist, or between the father and the girl's doctor. What topics would they likely cover?

5. **Make a Statement about Media Influence**   Cut and paste words and pictures that deal with the influence of media on the self-image of teenage girls or boys. Create a bulletin-board display with the collages, and have a class discussion about what messages teens get from the media regarding ideal body image.

> **PEER ASSESSMENT**
> - What did you think about the collages other students made?
> - Did other students make points similar to yours?

6. **Write on an Issue**   Pick another issue of concern to teens. Examples: the right to privacy, the need for positive role models, the importance of friends. Write about the topic thoughtfully in essay form.

Before you read, brainstorm a list of things society seems to expect teenagers to be and do. Create a separate list of things you expect of yourself.

As you read, summarize the feelings of the speaker about what it's like to be a teenager today.

What a Good Boy

Lyrics by Steven Page (of The Barenaked Ladies)

When I was born, they looked at me and said
what a good boy, what a smart boy, what a strong boy
And when you were born, they looked at you and said
what a good girl, what a smart girl, what a pretty girl.

We've got these chains that hang around our necks,
people want to strangle us with them before we
take our first breath
Afraid of change, afraid of staying the same,
when temptation calls, we just look away.

This name is the hairshirt I wear,
and this hairshirt is woven from your brown hair.
This song is the cross that I bear
bear it with me, bear with me, bear with me,
be with me tonight,
I know that it isn't right,
but be with me tonight.

Notes

The Barenaked Ladies are a Toronto-based rock group that has become very popular in Canada and the United States. Their catchy hits include "Brian Wilson," "If I Had a Million Dollars," "The Old Apartment," "Jane," and "One Week." Steven Page is a lead singer-guitarist and one of their main songwriters.

I go to school, I write exams.
If I pass, if I fail, if I drop out, does anyone give a damn?
And if they do, they'll soon forget,
'cause it won't take much for me to show that my
life ain't over yet.
I wake up scared, I wake up strange.
I wake up wondering if anything in my life is ever
going to change
I wake up scared. I wake up strange
and everything around me stays the same.

I couldn't tell you that I was wrong,
chickened out, grabbed a pen and paper, sat
down and I wrote this song
I couldn't tell you that you were right,
so instead, I looked in the mirror watched TV laid
awake all night.

We've got these chains, hang round our necks,
people want to strangle us with them before we
take our first breath.
Afraid of change, afraid of staying the same,
when temptation calls ...

When I was born, they looked at me and said
what a good boy, what a smart boy, what a strong boy
And when you were born, they looked at you and said
what a good girl, what a smart girl, what a pretty girl, hey

You take it from here ...

Responding

1. **Exchange Views**   Work with a partner to compare and discuss the lists you made before reading the lyrics. Are society's expectations different from your own? Why might that be? Formulate your own conclusions and present them in a class discussion.

2. **Consider Relevance** Keeping in mind your lists of expectations, reflect on the relevance of this song to teens today. How accurate are the song's views? Are some important issues not included? Express your thoughts in a written response.

3. **Discuss Meaning** In a group, review what the song has to say about the following:
   a) Who is "they" in stanza 1?
   b) What are the "chains" described in stanza 2? How do they "strangle" the speaker and his girlfriend?
   c) What is a "hairshirt"? How are the name, the girlfriend's hair, and the song like a hairshirt or "cross"?
   d) What fears are revealed in the poem?
   e) In what sense does the speaker "chicken out"?
   f) Why is the first stanza repeated at the end?
   g) How is the title "What a Good Boy" ironic?

   > **GROUP ASSESSMENT**
   > - What question was the toughest for the group to answer?
   > - What did your group learn about using the dictionary to answer questions?

Extending

4. **Write a Letter** In these lyrics, the speaker feels frightened and uncertain about the meaning and purpose of his life. Write him a letter trying to cheer him up and reminding him about the good things in life that balance the "bad" ones.

5. **Compose Lyrics** Write your own lyrics about the problems of being a teenager.

6. **Present a Mime** Find the song by The Barenaked Ladies on their *Gordon* album. With a partner, rehearse a mimed version of the song, then present it to the class.

Before you read, as a class, draw some conclusions about the role of effective listening in conversation.

As you read, write down what you think went wrong with this parent–teenager talk. Compare notes with another student.

For Better or For Worse

Cartoon by Lynn Johnston

You take it from here ...

Responding

1. **Examine Dramatic Irony**   *Dramatic irony* occurs when an audience is aware of something different from or opposite to what a character is aware of. What would be the example of dramatic irony in this cartoon?

2. **Focus on Detail**   With a partner, discuss what Mike is noticing while his mother talks to him. Is this realistic? Do teenagers have trouble listening to parents? Are they easily distracted? Comment.

3. **Analyze Visual Technique**   What is not shown in the conversation between the mother and son? Why does the cartoonist make that choice? Discuss in a paragraph.

4. **State Theme**   In one sentence, write the main idea of the cartoon. Write another sentence giving an example of the idea in the cartoon.

Extending

5. **Supply Dialogue**   Imagine and compose words for each of the four frames in which the mother is speaking.

6. **Explore Listening Skills**   With a partner, brainstorm the key elements of listening. What can people do to stay focused and not be distracted while listening? Create a guide or article offering advice on how to be an effective listener.

7. **Perform a Skit**   With one or two other students, rehearse and perform a skit portraying another familiar adult–teenager scenario focusing on the generation gap or communication.

> **TIP**
> - Check out Internet and library sources for additional ideas and tips on developing good listening skills.

> **Before you read,** discuss in a group what you would do if you were a parent of a teenager who was doing poorly at school.
>
> **As you read,** write your opinion as to whether you think Daisy is doing the right things for her son.

Teenage Wasteland

"For God's sake!" he said. "Don't you trust me?"

Short Story by Anne Tyler

Notes

Anne Tyler was born in Minneapolis and grew up in North Carolina. She took Russian studies at Columbia University in New York. Her eleventh novel, *Breathing Lessons*, won the Pulitzer Prize in 1988. Her 1985 novel, *The Accidental Tourist*, was made into a movie in 1988.

The title and phrase "Teenage Wasteland" come from the lines of a song "Baba O'Riley" by the 1960–70s British rock group The Who (from their album *Who's Next*).

Don't cry
Don't raise your eye
It's only teenage
  wasteland.
—Peter Townshend

He used to have very blond hair—almost white—cut shorter than other children's so that on his crown a little cowlick always stood up to catch the light. But this was when he was small. As he grew older, his hair grew darker, and he wore it longer—past his collar even. It hung in lank, taffy-coloured ropes around his face, which was still an endearing face, fine-featured, the eyes an unusual aqua blue. But his cheeks, of course, were no longer round, and a sharp new Adam's apple jogged in his throat when he talked.

In October, they called from the private school he attended to request a conference with his parents. Daisy went alone; her husband was at work. Clutching her purse, she sat on the principal's couch and learned that Donny was noisy, lazy, and disruptive; always fooling around with his friends, and he wouldn't respond in class.

In the past, before her children were born, Daisy had been a fourth-grade teacher. It shamed her now to sit before this principal as a parent, a delinquent parent, a parent who struck Mr. Lanham, no doubt, as unseeing or uncaring. "It isn't that we're not concerned," she said. "Both of us are. And we've done what we could, whatever we could think of. We don't let him watch TV on school nights. We don't let him talk on the phone till he's finished his homework. But he tells us he doesn't *have* any homework or he did it all in study hall. How are we to know what to believe?"

From early October through November, at Mr. Lanham's suggestion, Daisy checked Donny's assignments every day. She sat next to him as he worked, trying to be encouraging, sagging inwardly as she saw the poor quality of everything he did—the sloppy mistakes in math, the illogical leaps in his English themes, the history questions left blank if they required any research.

Daisy was often late starting supper, and she couldn't give as much attention to Donny's younger sister. "You'll never guess what happened at …" Amanda would begin, and Daisy would have to tell her, "Not now, honey."

By the time her husband, Matt, came home, she'd be snappish. She would recite the day's hardships—the fuzzy instructions in English, the botched history map, the morass of unsolvable algebra equations. Matt would look surprised and confused, and Daisy would gradually wind down. There was no way, really, to convey how exhausting all this was.

In December, the school called again. This time, they wanted Matt to come as well. She and Matt had to sit on Mr. Lanham's couch like two bad children and listen to the news. Donny had improved only slightly, raising a D in history to a C, and a C in algebra to a B-minus. What was worse, he had developed new problems. He had cut classes on at least three occasions. Smoked in the furnace room. Helped Sonny Barnett break into a freshman's locker. And last week, during athletics, he and three friends had been seen off the school grounds; when they returned, the coach had smelled beer on their breath.

Daisy and Matt sat silent, shocked. Matt rubbed his forehead with his fingertips. Imagine, Daisy thought, how they must look to Mr. Lanham: an overweight housewife in a cotton dress and a too-tall, too-thin insurance agent in a baggy, frayed suit. Failures, both of them—the kind of people who are always hurrying to catch up, missing the point of things that everyone else grasps at once. She wished she'd worn nylons instead of knee socks.

It was arranged that Donny would visit a psychologist for testing. Mr. Lanham knew just the person. He would set this boy straight, he said.

When they stood to leave, Daisy held her stomach in and gave Mr. Lanham a firm, responsible handshake.

Donny said the psychologist was a jackass and the tests were really dumb; but he kept all three of his appointments, and when it was time for the follow-up conference with the psychologist and both parents, Donny combed his hair and seemed unusually sober and subdued. The psychologist said Donny had no serious emotional problems. He was merely going through a difficult period in his life. He required some academic help and a better sense of self-worth. For this reason, he was suggesting a man named Calvin Beadle, a tutor with considerable psychological training.

In the car going home, Donny said he'd be damned if he'd let them drag him to some stupid fairy tutor. His father told him to watch his language in front of his mother.

That night, Daisy lay awake pondering the term "self-worth." She had always been free with her praise. She had always told Donny he had talent, was smart, was good with his hands. She had made a big to-do over every little gift he gave her. In fact, maybe she had gone too far, although, Lord knows, she had meant every word. Was that his trouble?

She remembered when Amanda was born. Donny had acted lost and bewildered. Daisy had been alert to that, of course, but still, a new baby keeps you so busy. Had she really done all she could have? She longed—she ached—for a time machine. Given one more chance, she'd do it perfectly—hug him more, praise him more, or perhaps praise him less. Oh, who can say....

The tutor told Donny to call him Cal. All his kids did, he said. Daisy thought for a second that he meant his own children, then realized her mistake. He seemed too young, anyhow, to be a family man. He wore a heavy brown handlebar moustache. His hair was as long and stringy as Donny's, and his jeans as faded. Wire-rimmed spectacles slid down his nose. He lounged in a canvas director's chair with his fingers laced across his chest, and he casually, amiably questioned Donny, who sat upright and glaring in an armchair.

"So, they're getting on your back at school," said Cal. "Making a big deal about anything you do wrong."

"Right," said Donny.

"Any idea why that would be?"

"Oh, well, you know, stuff like homework and all," Donny said.

"You don't do your homework?"

"Oh, well, I might do it sometimes but not just exactly like they want it." Donny sat forward and said, "It's like a prison there, you know? You've got to go to every class, you can never step off the school grounds."

"You cut classes sometimes?"

"Sometimes," Donny said, with a glance at his parents.

Cal didn't seem perturbed. "Well," he said, "I'll tell you what. Let's you and me try working together three nights a week. Think you could handle that? We'll see if we can show that school of yours a thing or two. Give it a month; then if you don't like it, we'll stop. If *I* don't like it, we'll stop. I mean, sometimes people just don't get along, right? What do you say to that?"

"Okay," Donny said. He seemed pleased.

"Make it seven o'clock till eight, Monday, Wednesday, and Friday," Cal told Matt and Daisy. They nodded. Cal shambled to his feet, gave them a little salute, and showed them to the door.

This was where he lived as well as worked, evidently. The interview had taken place in the dining room, which had been transformed into a kind of office. Passing the living room, Daisy winced at the rock music she had been hearing, without registering it, ever since she had entered the house. She looked in and saw a boy about Donny's age lying on a sofa with a book. Another boy and a girl were playing Ping-Pong in front of the fireplace. "You have several here together?" Daisy asked Cal.

"Oh, sometimes they stay on after their sessions, just to rap. They're a pretty sociable group, all in all. Plenty of goof-offs like young Donny here."

He cuffed Donny's shoulder playfully. Donny flushed and grinned.

Climbing into the car, Daisy asked Donny, "Well? What did you think?"

But Donny had returned to his old evasive self. He jerked his chin toward the garage. "Look," he said. "He's got a basketball net."

Now on Mondays, Wednesdays, and Fridays they had supper early—the instant Matt came home. Sometimes, they had to leave before they were really finished. Amanda would still be eating her dessert. "Bye, honey. Sorry," Daisy would tell her.

Cal's first bill sent a flutter of panic through Daisy's chest, but it was worth it, of course. Just look at Donny's face when they picked him up: alight and full of interest. The principal telephoned Daisy to tell her how Donny had improved. "Of course, it hasn't shown up in his grades yet, but several of the teachers have noticed how his attitude's changed. Yes, sir, I think we're onto something here."

At home, Donny didn't act much differently. He still seemed to have a low opinion of his parents. But Daisy supposed that was unavoidable—part of being fifteen. He said his parents were too "controlling"—a word that made Daisy give him a sudden look. He said they acted like wardens. On weekends, they enforced a curfew. And any time he went to a party, they always telephoned first to see if adults would be supervising. "For God's sake!" he said. "Don't you trust me?"

"It isn't a matter of trust, honey ..." But there was no explaining to him.

His tutor called one afternoon. "I get the sense," he said, "that this kid's feeling ... underestimated, you know? Like you folks expect the worst of him. I'm thinking we ought to give him more rope."

"But see, he's still so suggestible," Daisy said. "When his friends suggest some mischief—smoking or drinking or such—why, he just finds it hard not to go along with them."

"Mrs. Coble," the tutor said, "I think this kid is hurting. You know? Here's a serious, sensitive kid, telling you he'd like to take on some grown-up challenges, and you're giving him the message that he can't be trusted. Don't you understand how that hurts?"

"Oh," said Daisy.

"It undermines his self-esteem—don't you realize that?"

Teenage Wasteland

"Well, I guess you're right," said Daisy. She saw Donny suddenly from a whole new angle: his pathetically poor posture, that slouch so forlorn that his shoulders seemed about to meet his chin ... oh, wasn't it awful being young? She'd had a miserable adolescence herself and had always sworn no child of hers would ever be that unhappy.

They let Donny stay out later, they didn't call ahead to see if the parties were supervised, and they were careful not to grill him about his evening. The tutor had set down so many rules! They were not allowed any questions at all about any aspect of school, nor were they to speak with his teachers. If a teacher had some complaint, she should phone Cal. Only one teacher disobeyed—the history teacher, Miss Evans. She called one morning in February. "I'm a little concerned about Donny, Mrs. Coble."

"Oh, I'm sorry, Miss Evans, but Donny's tutor handles these things now ..."

"I always deal directly with the parents. You are the parent," Miss Evans said, speaking very slowly and distinctly. "Now, here is the problem. Back when you were helping Donny with his homework, his grades rose from a D to a C, but now they've slipped back, and they're closer to an F."

"They are?"

"I think you should start overseeing his homework again."

"But Donny's tutor says ..."

"It's nice that Donny has a tutor, but you should still be in charge of his homework. With you, he learned it. Then he passed his tests. With the tutor, well, it seems the tutor is more of a crutch. 'Donny,' I say, 'a quiz is coming up on Friday. Hadn't you better be listening instead of talking?' 'That's okay, Miss Evans,' he says. 'I have a tutor now.' Like a talisman! I really think you ought to take over, Mrs. Coble."

"I see," said Daisy. "Well, I'll think about that. Thank you for calling."

Hanging up, she felt a rush of anger at Donny. A talisman! For a talisman, she'd given up all luxuries, all that time with her daughter, her evenings at home!

She dialled Cal's number. He sounded muzzy. "I'm sorry if I woke you," she told him, "but Donny's history teacher just called. She says he isn't doing well."

"She should have dealt with me."

"She wants me to start supervising his homework again. His grades are slipping."

"Yes," said the tutor, "but you and I both know there's more to it than mere grades, don't we? I care about the *whole* child—his happiness, his self-esteem. The grades will come. Just give them time."

When she hung up, it was Miss Evans she was angry at. What a narrow woman!

It was Cal this, Cal that, Cal says this, Cal and I did that. Cal lent Donny an album by The Who. He took Donny and two other pupils to a rock concert. In March, when Donny began to talk endlessly on the phone with a girl named Miriam, Cal even let Miriam come to one of the tutoring sessions. Daisy was touched that Cal would grow so involved in Donny's life, but she was also a little hurt, because she had offered to have Miriam to dinner and Donny had refused. Now he asked them to drive her to Cal's house without a qualm.

This Miriam was an unappealing girl with blurry lipstick and masses of rough red hair. She wore a short, bulky jacket that would not have been out of place on a motorcycle. During the trip to Cal's she was silent, but coming back, she was talkative. "What a neat guy, and what a house! All those kids hanging out, like a club. And the stereo playing rock ... gosh, he's not like a grown-up at all! Married and divorced and everything, but you'd think he was our age."

"Mr. Beadle was married?" Daisy asked.

"Yeah, to this really controlling lady. She didn't understand him a bit."

"No, I guess not," Daisy said.

Spring came, and the students who hung around at Cal's drifted out to the basketball net above the garage. Sometimes, when Daisy and Matt arrived to pick up Donny, they'd find him there with the others—spiky and excited, jittering on his toes beneath the backboard. It was staying light much longer now, and the neighbouring fence cast narrow bars across the bright grass. Loud music would be spilling from Cal's windows. Once it was The Who, which Daisy recognized from the time that Donny had borrowed the album. *"Teenage Wasteland,"* she said aloud, identifying the song, and Matt gave a short, dry laugh. "It certainly is," he said. He'd misunderstood; he thought she was commenting on the scene spread before them. In fact, she might have been. The players looked like hoodlums, even her son. Why, one of Cal's students had recently been knifed in a tavern. One had been shipped off to boarding school in midterm; two had been withdrawn by their parents. On the other hand, Donny had mentioned someone who'd been studying with Cal for five years. "Five years!" said Daisy. "Doesn't anyone ever stop needing him?"

Donny looked at her. Lately, whatever she said about Cal was read as criticism. "You're just feeling competitive," he said. "And controlling."

She bit her lip and said no more.

In April, the principal called to tell her that Donny had been expelled. There had been a locker check, and in Donny's locker they found five cans of beer and a half a pack of cigarettes. With Donny's previous record, this offence meant expulsion.

Daisy gripped the receiver tightly and said, "Well, where is he now?"

"We've sent him home," said Mr. Lanham. "He's packed up all his belongings, and he's coming home on foot."

Daisy wondered what she would say to him. She felt him looming closer and closer, bringing this brand-new situation that no one had prepared her to handle. What other place would take him? Could they enter him in public school? What were the rules? She stood at the living room window, waiting for him to show up. Gradually, she realized that he was taking too long. She checked the clock. She stared up the street again.

When an hour had passed, she phoned the school. Mr. Lanham's secretary answered and told her in a grave, sympathetic voice that yes, Donny Coble had most definitely gone home. Daisy called her husband. He was out of the office. She went back to the window and thought awhile, and then she called Donny's tutor.

"Donny's been expelled from school," she said, "and now I don't know where he's gone. I wonder if you've heard from him?"

There was a long silence. "Donny's with me, Mrs. Coble," he finally said.

"With you? How'd he get there?"

"He hailed a cab, and I paid the driver."

"Could I speak to him, please?"

There was another silence. "Maybe it'd be better if we had a conference," Cal said.

"I don't *want* a conference. I've been standing at the window picturing him dead or kidnapped or something, and now you tell me you want a—"

"Donny is very, very upset. Understandably so," said Cal. "Believe me, Mrs. Coble, this is not what it seems. Have you asked Donny's side of the story?"

"Well, of course not, how could I? He went running off to you instead."

"Because he didn't feel he'd be listened to."

"But I haven't even—"

"Why don't you come out and talk? The three of us," said Cal, "will try to get this thing in perspective."

"Well, all right," Daisy said. But she wasn't as reluctant as she sounded. Already, she felt soothed by the calm way Cal was taking this.

Cal answered the doorbell at once. He said, "Hi, there," and led her into the dining room. Donny sat slumped in a chair, chewing the knuckle of one thumb. "Hello, Donny," Daisy said. He flicked his eyes in her direction.

"Sit here, Mrs. Coble," said Cal, placing her opposite Donny. He himself remained standing, restlessly pacing. "So," he said.

Daisy stole a look at Donny. His lips were swollen, as if he'd been crying.

"You know," Cal told Daisy, "I kind of expected something like this. That's a very punitive school you've got him in—you realize that. And any half-decent lawyer will tell you they've violated his civil rights. Locker checks! Where's their search warrant?"

"But if the rule is—" Daisy said.

"Well, anyhow, let him tell you his side."

She looked at Donny. He said, "It wasn't my fault. I promise."

"They said your locker was full of beer."

"It was a put-up job! See, there's this guy that doesn't like me. He put all these beers in my locker and started a rumour going, so Mr. Lanham ordered a locker check."

"What was the boy's name?" Daisy asked.

"Huh?"

"Mrs. Coble, take my word, the situation is not so unusual," Cal said. "You can't imagine how vindictive kids can be sometimes."

"What was the boy's *name*," said Daisy, "so that I can ask Mr. Lanham if that's who suggested he run a locker check."

"You don't believe me," Donny said.

"And how'd this boy get your combination in the first place?"

"Frankly," said Cal, "I wouldn't be surprised to learn the school was in on it. Any kid that marches to a different drummer, why, they'd just love an excuse to get rid of him. The school is where I lay the blame."

"Doesn't *Donny* ever get blamed?"

"Now, Mrs. Coble, you heard what he—"

"Forget it," Donny told Cal. "You can see she doesn't trust me."

Daisy drew in a breath to say that of course she trusted him—a reflex. But she knew that bold-faced, wide-eyed look of Donny's. He had worn that look when he was small, denying some petty misdeed with the evidence plain as day all around him. Still, it was hard for her to accuse him outright. She temporized and said, "The only thing I'm sure of is that they've kicked you out of school, and now I don't know what we're going to do."

"We'll fight it," said Cal.

"We can't. Even you must see we can't."

"I could apply to Brantly," Donny said.

Cal stopped his pacing to beam down at him. "Brantly! Yes. They're really onto where a kid is coming from, at Brantly, Why, *I* could get you into Brantly. I work with a lot of their students."

Daisy had never heard of Brantly, but already she didn't like it. And she didn't like Cal's smile, which struck her now as feverish and avid—a smile of hunger.

On the fifteenth of April, they entered Donny in a public school, and they stopped his tutoring sessions. Donny fought both decisions bitterly. Cal, surprisingly enough, did not object. He admitted he'd made no headway with Donny and said it was because Donny was emotionally disturbed.

Donny went to his new school every morning, plodding off alone with his head down. He did his assignments, and he earned average grades, but he gathered no friends, joined no clubs. There was something exhausted and defeated about him.

The first week in June, during final exams, Donny vanished. He simply didn't come home one afternoon, and no one at school remembered seeing him. The police were reassuring, and for the first few days, they worked hard. They combed Donny's sad, messy room for clues; they visited Miriam and Cal. But then they started talking about the number of kids who ran away every year. Hundreds, just in this city. "He'll show up, if he wants to," they said. "If he doesn't, he won't."

Evidently, Donny didn't want to.

It's been three months now and still no word. Matt and Daisy still look for him in every crowd of awkward, heartbreaking teenage boys. Every time the phone rings, they imagine it might be Donny. Both parents have aged. Donny's sister seems to be staying away from home as much as possible.

At night, Daisy lies awake and goes over Donny's life. She is trying to figure out what went wrong, where they made their first mistake. Often, she finds herself blaming Cal, although she knows he didn't begin it. Then at other times she excuses him, for without him, Donny might have left earlier. Who really knows? In the end, she can only sigh and search for a cooler spot on the pillow. As she falls asleep, she occasionally glimpses something in the corner of her vision. It's something fleet and round, a ball—a basketball. It flies up, it sinks through the hoop, descends, lands in a yard littered with last year's leaves and striped with bars of sunlight as white as bones, bleached and parched and cleanly picked.

You take it from here ...

Responding

1. **Focus on Motivation**   With a partner, go over the following questions:
   a) Why are Donny's parents concerned about him? How do they try to help their son? Why do their efforts fail?
   b) Give reasons for why Donny is the way he is. How does he see the world and his problems?
   c) What do you think finally prompts Donny to run away?
   d) What are Cal's methods for handling troubled teenagers? Do they work for Donny? Why do you think Cal has chosen to be a tutor?

2. **Write a Character Sketch**   Analyze the character of Donny's mother, Daisy. Use adjectives and examples to develop your analysis.

3. **Establish Relevance**   In a small group, answer the following questions:
   a) What sorts of problems cause some teenagers to quit school? What are some ways to resolve these problems? What light does the story shed on how to deal effectively with troubled teenagers?
   b) Is life more difficult for teenagers today than it was in your parents' teen years? What are some problems unique to today's teenagers? Are Donnie's problems typical of those faced by teens today?

Extending

4. **Write a Sequel**   Write a follow-up story in which Daisy either tracks down Donny, or Donny returns home of his own accord and tries to straighten out his life.

5. **Research Related Songs**   Find two or three songs that deal with the difficulty of being a teenager. Choose one to play for the class and be prepared to talk about how the song relates to the ideas presented in the story "Teenage Wasteland."

> **SELF ASSESSMENT**
> - What sources did you use to find a song?
> - How did you decide on which song to play for the class?

> **Before you read,** as a class, discuss what prompts some teenagers to run away and live on the streets.
>
> **As you read,** make a chart of the teens mentioned, identifying their problems and why they're on the street.

How many such kids are there in Canada? Who knows?

The Kids Who Make It in from the Cold

by Bob Levin

MAGAZINE ARTICLE

You can't see it, just looking. No nose rings, no Mohawk, none of the other spiky insignia of the street. Sitting in a Toronto sub shop, spooning her vegetable soup, she is a poised 20-year-old woman, smartly dressed, her brown eyes bright—a woman who was once a street kid and only a year and a half ago kicked her drug habit. A violent home, a resort to pot, booze, acid, and then the road time, sleeping on beaches or in a car in California and Vancouver, playing her guitar for change, stealing, getting beaten by her boyfriend, then the cocaine and the tortured escape to detox—she recounts it all with a controlled matter-of-factness, ashamed but somehow accepting, although parts she can't remember very well. "I was so wasted," she says.

Outside the restaurant, people bustle along the darkened sidewalk. Streetcars squeal, commuters honk. She is part of that world now, or almost, working in a bookstore and living in a rehab home. At her job, says Sally, which isn't her real name but one she picked for print, "I can go downstairs and pay five bucks for a sandwich and not worry about it: 'Oh, it's OK, I can afford it.' I think that's the most startling thing, to have all these, like, privileges. It feels weird." She no longer has to shoplift her Christmas presents; she will buy her mother something in a store. That part feels good.

Kids, holidays, home: they're supposed to be inseparable, a perfectly wrapped package, the season's holy trinity. They're a reminder of what street kids have lost and what people like Sally—the ones who struggle in from the cold—so desperately seek: a normal life. Sally is quick to say: "I don't really look back and think 'Boy, I'm a big success.' I think more like, 'I have a long way to go.'" But you get the feeling she'll make it, and hope she will, and she's something to consider as you hurry past a young panhandler or curse a squeegee kid (or listen to politicians talk about passing laws to force squeegees from the streets, which is like fighting disease by fining sick people). "These are kids in need," says Geraldine Babcock, Toronto co-ordinator of the Metro Youth Job Corps. "We have to find solutions and be compassionate. We're losing that."

It helps to know who these kids are—and aren't. They're *not* 1960s-style dropouts, slumming

334 Youth—The Awakening Years

for a while before returning to their middle-class lives; surveys show about three-quarters of today's street kids left home because of physical or sexual abuse. The Community Social Planning Council of Toronto, which published a report on street youth in 1998, said more than 80 percent had been on the street for over a year, surviving by panhandling, squeegeeing, prostituting, dealing drugs, getting welfare. How many such kids are there in Canada? Who knows? In Toronto alone (which, with a grandiosity only a megacity could manage, recently declared homelessness a "national disaster"), estimates range wildly from 2000 to more than 10 000.

So, naturally, there's no telling how many escape the street. There are stories, though—and they're worth hearing.

Shaun—his real name—left his troubled home in Saskatoon at 14, lived in foster care, worked as a carnie, then began a hitchhiking odyssey (Moose Jaw, Medicine Hat, Kelowna ...) that dragged on for years. Two summers ago, he lost his left eye in a Saskatchewan bar fight. He began drinking heavily, thinking "my life was over." But Shaun had an edge over many street kids: "one caring parent." Now nearly 23, he lives with his mother in Toronto and, after getting job counselling, works for a building maintenance firm, sweeping, mopping—and feeling good. "I can wake up and smile and say, 'Yeah, I like myself.' I couldn't do that for years and years."

Then there's Christina Wayvon, who was kicked out of her house in Windsor, Ontario, when she was all of 13. She eventually settled in Toronto, crashing on couches or in parks or, come winter, by indoor bank machines. She recalls Christmases: "You'd go into the Eaton Centre to get warm and it's everywhere, it's in your face—you remember the stuff you used to have, like a winter coat, and wonder if you'll ever have those things again. Then you get very angry at people who do, which of course isn't fair but you still get angry."

Christina's street life lasted six years, but "I don't want this to be some sob story—I'd rather focus on achievements." And Christina has achieved: scraping together borrowed cash and welfare payments, she took an apartment. She got counselling. She finished high school (straight A's). She's 26 now and a third-year university student, hell-bent on becoming a doctor to the poor and homeless. She still bridles at the stereotype that street kids are lazy: "That isn't true. They don't know how to get out of their situation, they have no life skills, so why isn't the focus on teaching them how to be presentable, to have confidence? How're they supposed to think they're better when everyone's telling them they're worse?"

There are no miracles here. Housing, money, dedicated street workers, old-fashioned values like tolerance and caring. And kids with the will to survive, to push on. "In spite of all the odds," says Steve Gaetz, health promoter at Toronto's Shout clinic for street youth, "in spite of all the crap, in spite of all the traps around drugs, a lot of them are strong and move forward."

Others, of course, sadly don't. Sally recalls returning to Toronto this year and running into a guy she'd known in 1992, still on the street. "I said, 'What're you doing here, man?' And he was like, 'I need money for ... whatever.' I couldn't believe it. I'd looked up to him back then—because he was nice, he was older than me, he seemed to be doing all right. Of course," and she smiles slightly, seemingly embracing the distance she's come, "I had a different concept then of what's doing all right."

You take it from here ...

Responding

1. **Respond Personally** Referring to the chart you made while reading, write your thoughts about each of these young adults and their situations. Do you have *compassion* (a sympathetic feeling) for them? Do you think more attention needs to be paid to the problem of young Canadians living on the street?

2. **Focus on Tone** With a partner, discuss whether or not the author takes a positive attitude toward young homeless people and their problems. Is the article a positive one overall? Quote examples of sentences to back your opinions.

3. **Examine Structure and Sequence** This is a well-organized piece of journalism. Write down the numbers 1 to 10 (for the paragraphs) and beside each number, explain what the topics and subtopics are for each.

Extending

4. **Conduct Research** Using the Internet, research information about teenage poverty, teenage runaways, or the urban homeless. Organize and present your findings to the class.

5. **Share Ideas** As a class, discuss circumstances that might lead someone to consider running away and/or live on the street. What choices might such a person have?

6. **Write a Poem** Using the voice of a teenager living on the street, write a poem presenting your view of the world.

Before you read, as a class, discuss what you expect from the selection based on the title.

As you read, record how the actual events of the selection compared with your earlier predictions.

"My Father Had Been Drinking"

No matter how bad it hurts, find someone to talk to.

Monologue from a book by William S. Pollack and Todd Shuster

Notes

William S. Pollack, Ph.D., is a clinical psychologist and assistant clinical professor of psychiatry at Harvard Medical School. He wrote *Real Boys' Voices* with **Todd Shuster** in 2000, a follow-up to his 1998 work, *Real Boys: Rescuing Our Sons from the Myths of Boyhood*. He is a founding member and fellow of the American Psychological Association's Society for the Psychological Study of Men and Masculinity.

Mickey, 17, from a city in the South:

Maybe a year ago, my father was drunk and slammed my brother's head up against the bookshelf. I was in the apartment with them, but I didn't see it. I heard him yelling, and then I heard my brother screaming, then crying. That's the only time he ever touched any of us, and I don't really care to know what happened. All I know was that my father had been drinking.

Our parents divorced when I was two and my brother, Ron, was four. We live with our mother and stepdad, but we see our father every few weeks. I was always the son that followed in his father's footsteps. He was an athlete, I was an athlete; my brother wasn't. My father connected with me through sports. We would enjoy sitting down and watching a football game together, but Ron didn't. I feel guilty about it because I've been able to have that kind of relationship with our father and my brother hasn't.

Neither of us was ever hurt except for that one time. He still drinks every once in a while, but he's giving it up. I see him every other weekend, and he doesn't drink when I'm around. But even though I can vent to him, I still don't feel like I can go to him with important things. His drinking just kind of rips us apart.

A few weeks ago I made a very bad decision when I was upset. My girlfriend and I had just broken up, and I found out that she was hooking up with this guy that had been trying to come between us ever since we started going out. That really made me mad, and I got pretty messed up on alcohol with three friends. We were all drunk, and we went to throw oranges and eggs at this guy's truck. But we didn't feel like that was enough, so we went back with a few cinder blocks and a screwdriver. That night we did three thousand dollars' worth of damage to his truck.

The next day I felt horrible about it, but it was too late. It's something that I'm not proud of, and I wish I hadn't done it. Messing up his truck is one thing in my life that I wish I could take back, but I can't. If I don't touch another drop of alcohol ever again, it'll be too soon.

That night I didn't think I needed to talk to anyone about how upset I was feeling. I thought I could handle it on my own, but I couldn't. If I knew anyone else in that sort of situation or feeling that upset, I would tell them to talk to somebody before they take any action. Separate yourself from the crowd and just think about what happened and why you're feeling the way you're feeling. No matter how bad it hurts, find someone to talk to.

There's pressure on us as guys to handle things on our own, but it all just balls up inside you, and eventually it'll explode. It exploded for me that night, and now all four of us are getting jobs to pay back the damages. Thank God they're not going to press charges.

I've always stood up for my own and wouldn't let anybody push me around. If you let them push you around, then they think they can do it any time they want to. When I have an issue with someone, or something is bothering me, I carry it with me until I deal with it. It's just how I am. I have a strong sense of justice, of what's right and what's wrong.

Male pride gets us in a lot of trouble sometimes. See, in a typical fight somebody insults you, then you respond, then he pushes you. Now, if you don't push back you'll get made fun of for God knows how long; people will call you a "wuss" or a "sissy." And that hurts anybody's pride, so you push back. In some ways it's better to get beat up to protect your pride than to take a punch and walk away. You show that you know how to fight and that you won't take it, so you won't end up getting teased. Of course, you still have to suffer the consequences of getting in a fight. You just have to decide which is more important: keeping your pride or staying out of trouble. Life is often very unfair.

You take it from here ...

Responding

1. **Assess Realism** Discuss in a group: Does Mickey's story sound true? What events suggest that these things really did happen to him? Does Mickey sound like someone you would like to meet or be friends with? Why or why not?

2. **Review Conflicts** With a partner, go over the monologue and answer these questions:
   a) How does Mickey's relationship with his father differ from Ron's? How does this difference affect the relationship between the brothers?
   b) Does Mickey trust his father?
   c) Why did Mickey get drunk and vandalize the truck?
   d) Find a sentence that reveals the pressure Mickey lives under.
   e) In your opinion, why is Mickey a fighter?

3. **Consider Cause-Effect** In a paragraph, tell about how alcohol has influenced Mickey and his family. How does this compare with what you know of the effects of alcohol on families and teens?

4. **Brainstorm Questions** In your notebook, make a chart of questions and answers. On one side, write down four questions you would like to ask Mickey. On the other side, answer the questions as you think he would.

Extending

5. **Compose a Sequel** Imagine this family in three years. What would it be like? Continue the story of Mickey, Ron, and their father.

6. **Analyze a Problem** Write an article reviewing what you think are the main causes of "broken homes" or dysfunctional families. In the second part of your article, suggest some positive solutions for these social problems.

Before you read, write a definition of "weekend parenting" and "visiting rights."

As you read, think about the good times you have had with a parent or guardian. Jot down a memory of one such time.

"Remember that time you ate a whole pizza?"

Write Me Sometime
by Taien Ng-Chan

MEMOIR

Notes

Taien Ng-Chan is a Montreal author of fiction and poetry.

Whenever I think of my father, I think of food. I think of the years we spent eating at McDonald's and the Old Spaghetti Factory and pizza parlours galore. From as far back as I can remember, I saw my dad only once a week, when he picked me up every Saturday afternoon to go out for lunch. I'd get to choose which restaurant we'd go to, and then he'd ask me about school, my mother, and assorted things that I can't remember now. I was probably too busy eating. My mother did come along with us at first, mainly to keep an eye on me, but she eventually stopped because she didn't want to deal with my father. I don't blame her.

When I turned ten, my six-year-old half sister started joining our Saturday excursions. Suddenly, I had a weekend sibling, which was strange because I had always thought I was an only child. The three of us would argue about where to go for lunch, but as my sister liked the same things I did, it wouldn't take too long for us to decide. Every now and then we'd let Dad choose, but we knew he'd just want to go for dim sum, which we thought was boring.

I used to look forward to these Saturdays because I could eat anything I wanted. As I got older, we started going out for steak and seafood, but for the longest time, I just wanted pizza. My mother never made pizza, or even spaghetti. Sometimes she made pork chops or shepherd's pie or soya sauce chicken and rice, which I liked well enough. But I loved pizza. Thin crust with extra sauce, sometimes ham and pineapple, sometimes all dressed but no olives. My dad and I were harsh pizza critics: the sauce had to be spicy, and the vegetables cut and arranged just right. An abundance of pineapple was a must, and the cheese had to pull away into long, thin strands between the slices. One particular restaurant failed abysmally to meet our standards and was forever dubbed

340 Youth—The Awakening Years

"The Yucky House of Pizza," which we'd shout every time we drove past it.

After lunch, we'd go bowling, or to the dinosaur park at the zoo, or paddle boating at Prince's Island in the summer, or skating and tobogganing in the winter. Sometimes, Dad would take us to Ikea and spend an hour pretending to look at furniture while we jumped around in the room full of blue and red plastic balls. Other times, we'd go to the bakery at the mall and each pick out two slices of cake, plus a couple for my mom. Chocolate cheesecake, fruit tarts, danishes. We'd make a pot of tea and pretend to have a party. Then, just before dinnertime, my dad and my sister would go home.

The images I have in my head of these Saturdays are blurry, happy pictures that go with my dad's stories like illustrations. There was the time he ate two slices of a pizza and I ate the rest. I must have been only six or seven at the time, and I see myself sitting small in the corner of a restaurant booth with dark brown vinyl seats, a huge pizza in front of me. "The whole pizza!" my dad exclaims every time he brings up that story.

Or the time we went for spaghetti, and the top fell off the container as I was shaking out some parmesan over the spicy meat sauce, spilling a ton of cheese like a snowfall over the entire plate. That's the picture I have, me with the container still in my hand, the lid in the spaghetti. From then on, we made a great ritual of checking the lids every time.

If I could just look at these pictures, I'd think my childhood was made up of fifty-two happy lunches a year. But somewhere along the way, I stopped looking forward to Saturdays. I'd listen to my sister talk about playing basketball with Dad after supper, or the way they both called grilled cheese sandwiches "grouchy" sandwiches. Or notice how my sister knew all the songs on the tape of Chinese opera that my dad liked to play in the car. It left me with the taste of something sharp and grey under my tongue, like a tiny piece of rock had slipped into my food. If I wasn't careful, I'd break my teeth on it. Once I told him not to bother coming any more, that I had lots of friends and needed more time to play with them. But I felt sad about it afterwards, remembering how his face had changed. After that, I seemed to go into automatic cheer whenever I saw him. Our Saturday lunch rituals continued right up until the time I moved out to go to university.

We live in different cities now, and I only see my father once or twice a year, when I come home to Calgary for Christmas or if he happens to come by Vancouver on business. I see my half sister even less, and I'm still apt to think of myself as an only child. I think she feels the same way, because we've never tried to stay in touch.

I don't know why I feel the need to keep in touch with my father, when he wasn't much more in my life than lunch once a week. But somehow I think that the lines have to be kept open. My mom thinks so too, oddly enough.

"Have you heard from your dad lately?" she says every time she phones. "What did he say? You should write him."

Write Me Sometime

And I do write him. I write him longer letters than I write my friends. I write him about what I've been doing, how my classes are going, what projects I've been working on. I sent him the entire movie script that I had gotten funding to write, and the last essay I researched about the effects of Darwinism on Victorian literature. I tell him about newspaper articles I've been reading on the controversy over the age of the universe, and what I've been thinking about our last conversation on artificial intelligence.

My father, you see, is a scientist. More precisely, a geophysicist. When I was younger, he used to tell me he sat at a desk and drank lots of coffee for a living. When I found out that he flew all over the world to look at rocks and stuff, I wanted to be a scientist too. Or an artist. "A scientist or an artist, I haven't made up my mind yet," I used to tell people who asked what I wanted to be when I grew up. In my letters to my dad, I guess I try to be both.

He hardly ever writes back to me, but every so often he calls. Every time we talk, we say that we should write more often, get to know each other better. And then I won't hear from him for another year. I feel as if I'm trying to communicate with outer-space life-forms, my satellite dish sending out signals just in case.

The last time I saw my father was about a year ago, when he was in Vancouver for a business meeting. He called me just before noon and wanted to take me out for lunch. I had already eaten an avocado and tomato sandwich.

"That's okay," Dad said. "You can eat more!"

"Well, maybe we can go for a walk instead," I suggested. "We could go to Stanley Park."

"I can't do too much walking," he said. "I've been having a little trouble with my feet lately. Your dad's getting old, you know …"

"Oh, Dad, you're not getting old," I said, as cheerfully as I could. "We can do something else. Maybe we can go to the art gallery. Or what else do you want to see?"

"I don't have too much time," he said. "Why don't we go have lunch anyway? We can go a little later if you like."

So I gave up and let him take me out for lunch. We ended up at a trendy restaurant on Robson Street, since it was close by, and Dad tried to order me everything on the menu.

"How about an appetizer?" he said, poking his finger at the description of the liver paté. "This sounds good. Or how about a salad? That's good for you. How are you eating these days? You should have some soup, too."

"I'm really not that hungry," I said. "I can't eat like I used to. What about you? What are you going to have?"

"I'm not too hungry either. I'll just have a beer," he said. I'd never seen him have a drink before. "Maybe we should've gone to the pub," I said jokingly.

The waiter came over and waited.

"I guess I'll have the spinach salad," I said, handing him my menu. "And a glass of white wine, please."

"I'll have a beer," Dad said. "Any kind."

The waiter nodded and smiled and went away. Dad looked at me funny for a second, probably because he'd never seen me drink before, either.

"Is that all you're having?" he said. "You should have an entrée. The veal looked very good."

"Veal ...," I said, screwing up my nose. "Dad, I'm a vegetarian."

"Oh. That's right." He scratched his head.

I could see him wanting to debate the issue, just as he had when I first explained to him why I was a vegetarian. I was back in Calgary for Christmas. I hadn't seen my dad or my sister in quite a while, and we were about to go out for lunch when I told them the big news.

"So," he had said, "that means you don't eat meat any more." My sister looked at me as if I was crazy.

"What about chicken?" Dad asked. "Do you eat chicken? Seafood?"

"No, Dad, chickens aren't vegetables. Fish aren't vegetables either."

"What's your reason for not eating meat? It's not just because you have to kill animals, is it? After all, death is a part of life."

"I know. If you went out and killed your own animal and ate it, that'd be fine with me."

I had launched into the whole thing about battery cages and steroids and how you could feed the world with the grain that goes to feeding cows and how the rainforests of Brazil were being destroyed for hamburgers. Dad countered each point. We ended by discussing the impact individuals could make, and why Buddhists didn't eat meat. My sister just looked on.

Finally, Dad asked us what we wanted for lunch. My sister suggested pizza.

"Uh," I said, "actually, I don't eat pizza much any more. I try to stay away from dairy products. Hard to digest."

But there weren't too many places to go in Calgary, so I compromised. "Wow," my sister said after lunch. "I never had a pizza without meat before."

When the waiter came back with our drinks and my spinach salad, there were bacon bits that I had to pick out. My dad watched me for a while and fiddled with his beer glass. Then he started what had become our usual routine.

"So," he began, "what do you think of what's been happening in the news lately?"

We had an ongoing discussion about politics and the economy and the state of the world—it gave us something to talk about. These talks always started and ended the same way. He would ask me what I thought about recent events, and then we would talk about the future, the need to adapt to change, the impact of technology. Dad always got very animated when talking about technology. I would bring up the need for human responsibility in science, and he would agree with me wholeheartedly. They were good conversations.

My father likes to debate things, to argue for the sake of argument. My mother said he had wanted to be a philosopher when he was young and idealistic. A lot like you, she said. That was when she first met him. That was before he decided there was no living to be made in philosophy and went into the oil industry.

"Arts," he said to me once, "are for the weekends."

I told him then that I wanted to be a writer.

"Journalism?" he said.

"No, writing," I said. "Stories and plays and stuff."

"Write for the newspapers," he said. "That's what you should do if you like writing."

I told him I would think about it.

But he never did ask me what I wrote about. And I never asked what he thought of the things I sent him, either. Except once, about the Darwin essay.

"Interesting," he said. "Very interesting. Why don't you write a book about the relationship between science and the arts?"

Write Me Sometime

I said I might do that. And we haven't mentioned it since.

By the time I had finished my salad, Dad had convinced me to have dessert. I mulled over the menu, torn between the chocolate hazelnut torte and the blueberry apple flan.

"Aren't you going to have any?" I asked, hoping we could swap bites. Dad shook his head.

"Why don't you get both anyway?" he said. "After all, how often do you get to have lunch with your dad?"

I settled for the flan.

The rest of the lunch was spent in polite enquiry. We had run out of politics and technology, so I asked him how his work was, and how my sister was. He asked me how my work was, and how my mother was. She's fine, we both said. Things are going fine.

After I had finished eating, we walked up Robson Street. We passed chocolate shops and pizza joints, and every time I looked in the window of a store, Dad would ask me if I wanted anything. When we passed a frozen yogurt shop he wanted to buy a tub of frozen yogurt for me.

"Yogurt's very healthy," he said. "I want you to eat right."

"But I just ate."

"You can eat it later," he said. "You're a growing girl!"

"Not any more," I said. "I haven't grown an inch in years."

"Remember that time you ate a whole pizza?"

"I was seven years old, Dad."

"A whole pizza! How about getting some pizza now? You can bring it home for dinner."

"That's okay."

"You don't eat much any more. Are you getting enough protein? You have to be careful, being vegetarian."

I nodded and smiled. "Yes, Dad."

We went on like this all the way up the street, with Dad ducking into a store every now and then despite my protests. By the time we reached my apartment, my arms were laden with bags of food. I invited him in, but he had had only a couple of hours to spare.

"Write me sometime," he said. "Let me know if there's anything you need."

I closed the door behind him, my insides feeling forlorn and empty. I went into the kitchen to put the pizza in the fridge, the frozen yogurt in the freezer, the chocolate in the cupboard. But I didn't feel like eating again for days.

When I told my mother about Dad's visit, she wanted to know all the details. Where we ate, what we talked about, what he had bought me.

"Did he give you any spending money?" she said. "Well, he should have. He's your father. And he can afford it."

"I don't want him to," I said.

I could hear her clucking her tongue over the phone. "You're his *daughter*," she said. "You shouldn't even have to *ask*."

I haven't seen my father since that lunch, although he did call me a couple of weeks ago. I was out at the time. When I came home, I found my father's voice on my answering machine, sounding almost querulous. He said that he'd call back some other time. I called him a few days later. The phone rang twice before he picked it up.

"Hi, Dad," I said, only to be greeted enthusiastically with my sister's name. "Uh, no," I said. I felt almost apologetic. "It's your other daughter."

"Oh," Dad said. There was a moment's silence, then he cleared his throat. "You sound very much alike."

"Well," I said, as cheerfully as I could. "We are sisters, after all." The conversation went downhill from there.

"Are you in town?" my father asked.

"No, I just called to say hi. And to return your call."

"Ah," he said.

I asked him how his work was, and how my sister was; he asked me how my work was, and how my mother was. She's fine, we both said. Things are going fine.

You take it from here ...

Responding

1. **Recall a Moment**   Share with a partner the special time you recalled while reading this selection. Explain why this time means something to you.

2. **Read Between the Lines**   With another student, take a second look at the selection. What conflicts do you see between the characters? What role does food play in creating conflicts?

3. **Analyze Character**   In two short paragraphs, analyze the characters of the narrator-daughter and her father.

> **SELF ASSESSMENT**
> - How did you organize your answer within the paragraphs?
> - What new information did you learn as you analyzed both characters?

Extending

4. **Investigate a Topic**   Find out more about vegetarianism. Why do people become vegetarians? What foods are eaten or not eaten? Is vegetarianism a healthy lifestyle? Share your findings in a class discussion.

5. **Script a Scene**   Write dialogue for the next meeting between the father and daughter.

Before you read, write about a moment when you did something adventurous that caused you to experience unexpected anxiety or fear.

As you read, write down in your notebook your opinions of the old man.

The Slave Fort

"Don't be afraid—I am not mad, as you believe."

Short Story by Ghassan Kanafani

Notes

Ghassan Kanafani (1936–1972) was born in Acre, Palestine. He was killed in Beirut when his car was sabotaged. He was a spokesman for the Popular Front for the Liberation of Palestine and taught and worked as a journalist in Damascus and Kuwait.

austerely: severely simple; harshly; sternly

convulsive: characterized by irregular motions of limbs

gelatinous: of a jelly-like consistency

jerry cans: water or gas cans

relapsed: fell back or sunk back

uncomprehendingly: without understanding

Had he not been so sadly shabby one would have said of him that he was a poet. The site he had chosen for his humble hut of wood and beaten-out jerry cans was truly magnificent; right by the threshold the might of the sea flowed under the feet of the sharp rocks with a deep-throated, unvarying sound. His face was gaunt, his beard white though streaked with a few black hairs, his eyes hollow under bushy brows; his cheekbones protruded like two rocks that had come to rest either side of the large projection that was his nose.

Why had we gone to that place? I don't remember now. In our small car we had followed a rough, miry and featureless road. We had been going for more than three hours when Thabit pointed through the window and gave a piercing shout:

"There's the Slave Fort."

This Slave Fort was a large rock the base of which had been eaten away by the waves so that it resembled the wing of a giant bird, its head curled in the sand, its wing outstretched above the clamour of the sea.

"Why did they call it 'The Slave Fort'?"

"I don't know. Perhaps there was some historical incident which gave it the name. Do you see that hut?"

And once again Thabit pointed, this time toward the small hut lying in the shadow of the gigantic rock. He turned off the engine and we got out of the car.

"They say that a half-mad old man lives in it."

"What does he do with himself in this waste on his own?"

"What any half-mad old man would do."

From afar we saw the old man squatting on his heels at the entrance to his hut, his head clasped in his hands, staring out to sea.

"Don't you think there must be some special story about this old man? Why do you insist he's half-mad?"

346 Youth—The Awakening Years

"I don't know, that's what I heard."

Thabit, having arrived at the spot of his choice, levelled the sand, threw down the bottles of water, took out the food from the bag, and seated himself.

"They say he was the father of four boys who struck it lucky and are now among the richest people in the district."

"And then?"

"The sons quarrelled about who should provide a home for the father. Each wife wanted her own way in the matter and the whole thing ended with the old man making his escape and settling down here."

"It's a common enough story and shouldn't have turned the old man half-mad."

Thabit looked at me uncomprehendingly, then lit the small heap of wood he had arranged, and poured water into the metal water-jug and set it on the fire.

"The important thing in the story is to agree about whether his flight was a product of his mad half or his sane half."

"There he is, only a few yards away—why not go over and ask him?"

Thabit blew at the fire, then began rubbing his eyes as he sat up straight, resting his body on his knees.

"I can't bear the idea which the sight of him awakens in me."

"What idea?"

"That the man should spend seventy years of his life so austerely, that he should work, exert himself, existing day after day and hour after hour, that for seventy long years he should gain his daily bread from the sweat of his brow, that he should live through his day in the hope of a better tomorrow, that for seventy whole years he should go to sleep each night—and for what? So that he should, at the last, spend the rest of his life cast out like a dog, alone, sitting like this. Look at him—he's like some polar animal that has lost its fur. Can you believe that a man can live seventy years to attain to this? I can't stomach it."

Once again he stared at us; then, spreading out the palms of his hands, he continued his tirade:

"Just imagine! Seventy useless, meaningless years. Imagine walking for seventy years along the same road; the same directions, the same boundaries, the same horizons, the same everything. It's unbearable!"

"No doubt the old man would differ with you in your point of view. Maybe he believes that he has reached an end which is distinct from his life. Maybe he wanted just such an end. Why not ask him?"

We got up to go to him. When we came to where he was he raised his eyes, coldly returned our greeting and invited us to sit down. Through the half-open door we could see the inside of the hut; the threadbare

mattress in one corner, while in the opposite one was a square rock on which lay a heap of unopened oyster shells. For a while silence reigned; it was then broken by the old man's feeble voice asking:

"Do you want oyster shells? I sell oyster shells."

As we had no reply to make to him, Thabit enquired:

"Do you find them yourself?"

"I wait for low tide so as to look for them far out. I gather them up and sell them to those who hope to find pearls in them."

We stared at each other. Presently Thabit put the question that had been exercising all our minds:

"Why don't you yourself try to find pearls inside these shells?"

"I?"

He uttered the word as though becoming aware for the first time that he actually existed, or as though the idea had never previously occurred to him. He then shook his head and kept his silence.

"How much do you sell a heap for?"

"Cheaply—for a loaf or two."

"They're small shells and certainly won't contain pearls."

The old man looked at us with lustreless eyes under bushy brows.

"What do you know about shells?" he demanded sharply. "Who's to tell whether or not you'll find a pearl?" and as though afraid that if he were to be carried away still further he might lose the deal, he relapsed into silence.

"And can you tell?"

"No, no one can tell," and he began toying with a shell which lay in front of him, pretending to be unaware of our presence.

"All right, we'll buy a heap."

The old man turned round and pointed to the heap arrayed on the square rock.

"Bring two loaves," he said, a concealed ring of joy in his voice, "and you can take that heap."

On returning to our place bearing the heap of shells, our argument broke out afresh.

"I consider those eyes can only be those of a madman. If not, why doesn't he open the shells himself in the hope of finding some pearls?"

"Perhaps he's fed up with trying and prefers to turn spectator and make money."

It took us half the day before we had opened all the shells. We piled the gelatinous insides of the empty shells around us, then burst into laughter at our madness.

In the afternoon Thabit suggested to me that I should take a cup of strong tea to the old man in the hope that it might bring a little joy to his heart.

As I was on my way over to him a slight feeling of fear stirred within me. However, he invited me to sit down and began sipping at his tea with relish.

"Did you find anything in the shells?"

"No, we found nothing—you fooled us."

He shook his head sadly and took another sip.

"To the extent of two loaves!" he said, as though talking to himself, and once again shook his head. Then, suddenly, he glanced at me and explained sharply:

"Were these shells your life—I mean, were each shell to represent a year of your life and you opened them one by one and found them empty, would you have been as sad as you are about losing a couple of loaves?"

He began to shake all over and at that moment I was convinced that I was in the presence of someone who certainly was mad. His eyes, under their bushy brows, gave out a sharp and unnatural brightness, while the dust from his ragged clothes played in the afternoon sun. I could not find a word to say. When I attempted to rise to my feet he took hold of my wrist and his frail hand was strong and convulsive. Then I heard him say:

"Don't be afraid—I am not mad, as you believe. Sit down, I want to tell you something: the happiest moments of my day are when I can watch disappointment of this kind."

I reseated myself, feeling somewhat calmer.

In the meantime, he began to gaze out at the horizon, seemingly unaware of my presence, as though he had not, a moment ago, invited me to sit down. Then he turned to me.

"I knew you wouldn't find anything. These oysters are still young and therefore can't contain the seed of a pearl. I wanted to know, though."

Again he was silent and stared out to sea. Then, as though speaking to himself, he said:

"The ebb tide will start early tonight and I must be off to gather shells. Tomorrow other men will be coming."

Overcome by bewilderment, I rose to my feet. The Slave Fort stood out darkly against the light of the setting sun. My friends were drinking tea around the heaps of empty shells as the old man began running after the receding water, bending down from time to time to pick up the shells left behind.

The Slave Fort **349**

You take it from here ...

Responding

1. **Reveal Context**   With another student, discuss
   a) what the Slave Fort is and why the young men have gone there.
   b) how the old man came to live near the Slave Fort and how he survives.

2. **Review Character Motivation**   Write answers to the following questions in your notebook:
   a) What upsets Thabit? What does he want to know?
   b) Why do the young men buy the shells?
   c) Why did the old man sell them the shells?

3. **Analyze Symbol**   In a group, analyze the deeper meaning of the shells as seen by the old man:

   "Were these shells your life—I mean, were each shell to represent a year of your life and you opened them one by one and found them empty, would you have been as sad as you are about losing a couple of loaves?"

   (Hint: Consider how the shells relate to the circumstances of both the old man and the young men.)

   > **GROUP ASSESSMENT**
   > - How did your group approach the task at hand?
   > - Did you go back to find lines in the text to support your views or to settle differences of opinion?

4. **Think about Purpose and Theme**   Write your response to the following:
   a) What does the narrator learn about life from the old man?
   b) How does the title relate to both the old man and the young men?
   c) What are your thoughts on the author's purpose and the story's main point?

Extending

5. **Relate an Anecdote**   In a group discussion, recount a memorable incident in which you learned something about life.

6. **Illustrate the Story**   Select a moment from the story to represent visually. Use lines from the story for a caption.

Before you read, tell about a time when you bonded with a friend or sibling.

As you read, write down words in your notebook to describe the feelings you got from reading the poem.

Celebration

Poem by Al Pittman

Driving along route three
to Fredericton
for my young brother
the first time out of his town
out of his province
the first time on his own
it is a day of beginnings
for me aware now
of the manhood flowing in his veins
it is an end of kind

not thinking any of this
just driving along nohow
we spy an apple tree
with fruit growing red
against the blue New Brunswick sky

we aren't hungry
have no appetite for apples
but stop anyway
climb the twisted trunk
shake the apples off
gather them in bushels
filling the back seat of the car
to a useless limit

the apples are rough
and pitted black on the skin
they are bitter to taste
and difficult to swallow
what we don't throw
at telephone poles in passing
we leave to rot on the back seat
yet our orchard thievery
is no futile act

it is an act of the blood
two brothers in a farmer's field
nowhere in New Brunswick
celebrating their brotherhood
their tribal communion
beneath the pale end
of one year's summer sky

You take it from here ...

Responding

1. **Explain Meanings** With a partner, interpret the following lines:
   a) "for me aware now
      of the manhood flowing in his veins
      it is an end of kind." (stanza 1)
   b) "filling the back seat of the car
      to a useless limit." (stanza 3)
   c) "yet our orchard thievery
      is no futile act" (stanza 4)
   d) "tribal communion" (stanza 5)

   Compare your views with those of another pair of students.

2. **Discuss Symbol** Brainstorm in a group: How are the apple tree and apples used as symbols in the poem? Then write a paragraph about the symbolism.

3. **Focus on Title** As a class, discuss how Pittman's poem is a celebration of youth and the joy of life.

Extending

4. **Recall a Similar Moment** Write your own poem, memoir, or story that describes a situation that reinforces the bond between siblings or friends.

5. **Have a Class Discussion** As a class, discuss what is special about the bonds between siblings. How do these bonds differ from those between friends? Are family ties generally stronger than ties between friends?

Reflecting on the Unit

Responding

1. **Respond to a Quotation**   Pick one of the quotations from the unit introduction and write an essay on it referring to 2–3 selections studied in this unit.

2. **Compare Themes**   Pick one of the following themes and write about what you learned about it:
   - values of teens
   - memories of the past
   - coming of age
   - the generation gap
   - teenage runaways
   - role models and influences

Extending

3. **Compose Diary Entries**   Compose three diary entries for three different characters or people from this unit.

4. **Analyze Media Portrayals**   Select two movies that feature teenagers, and present a review for each one, assessing and comparing how they portray teenagers. Include your thoughts on whether these movies have been popular with teenage audiences, offering reasons as to why or why not.

> **TIP**
> - You could select a scene from each movie to show to the class to illustrate your points.

> **SELF ASSESSMENT**
>
> Review what you have learned from this unit regarding
> - reading beyond the literal level
> - how information can be organized in nonfiction reading
> - how to pick out a theme
> - how to become a better speaker
> - how to listen critically
> - how media influence individuals' views and self-image
> - how to use technology to acquire information

UNIT 8

"Life has no meaning except in terms of responsibility."
—Reinhold Neibuhr

"The only place where success comes before work is in a dictionary."
—Vidal Sassoon

"To find joy in work is to discover the fountain of youth."
—Pearl Buck

"Find out what you like doing best and get someone to pay you for it."
—Katherine Whitehorn

Out in the World

This unit focuses on how young adults can prepare to enter the work world. As the quotations above suggest, career success depends largely on taking responsibility and being willing to work hard. They also remind us of the rewards of work. Work can keep us invigorated and mentally young, especially if we follow the ultimate formula for success by making a career out of doing something we love.

Attitude is central to success, and it is featured in the selections in this unit, along with practical information on topics ranging from interviews, résumés, and business correspondence to developing a polished visual "package" for promoting yourself and your ideas.

As you read this unit, think about the following:

1) What skills are necessary for success in the workplace?
2) How can job seekers and employees present themselves to advantage in work situations?
3) How can technology be used to promote personal skills and ideas?
4) What can be learned from self-help sources and self-evaluation?

Before you read, make a list of the characteristics of a successful job candidate.

As you read, discuss with a partner whether or not this applicant will likely get the job.

Herman

Cartoon by Jim Unger

"I've got two other applicants to see before I make my final choice."

You take it from here ...

Responding

1. **Express an Opinion**   Write a paragraph explaining whether or not the applicant will get the job. Give reasons to support your opinion.

2. **Discuss Theme**   With a classmate, discuss what you see as the main message of the cartoon.

3. **Analyze Effect of Medium on Message**   Select three details in this cartoon that support the cartoon's message. Write the message as a paragraph or slogan, incorporating the three details you noted. How does the different form affect the content of the message?

Extending

4. **Establish a Focus for Text Creation**   Identify an important "rule" for job seekers other than the one illustrated in this cartoon. Create a cartoon to convey that message.

5. **Write a Letter**   As the manager, write a letter informing the applicant of the final decision on hiring and responding to the applicant's suitability for the job.

6. **Develop a Skit**   With another student, role-play a scene for the class about another applicant who makes different mistakes at an interview. See if the class can spot the errors made by the applicant.

Before you read, write down a chart of do's and don'ts for interviews. Compare notes with a partner.

As you read, think of what other hints you could add to this article.

Be on time!

Preparing for an Interview

by GRAMMY ASIA LTD.

SELF-HELP INFORMATION

Remember to always dress professionally for an interview. Business dress is recommended. Pay attention to detail and always look your best. First impressions are very important and may affect the outcome of the interview!

It always pays to find out as much as possible about your prospective employer before attending the interview. It makes sense to utilize all the resources that are available to you! You can ask your friends who may work in the industry or obtain information from the company's marketing or public relations department. Your local business library may have current information, and, if the company has a Web site, you can explore it for up-to-date information.

Try to find out how long the interview is likely to last and try not to schedule any other events around the time of your interview. In general, the longer the interview, the better the outcome! Make sure that you have accurately written down the company's phone number and address and the names of anybody that you will have to see.

Be on time! It is extremely important that you are not late for your interview! Make sure that you know exactly where the interview is going to take place, how to get there, and how long the journey will take. Always allow yourself extra time in case you get caught in traffic or get lost. It may be appropriate to do a trial run if the interview is taking place in a location not familiar to you.

Take extra copies of your résumé with you to your interview, together with any relevant documents such as college diplomas, professional certificates, or references from past employers.

Bring a pen and notebook in case taking notes becomes appropriate.

Before an interview, think carefully about your work history, and satisfy yourself that you are able to discuss with confidence your responsibilities, performance and achievements or goals, and personal qualities. Always stress the positives and not the negatives about yourself. *Be prepared and ready to sell yourself!*

Review this information and anticipate the questions that may be put to you during the interview. Role-play with a friend will give you valuable interview practice and make you feel more confident at the actual event. In this competitive market, you owe it to yourself to prepare for the interview as much as possible. People who prepare for their interview are often far more successful than those who have not!!!

You take it from here ...

Responding

1. **Identify and Understand Key Points** Review the article and identify the key tips it offers. Choose any two of the tips you listed and for each one, write a paragraph explaining how it can contribute to a successful interview.

2. **Discuss Appropriate Attire** Have a class discussion about appropriate dress and grooming for an interview. What is "business dress"? How does it differ from casual, everyday wear? What grooming tips would you recommend for an applicant?

Extending

3. **Brainstorm a List of Questions** In a group, compile a list of questions to help prospective applicants get ready for their interviews. What would be the reason behind each question?

4. **Do a Personal Inventory** One of the points in the article is that it is important to "sell" yourself. Make a list of your own strengths. How could you use these to advantage in an interview situation?

5. **Plan to Follow up** In a group, discuss the different ways one can follow up an interview. What ways might be considered to be rude or "pushy" by a prospective employer? Are there any circumstances where such tactics might be appropriate anyway?

Before you read, tell the class about any food- or restaurant-based jobs you have had. Why is that a good area for young people to break into the world of work?

As you read, write in your notebook a definition of "job satisfaction."

Notes

Jim Daniels has worked as a clerk in a Dairy Queen and as a liquor store employee, as a stock boy, janitor, bookkeeper, assembly line worker, teacher— and short-order cook. He lives in Pittsburgh, Pennsylvania.

Short-Order Cook

Poem by Jim Daniels

An average joe comes in and orders
30 cheeseburgers and 30 fries.

I wait for him to pay before I start cooking.
He pays—
he ain't no average joe.

The grill is just big enough for 10 rows of 3.
I slap the burgers down,
throw two buckets of fries in the deep fryer
and they pop pop spit spit ...
psss ...
The counter girls laugh.
I concentrate.
It is the crucial point:
they are ready for the cheese.

My fingers shake as I tear off slices, toss
them on the burgers/fries done/dump/
refill buckets/burgers ready/flip
into buns, beat that melting cheese/wrap
burgers in plastic/into paper bags/fries done/
dump/fill 30 bags/bring them to the counter,
wipe sweat on sleeve, and smile at the counter girls.
I puff my chest out and bellow:
"30 cheeseburgers, 30 fries."
They look at me funny.
I grab a handful of ice, toss it in my mouth,
do a little dance, and walk back to the grill.
Pressure, responsibility, success.
30 cheeseburgers. 30 fries.

360 Out in the World

You take it from here ...

Responding

1. **Describe Attitudes**   In a paragraph, describe how the short-order cook feels about his work. Does he have a good attitude in dealing with the public? Why is attitude important for job satisfaction?

2. **Examine Techniques**   The poem uses an *idiom* (a figurative expression peculiar to a given language or culture). What does an "average joe" mean?

3. **Appreciate and Imitate Organization**   Use the information in the poem to write a step-by-step explanation of how to make 30 cheeseburgers and 30 fries.

Extending

4. **Write a Job Evaluation**   Assume you are the cook's boss. Write an evaluation of his work, and conclude with your recommendation as to whether or not he is ready for promotion.

5. **Do Job Research**   In groups of three or four, brainstorm a list of jobs in the food and hospitality industry, and then identify up to 10 businesses in your area that include these jobs. Create a directory for job seekers, identifying each business name, address, telephone number, and other available contact information (e.g., e-mail and Web addresses, name of person in charge of hiring). Post your directory on the classroom bulletin board, or collaborate with other groups to compile a central Job Search Directory.

6. **Compose Classified Ads**   Write two advertisements for a short-order cook. Stress the importance of responsibility for this line of work.

> **Before you read,** in a group, discuss the purpose of application forms and their role in job seeking.
>
> **As you read,** write down two questions you would ask the author about application forms.

"Can you tell me a little bit more about the position?"

Ten Steps to Completing a Successful Application Form
by Nancy Schaefer

INSTRUCTIONS

1) **Be prepared and look professional.**
   When you go out to pick up application forms, look your best. Bring along a notebook or pad of paper, plus a pen. You should keep track of every employer you visit and every employee you talk with. It'll help you remember if you don't hear back for a few weeks.

2) **Smile and be polite.**
   When you go into the place where you want to apply, ask if you can speak to a manager. Be very polite and speak clearly. If the manager doesn't want to be disturbed, then just direct your questions to the person you are already speaking with.

3) **Ask for two application forms.**
   Again, be very polite and ask if you can have two application forms. You can say something like: "I'm interested in applying for a job here. Is there an application form?" If there is an application, then say: "I'd like two copies if possible please." If you can't get two, then photocopy the form before you begin to fill it out. That way you'll have one to practise on first.

4) **Get as much information as possible.**
   Finding out more about the workplace will help you decide if this is the right job for you. If the person you're talking to seems friendly and isn't too busy, ask them about the position. You could ask if they know when they will be scheduling interviews, or how many hours they expect people to work. If they are busy, it is best to keep it short.

Just make sure to get the name of the manager in charge of hiring.

5) **Take the application home and fill it out.**
Do a thorough, very neat job. Make sure to get help from a friend or parent when filling out parts that you aren't sure about.

6) **Attach a résumé and cover letter.**
Even if the employer doesn't ask for a résumé and cover letter, do them anyway. It will make you look more organized. Try to include in your cover letter any information you collected when you picked up the application.

7) **Return the application directly to the person doing the hiring.**
Before you return your application, call first. If you weren't able to find out the person's name when you picked up your application, this is also a good time to find it out. Handing your application directly to the person doing the hiring will improve your chances of being chosen for an interview.

8) **Remember the name of the person who took your application.**
If the person in charge of hiring is not available, don't worry. Write down the name of the person who takes your application. Call back later or the next day to speak to the person doing the hiring and say, "I brought in my application yesterday and gave it to _____. I just wanted to make sure you received it."

9) **Don't try too hard or annoy the manager.**
If you're calling just to see whether or not they got your résumé, try not to ask for any other information. Hopefully you already know when they're doing the hiring. If not, that should be the only other thing you ask at this point. Don't ask for details about the job. You don't want to bother them and hurt your chances.

10) **Call back to check on your application a few days before they said they'd be interviewing.**
It's okay to call the person you know is in charge of hiring just to say, "I just wanted to check on my application." It will be clear that you are interested and that you're organized enough to have kept track. This will give a great impression at the critical time when they are deciding who to interview.
Warning: If you are told "Don't call us, we'll call you if you are chosen for an interview," or something similar, don't call. Always follow the employer's instructions.

~

What questions should I ask when I'm handing in the application form?

Here are some good things to ask and say when you're handing in your application. When you first drop it off, you might say:

- "Hi. I'm _____. I'm dropping off my application for the _____ position that is available. Can I please speak to the person doing the hiring?"

If you manage to get introduced to the person doing the hiring, try asking some questions:

- "Can you tell me a little bit more about the position?"
- "Do you have any idea of when you will be scheduling interviews?"

If you have an opportunity, tell them you are interested in the position:

- "As you'll be able to see from my application, I'm really interested in the position. This looks like a great place to work."

Always remember to dress nicely, smile, shake the manager's hand firmly, and confidently thank them:

- "I appreciate your taking a few moments to speak with me. I hope to hear from you soon."

If you think an employer has asked you an unfair question on an application, call or visit the Web site of your province's ministry of labour and find out. You can find the phone number in the "blue pages" of your phone book or by doing a search on the Internet. Know your rights.

Some applications just ask weird questions. If you come across a question that you think is irrelevant or strange, all you can do is try your best to answer it.

Do's and Don'ts of Application Forms

- ✔ Do take the form home and fill it in neatly, in blue or black pen, with no spelling errors.
- ✔ Do have someone you trust look it over for you.
- ✔ Do attach a cover letter and a résumé.
- ✔ Do try to speak to the person doing the hiring whenever you can.
- ✔ Do dress well when you are handing in your application form.
- ✔ Do keep track of the places where you've applied.
- ✘ Don't ever lie on an application form.
- ✘ Don't leave any parts blank or questions unanswered.
- ✘ Don't write, "See attached on résumé." Always fill it out in full.

What if they ask a question that I think is private or personal?

In Canada, there are laws that govern the relationship between you and your employer, and they take effect and begin to protect you even before you are hired, when you are applying for jobs. Although the laws differ from province to province, you always are guaranteed certain rights.

You take it from here ...

Responding

1. **Answer Questions**   Exchange with a partner the two questions you each wrote while reading. How do you think the author might answer your two questions?

2. **Respond to Instructions**   In a group, look over the headings for the 10 instructions. How are the instructions sequenced? Would you have changed the order of any of the steps? Can you think of any other steps you might add?

3. **Understand Reasons**   Write one or two sentences to explain the reasons underlying any three of the ten steps. Exchange your views with a partner.

> **SELF ASSESSMENT**
> - What did you learn by testing out your opinions on someone else?

Extending

4. **Write a Cover Letter**   The purpose of the cover letter is to explain why you are responding to the job opening. A cover letter can also briefly indicate why you might be qualified for that particular job. Imagine and write such a letter for a position of your choice.

5. **Create a Brochure**   Assemble a brochure visually illustrating the recommendations in this selection.

6. **Share Anecdotes**   In a group, recall and talk about your own experiences related to seeking work. Is the advice in this article sensible and useful? Comment with reference to specific points or examples.

Before you read, write a paragraph explaining what a résumé is and what typically goes into it.

As you read, note your personal reactions to the advice in the article. Are there any points you would add?

Be as objective and as honest as possible.

Preparing an Effective Résumé

INSTRUCTIONS

Nothing will go further toward getting you the job you want than a well-prepared résumé. It's the first impression a prospective employer has of you, and it's critical.

Here's advice on the art of résumé writing from a helpful booklet put out by Employment and Immigration Canada called *Creative Job Search Techniques*.

1) After your name, address, and phone number, state your job objective clearly and briefly, keeping it broad enough so that you might be considered for more than one position. Then use simple, forceful words to describe your background and achievements. Always be precise and to the point.

2) Write in the first-person and choose strong verbs that illuminate your accomplishments, such as "I instituted," "I organized," or "I designed."

3) Provide complete information on your job history, education (including specialties) and experience, using telegram style—that is, don't write in complete sentences. List all certificates and diplomas, and include your volunteer work as well as your paid work.

4) Type your résumé, and make the format straightforward and easy to read. Paragraphs should be short, with ample space between them. Résumés should run no longer than three pages.

5) If a strict chronological description of your job history doesn't work to your advantage, place your most relevant experience at the top of the résumé instead, and continue to follow that format.

6) Don't boast, but don't undervalue yourself either. Be as objective and as honest as possible.

7) Be neat. Double-check your spelling and grammar. Have a friend read your résumé over to check for errors you might have missed.

8) Avoid adverbs such as "rather," "slightly," or "fairly." Be specific. Instead of saying, "I'm fairly experienced in this field," say, "I have two years of experience."

9) Describe in brief but colourful detail the pastimes and personal interests that are relevant to the job for which you're applying. List every service organization and club you belong to.

10) Avoid gimmicks such as coloured paper or photographs. These single you out as an amateur who feels he or she must vie for attention.

11) If you provide references, choose them carefully, avoiding close friends and relatives. Seek people in various fields who know you well, and always alert them that they've been named.

You take it from here ...

Responding

1. **Discuss Purpose of Résumé**   With a partner, review the purpose of a résumé. Evaluate and explain its importance as a job-search tool.

2. **Elaborate on a Point**   According to the article, a résumé's importance is "critical" as it is "the first impression a prospective employer has of you." Taking an employer's perspective, write a few paragraphs describing what you believe you can tell about an applicant based solely on his or her résumé.

Extending

3. **Create Your Own Résumé**   As a class assignment, write a resumé for yourself using information recommended by this article.

4. **Compile a List of References**   List people you might use as character references and employment references. Be sure to include all relevant contact information for each person listed.

5. **Write a Poem**   Write a poem titled "Résumé" that tells others about the real you.

TIP

- Proofread your résumé before typing your final copy.

> **SELF ASSESSMENT**
> - What did you learn about yourself by transferring the content of your résumé into a poetic form?
> - What are your views about creative writing as a means to greater self-understanding?

Before you read, discuss with a partner what the following are: a letter of reference, an evaluation letter, an employee performance appraisal, and a letter of inquiry.

As you read, note the purpose of each communication.

"I sincerely hope you'll be able to stay with us, Marilyn."

Writing for Business

368 Out in the World

A. Letter Requesting Reference

3219 Crest Hill Drive
Medicine Hat, AB T1A 0P8

May 19, 20xx

Professor Pat McMahon
Western School of Business and Technology
1580 South Drive
Medicine Hat, AB T2L 3E9

Dear Professor McMahon:

Your course in office information technology was my introduction to the field, and your instruction provided an excellent background in this career area. Because you know this field well and because you also know my work as a student, may I use your name as a reference when I apply for employment?

As I will complete my course work at Western School of Business and Technology in June, I will be looking for employment shortly. Being able to list your name as a reference would assist my efforts greatly. Enclosed is a fact sheet listing information that may be helpful to you when you write about me.

I am grateful to you for the excellent foundation you provided in office technology and for any help you can provide in my job search. Please indicate your willingness to serve as a reference by mailing the enclosed postage-paid card.

Sincerely yours,

Natalie Kienzler

Natalie Kienzler

Enclosures

B. Memo to Employee

TO: Marilyn O'Riley
FROM: John Pearson, Manager
DATE: January 30, 2001
SUBJECT: ATTENDANCE AND PRODUCTIVITY WARNING

Over the past year, Marilyn, your attendance has been irregular, affecting your job performance and productivity.

For the six-month period of January to June of last year, you had 9 unauthorized absences and were late 16 times. From July to the end of the year you missed another 10 days and were late 14 times, according to our personnel records.

Other customer service representatives have complained that they must carry a heavier load of calls and correspondence when you are missing. Morale in your department is declining, and some reps are asking if an additional person can be hired to handle the workload.

At your performance review conferences June 4, 2000, and again January 5, 2001, you promised that your attendance would improve as soon as you settled temporary personal problems. I have not seen any change in your punctuality or attendance.

To remain with our organization, Marilyn, you must have no unauthorized absence or tardiness in the next three-month period. On April 30, I will review with you your attendance record and productivity. If they are unsatisfactory, we must release you and hire a new employee for your position. I sincerely hope you'll be able to stay with us, Marilyn.

C. Employee Performance Appraisal

LASER PRODUCTS, INC.
EMPLOYEE PERFORMANCE APPRAISAL

Last Name	First Name	Employment Division	Job Title
Mattheson,	Jim	Consumer Services	Customer Service Rep II

Group	Appraisal Period
T-9880	June 2, 2000 – June 1, 2001

Type of Increase

___ Merit   ___ Promotion   ✔ Merit and Promotion

Effective Date of Increase   June 2, 2001

Weekly Increase Recommended $50

I. PERFORMANCE

Quality of Work   Quantity of Work   Human Relations   Progress

   A(B)C D E   A B(C)D E   (A)B C D E   A(B)C D E

Where is employee's performance most proficient?

The quality of Jim's telephone work with customers is superior. He shows remarkable patience in answering customers' questions. He listens carefully to customers' questions, clarifies requests and problems, and provides articulate, courteous answers. Because he knows our product line well, he gives comprehensive responses, often volunteering more information than the customer requested.

The quantity of his work is satisfactory. When working the telephone lines, he averages 69 customer calls a day, which is slightly below our goal of 75 calls a day. Although he takes a little longer than most reps on each call, he provides good answers and generally is able to solve customers' problems.

C. Employee Performance Appraisal (continued)

In human relations Jim is well above average. He is pleasant and cooperative in working with customers, fellow employees, and management. He takes direction easily and seems to get along well with the entire team.

Since his last review, Jim has made progress in two areas. First, he mastered our new Infomax computer program. In fact, he learned Infomax so quickly that I asked him to give a demonstration for other customer service reps. Jim remains our expert on Infomax, and I am grateful for his enthusiastic support in implementing and troubleshooting this new system. Second, Jim attended two 10-hour in-service training seminars covering customer service goals, handling complaints, and sharing experiences.

Where does employee's performance need improvement?

When he switches to administrative work, which accounts for 25 percent of his assignment, Jim's performance falters somewhat. In working with correspondence, product mailings, and follow-ups, he has difficulty expressing his ideas in writing. Proofreaders return about half of his letters with errors in spelling, grammar, and punctuation. Other customer service reps average a correction return rate of only 5 percent. Because he must rewrite so many of his documents, his productivity in this area is low.

List employee's performance development goals and plans for the next evaluation period.

1. Jim will participate in an in-service training course in basic language skills.
2. He will also enrol in an evening college class in business writing.
3. Jim will reduce his correspondence correction return rate from 50 percent to 5 percent or less.
4. He will concentrate on increasing his customer-calls rate to reach the goal of 75 calls a day.

C. Employee Performance Appraisal (continued)

Overall Performance Rating (circle one)

A – Outstanding. Consistently exceeds job requirements. Sets example for others.
B – Excellent. Consistently meets job requirements and often exceeds them.
Ⓒ – Good. Consistently meets job requirements.
D – Acceptable. Meets most job requirements but occasionally needs assistance.
E – Unsatisfactory. Well below job requirements. Immediate attention needed.

II. ATTENDANCE AND PUNCTUALITY

Is attendance and/or punctuality a problem to the extent that this increase is reduced or deferred?   No

Expected date of next performance evaluation   June 2, 2002

Signature of Evaluator _____ *Craig C. Binsky* _____

Date _____ 6/1/01 _____

Signature of Employee _____ *Jim Matheson* _____

Date _____ 6/1/01 _____

D. Letter of Inquiry

560 No. Moorpark Rd. #236
Thousand Oaks, CA 91360

President
TOPPS BASEBALL CARD COMPANY
One Whitehall Street
New York, NY 10004

Jan 13, 20xx

Dear Topps Baseball Card President:

I have a valuable which I would like to donate to the great Topps card company because you stand for an American baseball institution. As a boy, I flipped your cards for hours.

In 1960, I was an employee of a hotel in Miami Beach, Florida, where Mr. Mickey Mantle was staying. About two in the afternoon, I was summoned to Mr. Mantle's room to deliver room service to him. He ordered an egg salad sandwich and an iced tea. I'll never forget it as long as I live.

As I was setting up the room service tray, I noticed Mr. Mantle clipping his toenails. I watched out of the corner of my eye as he clipped every toe. He had trouble with the last nail but eventually his diligence paid off. At that moment, the telephone rang and Mr. Mantle was called from his room. He told me to leave the egg salad sandwich and he would eat it later. I'll never forget his words for the rest of my life. He left the room. I dropped to the carpet and secured all the toenails that had been clipped off. There are almost ten toenails. Nine and some shavings but a full set.

I would like to donate this collectible to your card company. You have made children of all ages very happy. Perhaps this valuable could even be put on a card. They collect everything else! I think that Mr. Mantle was a great player. These toenails should be enjoyed by his millions of fans. Any time you can see something directly off a celebrity, that is better than any picture or autograph. This is something truly from his body.

Please write me and tell me who I should send this gift to for donation. Thank you.

Sincerely,

Ted L. Nancy

Ted L. Nancy

E. Response to Letter of Inquiry

National Baseball Hall of Fame and Museum, Inc.

March 12, 20xx

Ted L. Nancy
560 No. Moorpark Road #236
Thousand Oaks, CA 91360

Dear Mr. Nancy:

Si Berger, of the Topps Baseball Card Company, forwarded your letter of January 13th to the Hall of Fame and my attention.

We are very interested in your story of the Mickey Mantle toenails, and how you obtained them in Miami Beach in 1960 while delivering room service.

This is a fascinating tale, and we would like to know more about the condition of the nails, and what shape they are in. We have an Accessions Committee which meets periodically to review potential donations to the Hall, and we would be most interested in knowing more about the toenails, and why you wish to offer them to the museum.

If it is possible to send us a picture of the nails, we would be interested in examining them before we reach any decision.

Thank you for thinking of the historical importance of these items, and attempting to place them in an institution where they will be saved for future generations to enjoy.

Sincerely,

Peter P. Clark

Peter P. Clark
Registrar

25 Main Street, P.O. Box 590, Cooperstown, New York 13326–0590
(607) 547-7200 Fax (607) 547-2044

You take it from here ...

A. Letter Requesting Reference
Responding

1. **Discuss Purpose**   In a paragraph, discuss the purpose of Natalie Kienzler's letter. What has she done to ensure a response?

Extending

2. **Answer a Letter**   Assume you are Professor Pat McMahon and write a response to Natalie's letter.

B. Memo to Employee
Responding

3. **Discuss Context and Tone**   With a partner, go over the following questions:

   a) What has led to this warning?
   b) How can one tell that the manager is serious and annoyed?

Extending

4. **Take Positive Action**   In your notebook, write down what Marilyn should do to avoid being fired.

C. Employee Performance Appraisal
Responding

5. **Analyze Details**   List what you consider to be Jim's three most positive features as an employee. Write a paragraph describing how he could improve even more as an employee.

Extending

6. **Write Dialogue**   As Jim leaves work after getting this report, he phones his girlfriend on a cell phone. Write what he tells her about his evaluation.

D. and E. Letter of Inquiry and Response
Responding

7. **Analyze Satire**   What is the author of this spoof making fun of? What details add humour? Discuss with a partner.

Extending

8. **Write an Alternative Response** Decide on an alternative response to the "pitch" regarding the donation of this "valuable" to the National Baseball Hall of Fame and Museum, Inc. Two possibilities include a response demonstrating honest excitement about the prospect of possessing the "valuable" and expressing unconditional acceptance of the gift, or a brutally honest rejection letter. With a partner, exchange and assess each other's letters.

> **PEER ASSESSMENT**
> - Does your partner's letter clearly explain and support his or her position regarding the possible donation to the museum?
> - Is it written in proper letter format?
> - Was all spelling correct? Was punctuation used properly?

Before you read, in a class discussion, share your experience with looking for a summer job.

As you read, form your opinion as to the effectiveness of the brochure.

Youth Employment Strategy

Brochure by Youth Employment Canada

OUR JOB IS HELPING YOU FIND ONE.

IT'S A CHALLENGE

Finding a summer job can be one of the toughest jobs around. It's hours of pounding the pavement. It's scanning want ads. It's not knowing whether you're applying for the right job. But you can make it a lot easier on yourself.

TAKE THE PATH OF LEAST RESISTANCE

This year, start your search with us. We have countless detailed listings — from casual labour to career making opportunities — so you can focus your efforts on jobs that suit your individual needs. And best of all, it's free. You'll save time. You'll save money. And most importantly, you'll save your feet from terrible blisters.

We have more than 30 years' experience making the search for summer work easier. We've developed many effective programs and services designed to assist you. And the fact that we're staffed by students who've been in your position means we can relate to your situation. Plus because employers come to us looking specifically for students, there's a ready pool of jobs that require your skills, talents and energy.

Last year, we found jobs for 192,000 students across Canada and honed job search skills for 350,000.

SERVICES WE PROVIDE:

- Comprehensive job postings, including wage and hours
- Information sessions on career planning
- Résumé and cover letter assistance
- Job interview techniques
- Information on high growth job sectors
- Information on wage rates, employment stand and Human Rights

DROP BY TODAY

Finding a summer job doesn't have to be difficult advantage of our services. When you're looking f work, put us to work first.

HIRE a student.

You take it from here ...

Responding

1. **Examine Slogans**   With a partner, review the main headings of the brochure and discuss the meaning of each.

2. **Consider Style**   Take a second look at the word choice and sentence structure of the brochure. Write a paragraph describing the relationship between the writing style and the target audience.

3. **Understand Text Elements**   Write a paragraph describing how the visual features are used to appeal to the target audience.

Extending

4. **Develop a Brochure**   Put together a brochure instructing teenagers on how and where to find part-time, evening, weekend, or summer work.

5. **Describe a Past Job**   Recall one of your previous employment experiences. (If you have not worked as an employee, you can refer to work you do at home or in the neighbourhood, for example cutting grass, shovelling snow, or babysitting.)

   - How did you find the job?
   - What appealed to you about the work?
   - What were your responsibilities?
   - What did you learn from your job experience?
   - What personal qualities or special skills did you need for this job?

Before you read, in your notebook, define "graphics" and identify the purpose of graphics in publications.

As you read, take jot notes of the main points in the article.

"A picture is worth more than a thousand words."

Creating a Visual Package
by Marcelle Lapow Toor

INSTRUCTIONS

Notes

Marcelle Lapow Toor is a graphic designer and lecturer whose books include *Graphic Design on the Desktop: A Guide for the Non-Designer* and *The Desktop Designer's Illustration Handbook*.

"Visual language is already dominating verbal or at least written communication. If you think about it we've been growing up with a major change toward the visual, and computers have accelerated that change."

—John Waters, Print *magazine.*
September/October 1993.

You have come up with a design for your newsletter. It looks deadly. It's monotonous. It lacks colour and graphic interest. It needs some pizzazz. You are in a panic. Your budget is nonexistent. You can't even afford to have the piece printed professionally. It will be reproduced on a copy machine. What kind of cosmetic changes can be made to dress it up, to make it look appealing and colourful even though you can only use one colour? How can you create visual interest on the cover and inside pages so the person who receives the newsletter doesn't toss it into the trash without giving it a second glance? You need to turn your newsletter, brochure, flyer, poster, or magazine into a visual package—a successful marriage of illustrations and text.

Communication does not take place with text alone. Words do not have the same impact as pictures. "A picture is worth more than a thousand words" is an expression familiar to all of us, and it has even more meaning in today's world. The addition of good graphics will help enhance any printed piece. A good picture by itself will communicate. One that is well integrated with text can provoke an emotional response, make an impression, and help direct the reader through the layout of a page.

Visual images surround us in our daily lives. We see pictorial symbols in our homes on our microwave ovens, refrigerators, and answering machines. In our cars they inform and warn us when we are running low on gasoline or oil. Pictorial symbols are found on road signs. They speak a universal wordless language and make it easy for you to drive your car in a foreign country without knowing the language because they give you the information you need—deer crossings, sharp curves in the road. Graphic symbols are found in airports where people from different countries convene. They identify telephones, restrooms, restaurants, smoking and non-smoking areas. Symbols in the form of simple graphics speak a visual language and help us find information quickly.

The graphic or graphics you select for your printed piece should be a vital element in your brochure, newsletter, or flyer. A brochure that lacks in illustration must have a very powerful verbal message in order to make an impression. Pictures or graphic images attract attention. They can add a sense of reality to a publication, establish a mood, involve our emotions, and may even entertain in the process. Some events are better described with a picture than with words.

The choice of a graphic image is directly related to the audience, the printed piece, and the kind of message to be communicated. The quality of the image has the same importance as its appropriateness. The illustration you use should be an integral element and one of the main pieces that fit into the overall layout.

Graphics in a publication should

- Clarify the text
- Lead the reader through the text
- Attract attention
- Add a sense of realism
- Add a sense of fantasy
- Establish a mood
- Involve the emotions
- Entertain or explain

The best advice for using graphics is: keep it simple. A graphic should be easy to read and should be helpful in conveying important information. Research shows that photographs and other graphic images are used by readers as entry points onto a printed page. If the graphic you have selected does not contain information related to the text in your publication, leave it out and find another way to enhance the pages visually.

Tip 1
It is best not to use an illustration if you cannot find one that is appropriate.

Tip 2
It is best not to use a picture that is misleading or confusing.

SELECTING ILLUSTRATIONS TO ENHANCE YOUR PAGE LAYOUT

Making decisions

Before making a decision about the kind of illustration you need for the printed piece you are designing, you may want to consider the following questions:

1) **Who is your audience?**
   Identify your audience. What kind of person do you want to reach? Is this audience a specific age, gender, or income level?

2) **What is the content of the message?**
   What do you want to say to this audience? What is the tone you want to set? Is it serious or do you want it to have humour?

3) **Will an illustration enhance your page design?**
   Can you find an appropriate illustration that will make your newsletter or brochure look more interesting and easier to read?

4) **What kind of art will attract your audience to help them absorb the textual information?**
   Do some research to find out what kind of art appeals to your intended audience—what kinds of images they identify with. A good place to start is your local news-stand. Look at current magazines that appeal to your audience. A cartoon-like drawing may be the best way to get the attention of kids because kids like cartoons and most of them

Creating a Visual Package

watch TV. However, if the audience for your publication is the young professional, the sophisticated twenty-something crowd, or the thirty-something crowd, a photograph will attract better than a drawing.

5) **What type of illustration should you use?**
If you are designing a magazine spread for a short story, for example, a drawing or painting (oil or watercolour) may have a better "feel" than a photograph, since a story is based on fiction. On the other hand, if you are designing a brochure for a human services organization, photographs of actual people would be more effective. If you have to explain complex statistical information, a chart, table, graph, or bulleted list would be a better choice. If you are unable to find a picture that seems just right, you can always do some interesting things with type and typographic devices.

6) **Will the graphic attract attention?**
Find a graphic that will be appropriate to your printed piece and appeal to your audience using an image that is both familiar and pleasant. The picture you choose should attract attention but not detract from the editorial content of your printed piece. It should enhance the text and act as a guide to help move the reader through the information on the page.

7) **What kind of graphic image will reproduce well, given the printing process you will be using?**
If you are producing the entire publication on the computer for reproduction on a photocopy machine, you are limited in the kinds of illustrations you can use. Photographs reproduced on a copy machine, even one equipped to copy photographs, will not appear as sharp as when a professional printer creates a screened halftone. Simple line drawings and clip art, however, will reproduce quite well when photocopied from a laser printout. Your budget will influence the choice you make.

8) **Who will create the graphic?**
If you cannot draw and have a decent budget, you may want to hire an illustrator or photographer. If you are on a tight budget, stock art or clip art that comes on disk, CD-ROM, or in books might be the best solution.

WHAT ARE YOUR CHOICES?

All illustrations fit into two categories—line art and continuous tone art.

1) **Type and Typographic Devices**
When you are on a tight budget, type and typographic devices can be used very effectively as a means of illuminating text in a printed piece. Typographic devices include: dingbats, bullets, lines or rules, symbols, typographic ornaments, geometric shapes, large initial capital letters, patterned boxes, dots, and flags.

2) **Drawings**
Drawings fit into the category of line art. When we refer to drawings, we are talking about pictures rendered with pen and ink, paint, or pencil. If you can't draw, don't. A poorly executed drawing will make a potentially good publication scream, "amateur." Hire an illustrator if your budget will permit, or use clip art instead. Seasoned graphic designers use clip art when they need instant art. Clip art is available in many drawing styles, some quite sophisticated, and can be found on disks, CD-ROM, and in books.

3) **Photographs**
A photograph is made up of many grey tones, all the tones going from black to

white, and falls into the category of continuous tone art. Photographs are appropriate images to use when you want to document a real event or show actual people.

4) **Information Graphics**
Information graphics include: charts, graphs, diagrams, maps, and tables. An information graphic is a good way to present statistical information visually so that it is understandable. There are a number of software programs on the market that make it easy for you to create your own charts and graphs.

5) **Computer Generated Graphics**
The computer is replacing traditional drawing and painting tools for some illustrators. Many illustrators are using various painting and drawing programs to render complex illustrations.

Tip 1
It is better to use no art than art that is weak or poorly executed.

Tip 2
Allow plenty of time for the creation of your illustration whether you do it yourself or hire an illustrator.

Tip 3
Stick with a consistent art style throughout your publication.

Tip 4
Use your illustrations as a means of guiding the reader through the text.

Tip 5
Use graphics that relate to your printed piece, your message, and use ones that have some familiarity for your audience.

QUESTIONS TO ASK BEFORE SELECTING A GRAPHIC

- Is this the right type of illustration for my publication?
- Is this illustration appropriate for my audience and the message?
- Does the illustration tell a visual story related to the text?
- Will this graphic enhance the page layout and lead the reader through the textual information on the page?
- Will the size of the graphic help create a dramatic effect, or will it get lost on the page?
- Is the image unambiguous so that my readers will understand it immediately?
- Does the graphic have a credit line or caption as a means of identifying what it is and who created it?

Hints
- Keep a swipe file (examples of images from magazines and other publications) with illustrations that appeal to you. These samples can help with ideas when you are working with an illustrator or creating your own drawings.
- A good slogan to remember when using graphics is, "keep it simple."

ILLUSTRATIONS WILL

1) **Attract attention**
Readers will stop to read an illustration.

2) **Provide a place for the reader's eyes to rest**
Illustrations will provide relief from a page full of text.

3) **Help an audience remember your printed piece**
Strong images make a lasting impression.

Creating a Visual Package

4) **Establish an ambiance for your publication**
An illustration will help to reinforce the setting—the look and feel of your newsletter or brochure.

5) **Help the reader comprehend complex information**
Illustrations can lead the reader through the written text and explain information in a visual way.

You take it from here ...

Responding

1. **Review Points**   With a classmate, answer the following questions:
   a) What is the purpose of graphics?
   b) How does audience influence graphics style?
   c) What is "ambiance"? How can you create ambiance using graphics?

   > **PEER ASSESSMENT**
   > - What was your partner's best answer?

2. **Summarize Techniques**   In a paragraph, describe three visual techniques mentioned in this article, and explain how these can be as important as the printed text itself.

3. **Consider Implications**   In a written response, discuss how you can apply ideas in this article to your own work.

Extending

4. **Create a Newsletter**   Write and design a one- or two-page newsletter that focuses on an area of interest to you. For example, you could write an annual update of events for family and friends, or compile information for an interest group or organization you're involved in. Use some techniques outlined in this article to make your work visually interesting.

5. **Use Clip Art**   Using clip art or a computer illustration program, design a graphic for an imaginary product and a target audience of your choice.

6. **Create a Logo**   Imagine and design a logo for a school team, a band, or your family.

Before you read, discuss the short- and long-term effects of drinking or drug-taking on young people.

As you read, respond with a partner to the last line of the poem.

Notes

Gina Higgins lives in Newfoundland. "Hash for Cash" was published in 1994 as part of a Newfoundland Poetry Series collection of student poetry.

"Hash for Cash"

Poem by Gina Higgins

Here they are today, the adults of tomorrow,
Stoned to the eyebrows, and staggering around
    outside of a school, without a care.
Unable to care. Or even to think.
Lots of Money, perhaps unscrupulously gained.
"Hash for cash" scratched on a wall, meant as
    a joke.
Its reality startling.
Studies seem a waste of time, the future millions
    of miles and light years away.
Dope and hangovers today, time for work later.
But later takes its time in coming,
And when it arrives it snarls the unwary.
Tell me, what will happen to the children of today
    when they wake tomorrow, and discover that
    their chance was smoked away.

You take it from here ...

Responding

1. **Reveal Theme** With another student, discuss what the poem's main idea is. Compare your theme to one arrived at by another pair of students.

2. **Discuss Relevance** Consider how this poem fits into the "Out in the World" theme of the unit. Do you think it is relevant in the same way as the other selections? Comment in a paragraph.

Extending

3. **Compose a Poem** Write your own thoughtful poem about what youth values today.

4. **Deliver a Speech** Write and deliver a speech to the class on the importance of having goals and maintaining a clear mind to achieve them.

5. **Write a Song** Recast the poem's images into lyrics and, if possible, set them to music. In small groups, share your work.

Before you read, define "CEO" and "entrepreneur."

As you read, think of a person you know of who has applied McQueen's principles successfully.

You have the power to make of tomorrow exactly what you want.

How to Become a Millionaire
by Rod McQueen

SELF-HELP ARTICLE

Notes

Rod McQueen is an award-winning author and journalist. His books include *The Last Best Hope—How to Start and Grow Your Own Business.*

Lottery tickets are a waste of money. Everybody knows the improbable odds—one in 13 million. There's a better way to become a millionaire. You've already got everything you need—right inside. Here's the four-word secret: Start your own business.

Have you got what it takes?

After five years of interviewing the presidents of Canada's 50 best managed private companies, I've identified the top 10 steps to success.

1) **Find a need and fill it.** Have a plan and follow it. Newfoundland's Lorraine Lush concluded that her neighbours needed work skills. For 14 years she'd been a secretary, so she taught the first 65 students what she knew best: secretarial skills. Today, The Career Academy has 22 programs, 3000 students, and 15 campuses.

2) **Believe in yourself.** If you don't, who will? When free trade arrived in 1989, observers predicted the demise of Morrison Lamothe Inc., an Ottawa bakery begun in the 1930s. Third-generation president John Morrison didn't heed the so-called experts. The firm focused on private-label frozen dinners. Almost half of the product line is new in the last four years, and the firm is tackling the U.S.

3) **Exude optimism.** Nobody wants to deal with a dud. Geoff Chutter runs Whitewater West Industries Ltd. of Richmond, B.C., making waterslides and wave pools. Talking to this man is like taking a tonic. Despite having the best job in the world, Chutter has twice run for Parliament because he believes he can make a public policy difference.

4) **Be flexible.** Bend the rules. Take chances. Mining exploration fell two-thirds from 1987 to 1992 and with it went the drilling tool business in Fordia, of St. Laurent, Quebec. Fordia's Alain Paquet took a chance and chased customers in South America. "Your life is at risk when travelling in those areas," he says after being robbed in Venezuela. "You can get killed for nothing if you're not careful." He and the company both survived. Fordia now sells in 28 countries.

5) **Exercise vision.** This is the capacity to see the invisible. In September 1996, a stranger arrived at Crila Plastic Industries Ltd. in Mississauga, Ontario, promoting an unlikely

product, a plastic that looked and acted like wood. Intrigued, Crila president Peter Clark flew to Britain, obtained North American rights and now sells two million board feet of Extrudawood per month in an industry where a million board feet of anything in a year is a good sale.

6) **Accept help and advice.** Honour what people have to offer. Edmonton-based Fountain Tire doesn't just wait to hear ideas, it goes looking. Says CEO Brian Hesje: "It's more productive to be humbled by those that succeed rather than have the false sense of security that comes from visiting the less successful."

7) **Tap the passion within.** Be resourceful. Trust your instincts. "I believe entrepreneurs are being visited by divine inspiration," says clothing designer Linda Lundström. "I also believe an entrepreneur can visualize something and make it happen." How else to explain the moment when a bird-dropping spattered her car windshield while Lundström drove on an expressway. She combined that unhappy impact with a message she read on a passing truck and concluded that her La Parka line would do well. Her instincts were accurate.

8) **Fulfill customers' needs and exceed their expectations.** Glegg Water Conditioning, of Guelph, Ont., shipped a key component to a U.S. client but customs problems meant a 24-hour delay. A Lear jet was chartered to deliver the item that very day. "We'll do whatever it takes to look after our clients," says president and CEO Robert Glegg.

9) **Never give up.** True character means never accepting defeat. Robert Mills and his son, Ray, of Calgary, spent nine months in 1989 making 1000 sales calls. They sold only two of their pumps. In the tenth month, Ray sold 15 pumps to one company. Today, Kudu Industries Inc. employs 100 and has annual sales of $35 million.

10) **Dream it and do it.** Olympic cyclist Louis Garneau's racing gear and helmet business, based in St-Augustin, Quebec, began with one sewing machine in his father's garage. Montreal's Karel Velan filled his order book using a four-page leaflet before he'd manufactured his first valve.

Not every start-up succeeds; annual failure rates run to 20 percent. But what that also means is that out of 100 new businesses launched tomorrow, 30 will still be alive in five years. Of those, 20 percent will be scraping by, 60 percent will be doing middling well, but 20 percent will be spectacularly successful. Each of those six firms will have anywhere from 30 to 100 employees plus annual sales as high as $50 million. And each of those individual founders will be millionaires. Six millionaires for every 100 entrants. I like those odds. Don't you?

You have the power to make of tomorrow exactly what you want.

You take it from here ...

Responding

1. **Review Main Points**   List McQueen's 10 steps to becoming successful. Which did you find most convincing on the basis of its example? Explain in a paragraph.

2. **Examine Underlying Idea**   Look again at the 10 steps. Are they based on the influence of external situations and other people or are they based on self-motivation? In a written response, discuss the role of personal attitudes in determining success.

3. **Brainstorm Titles**   With a partner, brainstorm a list of at least 10 titles for other "How-To" articles you would like to read—or write—that could help people achieve their ambitions.

Extending

4. **Develop a Plan**   Choose one of the titles you came up with in Activity 3 and write the article.

5. **Design a Game**   Using the author's advice, develop a game called "How to Become a Millionaire."

Before you read, describe your feelings about questionnaires. Do you like them?

As you read, with another student, note the points that caught you off-guard or that were difficult to answer.

Are You a Risk-Taker?
by Marvin Zuckerman and D.M. Kuhlman

QUESTIONNAIRE

Read each statement. If it is true or mostly true circle the "T" and if it is false or mostly false circle the "F." It is important that you respond to *all* of the questions, even if you are uncertain of your answer.

1. T F I am an impulsive person.
2. T F I often feel unsure of myself.
3. T F I can't help being a little rude to people I don't like.
4. T F I like to keep busy all of the time.
5. T F I am a very sociable person.
6. T F I enjoy getting into new situations where you can't predict how things will turn out.
7. T F I frequently get emotionally upset.
8. T F When I get mad I say ugly things.
9. T F I like to wear myself out with hard work or exercise.
10. T F I tend to be uncomfortable at big parties.
11. T F I prefer friends who are excitingly unpredictable.
12. T F I tend to be oversensitive and easily hurt by thoughtless remarks and actions of others.
13. T F I have a very strong temper.
14. T F When I do things I do them with lots of energy.
15. T F I tend to start conversations at parties.
16. T F I often get so carried away by new and exciting things that I don't think of possible complications.

17. T F I often think people are better than I am.
18. T F If people annoy me I do not hesitate to tell them so.
19. T F I like to be doing things all of the time.
20. T F At parties, I enjoy mingling with other people whether I already know them or not.
21. T F I like "wild" and uninhibited parties.
22. T F I often worry about things that other people think are unimportant.
23. T F I am always patient with others, even when they are irritating.
24. T F I lead a busier life than most people.
25. T F Generally, I like to be alone so I can do things I want to do without social distractions.
26. T F I would like to live a life on the move, with lots of change and excitement.
27. T F I don't let a lot of trivial things irritate me.
28. T F When people shout at me I shout back.
29. T F I like complicated jobs that require a lot of effort and concentration.
30. T F I probably spend more time than I should socializing with friends.
31. T F I often do things on impulse.
32. T F I often feel uncomfortable and ill at ease for no reason.
33. T F When I am angry with people I do not try to hide it from them.
34. T F I do not feel the need to be doing things all the time.
35. T F I usually prefer to do things alone.

SCORING

Now score your test using the following key. Count one point on a scale each time your answer matches the one indicated below. If it doesn't match, do not add a point.

Impulsive Sensation Seeking (ImpSS):
1T, 6T, 11T, 16T, 21T, 26T, 31T Score =

Neuroticism–Anxiety (N–Anx):
2T, 7T, 12T, 17T, 22T, 27F, 32T Score =

Aggression–Hostility (Agg–Host):
3T, 8T 13T, 18T, 23F, 28T, 33T Score =

Activity (Act):
4T, 9T, 14T, 19T, 24T, 29T, 34F Score =

Sociability (Sy):
5T, 10F, 15T, 20T, 25F, 30T, 35F Score =

Scale Ranges

	ImpSS	N–Anx	Agg–Host	Act	Sy
Males					
Low	0–2	0	0–1	0–1	0–3
Med.	3–5	1–3	2–5	2–4	4–5
High	6–7	4–7	6–7	5–7	6–7
Females					
Low	0–1	0–1	0–1	0–1	0–3
Med.	2–4	2–5	2–5	2–4	4–5
High	5–7	6–7	6–7	5–7	6–7

If you scored in the high range on Impulsive Sensation Seeking (ImpSS), Aggression–Hostility (Agg–Host), and Sociability (Sy), you are a general risk-taker. If you scored high on two of them, particularly ImpSS and Agg–Host, you are more likely to take risks that could entail legal as well as physical consequences. If you scored high only on ImpSS, your risk-taking is likely to be primarily social, although you may also be tempted to dabble with drugs. If you scored low on all or two of these scales you may have a very cautious, risk-avoidant personality. If you also scored high on N–Anx, your avoidance may take the form of phobias or social avoidance.

You take it from here ...

Responding

1. **Discuss Results**   With a partner, compare notes and discuss the results of the questionnaire. How did you score? Do the results accurately describe you? Did you learn something new about yourself?

2. **Evaluate Criteria**   Write a paragraph expressing your opinion of this questionnaire. Do you think it would be helpful in determining whether one is a risk-taker? Why or why not? Overall, did you find it useful and interesting?

3. **Consider the Concept**   As a class, consider what it means to be a "risk-taker." Overall, is it a positive or a negative character trait? Explain.

Extending

4. **Design a Questionnaire**   Put together your own questionnaire for one of the following situations:
   - determining a person's musical tastes
   - determining the suitability of someone for a high-stress job
   - determining the qualities a person values in others

5. **Conduct a Survey**   Ask 20 to 25 people (perhaps students in another of your classes, friends, family) to respond to the questionnaire you designed in Activity 4. Tabulate the results of your survey and then summarize your findings. Present your findings to the class.

> **TIPS**
> - Decide on your target audience (age, gender, interests—if appropriate, etc.).
> - Include 10–15 questions.
> - Decide on the format: True or False, multiple-choice questions, or a scale measuring level of agreement (strongly disagree, disagree, neither agree nor disagree, agree, strongly agree).
> - Look in the library or on the Internet for examples and tips on questionnaire design.

Before you read, as a class discuss whether or not public speaking is a valuable skill beyond high school.

As you read, create three questions about the text. Ask a partner to answer them. Then discuss whether or not you agree with his or her answers.

How can you establish your credibility?

Speaking in Public
by Lucy Valentino

INSTRUCTIONAL ESSAY

Few people enjoy public speaking. I personally can face unanesthetized tooth extraction with more fortitude and less anxiety than I can face speaking in public. My hands begin to tremble, my voice gets higher (I'm a soprano, so it's fairly high already), and I begin not to perspire, but to sweat. I am not alone in this. Notice how many speakers keep their hands in their pockets!

Granted, you may not enjoy speaking in public, but you can survive without making a fool of yourself. *Just concentrate on your message and on your audience's need to hear it.*

Don't think of yourself. Think of the message. If you don't tell your audience what they need to hear, perhaps no one will. Think of how important your message is. Even if your hands do shake, and your voice does quaver, at least the audience will hear what you have to say. As well, you may be surprised to find that once you get started, it does get easier to go on.

What are the steps in preparing a speech? First of all, consider purpose and audience. What do you want your speech to do? What is your audience like? What is their attitude and level of knowledge about your topic now? What is their probable reaction to you? How can you establish your credibility? How can you get their attention?

Consider constraints of time and space. How long will you be speaking? Don't try to cram too much into a short space of time. Consider the room you'll be speaking in. Is it comfortable? Will your listeners start to shift after a few minutes on hard chairs or benches? Focus on what you most want to tell your audience.

Then organize. How can you most effectively get your message across? Prepare an outline, being sure to include examples and anecdotes that will be relevant to your audience. Remember that listeners' attention sometimes wanders. Make it simple, so that a returning listener won't be totally lost, but don't talk down to your audience. Respect them, or you really will be all alone up there.

Rehearse your speech, timing yourself and including visual aids. When it's showtime, take some cleansing breaths (it works for having a baby, but that may be easier), then get in there and deliver your message.

Here are a few basic rules to follow in giving a speech:

1) *Be prepared, but not overprepared.* Know your material, so that you are comfortable with it, but do not write out a complete speech. If you have a complete speech written out, the temptation is to read it, which is deadly. Never read a speech. Speak to your audience, don't read at them. If you are well prepared, you can sound spontaneous, paradoxical as that may seem.

2) *Look at your audience as you speak.* In this culture, it is customary to look at the person you are speaking to. What do we say about someone who doesn't? "He couldn't look me in the eye." It is essential to maintain eye contact when speaking. Don't look over people's heads, don't look down at the floor, don't stare at your visual aids—look at your audience. Think of your speech as a conversation. You would look at the other person then, wouldn't you? Looking at your audience personalizes your speech and, usually, makes it more interesting.

3) *Speak loud enough to be heard clearly, and use a natural pitch.* You aren't calling hogs, so you needn't bellow, but at the same time you must be sure to be heard. You may have a lovely, delicate voice, but if it doesn't carry past the second row you need to pump up the volume. People can't get your message if they can't hear it. At the same time, watch your pitch. Try to sound natural. Watch out for sounding tentative. In English, we raise the pitch of our voices at the end of a question; when making a statement, the pitch goes down. Say these two sentences out loud:

"Is that the book you borrowed from Kathy?"

"I borrowed that book from Kathy."

Notice the difference? What happens if your voice rises in pitch at the end of a statement? You sound like you're asking a question, which translates into sounding tentative and unsure of yourself. Do it enough, and you sound as though you're asking for approval, or else as though you don't really know what you're talking about. Watch your pitch.

4) *Speak slowly, but with enthusiasm.* Don't hyperventilate by rushing your speech out and setting a new record. Slow down. Slowing down helps to overcome your nervousness, and it certainly makes listening to your speech easier on your audience. Don't slow to a crawl, though. Be enthusiastic. Be real. Be careful not to speak in a monotone, putting everyone, including yourself, to sleep. And be sure to smile.

5) *Stand or sit comfortably, but don't slouch.* Don't touch your hair, don't drum your fingers on the table, don't rock back and forth, and don't touch your face. One of my students, an amateur boxer, gave a speech once and kept rubbing the bottom of his nose with his hand (the way fighters do while getting ready to land a punch). Unfortunately, from where I was sitting, it looked like he was picking his nose. Keep those hands away from the face!

There is one thing you should never do. *Never apologize.* You are doing the best job you can, and it's probably a good one. You know what you're talking about, and your audience needs to hear you; apologizing only undermines your credibility. Besides, there's not a person in the audience who would trade places with you. You're doing fine.

When you finish the speech, you breathe a sigh of relief, but then someone raises a hand. Just when you thought you were finished, there are questions. How do you handle questions?

Clearly, briefly, and simply. Look at the person who asked the question. Unless the questioner had a booming voice, repeat the question so everyone hears it, then look at the whole audience and answer *briefly*. You already gave a speech, and there's no need to give another one. What if you don't know the answer? Say so. Don't bluff, just admit that you can't answer a particular question, but say that you'll try to get the answer. People respect honesty. No one knows or remembers everything.

What if someone asks a stupid question, or one that you've already answered? *Never make fun of a question or the person asking it*. Not only is that unkind, but it's suicidal. The audience will turn on you. You will then either get really hard questions that no one could possibly answer, or else everyone will be afraid to ask a question for fear of being ridiculed. Either way, you've lost the audience.

You take it from here ...

Responding

1. **Add More Information** What else would you say to someone about how to become a better public speaker? Answer this question in your notebook or journal.

2. **Note Structural Features** This article makes effective use of italics, not just in the headings of rules. Find two instances where italics are used elsewhere and discuss with another student why these examples are effective.

3. **Explore Vocabulary** Using a dictionary, write the definitions of the following underlined words in context:

   "I personally can face <u>unanesthetized</u> tooth <u>extraction</u> with more <u>fortitude</u> and less <u>anxiety</u> than I can face speaking in public."

   "If you are well prepared, you can sound <u>spontaneous</u>, <u>paradoxical</u> as that may seem."

   Then rewrite both of these sentences in your own words.

Extending

4. **Give a Speech** Develop a two-minute speech on a subject of your choice and deliver it to the class.

> **TIPS**
> - Follow the advice that is given in the article.
> - Organize your information in point-form and talk from your point list.
> - Rehearse your speech with a partner.

> **PEER ASSESSMENT**
> - Did the presenters use an appropriate style of speaking during their speeches?
> - Which speeches did you find most interesting and entertaining? Why?

5. **Write a Factual or Fictional Anecdote** Write a short story or anecdote about the perils and pitfalls of public speaking, drawing on your own experiences (first- or second-hand). If you prefer, write a fictional story on the same topic.

Before you read, discuss as a class the importance of attitude in achieving success.

As you read, think about a person you know that the articles bring to mind. In your journal, put down your thoughts about why that person came to mind.

When adversity stares you in the face, give it a big smile.

A Is for Attitude!

FEATURE ARTICLES

GOOD NEWS FOR OPTIMISTS

Mix a spoonful of Mary Poppins's sugar into a glass half full, and you just may have an elixir for longevity. Not only does a positive and hopeful outlook yield a happier life, but a study at the Mayo Clinic in Rochester, Minnesota, shows that it can lead to a longer life.

A study of 839 Mayo patients ranked them on a pessimism–optimism scale according to how they tended to explain life events. After 30 years, survival rates for the optimist group were "significantly better" than expected, whereas they were 19 percent lower than expected for the pessimists.

Although the researchers say they cannot explain exactly how a pessimistic outlook puts a patient at risk, Mayo psychiatrist and lead author Toshihiko P. Maruta, M.D., says the study proves "that mind and body are linked and that attitude has an impact on the final outcome...." So, just as we suspected, it pays to subscribe to hope!

—Lane Fisher

BAD NEWS IS GOOD NEWS

Brace yourself—it may be best to expect the worst. So says James Shepperd, Ph.D., a psychology professor at the University of Florida (UF), whose recent research suggests that people tend to look on the bright side unless they're expecting feedback that challenges that bright outlook.

In Shepperd's study, presented at the American Psychological Society's annual meeting, UF students were told that, due to a university mistake, at least a quarter of them would soon receive a $78 bill. After asking them to predict their own chances of getting the bill, Shepperd learned that students engaged in "bracing," but only if the financial loss would seriously affect them. So while financially stable

Guarded Optimism

students tended to guess that their chances of receiving the bill were one in four, estimates of financially needy students were higher—some were even "sure" they'd get it.

According to Shepperd, setting up expectations is a protective behaviour. Low expectations mean less chance for disappointment—even from a negative outcome. In fact, he says, "a bad outcome can actually feel good if you expected something worse, and a good outcome can feel bad if you expected something better." Next, Shepperd hopes to determine which methods for delivering bad news work best—helpful knowledge to people like doctors, who have to tell others what they don't want to hear.

—*Jennifer Richler*

HEALTHY MIND, HEALTHY HEART

When adversity stares you in the face, give it a big smile. New research suggests that maintaining a positive outlook during distressing times can optimize not only your emotional well-being, but also your cardiovascular health.

In a study presented recently at the American Psychological Society's annual convention, researchers at the University of Michigan (UM) examined the ability of highly resilient people—those who react flexibly and resourcefully to stimuli—to recover quickly from stressful events. They gave nearly 60 participants only one minute to prepare a speech on a randomly assigned topic, leading them to believe beforehand that they would also have to deliver their speeches on videotape for later peer evaluation. No speeches were actually given, but the researchers monitored participants' blood pressure and other cardiovascular responses throughout the speech-writing period and for five minutes afterward.

The study's findings show that, in comparison to participants with self-reported low resilience, those who were more highly resilient not only appraised the task as less threatening than their counterparts, but also experienced faster cardiovascular recovery times. Says Michelle Tugade, a graduate student psychology instructor at UM and the study's co-author: "It's through the experience of positive emotions that these individuals are able to 'bounce back' quickly from a negative, stressful experience."

—*Alison Calabia*

You take it from here ...

Responding

1. **Give Personal Reactions** Share your impressions of these articles with the class. Are you surprised by any of the following points?

   - being positive and hopeful leads to a happier, longer life
   - low expectations mean less chance for disappointment
   - maintaining a positive outlook promotes cardiovascular health
   - people with positive emotions bounce back quickly from negative stressful experiences

2. **Discuss with a Partner** With a partner, review the article and consider how the cartoon supports the message of the "Bad News Is Good News" piece. Suggest other images you might have used.

3. **Focus on Allusion and Diction** What do the authors have to say about Mary Poppins, pessimism and optimism, longevity? Answer in a paragraph.

Extending

4. **Add a Visual** Create an appropriate visual for "Healthy Mind, Healthy Heart." Display your work in class.

5. **Draw Parallels** Make a list of famous people or characters who embody the attitudes mentioned in this article. Share your list with another student and compare notes.

6. **Create Humour** Use the following tag phrases and complete each in sentence form three times. "You know you're an optimist when … " "You know you're a pessimist when … "

Before you read, consider the meaning of the saying "If it doesn't kill you, it just makes you stronger."

As you read, decide how the saying pertains to the situation in this piece.

Raiding the North
From *What! A Magazine*

MAGAZINE ARTICLE

THE GAME
Raid the North, a 150-kilometre test of endurance and human dynamic. Twenty-two teams of four are under the gun to remain solid while navigating, trekking, biking, canoeing, and rappelling down deadly rock faces to cross the finish line inside a 36-hour time limit.

THE PLAYERS
Team Magi, from Manitoba, sponsored by *What! A Magazine*:

Jamie Falk, 25, and **Randy Grieser, 25**, both with extreme experience after charging through a '98 adventure race; **Michelle Sawatsky-Koop, 28**, three-time CIAU national volleyball champ and member of Canada's volleyball team at the '96 Olympics in Atlanta; and **Jeff Schmidt, 24**, a phys-ed teacher.

THE FIELD
Late June, Shuswap Highlands, north of Kamloops, BC. This is grizzly country, with plenty of dense bush, staggering altitudes, and utterly unpredictable weather conditions.

THE STRATEGY
Eight gruelling weeks of rope-and-pulley action, securing of knots, and propelling down jagged rock formations. Daily jogging, marathon canoeing, and mountain biking over rugged trails by day, down long stretches of highway by night.

THE OPPONENT
Not what you're thinking. Twenty-one other well-oiled machines and the perils of the

Canadian wild kept the game challenging. But nothing encountered would be more harrowing than having to conquer the most threatening enemy of all—themselves.

THE PAYOFF

For some, the goal is personal; others are driven by the thrill of the extreme, the adrenaline rush. In this contest of man versus himself, cash and trophies are the least of the rewards.

JEFF'S JOURNAL

Friday evening. Pack lightly.

There are 21 teams—some veterans, some rookies—and us, a mix. Some say they'd be satisfied to "race to finish." We're sticking with our motto—"race to win." We're pumped.

We're given our navigational map and checkpoint co-ordinates. We discover we have the trekking, rappelling, and canoeing legs to tackle, all before connecting with our support crew waiting with our bikes, a hot meal, and dry clothes. That means we'll have to haul our climbing gear, life jackets, helmets, etc. on our backs. Nearly 25 pounds worth.

After several hours of planning, preparing, and plotting, we manage to get a couple hours sleep.

6 a.m. Saturday. Go like hell.

A three-and-a-half-hour bus ride on an old logging road brings us to the starting point somewhere near the middle of nowhere. Towering pine trees surround us and a heavy mist hangs in the air. We can barely make out the mountains, meaning we'll have to rely on our compass, our map, and our instinct to navigate.

We line up and synchronize our watches. The countdown starts ... and we're off! Our team sets the pace, jogging at the front of the pack.

Everyone starts out on the main logging road. It's full of sharp switchbacks, and you never know when it's going to snake off in a

totally different direction. We make our first mistake—zigging instead of zagging onto another route altogether. We stop to find our bearings, and some other teams catch up to us. We figure out the way together.

We start climbing the mountain toward our first checkpoint. We pass one major river and, according to the map, we'll find another around the next bend. Check. We follow the river up to the lake, relieved that we're almost at the first checkpoint. But it isn't there. We search the alpine meadows frantically, looking for a sign of the checkpoint. No luck. Re-navigating our position, it suddenly hits us. We've climbed the wrong mountain!

Examining the map, you can see this peak is almost identical to the mountain next to it—where the checkpoint actually is. At this point, we've climbed nearly 4000 feet and we're standing in snow. Ten hours have passed since we left the starting line.

4 p.m. Saturday. Never give up.

We decide that returning to the starting line is the best way to point ourselves in the right direction. On the way down the mountainside, Randy falls and badly wrenches his knee. Up in the ridges, there are streams running beneath the snow, often littered with hidden logs. Those logs radiate heat, creating air pockets. When you step on the snow, your foot goes through the hollow pocket, jamming into the log underneath. They call it "stumping." That's what happened to Randy and now he's in excruciating pain. Jamie offers to carry his backpack and we continue on.

A couple of hours later we're back at the starting line and re-orienting ourselves.

6.30 p.m., Saturday. If it doesn't kill you …

We've prepared to go 15, maximum 20, hours before reaching our support crew, stationed with food and dry clothes. But the transition won't

happen till checkpoint seven, long after we finish the rappelling—over a 2000-foot cliff—and the canoeing legs of the race. And here we are, at the starting line, 12 hours already gone. It doesn't take a rocket scientist to figure out we won't have the provisions to keep us going until we reach our crew.

Finally going in the right direction, up the right mountain, we get a third of the way up—when suddenly the trail runs out. We're forced to hike through the brush. The forest is thick and heavy, wet from the mist, so we'd have to bushwhack our way in, getting drenched as we passed through. As it is, every time I take a step, my boot squashes and water squishes out.

Our feet are freezing, but if you just keep moving, you don't feel it. Michelle's lips are blue. Randy's knee—he says it feels like bones grinding—is in rough shape.

It's closing on 7 o'clock. We sit in the middle of the forest together for more than half an hour, debating what to do. There's clearly not enough food. It's very possible to get lost at night in these parts. And Randy says it's not worth continuing for him if it means wrecking his knee for life.

We sit in silence a long time.

Perhaps foolishly, I'm ready to risk freezing my toes off to hammer through for the full 36 hours and see how far I can get. Even if it's not completely safe. That's what I trained for, that's why we're here. Jamie wants to continue pretty badly too. But we have to make a team decision. Find the balance between pride—pushing on for the sake of saying we muscled through it—and safety—chalking this up to a great learning experience.

It's one of the toughest decisions we'll ever face.

The race rules state that as soon as the emergency radio pack is opened, your team is disqualified. So, after 13 hours in the bush, we

make the gut-wrenching decision to pull out the radio, call in, and call it quits. That really hurts—to surrender with seven simple words. "This is Team Magi, do you copy?"

When we flip the radio on, the airwaves are filled with other teams in distress. One is stranded on a ledge too far down to go up, too steep to go down, too tired to continue. Another is completely lost and has radioed for help. We hear of one girl whose ankles have actually frozen. It's shocking to hear the number of teams abandoning the race, but we find some relief in knowing we aren't alone.

We're all pretty quiet on the hike back. My mind is full of "We should've done this ... we could've done that...." Jamie reminds us that although we could pound ourselves with "shouldas" and "couldas," that's not what actually happened.

Sunday afternoon ... it just makes you stronger.

Randy: This was a case of having to push pride aside for reasons of safety. As hard as it was to say, "We're not going to make it, we have to quit," it was a good decision. We're four extreme competitors, and as frustrating as it was, we got back to the start and said, "let's start again," even though we were 12 hours behind in a 36-hour race. I was really proud of our team because, in that regard, we didn't quit like a lot of people would have. When all is said and done, I'm happy I was here. It's been a great experience.

Jamie: Nature is a beautiful thing, but when you're lost and tired and you want to win the race, it can turn really ugly. That's one way to lose an adventure race—to stop enjoying what you're doing by losing the passion that got you there in the first place.

Adventure racing is a roller coaster of emotions. You get really excited when things go well, but you can just as easily get upset when things don't. I suppose one way to be mentally successful is not to allow these roller coasters to exist to any extent. You have to deal with things as they come. And through this race and the whole experience, I think I've learned ways to look better at any situation.

Michelle: We took on a mountain, climbed to the top of it, then climbed all the way down when we found it was the wrong mountain. But I guess it became our mountain to climb, and we did it.

I learned that we each have our own adventures, and adventure racing is about that—you never know what's going to happen. The four of us need to be proud that we were brave enough to come here and do this. We persevered and that's the most important part. It's a wonderful thing to push yourself to a limit and go a lot farther than you ever thought you could.

Editor's Note: Seven teams out of 22 managed to complete what Frontier Adventure Racing has pegged an extremely difficult race under harsh conditions. Of these, only five crossed the finish line under Raid the North's 36-hour time limit.

You take it from here ...

Responding

1. **Discuss a Main Idea** In groups, share your thoughts about what "If it doesn't kill you, it just makes you stronger" means. In your opinion, are the competitors featured in this article stronger for their experience? Explain.

2. **Write a Letter** Think about other ways in which people stretch their abilities (e.g., through team and individual sports, music, drama) and what motivates individuals to push themselves to the extreme. Then take those ideas and write a letter to a friend encouraging him or her to join you and your team in a test of personal challenge like the one described in "Raiding the North." Exchange letters with a partner for review.

> **PEER ASSESSMENT**
> - Was the letter persuasive?
> - Was the spelling correct and was it properly punctuated?

3. **Analyze Teamwork** As a class, discuss the meaning of "teamwork" and find examples of it in the article. Examine how and why the team had difficulty making the decision to quit the race. Consider how the circumstances of each individual affected the outcome, and how the end result might have been different if the decisions had been made on an individual basis rather than as a team.

Extending

4. **Relate to Circumstances** Write a short story in which the main characters confront a test of endurance similar to the one faced by the Raiding the North team. Identify what that challenge was, how it was approached, and what successes and setbacks the characters encountered.

5. **Conduct an Interview** In groups of five (the four team members and the interviewer), present a talk show in which the team members share their feelings about their experience in Raiding the North and their future plans.

Reflecting on the Unit

Responding

1. **Make a List of Resources**   With another student, make a list of the many different ways a person can find a job.

2. **Develop a Personal Inventory**   Make a chart of your personal strengths and weaknesses. What are your best qualities? What do you need to work on or improve to get ready for the world after high school?

Extending

3. **Compose a Letter**   Respond to one of the unit selections in letter form. Choose from one of the different types of letters listed below:

   complaint   congratulations   inquiry
   thank you   reference   resignation
   invitation

4. **Write a Profile**   Research a famous and successful person you admire. Write a profile about the person, focusing on how and why he or she is successful. When you have finished, write a paragraph in your journal describing what you have learned from this person.

> **SELF ASSESSMENT**
>
> Review what you have learned from this unit regarding
> - the importance of having a positive attitude
> - how to conduct yourself in interviews
> - how to fill in forms
> - how to use language and visuals to achieve clear communication

GLOSSARY

alliteration repetition of consonant sounds usually at the beginning of a line or series of words

allusion brief reference to a person, place, or event from history, literature, or mythology

antagonist major character or force that opposes the protagonist

anecdote short narrative used to make a point or introduce a topic

antihero a protagonist who has none of the qualities normally expected of a hero; the antihero can be a humorous take-off of the traditional hero

assonance repetition of vowel sounds usually at the beginning of a line or a series of words

atmosphere prevailing feeling created by the story

audience who the selection is intended for: target readers, viewers, or listeners for a selection

autobiography nonfictional book which a person writes about his or her own life

ballad a poem that tells a story, often about a tragic event, popular legend, courageous act, or great love

bias predisposition or personal agenda toward or against something

biography nonfictional book about a well-known person written by someone else

brochure pamphlet or leaflet giving descriptive or helpful information

caption words that accompany a photograph, picture, or cartoon

cause-effect method for organizing an essay; cause looks at the reasons why something came to be; effects are the results or outcomes of an event or change

character a fictional person; realistic characters are complex and believable, while stereotyped characters (for example, a villain) are more predictable and one-dimensional

character sketch description of a character's or person's moral or behavioural qualities, including specific examples and quotations from the story

cliché stale, familiar phrase or pattern

climax highest point of emotional intensity, usually a turning point in the protagonist's fortunes

collage artwork made of selected pieces or a mix of various materials

compare to look at the similarities between two things, situations, or characters

complication event which starts or causes a conflict

conflict struggle between opposing characters or forces

content the ideas and situations of a selection; sometimes called "the what" or subject matter

context specific situation in which a word is used, or the personal or historical situation a person or character is in

contrast striking difference distinguishing two things being compared

convention rule of writing or familiar pattern within a genre

cover(ing) letter letter accompanying a résumé which often explains the applicant's special interest in or qualifications for a specific job

crisis moment of intense conflict

criteria various standards used to judge something

detail specific aspect or small part of the whole

dialogue   any conversation between characters or people

diction   word choice used by a writer

discrimination   negative action or attitude based on race, age, or sex

draft   rough copy or first attempt

dramatic irony   occurs when what a character says or believes contrasts with what the reader or other characters know to be true

dynamic character   protagonist who undergoes a significant, lasting change

editorial   personal opinion or stand written on an issue of interest

e-mail   electronic mail sent between computers

episode   incident or event which is part of the narrative or plot

endorsement   advertising technique in which a famous person recommends a product

evaluation   formal judgment or assessment of someone or something

fairy tale   exaggerated made-up story for young children

falling action   section of a story following the climax

fantasy   a highly exaggerated or improbable story that features events, characters, and/or settings that are not found in real-life experience

fiction   any narrative that is invented or imagined; because fiction may be based on actual events, it may seem very realistic

foreshadowing   a hint of events to come later; prepares the reader for the climax, denouement, and character changes

form   general term referring to the way in which a selection is put together, its "shape" or structure; sometimes called "the how" of the selection

frame   single, complete image in film, cartoons, or pictures; frame can also refer to the outside boundary of the image or what is contained within this boundary

free verse   poem that doesn't rhyme and has no regular structure

genre   type of text such as poetry, short stories, film

graphics   visual products of commercial design or illustration

hero/heroine   the protagonist, who possesses such admirable qualities as courage and honesty

idiom   an expression which uses language figuratively and which reflects a specific context or culture

image   words that form vivid sense impressions for the reader

imagery   repeated *pattern* of words that form sense impressions for the reader

improvise   to make up spontaneously; to ad-lib a scene

implication   indirect hint or suggestion

irony   two or more contrasting or contradictory meanings

italics   sloping kind of typeface used for emphasis

jargon   specialized language used by a group

juxtaposition   side-by-side or superimposed contrast for dramatic effect

logo   emblem or design used to represent and advertise a company or organization

marketing   planned selling and promotion of products or services

media   all-inclusive terms referring to means of mass communication, e.g., television, movies, newspapers, radio, magazines, books

memoir   a work of nonfictional prose in which the author reviews events in his or her life

metaphor   direct comparison between two unlike objects

mood   feeling created in the reader by a selection

moral   the stated or implied lesson of the story (moral should not be confused with theme)

motivation   what causes a character or person to do something

myth   imagined traditional story used to explain something in a given culture

narrator   person or character telling the story

narrative essay   essay that tells a story, either a made-up one to illustrate a point, or, more commonly, a true telling of actual personal or historical events

nonfiction   prose that presents actual happenings; examples include the essay (a brief presentation of ideas or views on a subject), biography (the story of a person's life, written by someone else), and autobiography (the story of a person's life written in his/her own words)

onomatopoeia   words used in poems that sound like what is being described

pan   reference to a camera technique in which a camera slowly swivels on a tripod from one side to the other laterally

pantomime (or mime)   drama without words, acted through gestures, face, and body movements

paragraph   a group of sentences that belong together, dealing with one thought or topic

parallel structure   usually refers to sentences which use a similar grammatical structure

paraphrase   to put a given text into your own or other words

parody   humorous imitation or take-off of something or someone's style

persona   mask or identity adopted by an author

personification   technique of giving human characteristics to abstract, inanimate things or nonhuman creatures

personal inventory (personal data sheet)   summary of information about an applicant

personal response   refers to the reader/listener/viewer's response to a selection; it usually includes personal associations, previous personal experiences that relate to the selection

plot   storyline or series of episodes

poem   a condensed, rhythmical form of writing using images and figures of speech, often organized into stanzas

point of view   perspective from which a story is told. The three most common points of view in short stories are (1) first person narrative (uses "I" and the perspective of the protagonist directly), (2) third person or limited omniscient narrative (uses "he/she/they" and presents the protagonist's perspective from "outside" the narrative), (3) omniscient narrative (story is narrated from several points of view, reveals the thinking of more than one character, or is narrated by an outsider).

précis   brief summary of a longer selection, usually the ideas of the selection

prejudice   hasty or automatic advance judgement of someone or something before fully experiencing or appreciating the person or thing in question

profile   piece of writing that reviews the life and/or career of a person

proofread   to read for and correct mechanical errors; i.e., grammar, spelling, punctuation, capitalization errors

pros and cons   arguments for and against an argument

prose   writing that uses ordinary language (not poetry)

protagonist   main character through whose eyes the story is told

public service ad   magazine, TV, or radio ad which serves a noncommercial community or humane cause or purpose

pun   play on words

purpose   reason the author wrote the selection

realism   refers to the use of qualities that make a selection life-like or believable

relevance   quality of a selection which relates it to the reader or audience

resolution   (sometimes called the denouement) part of a story when a conflict is resolved or a mystery is explained

résumé   summary of a person's basic data as well as past employment and education information, skills, hobbies, and references

review   personal analysis or commentary, usually about a play, movie, or book

rhyme   occurs when words have the same sound, often at the end of lines of poetry

rhythm   repetition and arrangement of stresses or beats especially in lines of poetry

rising action   incidents taking place before the climax

satire   use of irony to ridicule an idea, person, or thing, often with the intention of causing social change

science fiction   writing that speculates about the effects of technology, science, or the future on humans

sentence   the most basic unit of thought or expression in prose, containing a subject and verb; sentences can make statements, requests, commands, or explanations

sentence variety   using different kinds of sentence structures to create interest for a reader

sequel   an imagined follow-up to a story or poem

sequence   order and arrangement of a selection

setting   time and place of the story

short story   a brief fictional prose narrative; usually focuses on one character, has a limited setting and a single plot

simile   indirect comparison using "like" or "as" (for example, in poetry)

situational irony   when what happens is different from what is expected or considered appropriate

skit   humorous scene or dramatization

slogan   short catchy phrase used in advertising

speaker   person in a poem or play who is talking

spoof   humorous dramatization making fun of something serious or well known

stanza (or verse)   is the "paragraph" of poetry

static character   character who does not change

stereotyping   use of a fixed view or familiar pattern

storyboard   series of pictures used to help visualize a movie scene or to develop a cartoon

stream of consciousness   in stories, the presentation of uninterrupted thoughts and feelings of a character

structure   way in which a selection is organized

style   refers to the unique manner and approach a writer or artist uses in a selection

subconflict   minor conflict often related to the main conflict

subtheme   minor idea often related to the main theme

summary   a brief restatement or review of events or main points

surprise ending   the sudden unexpected change in a story's direction as it reaches its conclusion

suspense   reader's feeling of anxiety about the outcome of a situation

symbol   something which stands for or represents something else

tableau a still-life dramatic composition used to present a scene or an idea

technology today, generally referring to mechanical or electronic arts, or the tools used to accomplish a purpose

text language of a selection; this is broadly used today to refer to visual or electronic texts such as cartoons and films as well as print materials

thematic statement one-sentence statement that generalizes a story's message

theme central idea of a selection which is often implied rather than directly stated

thesis main idea of an essay usually found in the first paragraph

tone attitude of the writer or speaker toward his or her topic or audience

topic subject of a selection

topic sentence usually the first sentence of a paragraph, presenting the paragraph's main idea

trait characteristic, usually expressed as an adjective in a character sketch

verisimilitude life-like quality possessed by a story

Web page a page from a Web site

Web site place on the World Wide Web consisting of a home page and other files maintained by a particular organization

ACKNOWLEDGMENTS

TEXT CREDITS

UNIT 1

2: Herman ® is reprinted with permission from Laughing Stock Licensing, Inc., Ottawa, Canada. All rights reserved.

4: From ANNE FRANK'S TALES FROM A SECRET ANNEX by Anne Frank, copyright 1949, 1960 by Otto Frank. Copyright © 1982 by Anne Frank Funds, Basel. English translation copyright © 1983 by Doubleday. Used by Doubleday, a division of Random House, Inc.

7: Reprinted with permission of the Executor of the Estate.

13: "ONE OF THESE DAYS" from THE COLLECTED STORIES OF GABRIEL GARCIA MARQUEZ, Copyright © 1984 by Gabriel García Márquez. Reprinted by permission of HarperCollins Publishers, Inc.

17: Originally published by Theytus Books in ARCTIC DREAMS AND NIGHTMARES 1993. ISBN 0919441475.

21: Reprinted with permission of Peter Cole.

24: Reprinted with permission from SWALLOWING CLOUDS: AN ANTHOLOGY OF CHINESE-CANADIAN POETRY, edited by Andy Quinn and Jim Wong-Chu (Arsenal Pulp Press, 1999).

26: "The Man Who Finds That His Son Has Become a Thief" by Raymond Souster is reprinted from COLLECTED SOUSTER by permission of Oberon Press.

28: © Estate of Morley Callaghan.

33: Reprinted by permission of the author.

38: Permission from the *Coastline of Forgetting*, Pottersfield Press, 1995.

47: Reprinted by permission of International Creative Management. Copyright © 1981, Rod Serling.

UNIT 2

62: Copyrighted (01/11/98), Chicago Tribune Company. All rights reserved. Used with permission.

66: Universal Music Publishing Group.

68: Reprinted with the permission from the Ottawa Citizen. Margo Roston.

72: Reprinted by permission of Kathy Ullyott.

76: "Oprah Winfrey," by Deborah Tannen, Time, June 8, 1998, copyright Deborah Tannen. Reprinted by permission.

79: Courtesy of Time Canada Ltd.

82: Courtesy of Time Canada Ltd.

86: Courtesy of Ken Dryden.

91: From COLLECTED POEMS 1953-1993 by John Updike. Reprinted by permission of Alfred A. Knopf, A Division of Random House Inc.

93: "Poems by Giovanni Caboto" by Filippo Salvatore from THE ANTHOLOGY OF ITALIAN-CANADIAN WRITING, edited by Joseph Pivato, © 1998, pp. 166-168.

96: Copyright 1998 by the National Wildlife Federation. Reprinted with permission from INTERNATIONAL WILDLIFE magazine's September/October issue.

101: Courtesy of the Edmonton Journal.

105: Courtesy of the Edmonton Journal.

UNIT 3

110: © Salon.Com.

114: "It Was a Year Ago" by Grace Caguimbaga, reprinted with permission from *The World's Shortest Stories*, edited by Steve Moss, Copyright © 1998, 1995 by Steve Moss, published by Running Press Book Publishers, Philadelphia and London.

116: Reprinted with permission of the Estate of William R. Bird.

120: Courtesy of Max Haines.
124: "Flying Off the Handle" by Christopher Elliot. Courtesy of ABCNEWS.com.
127: "Heat Lightning" by Robert F. Carroll. Reprinted with permission of Samuel French, Inc.
136: Reprinted with permission of Stephen R. Biss, Barrister and Soliciter from the Internet website "The Great Young Offenders Act Debate" of http://www.lawyers.ca/tgyad.
140: © Winnipeg Free Press May 17, 1987. Reprinted with permission.
146: Herman ® is reprinted with permission from Laughing Stock Licensing Inc., Ottawa, Canada. All rights reserved.
148: Copyright © 1988 and 1989 by Bonnie Burnard. From WOMEN OF INFLUENCE (Regina: Coteau Books, 1988). Reprinted by permission of the author.
157: Courtesy of Rowan Books, The Books Collective.
159: Reprinted by permission of Betsy Willeford, 2001.

UNIT 4
168: Herman ® is reprinted with permission from Laughing Stock Licensing Inc., Ottawa, Canada. All rights reserved.
170: © AGC, INC., USED BY PERMISSION, AMERICAN GREETINGS CORPORATION.
172: Courtesy of TELUS Mobility.
174: Image courtesy of www.adbusters.org.
176: Courtesy of Nortel Networks Global Advertising Team.
179: Reprinted with permission of Bozell Worldwide, Inc.
182: Villard Books, a division of Random House Inc.
190: Courtesy of Gary Johnson.
194: Originally published on the Royal Canadian Mounted Police website. http://www.rcmp-grc.gc.ca. © 2001, RCMP-GRC.
197: Courtesy of George Bowering.
200: © The Canadian Press.
202: Copyright © 1991 by Jane Yolen. First appeared in *2041: TWELVE SHORT STORIES ABOUT THE FUTURE*, published by Delacorte Press, a division of Random House, Inc. Reprinted by permission of Curtis Brown, Ltd.

UNIT 5
212: "Conceiving the Stranger" by Nigel Darbasie, from FIERY SPIRITS & VOICES, edited by Ayanna Black. A HarperPerennialCanada book, published by HarperCollinsPublishersLtd. Copyright © 1992 by Nigel Darbasie.
214: Courtesy of Maxine Tynes: writer; poet; educator.
216: The Canadian Human Rights Commission, *Filing a Complaint with the Human Rights Commission*. © Minister of Public Works and Government Services Canada, 2001.
220: Reprinted by permission from SWALLOWING CLOUDS: AN ANTHOLOGY OF CHINESE CANADIAN POETRY, edited by Andy Quinn and Jim Wong-Chu (Arsenal Pulp Press, 1999).
223: © 1992 Karen Connelly, reprinted by permission from *Touch the Dragon*, Turnstone Press.
226: Rosemary Huggins.
229: Excerpted from *Aurat Durbar: Writings from Women of South Asian Origin* (edited) by Fauzia Rafiq, 1995; published by Second Story Press, reprinted by permission of Sumach Press, Toronto.
232: Courtesy of Tomson Highway.
235: "Arctic Plums" from CAPITAL TALES by Brian Fawcett © 1984, Talonbooks, Vancouver, pp. 67-70.
239: "Jamie" by Elizabeth Brewster is reprinted from *Selected Brewster* by permission of Oberon Press.

241: "Paper Matches" from CELESTIAL NAVIGATION by Paulette Jiles. Copyright © by Paulette Jiles. Used by permission from McClelland & Stewart, Ltd., *The Canadian Publishers*.
243: Courtesy of Universal Press Syndicate.
245: Hungry Minds.

UNIT 6
250: © W. Eugene Smith/BLACK STAR.
252: Reprinted with permission of Ed Kleiman.
256: Michelle McColm, author of ADOPTION REUNIONS, Second Story Press, Toronto, Ontario, Canada, 1993.
260: Reprinted with permission of Cynthia Reyes.
267: Reprinted with permission from Jennifer Champion.
271: "First Kiss—First Lesson" by Jennifer Braunschweiger. Jennifer Braunschweiger is a writer in New York City.
276: "Close to Home (aka First Date)" by John McPherson © 1995. Reprinted by permission by Universal Press Syndicate.
278: Reprinted with permission of Allison Mitcham.
281: From WELCOME TO THE MONKEY HOUSE by Kurt Vonnegut, Jr., copyright © 1961 by Kurt Vonnegut, Jr. Used by permission of Dell Publishing, a division of Random House Inc.
289: How Do I Love Thee? by Elizabeth Barrett Browning
291: PEANUTS is reprinted by permission of United Feature Syndicate, Inc.
295: Hal Leonard Corporation.
296: "Remember Africa?" by Jo Beth McDaniel, excerpted from *The Gift of Travel: The Best Travelers Tales*. Copyright © 1998 by Jo Beth McDaniel. Reprinted with permission. Http://www.travelerstales.com.

UNIT 7
302: Reprinted by permission with Ian Haysom, Southam News, 2001.
307: Published by Breakwater/St. John's Nfld.
310: Bumstead Productions, Susan Aglukark.
312: From *The Night in Question* by Tobias Wolff. Copyright © 1996 by Tobias Wolff. Reprinted by permission of Alfred Knopf, a division of Random House Inc.
317: "In the Past" is published with permission of the author, Lesley-Anne Bourne, and publisher, Penumbra Press, and is cited from the book *Skinny Girls*.
319: Warner Publications.
322: © Lynn Johnston Productions, Inc. / Distributed by United Feature Syndicate, Inc.
324: Reprinted by the permission of Russell & Volkening as agents for the author. Copyright © 1983 by Anne Tyler. Story originally appeared in Seventeen Magazine, November 1983.
334: "The Kids Who Make It in from the Cold" by Bob Levin, reprinted by permission from Macleans", © December 21, 1998, p. 87.
337: From REAL BOYS' VOICES by William Pollack. Copyright © 2000. Reprinted by permission of Random House, Inc.
340: Reprinted by permission of Taien Ng-Chan.
346: Denys Johnson-Davies, *Modern Arabic Stories*, © 1983, The Regents of the University of California.
351: Published by Breakwater/St. John's Nfld.

UNIT 8
356: Herman ® is reprinted with permission from Laughing Stock Licensing Inc., Ottawa, Canada. All rights reserved.
358: Courtesy of Grammy Asia.
360: Daniels, Jim. PLACES/EVERYONE. Winner of the 1995 Brittingham Prize in Poetry, © 1985. Reprinted by permission of the University of Wisconsin Press.
362: Material from *Good Job! A Young Person's Guide to Finding, Landing and Loving a Job*, copyright © 2000 by Youth Employment Service. Reprinted by permission of Stoddart Publishing Co. Limited.

366: Courtesy of Homemakers Magazine.
374: Copyright © by Ted L. Nancy's Hand-Dipped Productions. Introduction © 1997 by Jerry Seinfeld. Reprinted by permission of HarperCollins Publishers, Inc.
378: © Youth Employment Strategy Pamphlet, "Our Job is Helping You Find One." Reproduced with permission of the Minister of Public Works and Government Services Canada, 2001.
380: THE DESKTOP DESIGNER'S ILLUSTRATION HANDBOOK by Marcelle Lapow Toor, © 1996. Reprinted by permission of John Wiley & Sons, Inc.
385: Published by permission of Breakwater, St. John's.
387: Courtesy of the National Post.
390: Reprinted with permission of Marvin Zuckerman, 2001.
393: Courtesy of Nelson Thomson Learning.
397: Reprinted with permission of Hope Magazine Issue #24. 1-800-273-7447, www.hopemag.com.
397: Reprinted with permission from Psychology Today Magazine, copyright © 2000 Sussex Publishers, Inc.
400: "Raiding the North" from *What! A Magazine*, vol. 13, Issue 4, Sept./Oct. 1999, pp. 36-38. Reprinted with permission.

PHOTO CREDITS

UNIT 1
OPENER: © PhotoDisc; 4: © PhotoDisc; 5: © PhotoDisc; 8: © PhotoDisc; 10: © Earl & Nazima Kowall/CORBIS/MAGMA; 11: © PhotoDisc; 13: © PhotoDisc; 14: © PhotoDisc; 18: © Bowers Museum of Cultural Art/CORBIS/MAGMA; 19: © Wolfgang Kaehler/CORBIS/MAGMA; 21: © PhotoDisc; 22: © PhotoDisc; 24: © PhotoDisc; 26: © PhotoDisc; 29: © Mel Curtis/PhotoDisc; 31: © Mel Curtis/PhotoDisc; 34: © PhotoDisc; 35: © PhotoDisc; 36: © PhotoDisc; 38: © PhotoDisc; 39: © PhotoDisc; 42: © PhotoDisc; 45: © PhotoDisc; 47: © Bettman Archive/CORBIS/MAGMA; 47: Courtesy of Photofest; 48: © CORBIS/MAGMA; 50: © PhotoDisc; 51: © PhotoDisc; 53: © PhotoDisc; 55: © PhotoDisc; 57: © PhotoDisc; © PhotoDisc.

UNIT 2
OPENER (clockwise from top left): Canadian Press CP, Associated Press AP, Canadian Press CP, © Bettmann/CORBIS/MAGMA, © Reuters New Media Inc./CORBIS/MAGMA, © Bettmann/CORBIS/MAGMA, © Bettman/CORBIS/MAGMA, Canadian Press CP, Canadian Press CP, and Canadian Press CP; 63: © Neal Preston/CORBIS/MAGMA; 63: Associated Press AP; 64: Associated Press AP; 66: Associated Press AP; 69: © Lynn Johnston Productions, Inc./Dist. by United Feature Syndicate, Inc.; 73: Canadian Press CP; 74: Canadian Press CP; 77: © Bettmann/CORBIS/MAGMA; 79: © Kurt Krieger/CORBIS/MAGMA; 80: Courtesy of Caron MacMenamin; 82: Associated Press AP; 83: Associated Press AP; 84: Associated Press AP; 86: Canadian Press CP; 87: Canadian Press CP; 88: Canadian Press CP; 89: Canadian Press CP; 91: © PhotoDisc; 94: © Archivo Iconografico, S.A./CORBIS/MAGMA; 96: Canadian Press CP; 98: Canadian Press CP; 102: Canadian Press CP; 103: Canadian Press CP; 104: Canadian Press CP; 106: Canadian Press CP.

UNIT 3
OPENER: ALL © PhotoDisc; 111: © PhotoDisc; 114: © CORBIS/MAGMA; 117: © PhotoDisc; 118: © PhotoDisc; 121: © PhotoDisc; 122: © PhotoDisc; 125: © PhotoDisc; 128: © PhotoDisc; 129: © CORBIS/MAGMA; 131: David Samuel Robbins/CORBIS/MAGMA; 132: © CORBIS/MAGMA; 134: © CORBIS/MAGMA; 134: © PhotoDisc; 139: © PhotoDisc; 143: © Bettmann/CORBIS/MAGMA; 143: © Mark Jenkinson/CORBIS/MAGMA; 149:

© PhotoDisc; 151: © CORBIS/MAGMA; 153: © PhotoDisc; 154: © PhotoDisc; 157: © PhotoDisc; 161: © PhotoDisc; 163: © PhotoDisc; 164: © PhotoDisc.

UNIT 4
OPENER: © John-Marshall Mantel/CORBIS/MAGMA, Associated Press AP, Canadian Press CP, Canadian Press NATARK, Canadian Press CP, Associated Press AP, Canadian Press CP, Canadian Press CP, Canadian Press CP, PhotoDisc, PhotoDisc, and PhotoDisc; 191: © Universal Pictures/Photofest; 192: © Universal Pictures/Photofest; 195: © PhotoDisc; 197: © Canadian Press CP; 200: © PhotoDisc; 203: Anne Goodes/Nelson Thomson Learning; 204: © PhotoDisc; 205: Anne Goodes/Nelson Thomson Learning; 206: Anne Goodes/Nelson Thomson Learning.

UNIT 5
OPENER: © PhotoDisc; 212: © PhotoDisc; 214: © PhotoDisc; 216: © Comstock; 220: © PhotoDisc; 221: © Michael S. Yamashita/CORBIS/MAGMA; 224: © PhotoDisc; 224: © PhotoDisc; 227: © PhotoDisc; 230: © PhotoDisc; 233: © Michael Maslan Historic Photographs/CORBIS/MAGMA; 236: © PhotoDisc; 237: © PhotoDisc; 239: © PhotoDisc; 241: © PhotoDisc; 246: © PhotoDisc.

UNIT 6
OPENER: © PhotoDisc and courtesy of Caron MacMenamin; 253: Courtesy of the Heit family; 254: © PhotoDisc; 257: © PhotoDisc; 258: © PhotoDisc; 260: © PhotoDisc; 262: © PhotoDisc; 265: © PhotoDisc; 267: © PhotoDisc; 268: © PhotoDisc; 271: © PhotoDisc; 272: © PhotoDisc; 276: © PhotoDisc; 278: © CORBIS/MAGMA; 279: © CORBIS/MAGMA; 283: © PhotoDisc; 285: © PhotoDisc; 289: © PhotoDisc; 293: © Martyn Goddard/CORBIS/MAGMA; 297: © Alissa Crandall/CORBIS/MAGMA; 298: © PhotoDisc.

UNIT 7
OPENER: ALL © PhotoDisc; 302: © PhotoDisc; 303: © PhotoDisc; 304: CORBIS/MAGMA; 305: © PhotoDisc; 308: © PhotoDisc; 310: Canadian Press LDN; 310: © PhotoDisc; 312: © PhotoDisc; 314: © PhotoDisc; 317: © PhotoDisc; 319: The Canadian Press TRSUN; 319: © PhotoDisc; 320: © PhotoDisc; 325: © PhotoDisc; 327: © PhotoDisc; 329: © PhotoDisc; 331: © PhotoDisc; 334: © Paul A. Souders/CORBIS/MAGMA; 335: Canadian Press CP; 335: © PhotoDisc; 338: © PhotoDisc; 340: © PhotoDisc; 341: © PhotoDisc; 342: © PhotoDisc; 344: © PhotoDisc; 347: © PhotoDisc; 348: © PhotoDisc; 349: © PhotoDisc; 351: © PhotoDisc; 352: © PhotoDisc.

UNIT 8
OPENER: ALL © PhotoDisc; 358: © PhotoDisc; 360: © PhotoDisc; 362: © PhotoDisc; 364: © PhotoDisc; 366: © PhotoDisc; 368: ALL © PhotoDisc; 385: © PhotoDisc; 388: © PhotoDisc; 390: © PhotoDisc; 393: © PhotoDisc; 397a: © Bradford Veley; 397b: © Jim Sollers; 400: © Karl Weatherly/PhotoDisc; 401: top: © Karl Weatherly/PhotoDisc, bottom: © Kevin T. Gilbert/CORBIS/Magma; 402: Karl Weatherly/PhotoDisc; 403: Alex L. Fradkin/PhotoDisc.